Contemporary study of language and cognition in infancy and early childhood has received considerable, well-deserved attention; however, little effort has been directed to the means by which language becomes a cognitive and communicative tool, or to what the full implications of this development may be. The child's understanding of temporal concepts and language exemplifies the transition from language *and* cognition to language *in* cognition.

This book represents an integrative theory of cognitive development in infancy and early childhood, emphasizing the important role that language plays in taking the 2- to 5-year-old child to new levels of cognitive operations in memory, processing narratives, forming concepts and categories, and understanding other people's intentions. Biological evolution is discussed as the ultimate source of both language and culture, but it is argued that qualitatively different modes of thinking and knowing emerge therefrom. Aspects of cognitive organization (memory, concepts) and knowledge systems (time, psychosocial awareness) are considered within a model of collaborative construction that both retains and integrates individuality and social conventionality.

D0388140

Language in Cognitive Development

Language in Cognitive Development

Emergence of the Mediated Mind

Katherine Nelson

Graduate School and University Center
of the City University of New York

CAMBRIDGE
UNIVERSITY PRESS

PUBLISHED BY THE PRESS SYNDICATE OF THE UNIVERSITY OF CAMBRIDGE
The Pitt Building, Trumpington Street, Cambridge CB2 1RP

CAMBRIDGE UNIVERSITY PRESS
The Edinburgh Building, Cambridge CB2 2RU, United Kingdom
40 West 20th Street, New York, NY 10011-4211, USA
10 Stamford Road, Oakleigh, Melbourne 3166, Australia

First published 1996
First paperback edition 1998

Printed in the United States of America

Library of Congress Cataloging-in-Publication Data is available.

A catalog record for this book is available from the British Library.

ISBN 0-521-55123-4 hardback
ISBN 0-521-62987-X paperback

to Richard

Contents

IV   CONCLUSIONS

Preface

This book is about the role that language plays in early human development, from the period before the infant has access to the meaning system embedded in language to the point of relatively full access to linguistic messages conveyed orally. This early period (roughly 1 to 5 years of age) sets the stage for the acquisition of cultural knowledge systems and for entering into the literate cultural world as a full participant in all its technologies. My emphasis is not on the ways in which culture influences and forms children, but rather on the ways in which the child comes to participate in cultural and social activities, and the cognitive consequences of that participation at different levels and through different modes of representation. The focus of my story is the child in a social-cultural world, learning and using language for her own purposes, becoming a more skilled and better informed participant in the activities of that world.

The main theoretical ideas about cognitive development have been proposed and articulated by giants such as Baldwin, Dewey, Piaget, and Vygotsky; their intellectual descendents are alive and well, currently making substantial contributions to the field. Other writers have made connections between developmental psychology and contemporary linguistic, philosophical, and cognitive science theories. Yet what has failed to emerge, and what seems more remote now than ever, is a strong central theoretical viewpoint of what human development is and how it should be studied in its infancy and childhood phases.

I am not under the illusion that this book will fill this huge gap. But I do believe that at the very least what is needed is a bringing together of disparate views of the child's cognitive development from biological foundations, cultural contexts, mental constructions, and social influences. We need a model of cognitive development that goes beyond interactionism, whether that is conceived in terms of genes and environment, nature and nurture, individual and social. In going beyond, it is crucial to recognize the central role of communication, and in particular the role of language, in taking the human child beyond the solipsistic state envisioned by Piaget to the encultured mind of the human adult.

To understand the cognitive and social challenges that face the infant and young child, it is necessary to consider the gap between the child's cognitive resources and the world that she enters at birth. Many of the features of that world that we as literate adults take for granted, in our oral discourse with children as well as adults, have been documented by Ong (1982), who notes that they "are not directly native to human existence as such but have come into being because of the resources which the technology of writing makes available to human consciousness" (p. 1). Our own thinking as literate and scholarly adults thus is permeated by what writing and print (and more recently electronic media) have imposed on our consciousness. Moreover, the categories that have emerged from this literate way of thinking have in recent theorizing been imposed in a kind of back-formation onto the minds of young children, who live in a literate society but who are not themselves literate, indeed who for several years do not even command oral language for many of its common purposes. This move is, I am convinced, a major theoretical mistake.

Rather, I believe that we must begin with the recognition that human consciousness and cognition are not at base restricted to one particular way of thinking and are not equipped with the equivalent of literate adult categories, knowledge domains, or theories – recent claims to the contrary notwithstanding. The human mind-brain is an open system, with almost infinite plasticity and potential for reorganizing in the wake of new technologies, new language, new knowledge systems, new skills. Our challenge is not to identify the proto-categories in the infant mind that are the beginnings of literate adult categories, thus ultimately searching for their source in the genes. Rather, it is to understand how the open nonverbal, illiterate, and ignorant mind comes to acquire the knowledge domains and the categories and theories that Western culture (among others) embraces.

This view of the matter requires a stance toward understanding early childhood different from what is often presented by both professionals and the general media. The condition of young children in the modern world is analogous in some ways to that of illiterate adults in a literate society. It is often observed that nonliterate people make enormous efforts to disguise their condition and to pretend to know what is written on signs or instructions. A similar but more profound state of ignorance afflicts the young child, pretending to know what a verbal message means even when she is not able to decode it, or to know what is going on in a strange place when she is faced with novel activities (such as in psychological experiments). Young children often look so intelligent that we attribute deep knowledge, even theories, to them, although they are relying on entirely different kinds of knowledge – formulaic knowledge – to see them through. This is the perspective taken in this book; the ensuing chapters not only document the analysis of cognitive change that it implies but also present the accumulating evidence that supports this view.

There is little discussion here of the philosophical and general intellectual bases for the framework outlined. I recognize the profound significance and pervasive influence on my work of the ideas of Piaget, Vygotsky, Dewey, Wittgenstein, Bakhtin, G. H. Mead, Werner, and many contemporary theorists in many different fields – anthropology, linguistics, philosophy, sociology, psychology. A discussion of how they relate to the theory outlined here would have resulted in a different book, one that I fear would have obscured rather than illuminated the messages I want to convey. I believe that we need a central core of theory within which to do developmental work, and that none of the theorists mentioned (or our contemporaries) have produced such a theory. Explicating their ideas is an essential enterprise, and I have benefited greatly from the work of those who have undertaken this task. But I see my task as trying to make sense of where we are now in the enterprise. Thus I have made occasional reference to many theorists, past and present, but have not attempted the job of relating them in detail to the propositions set out here or of explicating their theories.

Development is an underground, unobservable process for which models of observable change are inadequate. An adequate theory of cognitive change must be constructed in terms of the "embodied mind," the "enactive mind," and the "social mind" – a tall order. This book aims to be a start in this direction.

There are other levels at which one can understand development, including cognitive development, besides that of lived experience, the focus here. Among these are the neurological level, the information-processing level, the educational or zone of proximal development level, and the construction of logic level. My claim is that by viewing children acting in social-cultural environments and by attempting to understand both the goals and the processes by which action is carried through in those environments – with what supports, and with what successes and failures – important insights into developmental issues can be gained that are not otherwise available. Furthermore, exploration of this level may shed important light on the complexity of organization of the hybrid literate adult mind. My conviction that these insights are important but not widely recognized in much contemporary work provides the impetus to introduce them to researchers and students in both cognitive development and in other fields where a developmental perspective on human cognition may have value.

Acknowledgments

Preparation of this book was begun while I was a Fellow at the Center for Advanced Study in the Behavioral Sciences at Stanford, California, from 1992 to 1993. I am grateful for financial support during the fellowship year provided by the John D. and Catherine T. MacArthur Foundation (Fellowship #8900078). I am especially thankful for the generous resources and helpful staff of the center, which facilitated the initial drafting of the chapters, including extensive bibliographic searches. Some of the research reported herein was supported orignally by grants from the National Science Foundation for work on the development of event representations, and by a faculty research grant from the City University of New York for research on the development of time concepts and language. Writing was also substantially assisted through a City University of New York Distinguished Professorship, which provides released time to devote to research.

In addition to the publications cited in the References, I benefited from the opportunity to prepare lectures for various forums, which contributed to the chapters in this book. Among those that remain unpublished in other forms were a keynote lecture on relevance in child language acquisition at the meeting of the British Child Language Association in Glasgow in 1992; a keynote lecture on "making sense" as a developmental theory, to the Human Development Conference in Atlanta in the same year; and a lecture series on narrative at the University of Oslo also in 1992. Coming as they did just prior to my beginning the writing of this book, these were welcome opportunities to try out my ideas. In addition, a symposium at the 1991 meeting of the International Society for Study of Behavior and Development provided the opportunity to compare general theories of representational change, forming the background for the discussion of these issues here.

Over many years I have been fortunate in having first-rate graduate students and postdoctoral fellows who have been true collaborators on research. Those whose work has contributed to and is cited herein (many of whom have gone on to distinguished independent careers) include in more or less chronological order: Leslie Rescorla, Janice Gruendel, David Furrow, Robyn Fivush, Judith Hudson, Joan Lucariello, Lucia French, Amy Kyratzis, Susan Engel, Tony Rifkin, Elena Levy, June Hampson, Minda Tessler, Sandra Sebris, Maureen Carbery, Younoak Yu, Roseanne Flores, and Elena Zazanis. Marta Korintus and Mariko Hayashi also participated in collaborative research as visiting scholars at the CUNY Graduate Center, and Lorraine Harner of Brooklyn College collaborated on the time studies reported in Chapter 9. Members of my current research group, including Lea Kessler-Shaw, Elena Zazanis, Daisy Edmondson, Calliope Haritos, Faye Fried Walkenfeld, Sarah Henseler, Daniella Plesa, and Sylvie Goldman, have not only collaborated on ongoing studies but also read and commented on early chapters of this book. I benefited also from bibliographic assistance by my students Calliope Haritos and Sarah Henseler. Sarah painstakingly checked the text and references for consistency and accuracy, for which I am very grateful. The contributions of all those cited to the research and theory discussed herein have been invaluable. This book would never have been possible without them.

During the writing of the book I benefited from discussions with many other scholars, in person and in correspondence, only a few of whom can be acknowledged here. During my year at the Center for Advanced Study at Stanford these included particularly Kurt Fischer, Paul van Geert, Betty Eisenstein, Paul Harris, Robbie Case, Alison Gopnik, and Shirley Brice Heath. At other points Liz Bates, Mark Bickhard, Lois Bloom, Ann Brown, Susan Carey, Annette Karmiloff-Smith, Jean Mandler, Keith Nelson, Josef Perner, and Mike Tomasello have been helpful in clarifying ideas as I was developing them. My colleagues at the Graduate Center share an important responsibility for the development of the framework presented here, especially through our ongoing faculty and postdoctoral fellow seminars devoted to discussion of critical theoretical issues in developmental and cognitive psychology and related areas. The contributions of Joe Glick and the late Sylvia Scribner were most influential there, but all my colleagues in developmental psychology, past and present, have helped to broaden this framework. Discussions during the 1980s with the New York Language Acquisition group (Jerome Bruner, Carol Feldman, John Dore, Daniel Stern, and Rita Watson) that resulted in *Narratives from the Crib* (Nelson, 1989c) were also influential in clarifying ideas and pointing to new directions.

My position as editor of *Cognitive Development* for the past five years has exposed me to the work of many authors, published and unpublished, and has thereby served as an important avenue for understanding issues central to the field today. Together with the many reviewers who have contributed critiques of their works, these authors have contributed to my knowledge of the variety of research and theoretical perspectives that are currently represented in this area.

Merlin Donald, whose written work plays an important role in this book, and who has been most generous in sharing his work, discussing ideas, and providing detailed critiques of versions of some chapters, deserves special thanks. Other readers who have provided helpful comments on different versions of one or more chapters include Janet Wilde Atkinson, Robbie Case, Bruce Dorval, Lucia French, Paul Harris, Joan Lucariello, Peggy Miller, Susan Oyama, Michael Tomasello, and four anonymous reviewers. I am grateful to all of them for their generous help, but I hold none of them responsible for the product.

Julia Hough, psychology and cognitive science editor at Cambridge University Press, has been a strong supporter of this project and has smoothed the way to its present concrete form. I am grateful for her support and help in the editorial process.

The collaborative construction of knowledge, a central theme of this book, is well illustrated by the citation of the contributions from all the individuals mentioned here, as well as others whose contributions may have been less consciously recognized. I have struggled for the past three years to integrate and make coherent my own thinking, drawing from the ideas of these others in the process making them my own. I take responsibility for the result, including any errors and infelicities, but any credit must be shared with the many colleagues recognized here, as well as with numerous others cited and uncited, including those who may take strong objections to what is said here.

My husband, Richard Nelson, an economist, has not only been an enthusiastic and steadfast supporter of this project from its inception, but also shared in the formulation of its ideas and has given critical readings to early drafts of chapters. In this he has continued the intellectual, material, and social collaboration that has sustained my work throughout my career. In long overdue recognition, this book is dedicated to him.

Katherine Nelson
Brewster, Massachusetts
July 1995

I. Perspectives

1. Language, Cognition, and Culture in Developmental Perspective

The basic premise of this book is that language is a catalyst of cognitive change during early to middle childhood. The multifunctional roles of language in cognition and communication during this important period of developmental change require deeper analysis than they have been given in contemporary theoretical writing. It is my conviction that to fulfill this goal the biological underpinnings and the sociocultural conditions of human development must be jointly analyzed in their contributions to the development of human cognition and language as a dynamic process.

Language is at the center of the theory to be outlined, because of its centrality to all of developed human life and thought. Despite the enormous place that language and its development occupy in linguistics, philosophy, and cognitive science, it is surprising how little attention is paid to language in current psychological theories of cognitive development. Relatedly, although in a different context, Wierzbicka (1994) commented: "Mainstream modern psychology . . . at times seems to behave as if language is irrelevant to the study of mind" (p. 431). This is particularly true in developmental psychology, where it sometimes appears that infant cognition has become the model for all human cognitive development.[1] Why this is so doubtless has many answers implicit in the history of the field itself, as well as in cognitive science more generally.

One source of the neglect of language in cognitive development surely comes from the legacy of Piaget. Much current theorizing in cognitive development derives directly or indirectly from the Piagetian model of cognitive construction. In this model, what is important are abstract logical operations independent of language, with a minor role assigned to symbolic representations, their emergence assumed to be dependent upon more basic processes of cognition. Although adherents to classical Piagetian theory are now diminished in number, many of today's theo-

3

ries have developed in response to its claims, from those who are characterized as "neo-Piagetian" (e.g., Case, 1992a; Fischer, 1980; Fischer & Farrar, 1988) to those who have positioned themselves in opposition (e.g., Carey, 1985; Spelke, 1991) and those who have diverged quite radically from it but have retained some of its most basic assumptions (Karmiloff-Smith, 1992; Mounoud, 1993). The relevant point here is that in each of these theories the independence of cognition from language has been maintained. There seems to be an implicit assumption among theorists that language is a communicative tool, and only that, or at most that it is the medium through which knowledge and cultural forms are conveyed. Language is assumed to exist as a separable system, either in the Chomskyan view, internally as a mental organ, or in the more general view, externally as a means of expression and reception of language-neutral "information."

As a result, language is recognized as an important communicative tool that children acquire and through which thoughts are expressed, but not something that affects basic cognitive functions or cognitive change. For the most part, in discussions of cognitive development, language is ignored altogether, except when its acquisition as a knowledge system is the focus. Indeed, the increasing acceptance of the modularity of mind has the effect of shunting language off into its own impenetrable module, while the central processor (where all the interesting activity takes place) carries on in terms of manipulating symbolic representations in its own innately specified Language of Thought (Fodor, 1983).

Although language is central to the story worked out here, it rests on prior nonlinguistic perceptual, conceptual, and social-communicative processes. Thus it is not separable from cognitive development generally, and the reverse is also true: Cognitive development is not separable from language. To understand these relations it is important, in my view, to take an experiential view of development in which individual development over time is the focus.

Understanding the Process of Cognitive Development: The Experiential View of the Child

The theoretical approach developed in this book is an *experiential* one. In this perspective, the child as an acting and interacting person is always in view. What the child represents of the world she[2] experiences is a function of the purposes enshrined in her current concerns, which change over time. The resulting representations constitute the filtered products of a developmental history, in turn providing the context within which new experiences are interpreted and represented.

One of the central claims of this approach is that *the primary cognitive task of the human child is to make sense of his or her situated place in the world in order to take a skillful part in its activities*. This is an imperative for the human child – unlike virtually all nonhuman animals – because of the highly variable conditions that may be met in human societies, beyond some very basic similarities.[3] The human child cannot know in advance the specifics of dwellings, infant caretaking practices, social roles and rituals, foods, geographical and climatological features, and language, among other things. All these must be acquired through experience in terms of *participatory interactions* within a social group.

Therefore, the first and most basic problem that cognitive developmentalists must address is this: How does an individual child begin to acquire knowledge of the specific circumstances of her life and world and to adapt to those circumstances effectively in order to take her part within its social and cultural activities? Note the difference between this basic question and that asked by Piaget, or by his contemporary critics, namely: How does the child construct or display knowledge of objects and their physical relations in space, time, and causality? From the present perspective, knowledge of the physical, object world is embedded within knowledge of the social-cultural world for the human child, and it is the latter that enables and guides the former.

The basic thesis is that the child begins to build representations of her world based on her experience in it. These representations, or models, are no doubt constructed according to principles that are "built in" to the human cognitive system, that is, that have an evolutionary, biological basis. For example, it is a premise here that events are parsed as sequences of actions through time and in space, that this is a basic characteristic of human cognition (and may be true of all mammalian cognition). It is a further premise that what is important to the infant are the events that she partakes in, with particular attention to those that lead to comfort (feeding, soothing, sleeping, socializing) and discomfort (pain, hunger, noise, cold). Primary caretakers – parents or others – play the most important roles in these events, and their habitual activities as displayed to the infant can be expected to enter as major constituents of her models.

The emphasis here is on understanding and predicting activities rather than – as in Piaget's view – on forming object schemas. Actions are important in both conceptions, but in the present view, actions of others, and interactions with important others, are as central – perhaps more central – to the child's knowledge schemas as the child's individual actions on objects. In other ways, though, the approach is somewhat similar to Piaget's, in that it is considered necessary for the child to build up abstract knowledge from specific concrete activities. The abstractions that are built up are not necessary logical constructions or operations, however, but generalizations of patterns and reorganizations of experience.

At all stages of development the child's knowledge state depends crucially on prior experience and present capacity to perceive, explore, and interpret situations. The central construct here is the idea of situational models that represent familiar experiences. Such cognitive models provide *cognitive context*, the context that is operational for the individual at any given time. The child acts within situations and activities, but the direction of that action is provided by the applicable internalized model of the situation (what fits from previous experience) in conjunction with specific present features of the situation (who, what, where, etc.). Together, these provide the cognitive context for action, and for the interpretation of the actions of others.

In the beginning the child's models are assumed to be representations of familiar significant repeated events, or general event representations (hereinafter termed *mental event representations*, or *MERs*). Over time, these become generalized into an elaborate *Child world model* that includes people, places, and a variety of activities – some pleasurable, others neutral, and some to be avoided. These situational models are amenable to operations of abstraction, so that generalizations across events, people, places, and objects may be made and entered into the growing complex knowledge system.

Experientialism is not equivalent to the traditional empiricist assumption that all knowledge is built up from sensation. Experience-based knowledge derives from varying sources: from action in the world, from perception, from biological dispositions to organize patterns of experience in specific ways, from social interactions and activities, and from cultural arrangements. It does not assume an unprepared or vacant mind, but it assumes that dynamic processes are in continual interaction with the experienced world, yielding ever-changing models of reality. These dynamic processes and the resulting changes in conceptual systems and world models are what need explication and explanation in our theories of cognitive development.

The experiential idea is nonetheless very different from the assumption that innate principles guide knowledge acquisition (at least beyond the basic parsing systems). It is not necessary to accept the idea of either a blank slate or radical social constructionism as a basis for rejecting the idea of innate knowledge. Recent research on what infants "know" (see Chapters 2 and 4) simply rules out theories that assume perceptual, conceptual, and enactive systems that are unconstrained by an evolutionary history of adaptation to an expectable human environment. The present view conforms with the ecological approach (e.g., Reed & Jones, 1982) in seeing infancy as a developmental period during which these basic systems are "tuned" to the actual world of experience (Gibson, 1982). That world has physical and social structure, some of it universally expectable, much of it highly variable. The infant is seen as becoming adapted to the structure of the environment through the exercise of the perceptual and motor systems. These systems are pre-adapted, but they depend upon the structure of the environment to develop epigenetically.

Beyond the developments of tuning perceptual systems and exercising motor systems, the conceptual system takes over an important role, and it is here that "knowledge" is activated. Indeed, it is a principal claim of the present argument that the conceptual system is designed at the most basic level to parse events that take place through time and space, thus to represent meaningful (to the infant) parts of the experienced world. This conception is described in more elaborate terms in succeeding chapters. What I want to emphasize here is the implication that, born without knowledge, the infant must acquire it in the real world. I dispute the currently popular idea that the infant is born with *"naive theories"* of physics, biology, or anything else (Spelke, 1991; Carey, 1985). Theories must be built on a data base of classifications of phenomena and are designed to explain the workings of and the function of those phenomena. Infants can better be seen then as collecting data, building an implicit data base that will later serve as the basis for model construction and even theory building. At the outset, like other closely related primates, infants attempt to represent the world in ways that provide guidance for action but do not seek to explain it. (More will be said about theories and alternatives to theories in Chapters 8 and 10.)

The infant's knowledge-constructing activity takes place within a social world, and part of the story here must be about how that world enters into the constructive process. In infancy and very early childhood the child can access very little of the adult's knowledge beyond what is directly displayed in and derivable from social interaction. The child's knowledge in this phase is *mediated* by virtue of living in a culturally arranged world in which caretakers direct most of the action. But the child's knowledge acquisition in a more basic sense is directed and *unmediated*, in that mediation through language and other semiotic systems is not yet possible. The establishment of an equivalent to the adult language representation system involves a long, dynamic process of establishing meanings that can be exchanged between people through the fuzzy symbolic system that is natural language.

The establishment of language as a representational and mediational system rests on four necessary contributions: (1) The biological basis of acquiring a linguistic system; (2) the psychological process that enables the child to construct a particular language system; (3) the social process that provides the communicative and linguistic model for the construction and that (4) supports its development. The discussion here is oriented to take into account the way in which these processes interact and contribute to the emergence of a new level of functioning – linguistic, social, and cognitive – during the latter part of the early childhood years.

Implications of the Experiential View

The experiential view takes the perspective of the child and focuses on individual cognitive development. Development of the individual child takes place within a bio-socio-cultural system, and contributions of each of these sources to developing knowledge content and organization must be accounted for, while recognizing as well the self-regulating properties of the active individual. Progress in understanding this system cannot be made on all fronts at once. But rather than breaking the child's mind into parts that can be examined piecemeal and ahistorically, the aim is to view the parts in their intertwined connections over an extended period of developmental time. The time period that is under examination here is that of the early childhood years, primarily between 2 and 5 years.

The thesis of the present work is that if we truly understand the evolution of human intelligence and language, the nature of human societies, and the nature of human infancy and childhood, we will come to a broader, albeit more complex, view of cognition and cognitive development that can predict more about children's actual capacities and developmental sequences than is presently the case. In particular, this kind of understanding would indicate how individuals build on their experience in the world to construct models that enable them to operate effectively in their current situations, whatever those situations are. And beyond this, such understanding would begin to show how this kind of experientially based knowledge feeds into more abstract systems that are grounded in evolutionarily specified cognitive structures, structures that reflect the kinds of intelligence that humans – and prehuman predecessors – have always displayed in natural environments, rather than structures that are modeled on logical conceptions of efficient machines or scientific theories. In this endeavor scientific theories are viewed as one of the premier cognitive achievements of the human species, but not as models of the most primitive cognitive structures of early childhood.

Analogies abound in contemporary developmental writing to the child as scientist, linguist, philosopher, or psychologist, or, in Piaget's theory, as epistemologist. The view here denies all these analogies and insists that the child's mind differs qualitatively from that of these adult models. The assumption that the child is like one of these Xs, but smaller and with less knowledge of the world, denies the cultural, historical, educational, and developmental histories of the adults who actually carry on these demanding scholarly activities. Viewing the infant and young child as in possession of "folk theories" is no improvement; this move simply denies that "folk" implies a community of shared meanings, meanings which the young child comes to share as language becomes a medium of communication and cognitive representations.

The explicitly experiential approach taken here stands in danger of being dismissed as superficial or commonsensical, or as reverting to "child study."[4] It is my belief that indeed we need more child study analogous to the natural history studies that formed the background of all modern science (Atran, 1990; Mayr, 1982). But I believe we are now at a point in understanding aspects of human development that makes it feasible to construct more adequate theories *if* we turn our attention to the developmental process itself. This move requires viewing that process in its complexity. Thus we can understand a moment and a place in a child's development only if we understand where the child has been and what the forces are that are propelling her into the future. Three points bear further emphasis:

1. As stated previously, the basic assumption is that the child's cognitive task is to learn from particular experience in a specific cultural environ-

ment, to "make sense." Thus it is necessary for psychologists to understand the nature of the child's experience at different points in development. This requires in part the specification of the environment, as in ethological and ecological studies; it requires as well, and specifically, an effort to understand the perspective of the experiencing individual. For example, it is important to understand what the child can see and hear, and how this changes as perceptual systems develop and as motor systems mature, enabling an immobile infant to crawl and then stand and walk. It requires the attempt to understand how prior experience bears on current experience in the child's interpretation of an event, as, for example, when a parent attempts to teach a new word, or when an experimenter hides an object, or when an experimenter presents a 3-year-old with a scenario of puppets who look for objects in the wrong place.

2. The second point implied in the first is methodological, involving the contrast that anthropologists have made between the "emic" (experientialist) and the "etic" (theoretical) units of analysis. The experiential view eschews the absolutist "objective" view of the experimenter in favor of asking how the child is experiencing the experiment or other activity. The objective scientist sets up the experiment and views the data that emerge as a puzzle demanding an explanation in terms of the scientist's prior theory. Not only are the data subject to possible misinterpretation (examples will abound in the chapters to follow) but experimenters may miss the relevant factors altogether because they have not taken the perspective of the experiencing child. To take one example, Gleitman (1990) has argued that verbs cannot be learned on the basis of their use in particular contexts because an unbiased observer cannot pick out the relevant components of meaning on the basis of the information present in the situation. But, of course, the child is not an unbiased observer. Indeed, this is Gleitman's point. The thrust of her argument is that the child must have special (innate) knowledge about verbs; whereas the experiential view recognizes special knowledge, based on history, of the situation. The experiential approach takes that history into account in formulating a theory of what the child brings to the experiment. This point was made forcefully by Donaldson (1978) and her colleagues (Grieve & Hughes, 1990) many years ago.

3. The third point is theoretical and is closely aligned with both the systems view (Van Geert, 1993) and the contextual/cultural view (Cole, 1991) of human development. Development is both teleological – the infant does develop toward a particular end with specifiable characteristics, adulthood, and eventually death in a cultural milieu – and historical and contingent – the individual who develops is uniquely constituted by virtue of a unique history of experience, a history that both supports development and forms a self. Although psychology may focus on a general course of development, or at most recognize variations among cultural groups, it must account for the fact that it is individuals who develop, and the more developed, the more unique each individual is (Salthe, 1993). Infancy is the most general of postnatal developmental stages, each succeeding stage being more historically informed. It is somewhat ironic that developmental psychology, with its roots firmly in the Western individualistic philosophical tradition, ignores

individuality in favor of universality. It is a strong virtue of systems theory that it recognizes development as an individual process and thus emphasizes longitudinal studies of individual children. The experiential approach shares this preference. Thus the experiential approach is a historical developmental approach. It focuses on the child who is developing, but it sees the child in a specific social and cultural milieu that makes possible the experiences that go into development.

Representation in Cognition and Communication

Enough has been said thus far to suggest that the subtitle of this book – "the emergence of the mediated mind" – incorporates two important principles: The notion of emergence implies levels of representation and representational change; the notion of mediation implies that the product of representational change is a result of a social mediational process. Some further explication of these ideas is important before plunging further into the heart of the argument.

"Representation" has been subject to differing interpretations in cognitive development research (Mandler, 1983). In Piaget's theory, for example, representation was equated with consciousness of what was represented. In contrast, a view that relates the function of representation across species rests on the assumption of a *"functioning isomorphism* between [an] aspect of the environment and some of the brain processes that adapt the animal's behavior to that aspect of the environment" (Gallistel, 1989, p. 156). In this perspective, representation is not a copy of reality, nor does it imply consciousness. Rather, perceptual systems represent aspects of the real world that are significant for creatures of a particular species, representations that enable the organism to move and act in the world. This representational function implies neither symbols nor an interpreter, but it does imply an "enactive mind" (Varela, Thompson, & Rosch, 1991). What is of particular interest is that seemingly simple animals (ants, rats, pigeons) represent such "abstract" aspects of the environment as position in space, duration of time, and number (Gallistel, 1989). There is every reason to believe that our own perceptual and conceptual systems are also designed to represent in specific ways these aspects of the real physical world in which we live. Conceptual systems represent higher-order relations derived by the cognitive system (in evolution or in development) on the basis of perception and action in the world. This level is interpreted, in the sense that inferences have produced new structures.

Language and Representation

In contrast to those theorists for whom language has disappeared into the role of information conveyer, George Miller (1990) has put language at the center of cognitive studies as follows:

> Human language is the happy result of bringing together two systems that all higher organisms must have: a representational system and a communication system. A representational system is necessary if an organism is going to move around purposefully in its environment; a communication system is necessary if an organism is going to interact with others of its own kind. . . . Human beings seem to be the only animals in which a single system serves both of these functions. (p. 12)

While emphasizing the unique significance of human language, this statement nonetheless maintains the dichotomy between cognition and communication that typifies discussions of language functions. The dichotomy implies that there is an internal representation unique to the individual, and that communication is "about" social interaction, something apart from "representation." But neither cognition, in the form of mental representation, nor communication can be so divided.

A major proposal of this work is that in development (as in evolution) language may *become* a representational system by way of its use as a communication medium for representing to other people. This point may seem incoherent to many cognitivists and needs to be spelled out. It is generally assumed that to communicate is to convey some observation (a representation) from one individual to another [see, e.g., Eco, Santambrogio, & Violi (1988)]. Thus from this perspective, representations must precede their communication. But from the developmental perspective, neither cognition nor communication is prior. The language representational system becomes established both cognitively *and* communicatively through a dialectical process. The focus of the analysis presented here then is on the emergence in development of language as a representational system, both for internal cognitive functions and for external communicative functions.

Human minds are equipped to construct complicated "mental models" that represent the temporary as well as enduring complexities of our social and cultural world. Human language reflects the demands of this process. For example, according to Jackendoff (1983, 1988) the major ontological categories of linguistic representations include places, directions, actions, events, manners, and amounts, as well as people and objects. These categories are neither objective realities nor simply categories of our languages; rather, they are the way that we construe the world. Jackendoff's system implies innate specific *linguistic* structures of meaning. This is not a necessary implication, however. From the perspective that language was a late invention of humankind, and was constructed for the function of communicating human representations between individuals, languages themselves must reflect to some degree prior adaptations in evolutionary time (see Chapters 2 and 3). In other words, languages must be adapted to human thought in both its basic representational and inferential conceptual forms as well as the social-cultural functions of human communication. This perspective on language, which is spelled out in more detail in Chapters 2 and 3, in no way detracts from its importance or complexity; it simply claims (in contrast to the reverse relation implied in many contemporary discussions) that *language is adapted to human minds and purposes.*

Representational Change

Levels of representation and cognitive change conceived in terms of the establishment of new levels of representation, including especially the possibility of representing in language, are important features of the theory that is outlined in this book. These ideas were introduced in two previous books (Nelson, 1985, 1986), and the presentation here takes the story further. Meanwhile, a number of other theories have been put forth that view development in terms of representational change, of which Karmiloff-Smith's (1986a, 1992) is the best known and the most thoroughly worked out.[5] There are many convergences between her model and the present one, as well as important differences. As a way of pointing out some of the issues that must be dealt with, it is useful to consider the major premises of her model.

Beyond Modularity. Karmiloff-Smith's theory combines a domain-general process with a domain-specific developmental approach, worked out from the twin perspectives of Piagetian theory and Anglo-American cognitive science. This model's basic level of representation is a product of interaction of a goal-directed system, analogous to Piaget's sensorimotor schemas. However, in contrast to Piaget, who viewed representation as an emergent function, based on later structural developments, Karmiloff-Smith's basic level is representational in Gallistel's sense and is the foundation for further representations. This nonsymbolic, nonpropositional base level is procedural, realized in the form of a connectionist network. Procedures are interactive constructions for solving problems; thus the base level represents direct knowledge constructed through interactions with the environment. At this level the child knows but does not know she knows. She acts on knowledge shaped by evolutionary forces but derived from direct individual experience in the world. To a large extent, this conception coheres very well with comparative and evolutionary views of development.

In Karmiloff-Smith's theory succeeding levels are assumed to change within knowledge domains (e.g., drawing, language, physics), so that a child might be at level 1 in one domain and level 2 or 3 in another. Cognitive change involves movement from the procedural to the computationally accessible (where procedures may be recombined or broken apart) and then to the consciously accessible (where the knower can consciously reflect on and manipulate procedures). The terminology of representational levels rather than stages implies that it is not the operations of the cognitive system that change, but the kinds of representations that are available to the system, within a particular knowledge domain. In this view cognition is a self-organizing system that is success-driven (rather than failure-driven, as in Piaget's theory); when a procedure becomes automatic and smooth it may become accessible to operations that analyze its parts and integrate it with other systems. The process of redescription and explicitation (making explicit at a higher level what was implicit at the lower level) is the central mechanism in this model. The dynamic systems view of development (e.g., Smith & Thelen, 1993) appears to be compatible with this theory based on its assumptions of levels, self-organization, and the emergence of new functions.

Karmiloff-Smith views development within language as similar to other cognitive developments. For example, the child's mastery of the articles and pronouns in French and English is analyzed from the procedural (correct use) to the computationally accessible phase (construction of a system) to the consciously accessible (reflection on the system). But beyond this, and critical to the present concerns, she suggests that the representational function of language enables movement to a new level of representational understanding. As many different representations are transformed into a linguistic code, new representational relationships can be drawn.

Karmiloff-Smith's theory is a powerful one, recognizing biological predispositions and modules, and going beyond them. The mechanism of change is somewhat vague, but many of her proposals fit well with the present views. Despite the many attractions of the theory, however, her stress on internal analysis and neglect of the influence of the external representations of others leaves the system analysis unfinished. In particular, the child's analysis of language cannot be independent of the context of the language in use. Thus the model does not take fully into account that language (and logic) are public constructions with private ramifications. Among the ramifications is the possibility of using language as a cognitive representational level with greater analytic power than any prior nonsymbolic representation system. It is the realization of this mental representation function of language that, according to the present argument, is the basis for the evident cognitive advances in the latter part of the preschool years.

Domain Specificity. The focus on development within specific domains in Karmiloff-Smith's theory obscures the view of possible interactions of domains and thus loses the full sense of a developing system, the sense that the experiential view provides. In general, domain-specific theories (see Hirschfeld & Gelman, 1994a, 1994b) break the mind into non-interacting pieces and tend to focus on one bounded period of development, often infants or 3- to 4-year-old preschoolers. This strategy loses a sense of what *function* any given domain is playing in the system under development, as well as the history and trajectory of the domain itself. It is a scientific strategy that is well adapted to the examination of nonreactive systems in a laboratory setting but is poorly adapted to the study of dynamic development. It is especially notable that often a particular problem has been extracted from a developmental course identified by Piaget and made into a focused investigation at a particular moment in its development without regard to prior or later developments (Fischer & Bidell, 1991; Chandler, 1988). Another common fallacy of this strategy is the assumption that a domain may be examined at one point and the lessons learned applied to other points without regard to the ongoing development of the cognitive system as a whole, much less of the embodied mind-in-context.

In contrast, the experiential perspective views representation as constituted of chunks of experience of events and activities, at a particular developmental time point, with derivations from those representations carrying forth the implications of the activities from which they are abstracted. The activities are always socially and culturally situated. This view has been spelled out in terms of MERs, summarized next.

Basic Event Representations

The basic function of a representation system is to guide action in the world, thus to provide information about present conditions and to anticipate future states. Such a system need not depend on memory for specific episodes, but rather needs to accumulate general knowledge about possible events, scenes, routes, predators and other threats, as well as conspecifics and satisfying situations. The *source* of such knowledge is the individual's experience in specific events, and the accumulation of such knowledge results in general event representations. That much human knowledge of the world – as well as the knowledge of other primates – is represented in this way needs little justification, although considerable experimental evidence has accumulated to show that scripts for familiar structured events play a powerful role in memory for specific episodes and stories, plans, decision making, and so on (Abelson, 1981; Bower, Black, & Turner, 1979; Graesser, Woll, Kowalski, & Smith, 1979; Mandler, 1983; Schank & Abelson, 1977). Extensive evidence exists as well that young children construct and rely on general event representations for understanding discourse, stories, and play (Nelson, 1986; Bauer & Mandler, 1992; Fivush & Slackman, 1986; Hudson, 1986).

The script construct developed by Schank and Abelson applied to both social (intermental) and individual (intramental) knowledge. In Nelson (1986), my colleagues and I differentiated among these levels, proposing general event representations (GERs) as a more general cognitive term not necessarily implying all the structural characteristics of scripts.[6] To make this differentiation more apparent, both specific and general mental representations of events are designated "MERs" in this work. The structure that MERs take no doubt reflects the fact that humans (and probably all mammals) have evolved to parse the world – that is, situations, events – in particular ways [see Jackendoff (1983, 1988)].

Thus MERs can tell us about the constraints on the basic structure of our experience. For example, research with adults as well as young children indicates that events come in packets with boundaries, beginnings, and endings (Rosch, 1978; Nelson, 1978a). What constitutes a boundary is not yet well-established; it seems likely that changes in locations or in the central components – actors and essential objects – constitute boundary conditions. Within an event, actions are sequentially organized; although in some events the possible sequence of actions is variable, in others it is invariant either by convention or through constraints on causal relations. Causal relations include enabling actions (setting up necessary conditions for an action) as well as direct cause and effect relations. Participants are often specified by roles (e.g., doctor, nurse, teacher, waiter/waitress) rather than by specific individuals, and different individuals may fill role slots on different occasions. Actions in the MER usually involve objects as instruments or objects of action, or simply as props in the situation. Objects can be variable, and the particular objects that fill an action-object role on a particular occasion may be thought of as "slot-fillers." Scripts are typically organized around reaching goals [although other organizations are possible, as Barsalou (1991) has pointed out], and those actions that are central to the achievement of a goal may be invariant constituents of a script. For example, "eating" is a central invariant action in a meal script, whereas the actions that surround it in the sequence may be variable and represent different possible pathways within the script.

Toddlers appear to construct their knowledge of the world in terms of familiar events, a process of "world-making" or model-building of "what happens" in the general case. Evidence comes from studies of very young children (3-year-olds) who produce verbal scripts for familiar events. General scripts are produced more readily at this age than specific memory accounts; indeed, when asked for a memory of a routine event (such as having dinner) children are likely to produce instead general scripts (Nelson, 1986). The fact that very young children report the same kinds of structures for events, in the same script-like terms as found for adults, indicates that they represent the same fundamental knowledge structures. For example, boundedness of events, goal orientation, sequential structure, causal relations, roles, and slot-fillers are all abstract knowledge constituents that are evident in the scripts of preschoolers. These are nontrivial constituents of human knowledge that appear first embedded in children's script constructions, before they are realized in more abstract and explicit forms.

Mental event representations are individual constructions of social situations (although a person may readily develop an MER for individual activities, such as toileting). Moreover, the MERs of older children and adults may be highly influenced by verbalizations of other people. And the same event may be conceptualized as a script in different ways by different people. By building representations of environments on the basis of individual experience, a general "world model" is constructed that guides individual action. Yet each world model is different from every other in subtle and sometimes startling ways. For example, family members generally assume that they share the same world model and the same experiences, yet comparison of memories of specific episodes often reveals extreme discrepancies in what happened as well as in the interpretation of the happenings (Bruner, 1990; Sebris, 1992). Discrepancies of this kind can usually be uncovered only through communication in language. Such variability within commonality poses the communicative dilemma of individual representations.

It is one of the primary advantages of human language that it enables the sharing and comparison of experience, thus the enrichment of understanding of the world for individuals. But the basic mammalian individual representation system does not allow such richness, being solipsistic and egocentric. The individual chimpanzee, for example, no doubt implicitly assumes that his own experience of an event is the same as everyone else's, or rather that everyone else's experience is the same as his. With no check on the details of experience from the report of other individuals, one's own representation of experience stands as a mirror of reality. That this is also the case for very young children has long been a theoretical presupposition in the construct of egocentrism (Piaget, 1926). Contemporary research has called many of the alleged implications of egocentrism into question, but many of its indications of cognitive isolation in early childhood persist (see Chapter 10). A goal of the present analysis is to show how individual MERs both support and are changed by and integrated with representations in language as the child meets and masters language. A missing link in this analysis will be found in the construct of *mimesis* put forth by Donald (1991), which enables the child to share aspects of the social semiotic world prior to becoming a competent language user (see Chapters 3 and 4).

Semiotic Mediation and the Sociocultural Context of Development

Study of the mind in context has gained increasing interest in cognitive and developmental psychology in recent years (Martin, Nelson, & Tobach, 1995; Resnick, Levine, & Teasley, 1991; Sternberg & Wagner, 1994; Wozniak & Fischer, 1993). Its roots in developmental psychology are deep, tracing back at least to the 1920s, when Luria and Vygotsky were working together, and the 1930s, when Vygotsky was writing *Thought and Language* (first published in English in 1962). But its influence on Anglo-American psychology has been only slowly advanced (Laboratory of Comparative Human Cognition, 1983). Over the past decade new advocates and new movements have pushed it further, moving it from cross-cultural psychology to cultural psychology (Shweder & LeVine, 1984; Stigler, Shweder, & Herdt, 1990; Valsiner, 1987).

Vygotsky's influence on developmental psychology has been variously interpreted (Cole et al., 1978; Rogoff, 1990; Wertsch, 1985a, 1985b, 1991; Van der Veer & Valsiner, 1991). In particular, Vygotsky's central premise has been taken to be internalization, as set forth in a famous quotation: "Each function in the child's cultural development appears twice: first, on the social level, and later, on the individual level; first, between people (interpsychological), and then inside the child (intrapsychological)" (Vygotsky, 1978, p. 57). In conjunction with the idea of the zone of proximal development (ZPD), which views the child as operating at one level on her own, but at a more advanced level when her problem-solving efforts are scaffolded by the adult, this maxim rests developmental change on the educational efforts of the adult. This emphasis contrasts with that on spontaneous organization in the individual child, as in traditional views of cognitive development, including both Piaget and information processing, as well as in most other contemporary cognitive theories. The divergence demands reconciliation.

In sociocultural psychology frameworks the environment is viewed variously as an activity context,[7] as an educational system, or as a parent–child system. Exactly how the knowledge existing in the environment is incorporated into the mind of the child tends to be neglected. Demonstrating that the environment is influential has been the primary goal of research efforts by adherents of sociocultural psychology, resulting in a deemphasis on individuality. Cultural differences are strongly recognized, but individual constructions have not been a major concern. In contrast, my emphasis here is as much on individual development – on what the individual contributes to and derives from the activity context – as it is on the constraints and supports of the activity itself.

In earlier work on event representations I introduced the idea of *participatory interactions*, referring to children taking part in activities without full understanding of what the activity was about or how it was structured. Through participation, they learn their parts and acquire knowledge of structure. The larger meaning or cultural significance of the activity, however, might not become apparent to the child for a long time, perhaps ever. The idea of "guided participation," elaborated particularly by Rogoff (1990) and her colleagues within an activity theory framework, is obviously related to this notion, but there is a difference, one that is apparent in the location of participation in the two phrases. In my construction, the child is the active participator in the interaction; in Rogoff's construction, the "guider" is the active participator, charged with overseeing the participation of the child. Similarly, in my construction, it is the child who constructs knowledge; in Rogoff's model, the critical process is constructing knowledge in the activity.

It is somewhat surprising that even among those who see the child essentially as a product of the social-cultural world, language per se is not for most a focus; rather, the emphasis is on the child's participation in activities guided by adults (e.g., Cole, 1991; Rogoff, 1990; Tulviste, 1991). Although theoretically language plays an important role via semiotic mediation of knowledge in this approach, its influence on cognition tends to be neglected. For most of these theorists development is guided by and is ultimately the province of the activities of adults. The topic of research is child cognitive development, but the focus is on the interplay of child and the social scene, from which emerges knowledge, socially shared cognition, and development of conceptual structures.

The semiotic mediation ideas of Vygotsky, focusing on the role of language itself in formulating knowledge (Wertsch, 1985a) and making meaning (Bruner, 1990), have, however, been the focus of some social-cultural theorists. Wertsch's recent writing (1991) has emphasized the notion of dialogic construction and the "diglossia" emanating from "voices in the mind," ideas based on Bakhtin (1986), the Russian literary theorist, as well as Vygotsky. This emphasis takes the influence of the representational function of language beyond Language to the varying languages that are found in different speech genres and different speakers in different activity contexts. These ideas present a highly dynamic view of the representational function of language that is in many ways consonant with the views developed later in this book.

The semiotic mediation of higher levels of thought and action was the central principle in Vygotsky's theory (1978, 1986). The idea of semiotic mediation found in Vygotsky's writings is obviously basic to the mediated mind construct; however, in most instantiations of these ideas, the emphasis is on the process of mediation itself – how semiosis is carried out – rather than on the effect on individual cognition. Vygotsky barely touched on the coordination problem, that is, the problem – in his terms – of coordinating scientific and spontaneous concepts. This is to my mind a central problem faced by the developing child, and the central problem of semiotic mediation (see Chapter 8). The focus in this book is on the entry into semiotic mediation in early childhood through the first language of everyday life. But, as Wertsch's (1991) discussion emphasizes, there are many different "social languages" or "speech genres" within the linguistic repertoire of a community. What the child learns to use first is the language of everyday experience. What schools use to teach about domains of cultural knowledge is a more formal language that employs linguistic objects as references and that provides a vocabulary for denoting abstract objects and relations.

Language and Collaborative Construction

It becomes apparent that very similar approaches to the social construction of knowledge differ in terms of the perspective that they take. My perspective obviously has its roots in the traditional "individual mind" view of knowledge in contrast to the assumptions of the "social mind" views. But, and this is the important point, my perspective sees the problem of *becoming* a "social-cultural mind" as a developmental problem for the human child; and by virtue of beginning as an individual mind, it retains that individuality in the context of its social and cultural infusion and participation. The problem is not solved by the child alone, as in cognitive constructionism, or by the social world or through social construction alone, but must be solved through a process of *collaborative constructionism,* in which the child's individual cognitive activity is as crucial as the interaction with the knowing social world.

The infusion of the social-cultural world by way of language has multiple consequences. Language is variously said to be a medium, a mediator, and a tool of thought, and these referents are often used synonymously. Yet the implications are different. As a *medium,* thought is held to be carried out in terms of inner speech. As a *mediator,* thought is formed by the categories and relations found in language, or the genres expressed in discourse. As a *tool,* language is used to articulate and manipulate thought and knowledge systems. Vygotsky discussed all these functions in varying ways, and they are all found in different forms in the chapters of this book. Together they bring out the generative power of language for the human mind.

The Socialcultural versus the Universal.   Given the generative power of language, is the mind only a product of the language in the way that Whorf's (1956) writings are usually interpreted?[8] Linguistic relativity and determinism imply that, given different languages and different cultures, different minds will result. To some extent this must be true, and it is also true that, given different experiences in the world and with different languages, individual differences in minds are brought about. However, there are also universals of mind that produce universals of language and culture; in turn, universals of cultures produce universals of mind and language. There is penetration from both directions throughout these systems, producing sameness within difference and difference within sameness.

Because of the widespread acceptance, covert or explicit, of nativist ideas in developmental psychology today, it is relevant to ask: Does the emphasis on social-cultural influences on children's cognition deny universals of human mind? The answer here is no, but with the qualification that universals appear to have been misinterpreted in many theoretical conceptions. To clarify, the following presuppositions lie behind the story presented here:

- All humans (normally endowed) share certain general perceptual and cognitive structures, predispositions, and potentials.
- All humans share social-cultural groups and environments wherein these structures, predispositions, and potentials develop.
- Infants are immature humans. Infants live in and experience a world like our own, but their experience *of it* differs because of their biological and social place in it and their goals and functions in it.
- Humans share functions and adaptations to the environment. Among these are cultural institutions, artifacts useful for food preparation, clothing and shelter, as well as the production of goods and services. These functions and artifacts are developed by groups of humans (i.e., not by individuals working alone). All have long histories.
- Humans, equipped with human minds, are capable of joining in the activities surrounding these functions.
- Infants are adapted to the support of human groups, and families are adapted to the support of infants and children. Part of the support involves socialization and pedagogy, teaching children how to be productive members of the group.
- Infant minds develop over years in the context of – and, so far as we know, only in the context of – the cultural surroundings of human groups situated in their own historical niches.

Given these assumptions, it follows that to search for the "natural human mind" in infants and young children is futile, although the search may turn up a "natural" infant mind (as Vygotsky thought). Similarly, to search for a "natural" human mind in nonliterate societies or in cross-cultural generalities is, if not futile, at least more challenging than generally considered, in that all groups reflect specific histories. No group product (e.g., folk classification of plants) reflects an individual human mind. All such products are social and cultural products, as all humans are social and cultural.

A suggested remedy for the nativist–universalist inclination in developmental theorizing is semantic: Substitute "humans" (both men and women) for "man" or "mankind." Substitute "human minds" for "the human mind"; substitute "languages" for "Language"; substitute "children" for "the child." (Of course, it will be observed that this is a cure that is difficult to take, as practice herein often reverts to the universal forms.)

Then it may be asked: If the purpose of the science of cognitive psychology and cognitive development is not to uncover universals of mind, what is its goal? Here the answer is straightforward: It is to study how human infants, children, and adults meet, master, and use cultural knowledge and cultural forms, for that is their destiny. Language takes its place here as the child comes to share the history and culture of the community, and as the child becomes aware of her own history. Through these processes the human child comes into her own as a thinking individual in a shared human culture. Without language she is cut off in essential ways from others and from herself. This essentially is the story to be told in the chapters to follow. It begins by asking what precedes language in phylogeny and ontogeny, and how does language come to play its essential role in our human cognitive and cultural lives?

Organization of the Book

The following chapters elaborate on the perspective taken, the evolutionary background, the developmental evidence, and the research and theoretical questions that are opened up thereby. As this introductory discussion has suggested, the perspective presented here focuses on how children represent the reality that they experience, and the modes of representation involved. Another focus is on the derivation of general or abstract knowledge from the representation of specific experience – in particular, the construction of concepts and conceptual systems of knowledge. A corollary of the present view is that concepts and conceptual systems change over developmental time, in response to changes in representational systems, and in response to operations of abstraction and organization, as well as in response to conceptual knowledge mediated through the language representations of others. A major problem for developmentalists is to document these changes, and to trace the source of the change to different influences, insofar as that is possible. In this work, then, I focus on the complexities that enter into the child's experiential models and the changes therein made possible when through language the child can take advantage of knowledge mediated by others who know more about how the world works. The thesis is that language when acquired changes cognition in important ways and opens up knowledge potentials not accessible without it.

The rest of the book is devoted to spelling out this story in more detail and providing the evidence and arguments for its basic claims. Chapters 2 and 3 complete the introductory section. Chapter 2 presents some evolutionary and biological background, together with alternative views on the implications of evolutionary history for psychological theory. The evolutionary perspectives discussed in Chapter 2 do not specifically address the question of the mediated mind, but rather focus on general processes and levels of intelligence and knowing, or on the specific domain of language. In Chapter 3, the proposal by Merlin Donald (1991) designed to explain the evolution of human cognition, inclusive of human language, is introduced and discussed in some detail. It provides a detailed model of representational stages in evolution that provoke developmental analogies. The purpose of using this model of the evolution of human cognition for a developmental analysis is to provide an integrated conceptualization of the biological in human cognitive development that coheres with (and does not compete with) the cultural. Donald's scheme is an attempt to do this on the phylogenetic scale; it is revealed to be highly compatible with the assumptions of the developmental theory developed here, and his themes reverberate throughout the remainder of the book.

Part II contains chapters on representation in and out of language. Chapter 4 sets the stage by considering prelinguistic basic event representations in the context of early social and cognitive development, culminating in the first steps toward language. These developments are shown to include important aspects of the mimetic skills that Donald's theory proposes as evolutionary precursors to language. Chapter 5 focuses on language itself, showing how it develops over the first 3 years to become a possible mode of representation. In Chapter 6 memory development in early childhood is traced, specifically the development of autobiographic memory and the end of infantile amnesia. Narrative plays a critical role in memory development, and has emerged as a distinctly human mode of thinking. Its development over the early childhood years is the topic of Chapter 7.

Part III considers conceptual development over the preschool years, in terms of the way that language enters into and changes preschoolers' understanding. Categorical or paradigmatic thinking has been contrasted to narrative (Bruner, 1986). Concepts and categories of objects are considered in Chapter 8, where it is shown that the two "modes of thinking" proposed by Bruner are in fact two faces of the same interdependent system. Time concepts and time language – generally neglected topics in developmental psychology – are considered in Chapter 9. Chapter 10 focuses on the currently "hot" topic of the child's theory of mind, otherwise understood as developing knowledge of self and the social world. Self-concept development is a continuing underlying theme throughout the chapters on language, memory, narrative, and time, as well as in Chapter 10. Rather than being treated as a separate topic, it emerges as a strand that ties the others together.

The topics treated here are obviously not inclusive of all the significant knowledge domains that develop during the early childhood years (omitting, for example, numbers and space); nor do they attempt to present an exhaustive review of research or an unbiased approach. The domains considered are ones that exemplify operations of the general model. One outcome of these considerations is a tentative identification of domains where language makes a difference and domains where it does not. At the end, Chapter 11 draws together the pieces presented and provides a summary of the theory of developmental change through collaborative construction in early human development.

2. Emergence of Human Minds in Evolution and Development

Humans are cultural and linguistic animals. There are no other animals of this type, with these characteristics. How did this come to be? Can we understand human development better if we understand our evolutionary history better? In this chapter I consider several perspectives on these questions. I argue that we must recognize both parts of the beginning proposition: On the one hand, we are animals that are closely related to other primate species, and understanding our development in comparison to theirs may shed important light on both basic processes and complex higher-order cognitive developments. On the other hand, the unique characteristics of the human species – language and the complexities of our social and cultural environments – may be better understood by considering the conditions under which these characteristics became established historically as well as developmentally. Underlying this proposition is the assumption that to understand the developmental processes that make language in cognition possible, it is necessary to understand the contributions of functions that precede and enter into its establishment.

Another justification for undertaking the survey in this chapter is the widespread acceptance today of what has been termed "neo-nativism," varying forms of which all embrace some type of genetic determinism. Many psychologists who reject genetic determinism tend also to ignore or reject biological or evolutionary theories in general as irrelevant to their concerns. However, there are important alternatives to genetic determinism in evolutionary biology, anthropology, and comparative psychology that are very relevant to understanding the basis for the development and processes of human cognition and language. Dynamic systems theory is emerging in developmental psychology as a kind of metatheory that is appropriate to the complexities of these processes (Thelen, 1989; Thelen & Smith, 1994; Van Geert, 1993).

The main reason for laying out – in however skeletal form – the bio-logical evolutionary and developmental basis for human cognition and language, however, is to provide the background against which to con-sider how the mind of the human infant becomes transformed into the fully cultural mind of the human adult. Research in infant cognition and adult cognitive psychology has filled in many blanks on both ends, but the transition between the two is very inadequately understood at pres-ent, and we lack general theories to explain the data we have. In con-trast, a powerful theory of the evolutionary transformations that led from a prehuman to a fully modern mind (Donald, 1991) is considered in detail in Chapter 3. The overall scheme presented there suggests impor-tant analogies to the developmental problems addressed here. In order to appreciate these analogies it is necessary first to confront some of the established knowledge and controversial claims about the prehistory of mind. The goal of this chapter then is to set the stage for the next, and in the process to whet the interest of those who may not yet have delved into these issues, some of which are passionately fought over in other branches of the social and biological sciences.[1]

Neo-nativism and Its Alternatives

In recent decades interactionism has been the widely accepted position of developmental psychologists. Although the term has many interpreta-tions, its usual meaning has been either developmental constructionism through interaction of the organism and the environment (e.g., Piaget-ian theory) or developmental determinism in terms of the interaction of genes and environment (the sociobiological view). Most developmen-talists have thus implicitly disposed of the nature–nurture question that has periodically vexed the field of psychology and have gone on to carry out research without worrying about the relative contributions of nature and nurture to the functions under examination.

This peaceful accommodation has been increasingly challenged, to the extent that a new and powerful force has been established within the developmental fold. A first challenge came from the theoretical argu-ments of Chomsky and Fodor against the constructivist position of Pia-get (Piatelli-Palmarini, 1980), with the strong claims that language, in-deed all concepts, must be innate, that is, not developed or learned. Behavior geneticists have contributed through population models of psy-chological traits, parceling out genetics and environment as independent and noninteracting components, and stressing the strong heritability of traits such as general intelligence.[2]

Perhaps most persuasive to many people has been the research on cognition in infancy, which reveals early and extensive understanding of the physical world, as well as abstract concepts like number, and cognitive processes of memory and categorization thought by Piaget and earlier psychologists to be advanced cognitive achievements. These findings have supported the related theoretical claims that (1) the brain is organized in terms of specialized modules for specialized knowledge systems, some of which – those mentioned here – emerge (full-blown) in early infancy; (2) such modules provide constraints on learning within a domain; and (3) knowledge in general is organized in terms of domain specificity, that is, that special processes apply to specialized knowledge domains (Hirschfeld & Gelman, 1994b). In the long run specific learning processes are assumed to become accessible to generalization and application to new domains (Rozin, 1976).

Further support for these claims has been viewed as coming from studies of learning and communication in nonhuman animals – for example, in the specialized systems for bird song acquisition, spider web creation, and honey bee navigation and communication – which are uniquely specified for the adaptive functions of particular species (Gallistel et al., 1991). For many of these systems it seems obvious to most observers that the acquisition of special competences is "coded in the genes." Then, to maintain that species-specific competences of humans – for example, language acquisition – are different seems obtuse from this point of view. Indeed, the degree of complexity of "innate knowledge" displayed by various species is enormously impressive. But there are, I believe, good reasons not to make the leap from bees and birds to human knowledge quite so readily.

Neo-nativists tend to ignore the contribution of developmental processes to the establishment of a psychological competence or physiological function. Rather, they see a direct route from genes to behavior. Much recent work not only ignores development but also denies significant cognitive change past infancy (e.g., Spelke, 1991) and considers culture as basically irrelevant to the study of psychological mechanisms (e.g., Tooby & Cosmides, 1992). In the latter view, both mind and culture are viewed as products of the genes, determined by natural selection for individual fitness. This view rests on an underlying model that Gottlieb (1992) terms predetermined epigenesis (see Table 2.1).

In the predetermined view both evolution and development are the

Table 2.1. *Two versions of epigenetic development*

Predetermind Epigenesis
Unidirectional Structure–Function Development
Genetic Activity ⟶ Structural Maturation ⟶ Function, Activity, or Experience (DNA ⟶ RNA ⟶ Protein)
Probabilistic Epigenesis
Bidirectional Structure–Function Development
Genetic Activity ⟷ Structural Maturation ⟷ Function, Activity, or Experience (DNA ⟷ RNA ⟷ Protein)

Source: Reproduced from Table 13-1, p. 160. G. Gottlieb (1992) *Individual development and evolution*. Oxford University Press. Used with permission of the publisher.

result of single-directional processes determined by a genetic code. Organisms are "vehicles" for genes and are adapted to unchanging environments. To the extent that development is considered at all, it is seen in terms of a set of developmental programs, organized by the genes as autonomous maturation instructions, thus as both necessary and sufficient for development. But, as Thelen (1993) states: "As development even at the embryonic level not only requires gene products but also a highly complex and contingent series of events including gradients, polarities, position and feedback effects, the causal chain is impossible to disentangle. Genes enable development to occur, but not more so than any other part of the process" (p. 102).

The alternative to predetermined epigenesis, with its unidirectional causes flowing forward from genes to behavior, is probabilistic epigenesis (Table 2.1) reflecting coaction between processes, with influences from activity at all higher levels flowing backward to affect the expression of genetic activity. In the probabilistic view evolution and development are multidirectional and multidetermined systems that include the environment as an essential component of the total system. Both organisms and environments change over time, and adaptation is a product of these changes. This view recognizes that perhaps the major problem for both evolution and development is the emergence of new forms – species in evolution and individuals in development – a problem with no satisfactory solution in the framework of genetic determinism (Gottlieb, 1992; Salthe, 1993).

How development relates to evolution is neither a simple matter of recapitulation nor an extension on the individual level of a history on the species level. Evolution can be understood as the novel emergence of new kinds of individuals, that is, species (Salthe, 1993). Each species is a unique solution to the organism–environment adaptive system. Development, on the other hand, is a process common (and to a large extent uniform) within a species. But each individual is also unique, with both a unique genetic heritage and unique epigenetic processes and experiences. Thus, whereas the processes that underlie development are universal across the species, each individual is a novel product of those processes.

Just as the result of evolutionary processes can be predicted only within very general constraints[3] of adaptation, so the result of individual ontogeny can be predicted only within very general constraints of biological development in specific environments. The implication is that we need to have a sound understanding of what those constraints are, as well as the potentials of the developing system as it encounters the equally important constraints and supports of the social environment.

Understanding individual development involves both understanding universal processes and the potential for diverse solutions to common problems. Such individual solutions can be thought of as analogous to the emergence of new species as the result of adaptations to new environments. The possibility of equipotential pathways to common products, such as language competence, is a necessary outcome of the dynamic systems approach. Thus, in evolutionary perspective human childhood may be viewed as a unique solution to the problems of developing within human environments. In this perspective the child is seen not as a product of genes plus environment (as in unidirectional views), but rather as a developing biological system within a cultural milieu.

Development considered as a dynamic system has implications for all the claims set forth previously in terms of the neo-nativist model. Infant cognition must be seen as part of the dynamic system of development, as related to prior individually organized biological processes, and to evolutionary processes of species organization. In place of innate fully specified modules we find open systems, flexibility, multi-determined processes, and neural plasticity dependent upon environmental experience. In this view, domain specificity and modularity are outcomes that are not explanatory of development. Development proceeds in concert with experience of the organism, and the social environment and cultural situatedness are essential components of human developmental processes. Therefore they are not competing with or separate from biology (including the genes) but are necessary parts of the system.

Human Infancy in Biological Perspective

Our species – *Homo sapiens sapiens* – belongs to the order of primates within the mammalian class. Other primates include the great apes (chimpanzees, gorillas, and orangutans), monkeys, and lemurs. Although each primate species is unique, a visit to the zoo impresses upon anyone the common structures and behaviors that each one shares with us. The basic design of human minds must then have a good deal in common with that of the other primates (and to some extent of mammals in general); indeed, most of the capacities recently observed in human infants are found in other primates in early infancy (Antinucci, 1990). A century and a half after Darwin put forth the basic theory of the evolution of species, this should not surprise anyone.

Thanks to the advances made in numerous infant research laboratories, almost every claim made by Piaget (1952) about development in the first year of life has been challenged in recent years. To give a superficial overview, we can note that infants of 6 months of age have been shown to expect objects to be three-dimensional, to be substantial, to occupy space, to fall to earth when dropped, and to cause other objects to move on impact[4] (Baillargeon, 1993; Spelke, 1988, 1991). In other words, infants live in and experience a physical world of objects much like our own. They do not construct physical knowledge from scratch, and there is little evidence of learning in this domain, as classically understood. These facts have shaken traditional conceptions of psychological development, but comparative and evolutionary studies imply that they should have been anticipated.

Given our close relationship with other primates, it is not surprising that comparative research has shown that chimpanzees, gorillas, and macaque monkeys all develop object concepts along a trajectory similar to that of human infants, with some variations in timing (Antinucci, 1989). This suggests two conclusions: First, structured knowledge of the object world was probably developed as a cognitive capacity far back in the primate line of evolution (and perhaps in mammals generally), long before humans branched off as a species. Second, such knowledge develops according to a sequenced organic program that has little to do with specific exposure to specific external environments.[5]

Even more striking, research has demonstrated infants' attention to the properties of number, generally considered an abstract idea (Starkey & Cooper, 1980; Starkey, Spelke, & Gelman, 1990; Wynn, 1992a). Impressive as these findings are, similar demonstrations among nonhuman animals of number perception and operations equivalent to arithmetic manipulations have been documented (Gallistel, 1989). For example, the evidence from conditioning experiments indicates that lower animals (rats and pigeons) are sensitive to numerosities up to about 50. Perception of numerosity thus does not appear to be as abstract as usually thought, nor is it a specifically human cognitive capacity. Of course, other species do not go on to develop arithmetic systems.

In other domains similar comparisons are found. Face recognition has been examined by Johnson and Morton (1991) in different species, and it appears that the human capacity for face recognition is if anything only a minor elaboration on a basic primate visual capability (Gomez, 1990). As for cognitive maps of foraging territory, rudimentary forms are found in rats as well as in our primate relatives.

These findings suggest some of what human minds – like other primate minds – are designed to extract from encounters with the environment, whether acted upon or only observed, whether available at birth or developing in interaction with experience in the world. Together they indicate an infant who is maturing within a physical environment that "makes sense" from a human point of view. Would not evolution have so provided? Why should we not have number detectors as well as color detectors? The "conceptual" capacities of human infants appear to be little different from the "built-in" abilities of other related species. The theoretical question this raises is whether human minds are constrained by these capacities in the same way that other species' behavior may be or whether these capacities provide the beginning point for more flexible functioning.

The results from infant research do not easily fit traditional empiricist distinctions between basic sensations (colors), perceptions (triangles), and abstract conceptions (number); therefore, they have seemed more compatible with rationalist or neo-nativist models. In an evolutionary perspective, however, infant capacities are no more surprising than the migration of swallows. Once we give up the outdated notion that all knowledge derives from sensations, the relevant questions become those that we can pose to evolutionary models of the primate and specifically human mind: How has mind evolved and what are the implications for its functions?

This perspective on individual development must be tempered, however, by the acknowledgment of a coacting system. Infancy in all mammals is a special period of preparatory development. In humans, it is characterized by the immaturity of all perceptual and motor systems, and maturation of these systems proceeds in concert with ongoing maturation of the central nervous system as well as with exploratory activity in the external environment.

Development of the Primate and Human Central Nervous System

Recent research on the development of the central nervous system (CNS) has underscored its fundamental plasticity and reliance on experiential feedback, supporting the probabilistic epigenesis view sketched in Table 2.1 In regard to these developments Gottlieb (1992) writes:

> Structural maturation [of the nervous system] refers to . . . the structure and function of nerve cells and their synaptic interconnections. The unidirectional structure-function view assumes that genetic activity gives rise to structural maturation that then leads to function in a nonreciprocal fashion, whereas the bidirectional view holds that there are constructive reciprocal relations between genetic activity, maturation, and function. In the unidirectional view, the activity of genes and the maturational process are pictured as relatively encapsulated or insulated so that they are uninfluenced by feedback from the maturation process or function, whereas the bidirectional view assumes that genetic activity and maturation are affected by function, activity, or experience. (p. 160)

The bidirectional view relies on feedback to signal the turning off and on of DNA for manufacturing protein, whereas the unidirectional view "calls for genetic activity to be regulated by the genetic system itself in a strictly feedforward manner" (p. 160). These comments apply to the basic biological processes of cell formation and function, and they apply as well to the macroprocesses involved in the maturation of the CNS over the infancy and early childhood years. Gottlieb (1992) reviews a century of experimental research supporting this view, including important demonstrations of developmental plasticity in the wake of varying experiential rearing conditions.

Furthermore, analysis of the development of the CNS in humans and other primates indicates progressive developments in neural maturation processes that relate advances in cognitive development with corresponding brain development. Much of the knowledge of brain development until very recently was based on studies of infrahuman primates, monkeys and apes. Such studies have been extremely valuable in tracing the general course of development in the primate brain, and in showing relations between species (e.g., Diamond, 1991; Goldman-Rakic et al.,

1983). For example, developments in both the CNS and problem solving that appear at 4 months for monkeys are observed in a similar relationship at about 10 to 12 months in human children. But the close comparison of cognitive achievements of monkeys and apes with humans can be extended only during the infancy period, after which human children take off in quite different ways. Thus the lessons that the primate data can provide are quite limited when one is trying to understand the specific contributions of later evolutionary changes in the human line. Anatomical studies of human infant brains are also quite limited, and recent advances in scanning methodologies, although provocative, do not yet provide a complete or coherent picture. From both older and newer studies, however, a general picture of early human brain development has emerged that includes the following significant sequences.[6]

Neurons are formed and migrate to different brain regions prenatally in the human, and a left-hemisphere bias for processing speech sounds is observed from birth, although the significance of this bias is at present undetermined. The human brain is notably immature at birth in comparison with other primates, and it remains extraordinarily plastic and subject to quite radical reorganization in response to trauma or experiential deprivation (and presumably enrichment) for several years and, to some extent, even throughout life. Processes of postnatal development of the human brain include hemispheric specialization, synaptogenesis, dendritic branching, and myelination. By 9 or 10 months most long-range connections in the brain have been established, and neural activity measured metabolically has reached adult levels in the frontal cortex. Myelination – the insulation of neural fibers – begins during this period and continues well into adulthood.

Rises and decreases in synaptogenesis over the early months and years appear to be most closely related to cognitive development. Between 9 and 24 months the density of synaptic connections rises to 150% of the adult human level. There is some disagreement as to whether the rise in synaptic connections is uniform across the brain, or whether it proceeds area by area from the sensory areas early in infancy with a peak in frontal cortex around 24 months of age (Bates, Thal, & Janowsky, 1992). A related increase in overall metabolic activity exists, which reaches a peak at about 48 months of age.

The most interesting aspect of the development of the CNS is that the peaks in neuronal numbers, connectivity, synapses, and activity are followed by decreases, often sharp decreases, to adult levels at later points in development. Neurons die, axons retract, synaptic degeneration follows synaptogenesis, and metabolic activity declines. In general, brain development seems to be primarily a process of pruning away excess. As Bates, Thal, and Janowsky (1992) put it, "The picture that emerges from recent research on brain development is one of *overproduction* (a relatively sudden process), followed by *selective elimination* (a relatively slow process that spans a longer period of time)" (p. 100). For example, at 2 years neuronal density in the frontal cortex is 55% above adult levels (although neuronal pruning has been proceeding since birth or before) and falls to 10% above adult level by 7 years. Synaptic degeneration falls gradually until sometime between 11 and 16 years. Similarly, metabolic activity declines from its peak at 4 years to adult levels in adolescence.

Are these developments more compatible with the unidirectional genetic determinism view or with the bidirectional, multidetermined epigenetic view? Although maturation is readily invoked by advocates of the former view, the rises and declines are more compatible with models of neuronal function that take account of the importance of experience in shaping brain structure and function postnatally, models that fit the bidirectional, probabilistic view outlined by Gottlieb (1992) in Table 2.1. Indeed, the openness of the CNS to the influence of the external environment over long periods of developmental time is consistent with the strong view of neural and cognitive plasticity in the human species. It is inconsistent with a strong deterministic view, whether seen in terms of genetic or neuronal structures. This is not to deny structural organization of the CNS, but to recognize the enormous plasticity and resulting individuality of that organization dependent upon postnatal experience.

Summary

In the present framework, the implications of studies of infant cognition and brain development for understanding individual ontogeny can be summarized as follows: (1) The neonate is prepared to analyze the world in specific ways, established through functions long enduring in evolutionary time. Infancy is thus a period of "tuning" the perceptual and conceptual systems to the specifics of the social and physical environment. (2) The brain – and mind – are open to, indeed dependent on, experience, and to reprogramming throughout childhood and into later life. (3) Specific human capacities come "on line" after infancy in collaboration with social-cultural experience. Language and cultural knowledge are products of this collaboration.

As Cairns (1993) notes, the integrated nature of development means that "although organisms are highly adaptive in immaturity . . . they are buffered from the enduring influence of these experiences. . . . The time between infancy and adulthood (a) permits restructuring because of the acquisition of alternative experiences, and (b) promotes reorganization because of inevitable maturational changes" (p. 79). In brief, postnatal experience throughout childhood is critical to the development of brain and mind.

As noted previously, finding that human infants are "predesigned" to deal with their environments – physical, social, and linguistic – in intelligent ways has appeared to support the idea that the human mind is constrained by innate modules to learn in specific ways within specific domains of knowledge. However, a broader evolutionary perspective contradicts this conclusion, as the following section argues.

The Perspective of Evolutionary Epistemology

The ideas of evolutionary epistemology rest on an abstract model of levels that provides an important perspective on the evolution of human learning, cognition, and language. D. Campbell (1982/1974, 1990) outlined the theoretical postulates of this position and the research supporting it. Plotkin (1982, 1988, 1993) elaborated this approach to the evolution of intelligence and culture, analyzing their place within a wider evolutionary framework. Of interest to the present account is the proposal of a hierarchy of processes in gaining knowledge. Campbell (1982/1974) proposed 10 levels from genes to learning, thought, and science. Plotkin posits four fundamental levels, outlined here.

1. Genetic programs constitute the most fundamental level of knowledge gain about the environment that is useful to the particular organism in its functional tasks. This level is temporally restricted by generation turnover time. If environmental events of significance to the organism occur at a more rapid temporal pattern than one generation, pressures exist for the organism to adapt new forms of information acquisition and retention. Adaptation to environmental conditions that do not change over eons may be specified in the genotype. For long-lived species such as humans in which generational time is extended, alternative information utilization possibilities are essential and can be found at both the individual and the social group levels.
2. Environmental conditions that vary during the lifespan of the individual must be adapted to either through variable developmental programs (level 2) or through individual learning processes (level 3). It is now a well-established biological principle that epigenetic processes are based on self-regulation and self-organization. Concepts that have linked morphological development to evolution include neoteny (developmental

delay), acceleration (early development), and heterochrony (a mixture of early and delayed development across different components of a system). These concepts may be applied also to behavioral (including cognitive) developments. Cairns (1993) suggests, "A modest heterochrony, or the mix of the developmental trajectories of component features, can rapidly bring about new behavioral adaptations. Human beings, for example, can be neotenous in motor development yet accelerated in cognitive development, conditions that give rise to distinctively human language" (p. 67). Gottlieb (1992) emphasizes that development is the key to all expression of the genome.

3. Individual learning is the most general mode through which organisms adapt to variable conditions in the environment that are not predictable over generations. Learning through habituation, classical, or operant conditioning can be found among all complex, even in some form in some very primitive, organisms. Individual learning in interaction with the environment is obviously of importance to all complex creatures, including humans, at all stages of development.

4. Adaptation to varying conditions on the group level through using communication systems to share information is a further development that is found among the social insects, as well as birds and mammals, and is characteristic of all primate groups. However, recent analyses suggest that human learning differs from that of other primates in significant ways (Tomasello, 1990; Tomasello, Kruger, & Ratner, 1993). In particular, Tomasello claims that other primates do not engage in true imitation as do humans, who model their actions closely on others. Chimpanzees, for example, attempt to meet the same ends that they see others achieving, using sticks to fish for termites without attending to the specific skills involved. Moreover, he concludes, "The vast majority of chimpanzee communicatory signals are learned by conventionalization" (p. 302). What he means by conventionalization is that "Each signal is created anew from individual, though perhaps common, social interactions, with no attempt to reproduce the behavior of a conspecific . . . Overall imitation plays a minor role in chimpanzee communication, and thus there is little, if any, cultural transmission" (p. 302). Rather, he suggests, learning by chimpanzees is basically a question of shaping behavior, either by the reactions of the interactant in a social situation or by the conditions of the physical environment, as in standard operant conditioning.[7] In an extension of this argument, Tomasello, Kruger, and Ratner (1993) propose that cultural learning is specific to human beings and is one of the characteristics that distinguish humans as a species.

These four basic epistemological levels are displayed by many species, albeit the last in rather restricted ways compared to humans. Plotkin (1988) asserts that the evolutionary epistemological proposal "begins to resolve the age-old nature-nurture issue. . . . It does this not by having recourse to the pseudo-explanatory device of 'interactionism', but by an entirely different kind of conceptualization of nested processes, hierarchically organized" (p. 80). According to Plotkin, "Tabula rasa learning is impossible because the third level evolved out of a failure of the first and second levels to deal with changes occurring above a certain frequency; and having evolved out of this failure . . . it is rooted within and constrained by those more fundamental levels of the hierarchy" (p. 85).

This conception bears on the observation of innate capacities to learn only certain things. For example, Marler (1991) and others have stressed that organisms are programed for specific acquisitions, as songbirds are programed to learn their songs from conspecifics. This idea, known more generally as "constraints on learning," has played an important role in contemporary theories of human infant learning (Gallistel et al., 1991). Questions for developmental theory to answer are: To what extent do *specific* learning programs direct learning at any stage of life, and to what extent does their operation (in infancy, for example) relate to more general intelligent functioning (e.g., in later childhood)? Recognizing the evolutionary bases for species learning, even species-specific programs, does not require the strong form of constraints that this recognition is often thought to imply, according to Plotkin's analysis of hierarchical processes.

Once intelligence evolves, it may become detached from its origins. Plotkin offers the example of manual dexterity in chimpanzees, which enables them to manipulate the environment at a high rate. But once this capability evolved, it could no longer be tracked by genetic mechanisms; thus the variability produced through these manipulations, restricted to the manual domain, leads to new knowledge. Plotkin (1988) generalizes this argument to the use of language in humans: "The human brain is a prodigious generator of variants in the linguistic sphere" (p. 85). Plotkin concludes, "The foci of intelligence in any intelligent species has evolved. . . . *This line of argument does not, however, confine intelligence only and directly to its original source of adaptation*" (p. 86, emphasis added). Evolutionary epistemology then differs from the adaptationist position of genetic determinism. It links learning and culture with the genetic level as extensions of a general epistemological process, but it does not limit them to genetic determinants. Instead, it focuses attention on the way that development and learning may take over adaptive processes for the organism during its lifetime.

Plotkin's four-step version of Campbell's epistemological scheme truncates evolution at the social learning level, a level that arguably applies as well to bees, birds, and chipmunks as to apes and humans. In fact, Plotkin's 1993 exposition stops at the level of the brain and as a result is inadequate in its handling of culture and communication (including language). As previously noted, Tomasello and his colleagues (1993) have made a distinction between social learning and cultural learning that attempts to fill out this gap. Campbell (1990) himself elaborated these steps further into language, cultural cumulation, and science. From the present perspective it is important to consider at least the emergence of a fifth level of knowledge accumulation:

> 5. The next level of adaptation via knowledge gain is available to humans through cultural representation and semiotic cumulations, such as oral traditions and libraries, which human language has made specifically possible.[8] This level can hardly be ignored as the definitive differentiator between humans and other species. Moreover, this level depends critically on the availability of complex human language, as the remainder of this book argues. This observation raises an obvious question: Is this the only difference between humans and other closely related species?

What's Different about Humans?

Despite the many similarities between humans and other primates, and the vast amount of genetic material (DNA) that we apparently have in common with our closest relatives – the chimpanzees (estimated at 99%) – it is hard to overlook the enormous gap between us and them. Questions then arise: What makes humans different? Why did they diverge in the path that they did? These questions have been raised continuously since the eighteenth century and have motivated the ongoing search for human origins by paleontologists, anthropologists, and comparative psychologists.

One notable characteristic that differentiates humans is that their rate of development is slower than that of other species. Humans spend a relatively long time in the womb before birth but are nonetheless born at an earlier stage of development than other primates, and mammals in general. Human infancy lasts two years (compared to one for the chimpanzee), during which both sensory and motor control are achieved, including independent locomotion, and the brain undergoes extensive development (as discussed earlier). During the long period of prenatal and postnatal development the infant is almost totally dependent upon others for basic needs. The many years of childhood dependency associated with extensive physical and mental development is a specific characteristic of the human species that has often been related to other species characteristics, such as highly developed skills and intelligence. Slow growth and development are surely significant, but the length of childhood in humans is only quantitatively different from that of the other great apes. Female chimpanzees, for example, reach sexual maturity at about 12 years but are sterile until about 14 years, not different from contemporary human females.

Humans are clearly differentiated by the high intelligence associated with increased brain capacity, particularly in the development of the neocortex. Proportionately, human brains have tripled in cortical volume (Passingham, 1982) from the general ape model. The observed differences in brain size are accompanied by an increase in neocortical plasticity, noted in the previous discussion of brain development. These developments are extensions of the structure of the brain of other primates, not qualitatively different from theirs, however, in that the extraordinary plasticity of the human brain is more marked but not discontinuous with that of other primates.

Thus these three characteristics – high intelligence, plasticity of neural development, long childhood – can be seen as intensification of general primate features rather than novel pathways. Further, the social groups that are characteristic of all human environments, and that are necessary to sustain the arrangements that make long childhood possible, are also found, although clearly in less complex forms, among our primate relatives.

Although there is considerable similarity between young primates of all species, no one would doubt that humans are different. If the biological difference is only quantitative, what underlies the observed qualitative difference, the intuitive sense of discontinuity? Anthropologists and other observers have long identified culture, tools, and language as specifically human inventions or emergent capacities. Recent studies of apes have identified primitive tool use, such as the use of sticks to search for termites; also, claims have been made that monkeys and apes pass on specific cultural inventions over generations, differentiating one group from the other (Gibson & Ingold, 1993). However, there can be little question that human tools and artifacts, and human cultural groups, practices, and institutions, differ from the tools, artifacts, and "cultures" of other primates in qualitatively discontinuous ways. As for language or communication, human languages are unique and have little in common with the vocal signals of other primates. In addition, organized pedagogy is generally recognized as unique to humans, and it appears that cultural modes of learning are specific to humans (Tomasello, 1990; Tomasello, Kruger, & Ratner, 1993).

As Donald (1995) has remarked, the "massive changes [that mark human cognitive functions in comparison with those of other primates] were apparently achieved with about a 1% change in DNA. This fact alone hints at the special nature of human cognitive evolution. . . . Chimpanzees are genetically much closer to humans than they are to most other primates, and yet their cognitive profile is far closer to that of other primates than it is to that of humans. This suggests that we need to invoke something more than genetically entrenched changes in individual capacity in the case of hominid cognition" (p. 8 of manuscript). What can evolution studies tell us about this "something more"?

Evolutionary History of Human Cognition

Evolutionary models of human cognition are based mainly on the phylogenetic history of the human brain, involving a comparison of cranial capacities in early hominid fossils with those of living apes and with those of later *Homo sapiens* fossil skulls and modern humans. Reconstruction of this history has been quite recent, requiring extensive analysis of skeletal and skull structure from fossil fragments. The results are controversial, but a strong pattern of evolutionary change has emerged, which can be summarized as follows.[9]

The hominid line branched off from the primate line shared with the great apes about 5 million years ago. The first human ancestors included two or more species of *Australopithecus*, but these early forerunners were still relatively small-brained creatures, equivalent in this respect to present-day chimpanzees, the primates to whom we are most closely related. *Homo habilis*, found in sub-Saharan Africa dating from about 2 to $2\frac{1}{2}$ million years B.P. (before present), initiated a different branch of the ancestral tree, leading eventually to *Homo sapiens*. The mean brain size of these ancestors (400–500 cc) was about one-third that of *Homo sapiens*. Of more significance than brain size is the brain/body ratio, or encephalization quotient (EQ), which ranges from 1 for the Colobus monkey to $2\frac{1}{2}$ for *Australopithecus* (not different from the chimpanzee), to about 4 for *Homo habilis*, and reaching approximately 7 for *Homo sapiens* (Passingham, 1982).

Over the next 2 million years human ancestors engaged in a hunting-gathering way of life in the savannahs of Africa, where the earliest stone tools were formed and used. *Homo erectus* emerged, more than 1,000,000 years B.P.; mean brain size for *erectus* doubled to around 1,000 cc, but EQs were not much greater than those of *H. habilis* (Gamble, 1994).[10] About 200,000 years ago archaic *Homo sapiens* arrived with brains of about present size (1,400–1,500 cc). Of equal importance is the relative

Table 2.2. *Approximate time table of human evolution*[a]

Years Before Present	
5 million	Branching from main primate line
	Australopithecus
$2\frac{1}{2}$ million	First hominids – *Homo habilis*
$1\frac{1}{2}$ million	*Homo erectus*
	Stone tools, fire
200,000	Archaic *Homo sapiens*
125,000–40,000	Modern *sapiens*
	Language
50,000–10,000	World colonization
	Cultural explosion

[a]Years cited in the table are averages derived from those frequently given in the sources cited in note 9, but they are subject to modification with further exploration and study of origins.

growth in the different areas of the brain, compared with chimpanzees. Passingham (1982) notes that the human hippocampus is two times the size of the chimpanzee hippocampus, the cerebellum is three times the size, and the neocortex is about five times the size. Thus the increase in brain size has been primarily in the integrative areas, sites of higher cognitive processes.

Homo sapiens sapiens, anatomically modern humans, date only from about 40,000 to 125,000 years B.P., achieving brains of the present shape and structure about 50,000 years ago. The biological evolution of humans as a species was largely complete at that time. Whatever further genetic changes have occurred have not altered the basic structures of the body and its organs, including the brain. As this brief overview indicates, the greatest evolutionary change in terms of the brain occurred in the relatively recent period with the emergence of *Homo sapiens* as a species over the last 50,000 to 200,000 years. Table 2.2 provides an approximate time line summarizing these changes.

It is not only in Africa that early hominid fossils have been found. Some of the *Homo erectus* and Neanderthal specimens have come from Europe and Asia, dating back as much as $1\frac{1}{2}$ million years B.P. However, it is now generally agreed that ancestors of modern humans originated in Africa and left that continent beginning around 800,000 years ago; by 50,000 to 10,000 years ago they had colonized most of the land mass of the world, including the Asian subcontinent, the Pacific, Australia, and the Americas. Regardless of their origins in eastern and southern Africa, *Homo sapiens* were clearly never confined to a particular diet, climate, geographical area, or type of living site. Moreover, although the most primitive stone tools are found in Africa, dating from as far back as $2\frac{1}{2}$ million years ago, there was little change in tool making for more than a million years. It was after the migration to new sites that major advances in tools, use of fire, and cultural innovations of all kinds are found. From around 35,000 to 50,000 years ago in Europe, social and cultural complexity expanded dramatically.

Gamble (1994) emphasizes that the climatic changes that took place during humans' most recent history are important to understanding how and why humans may have colonized the earth so successfully. Of most significance were the recurrent glacial periods from about 300,000 to 15,000 years ago. These fast-changing climates in Europe and Asia (some shifts from glacial to interglacial periods were as brief as one human generation) affected the forests of Africa as well by cooling and drying, thus shifting forest to savannah and confining species adapted only to forest ecologies to narrow bands. Early humans were able to meet these climatic challenges because of what Gamble refers to as a "suite" of adapted elements: bipedality, big brains, omnivorous diets, large size, and cultural innovations. Several of these – brains, diets, culture – reflect the advantages of generality and related flexibility. More specialized related species retreated to environments that could support their unique lifestyles, particularly their dietary needs. It is no doubt significant that none of the earlier hominid species (e.g., *Homo habilis*, *Homo erectus*) survived to the present day, although other primates, such as the chimpanzees, have remained in their special ecological niches over millions of years.

Clearly, the increases in brain size indexing hominid evolution indicate the potential for increasing cognitive power. An issue of current debate and strong interest to the present story is when and why language entered the picture. The anatomical adaptations for speech were not complete until the later stage of modern *Homo sapiens*, about 40,000 years ago (Lieberman, 1984). This timing suggests that language emerged in something like its present forms in conjunction with the emergence of more complex culture, including a vast increase in varieties of manufactured tools, followed by cave art and work with ivory, bone, and clay. The flowering of culture came after a long period (more than 2 million years) of cultural stasis of our hominid ancestors that included the use of only a few primitive stone tools.[11]

Dramatic change in the culture of *H. sapiens* emerged after the changes in their brain size (Durham, 1991; Gamble, 1994). Expansion of the neocortex, especially the frontal lobes, critical to integration of information, enabled increased capacities for differentiation and construction, applied certainly to tools, and inventively to many other aspects of the environment (Parker & Gibson, 1990). The capacity to differentiate aspects of the environment and to construct new tools from old parts would also have transformed the nature of the environment. The physical environment of human groups changed significantly because of climatic changes associated with glaciation and worldwide migration, and also because increased use of tools, fire, and decorative and utilitarian artifacts itself provided a different human environment than that of earlier hominid hunter-gatherers. Not least, the emergence of language use would certainly have provided a vastly different social environment for early *Homo sapiens* than that of earlier species. Thus modern humans are not simply the result of a long, static period of adaptation to an unchanging environment, but rather emerged from a period of a relatively rapid series of changes, including not only changes in the physical environment but elaboration of both culture and language.

Social Origins of Intelligence

Important aspects of the human condition that are neglected in studies that concentrate on skeletal fossils, physical artifacts, and knowledge of the physical world are social organization and social knowledge. These are less amenable to reconstruction from the fossil evidence, but they have been analyzed in terms of comparative studies of present-day primates. Many authors in recent years have claimed that complex human cognition evolved specifically to solve the problems posed by life in complex social groups (e.g., Byrne & Whiten, 1988; Cairns, 1990; Gamble, 1994; Humphrey, 1976; P. J. Wilson, 1980). The basic claim is that primate – including human – intelligence is social intelligence. The assumption that human intelligence evolved as social intelligence has enormous implications for how we view human cognitive development.

That human brain capacity was used in the first place to manage life in social groups, including communication, organization for the exploration of new feeding sites, social alliances, planning hunts, and other vital activities, also sheds light on human ability to subsist in varying ecological niches. Gamble (1994) notes, "Selection for generalists produced the savannah lineage of *Homo*" (p. 116). However, this did not provide the wherewithal to colonize the world. Rather, he claims:

> The evidence . . . is conclusive that the extension of range, which occurred after a million years ago, was the product of selection on the social organization of these savannah groups not on their skulls and brains. An expanded web of relations . . . alliances, incidentally overcame some of those barriers to migration. . . . The construction and constitution of these alliances using the elements of omnivory, mobility, dexterity, social intellect and its effect on memory and manipulation produced unintentional results. (p. 116)

Mind and Culture

With little effort, the list of special human qualities noted in the previous section could be extended to include clothing, agriculture, constructed shelters, cooked food, written and graphic symbolic systems, art, music, and technology. But this list would only extend the notion of culture from its primitive beginnings to its more complex forms. Cultural development or evolution is important to understanding modern human intellect, but it is at the same time both a biologically potentiated and supported system and a process distinct from biological evolution. The evolutionary perspective implies that humans everywhere and throughout history are – more or less – the same, with the same developmental potential. Yet cultural differences in the ways that potential is realized are sometimes quite striking, even extreme. The evolutionary perspective taken here does not override or ignore cultural differences, although it recognizes as well human universals. Both must be accounted for within a developmental model.

In a contrasting approach to the place of evolution in psychological science, Barkow, Cosmides, and Tooby (1992) have developed a wide-ranging program based on sociobiological concepts applied to psychological problems, including especially issues of cognition and language, which they call the "new evolutionary psychology" or the psychology of the "adapted mind." Sociobiological theorizing was initiated by E. O. Wilson (1975) and has since been extended by others (e.g., Dawkins, 1976). Sociobiologists embrace the neo-Darwinian synthesis in which inclusive fitness, equivalent to reproductive success measured in terms of gene survival, is the fundamental unique evolutionary mechanism. In consequence, Cosmides, Tooby, and Barkow (1992) hold as premises that "Evolved psychological mechanisms are adaptations, constructed by natural selection over evolutionary time . . . adapted to the way of life of Pleistocene hunter-gatherers, and not necessarily to our modern circumstances" (p. 5). Cosmides and Tooby (1994) argue further that evolutionary biology supports the assumption that the mind/brain is structured in terms of domain-specific modules, not domain-general processes, such as general learning processes or neural-net connectionism. Their view derives domains or modules from theoretical sociobiological concepts and from speculations about the ecological demands of the hunting-gathering hominids of 2 million years B.P.[12]

Gamble's (1994) analysis of the conditions that led to the migration of early *Homo sapiens* leads to conclusions quite different from those of Cosmides, Tooby, and Barkow. As noted previously, he emphasizes the advantages incurred by generality in enabling existence in a variety of different environments. Rather than adaptation, which puts the burden on outside forces (i.e., changing environments) to shape goodness of fit between form and function in the organism, he invokes the principle of *exaptation*. Exaptation was introduced by Gould and Vrba (1982) to note a process by which a form that originally served one function comes to be opportunistically applied to a different function. The most familiar example is that of feathers, originally serving to sustain warm temperature, then adapted to wings for flying.

What is missing from the Cosmides, Tooby, and Barkow (1992) account, and others of the same type, is [in Gamble's (1994) words]

> the interface between an organism's genetic structure and the environment it has to make a living in. This buffer is, of course, provided by behavior. The interesting point is not that evolution is driven by genetic laws but rather that it is infinitely varied as a result of dealing with survival through the fuzzy medium of behavior. Certainly, animals are engaged in reproductive strategies where Darwinian selection demonstrably takes place. But they are not just machines to replicate genes. They are social as well as reproductive units for the simple reason that social life is where such strategies are played out. (p. 100)

Cosmides and colleagues (1992) state, "The most reasonable default assumption is that the interesting, complex functional design features of the human mind evolved in response to the demands of a hunting and gathering way of life" and, "Behavior generated by mechanisms that are adaptations to an ancient way of life will not necessarily be adaptive in the modern world" (pp. 5–6).[13] The impression this description leaves is of an optimally adapted species existing over millions of years, whose adaptations have become disrupted in the modern era by the irrelevant demands of civilizations that are unlike those of hunter-gatherer societies.

This view is hardly novel, being essentially the same as earlier ethologically based claims such as Lorenz's (1966) regarding the aggression built into our genes. But the impression created is misleading on several counts. First, *Homo sapiens* is not the same species as those hominids that lived 2 million years ago; many changes in body and brain, and presumably behavior as well, resulted from the evolutionary processes that produced the modern species, which appeared in anatomically modern form about 40,000 to 50,000 years ago. Second, the major characteristic of the Pleistocene epoch (from about 2 million to 10,000 years ago) was that of catastrophic climatic changes during glacial and interglacial periods. As previously noted, in the latter part of this time period humans migrated over large distances in response to these changes, and of necessity they adapted their food-gathering and hunting patterns to new ecological sites. Toward the end of the Pleistocene they were already reaping grain; soon after, settled agricultural societies grew up and production of tools and other artifacts exploded. Cultural explosion is the differentiator of our species in comparison to others of prehistory. Rather than the 2 million years that Cosmides, Tooby, and Barkow (1992) see as a static period during which the human brain was narrowly adapted to a specific type of hunting and gathering way of life in a particular environment, the African savannah, the actual timetable (reviewed previously) provides a different picture. It reveals growth and change in both organism and environment, including the evolution of the brain during the million or so years leading from *Homo erectus* to *Homo sapiens*, changes that were associated late in the period, after the emergence of *Homo sapiens*, with the rapid evolution of cultural forms.

Rather than dealing with the requirements of interconnected generations and social groups in providing for survival, Cosmides and associates deal with culture primarily from the stance that culture reflects functional "mind design" features. Thus social groups and cultures are viewed by them from the perspective of individual survival and reproduction, based on the claim that the gene selection by the environment is the only mechanism of evolved structure (by this reasoning, all structures are adaptive). This view of evolution sees the organism as the tool (or vehicle) of the genes in the competitive struggle for survival. But rather than the single-direction process implied in the adapted mind model (and other genetic determinism models), human evolution requires a multidirectional systems analysis such as Gottlieb (1992) provides. Alternative biological views (e.g., J. Campbell, 1985; Depew & Weber, 1985; Gamble, 1992; Gould & Lewontin, 1979) recognize nonadaptive (neutral) traits, and mechanisms of self-organization in organismic development. Alternatives to the sociobiological model may be found in modern views of evolution and individual development that posit levels of selection and processes of organization above the level of the gene that affect the organism's success in survival.

Human social and cultural environments are of special kinds that both offer protection for the developing child and make demands of her. Within human societies, development of the cognitive and action potentials that enable the child to reach adulthood prepared for the adult tasks of production, reproduction, and maintenance of the community are of signal importance. Each human environment is different from every other, and the human child must be flexible enough to adapt to all such viable environments. In turn, human cultures must be adapted to the constraints imposed by human childhood – and by mature human cognition – if the culture itself is to be maintained. Thus the general structures of human environments – that is, cultures – are invariably such that general adaptive strategies of human children may succeed within them. Among these adaptive strategies, one may assume, are attachment to primary caretakers/parents, attention to and exploration of characteristics of the physical world that are significant for and perceptible by humans, ready interaction with and enjoyment of social others in playful activities, and acquisition of human communication systems, primarily the language of the community. Armed with these biologically potentiated strategies, the human infant/child is prepared to acquire knowledge necessary to adapt to varying conditions and to become a participating member of any human group.

It is simplistic to equate the evolutionary heritage of the human species with its genetic component alone. Humans live today and are adapted within complex cultures. Any claims that their intelligence, language, and learning are constrained by specific adaptations for a particular simpler cultural existence must be established on a case-by-case analysis rather than assumed on general theoretical grounds.

Evolution of Language

The evolution of language is a specific problem for those who seek to understand both language and cognition from a functional perspective. Identifying the evolutionary mechanisms that may have led to the emergence of human language, whether in the service of individual higher cognitive processes, pragmatic communicative needs for managing work activities such as tool-making and hunting (or foraging), or for social functions of managing larger social groups, has been the basis for much speculation. Alternative views emphasize the demands of socializing children, sharing food, and planning activities as contexts for language emergence, or talking about abstract concepts such as temporal relationships. Of course, any of these communicative pressures may have facilitated the development of language once its basic potential was in place.

Gamble (1994) summarizes the issue neatly:

> Communication existed among all [early hominids] and the social context provides the exaptive process to upgrade this to language. The link between, on the one hand, exploration and the use and knowledge of space, and on the other the scale, depth, and complexity of social life is irrefutable. . . . Viewed exaptively the origins of language escape from the adaptive problem of the chicken and egg. Which came first, social relationships requiring memory and the ability to juggle time and people? Or language, making possible intricate socializing interrupted in time and place and complicating by fluctuating numbers? . . . They were adapted/exapted to satisfy current needs and not to meet an unknown future goal. (p. 174)

The basic mode of natural language is speech, involving the production and perception of combinations of elementary sounds realized in different languages as phonemes, sounds that "make a difference." Speech is a distinctly human capacity, not shared by other animals; evidence for the completion of the modern form of the vocal tract that makes production of speech sounds possible is confined to the last 100,000 years of *Homo sapiens*, compared to the $3\frac{1}{2}$ to 4 million years of hominid evolution beginning with *Australopithecus*.[14] Evidence for skills related to human language in chimpanzees (i.e., use of symbols provided by humans and combinations of these symbols) does not imply a genealogical relationship, although it may imply a common underlying *cognitive* structure from which language capacities might have evolved. To the extent that the learning processes of a primate like the pigmy chimpanzee Kanzi may be similar to those of human children acquiring language (Savage-Rumbaugh et al., 1993), we might conclude that there are general learning programs that may be used for acquiring complex symbol-like systems (including English) that are not unique to humans. But this evidence would not speak to the evolution of language, or even to the evolution of symbolic systems, since no other animal that we know of has invented or evolved a symbolic system for communication or for any other purpose.

The system for producing and perceiving speech clearly evolved through natural selection (Lieberman, 1984; Studdert-Kennedy, 1991). Lieberman shows that the physical evidence implies that the evolution of the laryngeal changes that made human speech possible took place gradually over 1.5 million years. Evolution of the speech capacity involved significant modification of the larynx, pharynx, and mouth cavity from the general primate model, which enabled the production of modulated speech sounds. In addition, the tongue receded to form the flexible mouth cavity. These changes are recapitulated in human infancy.[15] Lieberman points out that the result was a significant survival disadvantage in that humans past infancy, unlike other primates, maintain open pathways to the larynx, which poses a constant threat of choking on food. Beyond the structural changes, the capacity for flexible motoric movements involved in the production of speech had to be developed to make possible the rapid recombination of sounds demanded by the infinitely expandable lexical-morphological system. In addition to the physical changes, underlying speech cognitive mechanisms required for language include the representation, memory, and analysis of rapid sequentially ordered speech sounds.[16] The accompanying developments in language structure could not have preceded these developments.

The evolution and development of the speech system cannot be questioned (although the precise dates and changes cited by Lieberman have been questioned), but when theorists debate the question of whether *language* has evolved through natural selection it is not always clear whether they are talking about speech or the abstract structure of languages that serve to connect speech sounds to meaning. These two are of course intimately intertwined but they are not the same. Languages can be expressed in other forms (e.g., sign language, writing). The brain is involved in both aspects of the speech/language system, but usually when the brain, or the cognitive, basis of language is discussed by linguists and psycholinguists it is the abstract structure of language, not its physical realization in speech, that is the topic and that is subject to controversy. Indeed, many cognitive scientists view language as simply an outcome or a necessary component of complex cognitive processes, a position shared by Chomsky (1988) and Fodor (1981), among others.

All human languages call on a set of abstract symbols and categories for their structure. They involve such things as lexical categories (e.g., noun, verb), noun phrase and verb phrase categories, structure rules, order rules, affixes (as for tense), and a number of others [see Pinker and Bloom (1992) for discussion]. The major issue that arises from the consideration of these structural categories is how symbols, symbolic categories, and phrases for expressing propositions emerged from prior nonlinguistic thought structures. Researchers in cognitive science and linguistics have for the most part assumed the computational model of human representation and thinking, where computations are manipulations of symbols, akin to natural language, thus avoiding this issue (see Donald, 1991) without solving it.

Pinker and Bloom (1990, 1992) have presented a case for the Darwinian evolution of the universal grammar of natural language, in opposition to the views of Chomsky (1988, 1991) and Piattelli-Palmarini (1989) that language could not have evolved but emerged (full-blown) as a by-product of some other process – allegedly one of Gould and Lewontin's (1979) spandrels.[17] Pinker and Bloom (1992) work from within the generative grammar tradition of Chomsky (1965, 1991), providing an outline from that perspective of the design of human languages. They note, "Human language is a device capable of communicating exquisitely complex and subtle messages, from convoluted soap opera plots to theories of the origin of the universe," and thus "It would have to have rather special and unusual properties suited to the task of mapping complex propositional structures onto a serial channel" (pp. 463–464). They argue that the complex design of language to suit functional purposes – of expressing propositional thoughts – can be accounted for only by genetic adaptation mechanisms.

In arguing that Universal Grammar as conceived in Chomsky's theory evolved through the process of natural selection, Pinker and Bloom (1992) deny that a grammar would have to evolve as a whole structure all at once. Their discussion of this point is worth quoting:

> The assertion that a natural language grammar functions either as a whole or not at all is surprisingly common. But it has no more merit than similar claims about eyes, wings, and webs that frequently pop up in the anti-Darwinian literature . . . and that occasionally trigger hasty leaps to claims about exaptations. Pidgins, contact languages, Basic English, and the language of children, immigrants, tourists, aphasics, telegrams, and headlines provide ample proof that there is a vast continuum of viable communicative systems displaying a continuous gradation of efficiency and expressive power. (p. 479)

Note that this caution in itself undermines the necessity of the conclusion that language structures as we know them were a product of human biological evolution. Rather, it suggests the possibility that language may have evolved biologically as a kind of communication system producing telegraphic-type utterances that was subsequently elaborated in the process of cultural evolution.

Indeed, at least two proposals have been advanced that suggest this possibility. Greenfield (1991) proposes a model based on homologies in neurological and behavioral levels, specifically object manipulations by human children and chimpanzees. She envisions an early stage of proto-language undifferentiated from the hierarchical structures underlying object handling, equivalent to the productive language abilities of modern 2-year-old humans. A later stage of language modularization encapsulating complex syntax is thought to follow this early stage, to be in some sense equivalent in structure to recursive subassemblies of objects, and to be unique to the human species. Bickerton's (1984, 1990) distinction between pidgin and creole languages is similar to Greenfield's proto-language and true language; both see the second more complex development as a biological adaptation specific to humans. In contrast, Donald (1993b; see Chapter 2) suggests that both the proto-language and more complex grammar were human inventions, products of an earlier biological evolution of symbolic forms, that subsequently have served to shape the human brain epigenetically.

Pinker and Bloom (1992) note the usefulness of language in learning and in pedagogy, stating, "Presumably there is a large selective advantage conferred by being able to learn in a way that is essentially stimulus-free. . . . Children can learn from a parent that a food is poisonous or a particular animal is dangerous; they do not have to observe or experience this by themselves" (pp. 481–482). Of course, the advantages of language-based pedagogy go far beyond such cases.[18] Both contemporary (!Kung) and early hunter-gatherer groups may have found language advantageous not only for hunting but for other purposes, including telling stories about their adventures. Or, as Raeithel (1994) suggests, they may have found language essential for tracking the seasons of the year, important in planning foraging and hunting, as they migrated to new climates or adjusted to the changes of glacial periods. These speculations align with Gamble's conclusions quoted above. However, what is missing from the Pinker and Bloom account is the consideration of social complexity. As Savage-Rumbaugh and associates (1993) point out, great apes plan their routes for locating food sources and must have cognitive capacities for keeping in mind foods that are plentiful at different times, and they do this without the advantage of human language. Similarly, wolf packs coordinate their hunting activities successfully without language. These primitive food-gathering and hunting activities obviously do not require complex language.

Pinker and Bloom (1992) note, "Devices designed for communicating precise information about time, space, predicate-argument relations, restrictive modification, and modality are not wasted in such efforts [i.e., planning hunts]. Recursion in particular is extraordinarily useful" (p. 482). These claims are right on the money; they are surely true, and their validity is part of the motivation for spelling out the role that language does and does not play in early and later cognition, the topic of this book. But the usefulness of complex grammar to the linguistic constructions of present-day humans (even present-day hunter-gatherers) does not speak to the functional pressures that lay behind the evolution of language in the first place, or to the form of language or communication that might have preceded and led into the design of human languages, or to the variety of functions of language today.

As noted previously, the human species evolved as the most generalized primate, where the primate order is the most generalized among mammals (P. J. Wilson, 1980). Generality enables adaptation to extremely variable environments, such as those met by hominids during the Pleistocene, and variability is the prime characteristic produced by different human cultures and by different human languages. Despite the claims of Universal Grammar, the actual diversity of grammars in languages is very great: Maratsos (1990) claims that the only structural characteristic common to all languages is predicate-argument configuration. Applying these insights to the language evolution problem, one may agree with Greenfield and others (e.g., Savage-Rumbaugh et al., 1993) that the human language capacity was an elaboration of neural structures underlying cognitive capacities possessed by early primate ancestors common to humans and the great apes. Certainly, it is clear that the human species evolved specific articulatory mechanisms and neural structures for the production and interpretation of speech. However, the vast proliferation of diverse languages and cultures suggests that these capacities were used for creating and elaborating languages for social and cultural purposes, each with unique variable structure, constrained only by the capacity for human infants (and, it appears, some other primates) to learn them. The commonalities among the morphologies of creole languages that Bickerton (1984) emphasizes are, as he notes, those that are useful in talking about objects and events central to the concerns of humans in groups – specifying objects, locating events in time and space, and noting completion or ongoing action. Constraints on the structure of human languages from the joint operation of their basis in general neural/cognitive structures, communicative requirements, and need to learn seem quite sufficient to ensure the limited degree of common structure that has been uncovered in the past half century.

These views by no means deny the biological basis for language structure, but set it into a different framework, where cognizing and communicating are about human purposes and within human groups, and where learning by human children, using available learning principles and mechanisms, is taken for granted. It is beyond reason to believe that humans would have invented languages, and that these would have spread within and across groups, that could not have been learned by their progeny.

A final caveat regarding the claims of the evolution of human *language structure* is this: Evolutionary epistemologists have argued that genetic programs and learning processes are alternative knowledge-gaining devices, as brought out in an earlier section of this chapter. The former program is adapted to very long-run retention of information that is useful in invariant environments unchanged over evolutionary time (e.g., millions of years); the other learning system is useful for acquiring information (representations of the environment) for features that vary in different environments that might be encountered and that change over short periods of time (e.g., from thousands of years to single lifespans). Language belongs obviously to the latter type of information system. A proposal based on these considerations is that children are innately prepared to learn language, but that this preparation does not consist of the kinds of innate categories and structures conceived of in Universal Grammar; rather, they are prepared with modes of analyzing and reconstructing phrase structure rules on the basis of the speech that they hear (Bates & Carnavale, 1993). The claim that language was invented by humans for human purposes and is in part reinvented anew in each generation captures this idea. Language is seen then as a cognitive-communicative invention for representing and exchanging ideas. The invention was constrained by the speech mechanisms used to fashion it, which in turn evolved under joint mechanical pressures of erect posture and functional pressures of the use of the vocal channel for communication.

Pinker and Bloom's evolutionary case (as well as Chomsky's denial of evolutionary processes) appears to confuse phylogenetic and ontogenetic adaptation to the surrounding environment. Human children now live in environments surrounding them with language, pressuring them to adapt to such environments. Their brains (and, more generally, their psychologies) must then be of a form and function to be able to learn language [this is a claim that Chomsky (1965) has made, but without the adaptationist corollary]. This proposition assumes the existence of language independent of the individual, which is true in ontogeny. However, in phylogeny, in the evolution of the species, languages, like tools, were an evolving product of mind (and hand or mouth), an essential part of the organism–(social)environment exchange. To push this point further, it seems as likely that human minds were adapted to the structure of language via biological/genetic evolution as that human hands were genetically adapted to the shape of hammers, screwdrivers, knives, and spears. The upshot is that languages must be designed to be learnable by human children (rather than the reverse – that children must be designed to learn language), but because languages developed from human invention for social exchange the conditions of development ensured their learnability in individual lifespans.

Beyond the question of how language structure evolved, what most of the authors writing on this topic fail to discuss is how language enters into human cognition; how the reorganization of cognitive structures might have been affected by the use of language for various functions; or how the higher mental processes might have emerged from language experience. These topics are considered in the next chapter.

Implications of Biological and Cultural History for Cognitive Development

The cultural embeddedness of all human activity represents a truly novel emergence of a new level of existence. Thus we may conclude that culture propagation is a natural product of the modern human species. The flourishing of complex culture coincided with the emergence of complex natural human speech/language, and the two are clearly intimately connected. Perhaps because language appears to belong to individual speakers in a way that culture does not, psychologists have paid more attention to the evolution of language as a distinct species characteristic than to the evolution of culture. Culture and brain coevolved in human evolutionary time (Durham, 1991). Culture was not simply an add-on to a brain that happened to evolve to enable complex cognition, any more than environment is simply an add-on to the biological organism. Nor is modern culture an aberration for which humankind may be poorly fitted because we evolved in an earlier epoch. By no means is this a claim that modern culture is adaptive to modern humans, or that modern humans are well adapted to modern culture. But the evolution of culture must be understood in terms of the functions it serves for humans, just as the evolution of organisms must be understood in terms of the functions that an adaptation serves.

These functions – of biological adaptation and cultural systems – need not have the same basis. The functions that cultures serve need not be confined to those of promoting survival and reproduction of individuals. Gould and Lewontin's (1979) notion of "spandrels" (see note 17) seems ideally applicable to cultural evolution in the following way: The evolution of neocortex, intelligence, and language in *Homo sapiens* can no doubt be demonstrated to promote survival and reproduction in the late Stone Age through improved communication, group solidarity, production of tools, and so on. But these very developments also produced complex cognitive potentials that were not confined to the solution of the original problems that led to their development. [See Plotkin's (1988) similar analysis of chimpanzees' manual dexterity extended beyond its original functions cited earlier.] New capacities were used to construct new cultural environments, including clothing, decoration, agriculture, music, dance, stories, and religion, among other things. The proliferation of these cultural forms did not in themselves necessarily promote survival and reproduction of individuals but may have promoted the survival of groups (Durham, 1991; Gamble, 1994), which in turn enabled the survival of individuals within the group.

The implication of this line of argument is that the cognitive capacities that were evolved during the Stone Age have produced not only a proliferation of cultural forms, skills, and knowledge but also their own cognitive imperatives. These imperatives impel human children to learn about the world and its inhabitants, seeking knowledge almost compulsively, and engaging in cognitively demanding activities such as inventing games to fill their time and practicing skills like hitting targets with stones (Parker & Gibson, 1979; Donald, 1993b). Such activities are characteristic of humans, unlike other primates, who may throw stones at a specific target to attain a goal but do not spend time practicing the skill. These considerations underscore the need for a better analysis of the relation between the complexities of cultural environments and cognitive development.

As formulated by "adapted mind" psychologists, the evolutionary task posed by neo-Darwinians is simply that of surviving to become sexually mature and to reproduce. But it is noteworthy that the complex cognitive capacities and complex cultural systems of humans provide their own developmental imperatives. It is not simply that evolution has provided humans with complex cognitive capacity, including the capacity for learning and using symbolic languages, but that that capacity in itself directs human cultures toward complex societies and semiotic systems. The evolutionary task for the human child is thus precisely the culturally specified task: to grow within and adapt to the needs of a human society; to acquire and use the language and tools of that society; to share in its social structures that support life; and to engage in the regeneration of both individuals and knowledge, and the generation of new forms of the latter. Thus education, productive work, the pursuit of knowledge, the creation of art and science are all part of the child's evolutionary task. One may note that the problems and complexities of achieving solutions to these tasks have long been well recognized and described by social and psychodynamic theorists such as Freud and Erikson, although less commonly by cognitivists.

Many theorists of cognitive development have viewed the implications of complex cognitive capacities very narrowly, primarily in terms of the acquisition of knowledge and the solving of problems within domains that have been specified by the parceling out of science and philosophical thought in Western academies. Cognition and cognitive development, then, have been viewed principally in terms of the achievement of physical principles, mathematics, and logic. Models of social knowledge, such as the understanding of other people's intentions and beliefs, have been viewed as abstract logic systems or theories, on the model of physical knowledge structures. These views project no important differences between the thought of infants and young children and that of scientists and philosophers. They see infancy not as a period of tuning but as a source of knowledge and a constraint on learning. They have taken Piaget's search for the origins of logic and located it in the neonate (Bower, 1989).

In contrast, in the present view the function of human childhood can be seen as that of making sense of the specific world conditions within which the child lives. All primates learn, but children acquire cultural knowledge. They are engaged in learning from their parents about tools as well as the social world; teaching and learning are prime contexts for developing language. Once language emerged as a communicative tool it would be useful for a cognitive and, indeed, for an introspective tool, as Mead (1934) and Vygotsky (1986) each suggested. It is inconceivable that the artifacts and symbolic systems of cultures would have proliferated in the absence of complex language. Unfortunately, like all else concerned with the "soft" side of human evolution, this claim remains speculative.

In the next chapter a compatible, quite detailed account of the evolutionary relation between language and cognition is laid out, and its implications for issues of language and cognitive development are considered.

3. Evolution and Development of the Hybrid Mind

In contrast to the evolutionary perspectives found in Chapter 2, which focused on general processes and levels of intelligence and knowing, and on the specific domain of language, Merlin Donald's (1991) proposal for the evolution of the modern mind provides a detailed model of representational stages in evolution that provoke developmental analogies. In this chapter that model and its developmental implications are considered in some detail.[1] The purpose of using this model of the evolution of human cognition for a developmental analysis is to provide an integrated conceptualization of the biological in human cognitive development that coheres with (and does not compete with) the cultural. Donald's scheme is an attempt to do this on the phylogenetic scale. As forecast in the previous chapter, the biology of the human individual is seen as potentiating the cultural achievements of the group, thereby making possible the more complex cognitive achievements of individuals within the group. There is no possibility of divorcing biology from culture in this scheme. Similarly, there is no possibility of divorcing the mind from the body, or ideation from activity.

Donald's Theory of the Evolution of Human Cognition and Language

The goal of Donald's (1991) original theory of the phylogenetic evolution of human cognition is to find a satisfactory solution to the problem of how human cognition evolved over a brief period of time (speaking paleontologically) from a basic general primate structure to the far more complex and differentiated – and thus powerful – human kind. He notes at the outset what is often overlooked in our enthusiasm for seeing parallels, analogies, and beginnings in earlier forms: "Despite our close genetic relationship to apes, the cognitive distance from apes to humans is extraordinarily great, much greater than might be imagined from comparative anatomy" (p. 3). Then:

> The essence of my hypothesis is that the modern human mind evolved from the primate mind through a series of major adaptations, each of which led to the emergence of a new representational system. Each successive new representational system has remained intact within our current mental architecture, so that the modern mind is a mosaic structure of cognitive vestiges from earlier stages of human emergence. (pp. 2–3)

These vestiges are supplemented by new symbolic devices that have radically altered the organization of the human mind. In essence, Donald attempts to provide the "conceptual framework within which our continuing mental evolution may be viewed" (p. 4). His claims are grounded in the literature on primate and early human physical and cultural evolution reviewed in the previous chapter. Although the ideas expressed are admittedly speculative, they are necessarily so by the nature of the evidence. What follows is a summary of the main theses of Donald's proposals as a background to the developmental implications suggested by them, which are considered in the latter part of the chapter.

Stages in the Evolution of the Modern Human Mind

Donald's conception is that culture and cognition are mutually constitutive, and in his theory the major stages of the evolution of mind are defined in terms of cultures, with cognitive (and biological) characteristics derivative therefrom. Note that this use of "culture" is essentially synonymous with "human (or primate) environment," without necessarily implying artifacts, activities, or practices typical of human societies. The emphasis is the same as that expressed in the previous chapter – that organism and environment are mutually defined.

Episodic Culture – the General Primate Mind

What kind of representational intelligence might we ascribe to the ape mind? As we saw in the last chapter, comparative research has documented considerable commonality between the cognitive abilities of apes and humans in infancy. Moreover, much recent work has been devoted to exploring the extent to which some apes (mainly chimpanzees) may be taught to use symbol systems of varying kinds (e.g., American Sign Language, computer icons). Although there are conflicting conclusions on this issue, there seems to be little doubt that apes can learn to associate a large number of symbols (in the low hundreds) with objects, events, people, and relations, and can use them in their interactions with humans to express desires and intentions, up to the level approximately of the 2-year-old child (Savage-Rumbaugh et al., 1993). However, no primates except humans have ever invented symbols. It is Donald's contention that the "episodic culture" of the primate mind did not provide the basis for such an invention.[2]

Donald elaborates this argument as follows: "The episode is the 'atom' of ape experience, and event perception is the building-block of episodic culture" (p. 153). This statement highlights important differences from the classic conception of objects as the units of "basic cognition." "Event perception is, broadly speaking, the ability to perceive complex, usually moving, clusters and patterns of stimuli as a unit" (p. 153). Furthermore: "Animals that we call intelligent are those that respond to events of increasing complexity and abstraction" (p. 154). The simplest events are "close to" object perception. In other words, event perception incorporates more complexity than object perception (which is customarily taken to be the "basic building block" or "atom" of human – and presumably primate – cognition). Object cognition is simply a special case of event cognition – slowed down to a stop, as it were.[3] This position is consistent with the emphasis on events in Gibsonian ecological perception (J. J. Gibson 1979; Shaw & Hazelett, 1986) as well as the event knowledge perspective set forth in Nelson (1986; Nelson & Gruendel, 1981), outlined in Chapter 1.

Ape behavior is nonetheless unreflective, concrete, and situation-bound. "Their lives are lived entirely in the present, as a series of concrete episodes, and the highest element in their system of memory representation seems to be at the level of event representation" (p. 149). Episodic memory consists of the "specifics of an experience: the place, the weather, the colors and smells, . . . such memories are rich in specific perceptual content. By definition, episodes are bound in time and space to specific dates and places" (p. 150). Donald contrasts this type of memory with human semantic memory [following Tulving (1983)], that is decontexted from time and place. He concludes: "From a human viewpoint, the limitations of episodic culture are in the realm of representation. Animals excel at situational analysis and recall but cannot re-present a situation to reflect on it, either individually or collectively" (p. 160). In contrast, "The cognitive evolution of human culture is, on one level, largely the story of the development of various semantic representational systems." What he emphasizes with respect to memory differences in ape and human is that episodic memory in apes enables the storage of situational information, but that its recall depends upon environmental triggers, whereas in humans recall is under voluntary control.[4]

It is important to distinguish "event memory" from what has been commonly termed "procedural memory" (Sherry & Schacter, 1987). Procedural memory retains procedures for carrying out actions and is usually considered to be shared by most (all?) species of mammals. In some theories procedural memory is characteristic of human infants and is contrasted with declarative memory, which is representational and therefore accessible to recall and reflection (Mandler, 1984a). Donald considers one of the primary distinctions between procedural memory and episodic memory to be level of generality, with procedural storing generalities and episodic storing specifics and not the general. Following Sherry and Schacter (1987), he claims that the two functions are incompatible, and that the same neural mechanism could not do both.[5] The important point – shared here – is that event memory is a form of representation that involves a degree of conscious awareness.

However, the degree of conscious awareness involved in event representation is not, Donald asserts, a sufficient basis for the emergence of language. The limitations of the cognitive capacities of the great apes can be viewed in part in terms of the difference between generating or inventing symbols in contrast to simply acquiring their use. This important point is a key to Donald's theory: "Invention was, of course, the key piece of the puzzle; the first user of specific gestural signs had to be able to invent them *de novo*. And invention is also a key aspect of human language capacity. . . . Language would not have emerged in humans, and probably could not have been sustained, unless each succeeding generation was capable of reinventing it" (p. 134); and, "To proceed from the limited representational capabilities of apes to the next level of symbol use required a qualitative cognitive change, a move towards symbolic invention, with the concomitant cultural change such a capacity would imply" (pp. 136–137). What is the nature of this cognitive change, and when did it emerge? Donald speculates (together with many other recent writers; see Chapter 2):

> Since language is a social device first and foremost, it is logical to expect the growth of language to be tied to the evolution of social structure. As social groups increase in complexity and size, the control and stabilization of group behavior, as well as the sharing of knowledge, becomes important. . . . Whatever forms preverbal

social intelligence may take, it is clear that language was the final step, and that presymbolic forms of social intelligence must have been its foundation. (p. 137)

In addition to social intelligence, tied to the complexity of social groups, Donald invokes *self-awareness* as a step beyond simple awareness and even the consciousness associated with episodic memory (see the discussion in Chapters 4 and 10). Self-awareness has been shown to be very limited in nonhuman primates, as demonstrated through experiments with different species concerning self-recognition (Gallup, 1970; Parker, Mitchell, & Boccia, 1994). Human infants achieve this minimal level of self-awareness during their second year.

Mimetic Culture: The Mind of Homo Erectus

Both social intelligence and self-awareness are critical to the transition to the next cognitive/cultural stage posited by Donald. His conception of mimetic culture and its cognitive correlates is his most original proposal. Because the paleontological record of hominid evolution is confined to physical evidence of morphology and cultural artifacts (when these are found), constructing a history of cognition is of necessity a highly speculative enterprise. On the basis of the phylogenetic record of brain growth in successive species of hominids, together with evidence of emerging complex culture, Donald has identified "a category of archaic but distinctly human culture that mediated the transition from ape to human" (p. 162). He terms this culture-cognition form "mimetic" on the basis of what he views as its dominant or governing mode of representation.

What is mimesis? According to Donald, it is a kind of imitative skill, but it is distinct from other types, such as mimicry, which is a literal attempt to produce an exact copy of some behavior, and which some birds are capable of. Imitation is less literal than mimicry and is engaged in to some extent by monkeys and apes[6] – it involves replicating a behavior to perform a similar function, as when offspring imitate the behavior of parents. *Mimesis,* according to Donald, incorporates mimicry and imitation to a higher end, that of *re-enacting and re-presenting* an event or relationship. That is, mimesis is fundamentally representational; it is representation through action. In this respect it is consistent with Piaget's (1962) descriptions of early imitation. Moreover, it involves "the *invention* of intentional representations" (p. 169), and "When there is an audience to interpret the action mimesis also serves the purpose of social communication" (p. 169). However, it is not confined to communication.

One may rehearse and refine a skill, and the act itself may be analyzed, reenacted, and reanalyzed, that is, represented to oneself. This also counts as mimesis.

The important point is that the properties of mimetic acts include "intentionality, generativity, communicativity, reference, autocueing, and the ability to model an unlimited number of objects" (p. 171). This list dovetails neatly with the characteristics associated with human language, and thus may set the stage for the emergence of speech. It is critical that mimesis is both shared – communicative – and individual – cognitive – as is language itself.

Mimetic culture consists of the forerunners of those "significant parts of normal human culture" (p. 167) that function without much involvement of symbolic language. These include trades and crafts, games, athletics, art forms, aspects of theater, and social ritual. Donald's claim is that early social intelligence of *Homo erectus* (1.5 million to 0.3 million years ago) developed forms of social life that involved mimetic skills such as are employed in these cultural forms today. This evolutionary claim is based on "one of the basic principles of evolution . . . the conservation of previous gains in adaptation. The human sensory and motor apparatus has remained essentially similar to those of primates presumably because the primate sensory apparatus continued to serve its purpose perfectly well. Changes in our brain, by contrast, were driven by a different level of selection pressure" (p. 165). Donald adds, "A cognitive culture that was successful in inventing, transmitting and maintaining complex social and technological skills would continue to be useful even after language had been adopted" (p. 165). Thus there is the evidence of cognitive vestiges of *Homo erectus* in athletics, rituals, games, dance, and so on in human life today.

The social consequences of the development of mimetic skills and the emergence of mimetic culture are numerous. Mimesis provides the possibility of modeling social structure or sharing knowledge without the necessity of every group member reinventing it. Thus there may emerge and persist a collective conceptual "model" of society, including its social roles. One sees the corollary in human childhood, where children rehearse and model society, acting out not only their own roles but those of other players. Group play in the "housekeeping corner" of any early childhood center reveals this rehearsal in action, even prior to incorporating language into it [French, Boynton, & Hodges (1991); see Chapter 4]. In addition to such overt modeling, mimesis enables playing reciprocal mimetic games and group mimetic acts, and evokes conformity and coordination within the group. Mimesis provides the basis for innovation and generativity, as well as nonlinguistic forms of pedagogy. The uses of mimesis in facial expression and vocal expression are special cases particularly relevant to the emergence of speech.

How did mimesis develop? One of the obvious routes is the freeing of hands – following attainment of upright posture – for technological skills, childrearing, toolmaking, gathering and hunting, sharing food and other resources, and constructing and sharing shelter. Mimesis is not confined to the hands, however; essentially it involves the integration of motor modalities, and in this integration the use of rhythm is critical.

Like language, mimesis as a representational system has two sides. Its social side is seen in its use in the control and coordination of *social* activities. But as an individual *cognitive* system of representation, it goes beyond the event representation possibilities of the primate system. Now the individual's own body, and its representational movements through space, can be re-represented in the brain, providing "a conscious map of the body and its patterns of action in an objective event space" (p. 189). Donald speculates that the parsing of event sets is central to what he calls the "mimetic controller." This level of representation is capable of "integrating models of self and the external world and expressing these relations through the movement systems" (p. 193). The potential of this level has much in common with Karmiloff-Smith's (1986a, 1992) first level of "explicitation" (summarized in Chapter 1). Table 3.1, based on Donald's table 6.1 (p. 198), summarizes the skills, social consequences, and cultural potential and achievements of this period of human evolution.

Readers may identify a missing piece between this description and the next stage – the piece that is customarily identified with the beginning of language, namely the first production of speech sounds in the form of words or speech symbols, which it might seem natural to attribute to the early *Homo sapiens* in this mimetic cultural milieu. Despite the strong intuition that early language must have begun with single word-like productions (as does early child language), there is no available evidence on this point. Mimesis as a symbolic system and single words are not necessarily competitive but may have been convergent or coordinated. Indeed, the physical evidence (Lieberman, 1984; Studdert-Kennedy, 1991) strongly suggests that vocal productions must have been part of this evolutionary period of development.

Table 3.1. *Elements of an archaic hominid mimetic adaptation*

Episodic Culture Primates	
+ Mimetic Skill	Intentional representations
	Generative, recursive capacity for mime
	Voluntary, public communicative system
	Differentiation of reference
	Unlimited modeling of episodic events
	Voluntary autocued rehearsal
+ Social Consequences	Shared modeling of social customs and hierarchies
	Reciprocal mimetic games
	Enhanced conformity and coordination
	Group mimetic acts
	Slow-paced innovative capacity
	Simple pedagogy and social attribution
= Mimetic Culture	Toolmaking, eventual fire use
	Coordinated seasonal hunting
	Rapid adaptation to climate, ecology
	Intricate social structure
	Primitive ritual (group mimetic acts)

Source: Donald (1991, p. 198). Reprinted by permission of the publisher from *Origins of the Modern Mind: Three Stages in the Evolution of Culture and Cognition* by Merlin Donald, Cambridge, MA: Harvard University Press. Copyright ©1991 by the President and Fellows of Harvard College.

Mythic Culture: Stone Age Homo Sapiens

A major cultural change can be observed beginning around 35,000 B.C., when the Upper Paleolithic *Homo sapiens* are contrasted with *Homo erectus* and primitive *sapiens*. Among the Stone Age peoples are found the characteristics of all true human cultures: the manufacture of clothing, fabric, sewing, transporting heavy objects, constructed shelters, implements, and weapons. There is also evidence of knowledge about the growth, selection, and preparation of food; use of fire; and navigational skill. Complex social and religious life is found, including dance, chants, masks, costumes, self-decoration, and semiotic devices to indicate clan, status, and totemic identification. This rapid proliferation of cultural achievements calls out for explanation, and the contemporaneous emergence of complex language must have played some role therein.

Donald has two important claims to make with respect to the emergence of human language. The first is that mimetic culture was a necessary precursor and foundation; the second, and relatedly, is that "Above all, language was a public, collective invention" (p. 216). In this view, language was invented to serve social purposes (see also note 18 in Chapter 2 for Konner's 1982 description of talk among the !Kung). Even more important, the essential functions served by language according to this theory were integrative and thematic, supplying a unifying synthesis to formerly disconnected time-bound snippets of information. This observation is highly relevant to the developmental story told in the subsequent chapters of this volume.

Donald's claim is, "The most elevated use of language in tribal societies is in the area of mythic invention – in the construction of conceptual 'models' of the human universe" (p. 213). Myth attempts to explain, predict, and control, going beyond the mere representation potentials of mimetic culture. Myth is integrative, deriving general principles and extracting thematic content. The claim, then, is that the "natural product" of language is narrative. According to this claim, language did not emerge primarily to name things but to integrate models of the world. Language adaptation was not simply a matter of the emergence of symbols or grammars.

> Possession of symbols alone . . . would change nothing. It is the representational intelligence underlying the symbol that defines its power and leads to its invention. It is thus the nascent mental model that cries out for the perfect symbol . . . to express its as-yet-uncaptured concept. . . . Symbols could not have come first and triggered language and thought by their invention. The invention of symbols, including words, must have *followed* an advance in thought skills, and was an integral part of the evolution of model building." (p. 218)

This is a strong, original, and provocative thesis. It has serious implications for how we think of human development.[7] The central importance of this claim is clarified in Donald's observation that

> Episodic minds (as in apes) can use symbols when provided with them, and mimetic minds employ symbolic mimetic displays; each uses symbols in its own way. Modern humans, similarly, use symbols in our own way. The value of a symbol depends on the kind of mind putting it to use. Episodic minds create episodic models of the world, mimetic minds create mimetic models. Signs and symbols, given to such minds, possess no magical powers to change this. By extension, modern minds create the kinds of symbols that they do because their thought processes are different." (p. 225)

Modeling is a key concept in Donald's theory about the evolution of language: "Thought and language are so closely related as to be two sides of the same coin; there are many forms of thought that are literally unthinkable without language and other semiotic devices. Most importantly, where humans differ from apes and other mammals is not so much in their possession of signs and symbols but in the types of mental models they construct" (p. 233).

Donald's construction of the emergence of language is based on the paleontological evidence [following Lieberman's (1984) reconstruction]. However, he departs from the usual story in his conception of the functions and products of language, as well as in his conception of the cognitive basis for the language adaptation.

First, the emphasis is placed squarely on speech as a semiotic device that was necessarily prior to any derivative form (e.g., sign language, written script, etc.). Note that the mimetic cognitive system incorporated primitive semiosis. The addition of the speech system built on this base and enabled the human symbolic capacity to move beyond it to develop complex language dependent on high-speed processing capacities. The function of language as a discourse mechanism, integrating thought over extended thematic passages, stands in contrast to the idea of language as a device for categorizing objects of the world. Of course, it is necessary to construct discourse from parts (phonemes, words, sentences) and to analyze it in terms of parts in order to recover meaning. And it is necessary to invoke categorizing skills for each of these processes. However, the primary function of language, in Donald's view, is integrative. It is this function that drives the selection pressure toward a high-speed system requiring additional memory capacities as well as rapid production and analytic devices.

Language brings mental models under symbolic control. "Different kinds of models, in which the event structure of the world has been differentiated and the components made independently accessible in memory" (p. 252) become possible. This representational function of language is critically important to the developmental story. It is because the models constructed through language encompass words used in their definition and that words are an integral part of the definition of the model that the parts can be independently manipulated and entered into new constructions never before experienced in the world. Mental models thereby move beyond human experience into new possible worlds. This claim for the potentiality of language beyond that of prior human cognition is implicit in much thinking about the relation of thought and language, but making it explicit provides a clearer perspective on the function of complex language forms. Donald goes further:

> Once the mind starts to construct a verbally encoded mental "world" of its own, the products of this operation – thoughts and words – cannot be dissociated from one another. . . . The models and their words are so closely intertwined that, in the absence of words, the whole system simply shuts down. There is no surviving "language of thought" from which the words have become disconnected. No symbols, no symbolic thought, no complex symbolic models. (p. 253)

The implications of this claim for contemporary models of cognitive science (e.g., Fodor, 1975, 1983; Newell, 1980) and for developmental psychology appear to be enormous. Among others, the claim implies that the language "center" in the brain does not in itself contain symbols independent of the language learned in ontogeny. Symbols come from outside the individual, from the group, although the potential for acquiring, using, and inventing symbols is part of the human cognitive (brain) system.

As stated earlier, Donald sees narrative as "the natural product of language." Narrative evolved from mimetic culture and drove the evolution of language: "Narrative skill is the basic driving force behind language use, particularly speech: the ability to describe and define events and objects lies at the heart of language acquisition. Group narrative skills lead to a collective version of reality; the narrative is almost always public" (p. 257). This statement incorporates the central themes of Donald's thesis. Language is public, a human invention for the purpose of integrating thematic constructions of events. Stories, histories, memories are enshrined in narrative to be shared with others.

Myth is a major product of narrative; therefore, this linguistically defined cultural epoch is termed "mythic." Myth represents the authoritative version of reality for the group; it is a filtered product of generations of narrative interchange. When mythic narratives became possible they complemented the mimetic representations already existing in ritual, song, dance, and games, and took over a controlling role in these group representations. Through narrative the group could share in a common understanding that existed through time as well as across individuals within the group; it could be passed on from generation to generation. The mythic culture enshrines a shared vision of both past and future that does not simply reconstruct human experiences but attempts to explain them in more encompassing terms.

By the end of the Paleolithic epoch, language was fully evolved and mythic culture fully ensconsed, as it is in hunting and gathering cultures in the contemporary world. As noted in Chapter 2, from every indication that we have, biological evolution of the human species was complete at the time that language and myth arose (35,000 years ago). Donald concludes: "The human mind had come full circle, starting as the concrete, environmentally bound representational apparatus of episodic culture and eventually becoming a device capable of imposing an interpretation of the world from above, that is, from its collective, shared, mythic creations" (p. 268).

What could be next? What is the alternative to narrative as the primary product of language? Bruner (1986) has contrasted "narrative thinking" with "paradigmatic thinking," the prototype of which is analytic thought, based on logical categorical construction, construction that is abstracted from events in the world. Although much discussion in both cognitive science and cognitive development appears to assume that paradigmatic thinking is the premier function of language, Donald sees such a function as waiting for the next stage of development, theoretic thinking.

Theoretic Culture: Modern Human Mind

Donald's final radical proposal about the evolution of human thought, memory, and representational systems is that further cognitive change was a product not of biological change but of cultural invention. He notes first that three "crucial cognitive phenomena" were underdeveloped or nonexistent in mythic (oral) culture: graphic invention, external memory, and theory construction. The major products of analytic thought, including formal arguments, systematic taxonomies, formal measurement, and logics, were generally absent. The transition to the next stage culminated in formal theories. Whereas the myth integrates and typifies, the formal theory is an integrative device that predicts and explains. This third transition in human cognitive evolution was not biologically supported – biological evolution was complete in the previous stage – but was dependent on technological evolution, and specifically on the development of external memory devices. Among the first and most important of these were forms of written language, usually thought of as communicative rather than memory devices.

The first externalization from the human body was the visuographic representation in pictorial form, evident in the great detail found in cave paintings. This observation implies that external representation through (oral) language preceded external iconic representation. A second much later move was the ideographic representation, which began as a kind of pictorial narrative (as in the Egyptian tombs) and evolved into a representation of lexical concepts. Note, however, that this original visuographic representation denoted concepts directly, and not through the speech system. These were in effect, alternative language systems.[8] The invention of the phonetically based alphabet in the first millenium B.C. was the first attempt to translate speech/language directly into written form.

These external representations – and especially the last – then served as a kind of "external memory field" (EXMF) through which events could be interpreted. With the possibilities opened up through written script, the long-term storage of speech-based language became a source of shared knowledge systems that could be maintained over time in the same form, thus less dependent upon interpretive shifts in conceptual systems.[9]

External symbolic storage (ESS) systems include books, libraries, and records of all kinds. Both science and art depend upon external memory devices involving such storage systems as musical notation, maps, and geometry. The primary characteristic of this advance is that the system is external to the biological representation or memory of any given individual. But the individual functions within the culture only with the assistance of such systems. Thus memory can no longer be thought of as having clear biological boundaries, as psychology traditionally assumes. According to Donald, external memory "is the *exact* external analog of internal, or biological memory, namely a storage and retrieval system that allows humans to accumulate experience and knowledge" (p. 309).

> The memory system, once collectivized into the external symbolic storage system, becomes virtually unlimited in capacity and much more robust and precise. Thought moves from the relatively informal narrative ramblings of the isolated mind to the collective arena, and ideas thus accumulate over the centuries until they acquire the precision of continuously refined exterior devices, of which the prime example is modern science. (p. 311)

Donald views ESS as being encoded in terms of "exograms" in analogy with the traditional "engram" of memory studies. The similarities and differences between the two are outlined in Table 3.2 [from Donald (1991), table 8.1, p. 315]. As is evident from this table, Donald sees the invention of external means of information storage as providing almost unlimited potential for human cognition. As long as cognition is conceived to consist of operations on information represented in memory

Table 3.2. *Some properties of engrams and exograms*

Engrams	Exograms
Internal memory record	External memory record
Fixed physical medium	Virtually unlimited media
Constrained format	Unconstrained and reformattable
Impermanent	May be permanent
Large but limited capacity	Virtually unlimited
Limited size of single entries	Virtually unlimited
Not easily refined	Unlimited iterative refinement
Retrieval paths constrained	Retrieval paths unconstrained
Limited perceptual access in audition, virtually none in vision	Unlimited perceptual access, especially in vision; spatial structure useful as an organizational device

Source: Donald (1991, p. 315). Reprinted by permission of the publisher from *Origins of the Modern Mind: Three Stages in the Evolution of Culture and Cognition* by Merlin Donald, Cambridge, MA: Harvard University Press. Copyright ©1991 by the President and Fellows of Harvard College.

(and no alternative to this conception seems available), then it follows naturally that the enormous increase in potential that ESS systems have made possible must be the source of the enormous advances in cognitive achievements of the historical period.

It must be emphasized, however, that both engrams and exograms are interpretable only by the human mind; the latter were indeed invented for interpretability. Only the individual human can provide a referential basis for understanding the memory record, whether it is a biological or an external record. The properties of exograms listed in Table 3.2 emphasize the open-ended, relatively unconstrained and unlimited capacity available through ESS systems, which are, of course, continuously being reinvented and refined, thus continuously adding to the already available potential.[10] Cognitive scientists often cite with awe the extraordinary potential of the human neural networks; Donald's point – seemingly obvious yet scarcely noted by most cognitive psychologists – is that this potential is vastly augmented and amplified by the external systems that humans have come to rely on in carrying out cognitive processes. For example, most human memory operations do not rely on biological storage alone, but on the accessibility to the biological system of technological forms of storage. Yet studies of unaided memory in the psychological laboratory do not tap into this system, and thus present a very limited picture of human cognitive potentials.

Formal education systems have been designed primarily to teach skills for using ESS systems, beginning with reading, writing, and arithmetic. Beyond these basics, students are taught how to *manage* the joint biological/technological memory system, to acquire knowledge in a domain in an organized form such that the two parts can be used effectively in tasks requiring that knowledge. Sometimes the biologically stored knowledge will be sufficient to the task, but often input from an external source (e.g., reference books) will be needed to supplement. In any complex cognitive task external tools – written notes, equations, diagrams – will serve as temporary memory stores for the working out of problems and implications. Thus ESS systems serve as both short-term and long-term memory amplifiers; each serves a vital purpose in modern human cognition. Biological memory becomes the loop in the thought process that performs transformations and analyses on the data base provided by external symbols. "External symbolic stimuli not only drive the thought process; they serve as the brain's holding tank while its various systems go about the business of processing and altering the symbolic environment" (p. 332).

The culture that has emerged in conjunction with the invention of the succession of more and more powerful technological systems is termed by Donald "theoretic culture." Biological memory "could not possibly have supported the type of theoretic development that humans have come through during the past four millennia. Working memory is too transient, too vulnerable to distraction, and too limited in capacity to manage a major cognitive project that may eventually result in theoretic products. . . . This symbiosis of human working memory and the [external memory field] is basic to modern thought" (p. 331).

Donald's claim is not simply that the human mind in its reflective mode felt the need to invent external systems to aid that reflection; rather, the invention of such systems made possible a new kind of cognitive stance of reflection, and thus enabled new possibilities of modification and refinement. This process led eventually to systems of logic, mathematics, philosophy, and science. For example, "Logic evolved out of an external, formalized process of verifying the 'truth' of propositions. The 'rules' of logic are themselves a working model of the verification process. The development and acquisition of purely symbolic – that is, logical – verification has a long and arduous history of symbolic invention; it was the furthest possible thing from an innate process" (p. 353). Moreover, "No major graphemic products – things such as novels, scientific theories, economic forecasts – have an equivalent in purely oral expression. They are products of hybrid minds with extensive ESS linkages" (p. 354).

Not everyone who has compared oral and literate cultures would agree with these statements, but it is important to recognize that Donald's claims refer not to thought processes per se but to the power that results from complementing basic human cognition with external and shareable representations.[11] He sees in this development radical cognitive change resulting, not from biological evolution, but from the cultural evolution that the biological potential for generativity – invention – of symbolic forms made possible. The conclusion to this story follows:

> Our modern minds are thus hybridizations, highly plastic combinations of all the previous elements in human cognitive evolution, permuted, combined, and recombined. Now we are mythic, now we are theoretic, and now we harken back to the episodic roots of experience, examining and restructuring the actual episodic memories of events by means of cinematic magic. And at times we slip into the personae of our old narrative selves, pretending that nothing has changed. But everything has changed. (p. 355)

Developmental Parallels and Implications of the Evolution of the Hybrid Mind

Donald's cognitive evolution proposal posits representational change as the fundamental advance from primate to human cognition, eventuating in the modern hybrid mind. The proposed stages in human evolution imply the possibility of a developmental parallel. The idea that the hybrid modern adult mind contains episodic, mimetic, oral narrative, and theoretic representations altogether suggests that modes of cognition may emerge at different times and in different combinations in the course of human development. If this is so (and, of course, it remains to be shown) it would have important implications, not only for developmental theory but also for, among other things, educational practice. Such a possibility certainly seems worth examining. To recapitulate briefly, the following themes are basic to the proposal, and they each suggest developmental implications.

- *Emphasis on event memory as basic in the primate line.* This proposal suggests that a similar level of representation would be found at the earliest stages of human development, as well as throughout life, although the dominance of event memory would be expected only in the first stage.
- *Emphasis on the dynamic relation between cognition, cognitive potential, and the*

culture within which it operates, especially in its social functions. This emphasis clearly suggests that a developmental theory ought to include as a significant component the cultural milieu of the individual, and to the extent that the relevant aspects of culture vary, concomitant variations in cognitive functioning would be expected.

- *Emphasis on model building as a driving mechanism in cognitive advance.* Here one would expect a theory to specify the content and structure of cognitive models as they change with development.
- *Emphasis on layers of representation in the developed hybrid mind.* Rather than focusing on one kind of representation (scripts or theories, for example), a theory should take into account that information may be processed and represented in different ways for different purposes, and in more than one way simultaneously.
- *Emphasis on the role of language in cognition.* A theory ought to be explicit in spelling out how language enters into cognitive processing and representation, and how language changes cognition.
- *Emphasis on external support systems, such as written materials, for complex cognitive processing and representation.* One would not expect nonliterate children or adults to perform at the same level of complex cognitive operations as literate people. In particular, one would not expect theoretical systems to emerge without external symbol systems. And, one would not expect individuals of any age to perform at the same level of complexity without external aids as they could perform with such aids.

A developmental analog of the evolutionary scheme might present the following view: The human child is first seen as growing within a social/collective community that provides a rich array of semiotic meanings that the child encounters "naturally" in the course of growing older. Second, the child is seen as moving through a series of representational potentials, beginning with the simple acquisition of event knowledge, which implies a dynamic functional system at base, and developing mimetic forms of representation. Third, the revolutionary impact of language representation on the more primitive systems is revealed, both in the "natural" narrative form and in the fully developed abstractions of the theoretical forms. In addition, the impact of all the cultural technology of external support systems is recognized, together with the implications of these supports for the later stages of cognitive development. Finally, the open-endedness of the human cognitive system is brought into full focus. The telos of modern mind can be recognized as a moving target, now amplified by technology but open to further possibilities as technology advances. At the same time, the constraints on the biological potential of the human cognitive system bring into focus the limitations of any individual within the collective culture. The human mind today is as much a product of its culture as – and perhaps more so than – it ever was in the past. Before proceeding with this version of the developmental story, some limitations on the analogy must be noted.

Phylogenetic and Ontogenetic Analogies: Cautionary Considerations

Biologists (Haeckel, 1905) and psychologists (e.g., Hall, 1904) of the nineteenth and early twentieth centuries found the parallel between evolutionary progression and ontogenetic development to be compelling (Cairns, 1983; Gould, 1977). Since then, in both biology and psychology, this parallel – incorporated in the familiar aphorism "ontogeny recapitulates phylogeny" – has been discarded for good reasons (Gottlieb, 1992). Yet the claim of an evolutionary progression in cognitive power in the human line compels an examination of the evidence for the survival of vestiges of the earlier forms – especially given Donald's claim of the hybrid adult mind, which retains aspects of four representational systems – and requires confronting the hypothesis that earlier stages of human thought might be more clearly visible in the earlier stages of human ontogeny. Of course, any developmental analog of an evolutionary model must take into account certain well-understood cautions about drawing lessons for ontogeny from phylogeny.[12]

Child in Culture.   The first cautionary note is that, unlike the development of earlier hominid species and early *Homo sapiens*, modern human development takes place within a modern cultural milieu (assuming the contemporary culture of the developed and developing world). Donald's thesis is that cognition and culture are mutually definable and dynamically interdependent. But the contemporary human infant is not born into a culture that is first episodic, then mimetic, then mythic, and finally theoretic, as the phylogenetic proposal implies. Indeed, modern educated parents confront their progeny from the beginning with representations from cultural materials of an advanced technological society; books, museums, and computer programs are part of the world of the very young in much of modern society. Could an episodic or even mimetic mind adapt to a theoretic culture? How would such adaptation look? Of course, as Donald points out, the adult mind is hybrid, and adult culture is hybrid as well. Thus as the infant mind developed it might adapt selectively to those aspects of adult culture that it could encompass. The important point remains, however, that the modern complexity of the culture of childhood must become part of the system within which we describe development.

Teleological Development. A second caution must come from the related point that the modern human child develops toward the end point of the modern human with a hybrid mind, including the potential for engaging in the highest forms of human cognition in conjunction with all the external representational apparatus available. This means that the devices, both biological and technological, that come to support the most advanced thinking must be developing, coming into existence, and being perfected prior to their final expression in adult thought. The educational process is only one aspect of this part of human childhood. The expectations of parents and other adults that the child will grow into the competent adult must provide a social milieu within which the early cognitive capacities of the child operate that is vastly different from that in which similar capacities might have operated for adults in earlier species and subspecies in the hominid line. In particular, as is explicated in more detail later, learning to speak and understand one's language is prerequisite to its functional use as a representational system, but during the learning period the cognitive system may continue to operate principally in terms of an earlier developmental system. The idea that biological development of the cognitive system is succeeded by and interdependent with cultural development raises the possibility that growth may be a function of different processes at different points in development. At the same time, the underlying self-organizing principle must be operating throughout.

Developmental Chronology. The evolution of human cognition occurred over several million years. Even the most recent stage in Donald's scheme (i.e., writing) has occupied several millenia. The human child, in contrast, progresses from neonate to adult status within about 16 to 20 years. This is not just a compression of the sequence; rather, the question must be asked as to whether the sequence could be the same under both time schemes. To take language again, first words and first pretense tend to occur at about the same time in human development. Yet Donald's claim is that in evolutionary time, games, routines, and rituals preceded symbolic speech, and that when speech emerged it served as a vehicle for narrative. Does the developmental evidence bear on the evolutionary hypothesis? Or does the fact of different chronologies implicate different developmental orders? These questions can only be raised at this point, not answered.

Biological Evidence.   The cautions articulated above are meant to forestall too easy analogies from phylogeny to ontogeny. In addition, Donald's evolutionary speculations are based on detailed evidence about the increase in cerebral cortex in the hominid line in comparison with other primates, and on evidence of hemispheric specialization and the development of language centers in the left temporal lobe. It might be asked what the theory would predict with respect to the neurological basis for the development of three stages of cognition beyond the basic event representation stage. The following speculations are based on the evidence reviewed in Chapter 2, but given the fast-changing state of studies in developmental neurobiology, they should be taken as purely suggestive.

First, the initial foundation should look and function much as the primate brain does. This condition is well substantiated in the brain-behavior literature (Goldman-Rakic et al., 1983; Diamond, 1993) focused on the development of object concepts and relations. Second, the emergence of a level of imitative, mimetic representation should be signaled by maturation of activity in the frontal (integrative) lobes, following after the maturation of motor areas (which make such mimesis possible). Third, maturation of the language-processing areas should signal the development of early language learning. This should be followed by new activity in the integrative frontal lobes as integrated language representations become possible. The next level of activity should be observed as learning of external symbolic systems (reading, writing, arithmetic) proceeds. This activity should be dispersed to areas eventually devoted to mathematical or written language processing. A final level of activity in the frontal lobes should be observed as integration of ESS systems is developed. With highly educated subjects, further bursts of activity might follow as domains of knowledge became subjected to theoretical systematization and creativity.

This sequence of maturational activity cannot be specifically validated with current data, and it would be desirable to have much more specific hypotheses about what areas should be developing in what ways at what times. At present, however, the data look promising from both brain and behavior directions, and suggest appropriate ages at which to look for the relevant developments, which are consistent with those summarized in the previous chapter.

There is no evidence that any particular brain structure, area, or function subserves any specific mode of representation, aside from the well-established localization of language-processing centers (Broca's and Wernicke's) in the left temporal lobe. Donald suggests that prelinguistic mimetic symbolic processing may have been (and still might be) situated close to the language-processing centers.. The speech and language centers, so far as we know, subserve the *processing* of language – its production and interpretation – not its possible function as a system of content representation or model building. But even the storage of words and word knowledge, thought to be centered in Wernicke's area, is not the same as a center for representing thought in language, as in narratives about events.

It may be speculated that the early developments in brain maturation at 18 to 24 months (activity, synaptogenesis) are symptomatic of the advance in *learning* language and *using* symbolization in general. In contrast, the peak in neural activity at age 4 to 6 years might correlate with the potential to *represent* in language. Another peak at 7 to 8 years might be associated with external symbolic acquisition and development, which becomes consolidated as a representational system at 11 to 12 years, and which might lead to theoretical potential at about age 15 to 16.[13] These peaks in brain development have all been documented in recent work (see Dawson & Fischer, 1994; Johnson, 1993).

Beyond the speculative nature of this discussion, the point is simply that after we leave the rather neat fits between brain and behavior demonstrated for infrahuman primates (which have been shown to map onto human development at somewhat later ages in infancy) there is very little to sustain any specific theory about cognitive change beyond the peaks and valleys of metabolic and EEG activity. But, as Fischer (Fischer & Rose, 1993) and Case (1992b) and others have argued, the ages at which these changes take place are consistent with both classic and neoclassic stage theories of development.

The Stage Question in Developmental Psychology. Although at present general stage theories of cognitive development are not popular, until recently it has seemed natural to most students of development to think in terms of stages, whatever one's theory of structure, function, or process might be. Even the most stringent behavioral psychologists of the 1950s and 1960s recognized stage differences early in development (Bijou & Baer, 1965). But stages then were considered somewhat ad hoc to those who believed that a single process – learning – explains developmental change throughout life. The idea of stages was tainted by the maturational "explanations" associated with Gesell (1940), which were generally held to be circular and nonexplanatory [see Kessen & Kuhlmann (1962) for discussion]. These biases were projected onto Piaget's proposals when they came to the wide attention of American researchers in the 1960s. Although the idea of cognitive stages was certainly not new (Piaget's echoed Baldwin's from earlier in the century), Piaget's elaboration of them met widespread skeptical resistance among American researchers schooled in learning theory.

The "stage question" as represented in Piaget's theory persisted into the 1970s, even as Piaget's thinking was permeating the field of developmental psychology (e.g., Gelman & Baillargeon, 1983; Brainerd, 1978). One of the results of the confrontation with Piagetian work was the widespread effort to find earlier and earlier evidence and precursors of cognitive capacities that were held to be characteristic of a particular stage in Piagetian theory, for example, with respect to the conservation of number (Gelman & Gallistel, 1978) and logical classification (Donaldson, 1978). These efforts appeared to doom the discontinuity assumption of the stage notion, leaving only a shell of the former claims. Except for orthodox Piagetians and neo-Piagetians most developmentalists since have either avoided the stage question altogether or have opted for a kind of middle ground, admitting stages of development within domains, but not "of the whole" as in Piaget's theory. The debate today is not usually about stages per se, but about conceptual change and its mechanisms within domains or modules. If major changes persist in being identified with the classical periods of childhood and adolescence, that fact tends to remain unacknowledged.

But through it all, stages will not go away. Shakespeare, Freud, and Erikson, as well as Gesell and Piaget, not to mention developmental biologists, have all noticed dramatic changes from infancy to early childhood, to middle childhood, to adolescence. Do adolescents think differently from preschoolers? Most laypeople, most educators, and, in their nontheoretical modes, most developmental psychologists would not hesitate to answer affirmatively. The question is: How can the differences be characterized and to what can they be attributed?

Ontogenetic Parallels with Phylogenetic Stages

At first glance, the evolutionary story that Donald has set forth presents an obvious parallel with standard stage accounts of human cognitive

Table 3.3. *Parallels between Donald's phylogenetic stages and developmental stages*

Age Stage (Phylogeny)	Age (yrs.)	Cognitive Stage		
		Piaget (1970)	Bruner[a] (1966)	Vygotsky (1962)
Infancy (Primate)	0–1½	Sensorimotor	Enactive	Natural
Early childhood (*H. erectus*)	1½–5	Preoperational	Iconic	Preconceptual
Middle childhood (*H. sapiens*)	6–11	Concrete operational	Symbolic	Conceptual
Adolescent (Modern mind)	12–adult	Formal operational	?	Scientific

[a]Bruner, Olver, & Greenfield (1966).

development. The parallels with three general theories are displayed in Table 3.3.

This table does not begin to suggest the commonalities and distinctions among these different theorists, or the major content of their theoretical stages. In particular, Bruner and his colleagues (1966) did not elaborate beyond the symbolic to an adolescent stage, and Vygotsky did not lay out such a scheme in so many words – rather it is implicit in his description of phylogenetic and ontogenetic conceptual developments.[14] However, what the table does suggest is that these theorists saw different kinds of cognitive functioning emerging at similar points in development, although their characterization of the differences varied considerably.

There are obvious problems with this kind of direct analogy. The first and simplest problem is that none of the ontogenetic cognitive stages proposed are directly analogous to Donald's evolutionary stages. Event representations are not the same as sensorimotor schemes (Piaget, 1970), nor are they the same as enactive representations, which are more like procedural memory than episodic memory (or general event memory). The early childhood stage was considered by Piaget to be the first representational stage, reflecting the onset of symbolic representation. In his theory imitation played a central role in the establishment of symbols; thus there may be a convergence with Donald's idea of mimesis. Nonetheless, the parallels are not strong. Even less strong is Bruner's stage of iconic representation, the idea in his theory being that preschool children are "centered" on perceptual figures, but when deprived of perceptual representations (e.g., pictures) they can operate on a more abstract level.[15]

Piaget's stage of concrete operations is conceptualized in terms of the emergence of logical thinking, quite a different proposition from Donald's proposal of mythic/narrative thought. In his 1966 theory Bruner followed Piaget rather closely in his descriptions of thinking at the symbolic level (for example, in the achievement of inclusive classification systems), thus also stressing logical thought. More recently, Bruner (1986, 1990) has emphasized narrative thinking as a basic form of thought, thus mapping more closely onto Donald's thesis.

Piaget's final stage of formal operations would fit more closely with Donald's last stage of theoretic thought; both are found to depend on the availability of language, and in Donald's case (less clearly in Piaget's) external representations. Bruner and colleagues' (1966) theory was not developed beyond the symbolic stage. Thus overall and specifically the first approximation of cognitive stage theories to Donald's evolutionary stages moving toward the hybrid modern mind does not work. But Vygotsky's theory appears to offer a closer match than the others, whether considered from the perspective of stages of semiotics. Note first, however, that none of the cited developmental stage theories are integrative in the sense of one stage being incorporated into the next; rather, they all fit the levels and layers of the hybrid mind model.

Vygotsky's Program in Thought and Language *(1934)*

The program that Vygotsky set forth in what is widely considered to be his classic statement of cognitive development and the relation of thought and language [or closer to the Russian meaning, "thinking" and "speaking" – Kozulin (1986)] had much in common with the evolutionary perspective outlined in this chapter. Vygotsky began with phylogeny, considering what was then known of ape cognition and communication, based on the research that was available in the 1920s. The "natural" course of development exemplified by nonhuman primates gave way in his view to the sociocultural when language entered thought. Words and word meanings were for him the basic units of analysis of thinking.

In contrast to the universalism of Piaget, Vygotsky saw cognitive development unfolding within a cultural-historical framework. Cognition in this perspective would develop in different ways (and to different levels) depending upon its cultural conditions. The social-communicative function of language played the central semiotic mediation role in cognition. Culture and cognition were internalized by the child through externalized transactions with adults – parents or teachers – who made implicit relations manifest in learning situations. Scientific thought in particular was seen as imparted from the culture to the child in pedagogical situations; the child's problem was to reconcile the spontaneous concepts, formed on the basis of pragmatic experience, with the scientific concepts externalized by the culture. Luria's (1976) studies based on these ideas have been extended by Tulviste (1991), who provides a good summary of them.

Vygotsky (1978) also viewed external aids in memory and attention as mediators of thought in a way that is similar to Donald's ideas about ESS, emphasizing the cultural history of such aids, and their different distribution across historically differentiated cultures. People in different societies could be expected to think differently according to the availability of mediational means. These ideas, again, are quite consistent with Donald's views. In addition, Vygotsky's idea of scientific thought had much in common with the theoretical culture espoused by Donald, and his emphasis on language and on semiotic mediation is also highly compatible with this view. Neither Vygotsky nor his present-day followers, however, considered the role of mental model building, in layers and levels of representation, or the idea of the hybrid mind. Rather, Vygotsky viewed the "higher mental processes" as culturally developed, taking over the function of "lower" "natural" processes, which could be revealed again in cases of brain damage. Nonetheless, Vygotsky recognized the importance of writing, and of material aids, tools and other cultural artifacts and technology to thinking, consistent with Donald's focus on the significance of external support systems [see Raeithel (1994)]. Moreover, Van der Veer and Valsiner (1991) point out that in considering child development as a science, Vygotsky stressed that the individual experiences the environment differently at different ages or developmental stages.

Overall, Vygotsky's theory has much in common with the Donald proposals. Indeed, Van der Veer and Valsiner's (1991) tracing of the history of thought in the late nineteenth and early twentieth centuries, on which Vygotsky drew in developing his own theory, evokes the point that Donald's thesis is a modern version of the historical approach to understanding mind, common to Darwin, Baldwin, and others of the earlier period, and reconstituted in Vygotsky's mature work. In further exploring these connections it becomes clear that the present work is quite close to Vygotsky's general approach, and to some versions of present-day cultural theory, derived ultimately from the same source.

Many other theorists recently have proposed alternatives to standard cognitive theories, with their emphasis on the disembodied autonomous mind. In reaction they have stressed that the mind must be situated in the body, and the body must be situated in the world (e.g., Varela, Thompson, & Rosch, 1991); and when the body is a human body, it becomes important that the world is both social and cultural. "Enactive cognition" [Varela, Thompson, & Rosch (1991); see also Bickhard (1987); Lakoff (1987); Johnson (1987)] addresses some of the same issues as the evolutionary concerns expressed by Donald, based on the premise that individual cognition begins with experience and experientially based knowledge. This perspective does not deny that either acquisition or organization is constrained by humanly possible structures, but stresses that the constraints and potentials in the system may come as readily from outside the organism as from within it.

Experientially Derived Event Knowledge

As outlined in Chapter 1, studies of event knowledge in infants and young children were the basis for earlier versions of the model developed in this book organized around the proposal that general event representations are the "basic building blocks of cognition" (Nelson & Gruendel 1981; Nelson, 1986). This idea is echoed in Donald's statement that "the episode is the 'Atom' of ape experience, and event perception is the building-block of episodic culture" (p. 153). Our basic thesis was that infants and young children represent the important events that they participate in in a general format that enables them to take part in the social activities of their familiar settings. Important events are those in which they are participants, whether actively or passively; that recur frequently, such as caretaking routines and simple games; or that evoke significant affective responses.

Event representations are basic to adult human everyday knowledge systems, as well as those of apes, infants, and children. We do not outgrow our dependence on expectable event knowledge; it forms an important part of our hybrid cognitive system. However, as Donald noted, "Animals excel at situational analysis and recall but cannot represent a situation to reflect on it, either individually or collectively" (p. 160). To become a cognitive building block, the event representation must become accessible to reflection. It must also become integrated with, and somehow receptive to, a system of symbolic representation. This development was implicated in the event representation work, where event representations were seen as the source of concepts and categories and the support of language acquisition. Later chapters of this text spell this out. The idea of layers and levels of representation was also an important part of the event representation story (Nelson, 1986). Moreover, language was seen as learned and developed within well-understood, familiar event routines. All of these proposals appear consonant with Donald's suggestions, and they are elaborated in the chapters to follow.

Preliminary Synthesis and Thesis: The Hybrid Mind in Development

Invoking a developmental approach to the problems raised by Donald's theory requires taking the view that the developing individual constitutes a system of developing strands – skills, capacities, interests, emotions, activities, situations, physical strength and size, social settings and partners, concepts, memories, and other strands recognized and unrecognized as contributing to the developing mind. As the study of nonlinear systems has revealed (e.g., Van Geert, 1993), from the convergence of strands or separate influences there may come the emergence of new levels of organization. This kind of emergence of more complex organizations from the combination of independently changing components without the necessity of a single mechanism or push is clearly compatible with the observations and theses of stage theorists. Although in most cases of cognitive development it may be difficult or impossible to trace the contributions of each bit to the whole and to model the developments accurately, nonetheless the framework is appealing.

In language, in memory, in conceptual growth it is clear that there are no single effective pushes to the developing system but rather a combination of influences that lead to observable change. It is a major challenge to the field to break away from the search for single causal mechanisms and to trace instead the independent and interacting forces that operate within each developing domain of interest. In the areas under examination here a major role is assigned to language as a representational medium, but this role is conceived to be at once a product of ongoing communicative and cognitive developments and a catalyst for further change, in ways that are quite similar to, but on a different scale from, what Donald has traced in the evolutionary scheme.

Table 3.4. *Developmental stages mapped onto evolutionary stages*

Stage	Age	Cognition	Language
Infancy/*episodic*	$0-1\frac{1}{2}$	Event reps.	Sounds, first "words"
Early childhood/ *mimetic*	$1\frac{1}{2}-4$	ERs with words Games, play, songs, social rituals	Dialogue Grammar developing, language in mimetic reps.
Middle childhood/ *narrative*	4–10	Narrative thinking, personal memory, cultural learning	Narrative Beginning reading and writing, math, categorical schemes
Adolescent/ *theoretic*	10– adult	Logical abstractions Deductive systems Extensive use of external systems Acquisition of "scientific" social-conventional knowledge	Logical abstractions, argument and scientific reading and writing, specialization

Table 3.4 instantiates one form of a developmental analogue to Donald's scheme, mapping hypothesized developmental periods onto the evolutionary scheme. Donald's labels for the different stages (episodic, mimetic, and theoretic) are included here for heuristic purposes. Although as noted previously we could not expect the human child today to proceed through the same stages in the development of representational systems as in evolutionary time, retaining the labels is a reminder that earlier forms of representation exist and are operative throughout development, and the possibility exists that a particular type of representation might emerge and dominate during a particular period of ontogenetic development.

For each stage aspects of cognition and language are sketched in. There is no implication here that the developments listed are in any way exhaustive of thinking during the period. For example, conceptual development and number are absent from the table, although the former will be considered in some detail in a later chapter. What the table is meant to convey is that some developments that seem to be interconnected and perhaps intertwined, and that are related to those that were significant in the evolution and history of complex cognitive systems, are developing together over periods of developmental time.

Note that the major transitions are associated with acquisition of linguistic forms (grammar, written language) and with new language functions (dialogue, narrative, formal argument). The implication through all of this is that it is human language and its potential for different ways of formulating thought that has driven and continues to drive human cognitive development on both the evolutionary and the individual scale. It must be emphasized, however, that this claim does not imply that human cognition is totally dependent upon language; there is every evidence that cognition without language is complex and powerful. But at every point, language amplifies and advances thinking in directions that it would otherwise not be possible to go.

Of the potential power of language and its derivatives (graphic forms, printed documents, computers), by far the most significant is the potential that it provides for sharing representations with other people and deriving benefit from the knowledge constructions of others. This power is observed at every step in development from first words to scientific theory making. What is remarkable is how little heed developmentalists, and psychologists in general, have paid to its significance for cognitive growth, knowledge acquisition, and theory construction. In the remainder of this book these connections will be spelled out in more detail, whereas the biological foundations are hereafter assumed but not further explicated.

The discussion in the chapters to follow concentrates on developments during the transition from the prelinguistic representation stage (0 to 4 years) to the oral language representation stage (4 to 10 years). Developments during this transition period (roughly between 3 and 5 years) are quite dramatic in a number of domains; recent research has concentrated on this period, projecting explanations for the changes observed from different theoretical positions. The thesis here is that many of the changes observed during these preschool years result primarily from the emerging potential to represent knowledge in linguistic formats, and the corollary potential to exchange knowledge with others, in particular with more knowledgeable adults. Some attention must be paid as well, however, to developments that may not be dependent upon language representations. Identifying examples of each kind will help in developing a theory adequate to explain developments in this particular stage of life.

Later transitions are thought to represent more variable, more technologically and educationally dependent pathways. There is no implication here that early developments are critically deterministic of later potentials, in the sense of setting trajectories, but the initial shift to language representations is crucial to subsequent developments of written language and thought, including both narrative and theoretical knowledge structures. This brings out a point that is too often hidden in our theories. Development is teleological, and to prepare for language representations, one must first learn language, just as to become a scholar one must first learn to read and write. Many tasks of childhood do not serve the immediate goals of that period but are preparaatory for the next stage. This poses a challenge to our theories that has not been met by any that focuses solely on the individual mind or on specific domains of knowledge.

In the course of the consideration of the developments traced here, two issues emerge that will receive some illumination. One is the issue of conceptual change, which has been the focus of debate in recent years (e.g., Carey, 1985; Carey & Gelman, 1991). What is the mechanism of change? What drives the developmental system? The real task for stage theories is not to describe stable states (which may never exist) but to trace the dynamic of change. The other central issue is the conceptualization of the social mind: How is the psychological to be reconciled with the social-cultural world without becoming its puppet? How is psychological integrity to be maintained in the face of overwhelming social semiosis? It has been intimated in the preceding discussion that the solution from cognitive science has been to shut off the mind from outside influences, to consider the mind as an autonomous encapsulated organ, operating on decontextualized "information." When this move is viewed as illegitimate, as it is here, what is left of individuality? These questions will be set aside while the more prosaic and pragmatic developments are unfolded in the chapters that follow, but they will be raised anew in the final chapter.

II. Developing Representational Systems

4. Early Cognition: Episodic to Mimetic Childhood in a Hybrid Culture

Walk into any preschool serving children between the ages of 2 and 4 years and you will find the mimetic society in miniature. Language is heard, as children direct each other in play, exchange comments, sing songs, yell in triumph or tragedy in the play yard, listen to the stories read by caretakers, follow directions for cleaning up, getting food, laying out cots for naps, and so on. But despite the language noise, and with the exception of the story reading, language is used in, as part of, and in conjunction with these activities, and not primarily as a medium of conveying knowledge from one person to another. Its primary use is pragmatic, not symbolic. Symbolic activities proliferate in games, songs, pretense play, building, painting, modeling with Play-Doh, working with number boards, looking at picture books, and so on. Narratives of everyday life and of imaginary situations are literally played out, using the props of the housekeeping corner, the play yard, blocks, and trucks. This is the episodic/mimetic world of the young child. Within these activities language is learned, used, and extended.

The hypothesis to be explored in this chapter is that in human childhood, the episodic/mimetic world enables the linguistic/narrative world to emerge, and that the first three years of life encompass the transition from the first level of representation in terms of events or episodes to the second, in terms of socially shared motorically expressed representations relevant to actions in the real world, *mimesis* (Donald, 1991). In modern human childhood these representations include participatory routines, imitation games, symbolic play, gestural communication, songs, and so on. The claim here is that speech at first is a part of this episodic and mimetic system of functioning. Language uses in these shared activities help to mark them, to move them forward, but language is not initially used to *represent* them as such in the child's cognitive or communicative productions. Communication between participants gradually moves toward greater use of linguistic forms and formulas, but language is more of an accessory to the activity than an essential part of it during these early years.

In this chapter, as in the rest of the book, representation is used in both its internal, individual sense, and in its external, social sense. One of the purposes of the discussion is to show that these two are inextricably related. Even without language those things that are represented by the culture through its semiotic systems, and are re-represented by cultural members through social activities with children, become part of the individual representations of both child and adult within the culture. In this sense, the human child possesses a mediated mind from birth. But in another sense, the child's mind is inaccessible to the direct mediation of other minds as long as language of some kind is not available. Without representational language, social partners can convey bits of knowledge, can guide participation in activities, but cannot provide a window into other minds or construct a thematic whole. This point has important implications for thinking about children's understanding of others' intentions and interpretations. Without language but with the wide range of social experiences that children have, they should be able to predict what people will do, where they will look for things, and so on, but they will not know that what other people think may be different from what they think about a commonly experienced event (see Chapter 10). Children display a broad range of specifically human capacities socially and individually during this period of development, including the acquisition and use of complex language. These developments prepare for the next major transition to cognitive and communicative language in all its multifunctional forms.

Thus in this chapter development between 1 and 3 years of age will be interpreted in terms of a basic event representation system developing into a mimetic system with elements of the linguistic symbolic system embedded in these. To set the stage, consider the following sketch of the developing child within the hybrid culture of modern life.

Children in a modern culture enter a world organized in terms of symbolic forms. They are surrounded by cultural artifacts from the beginning of life, artifacts that have symbolic value in the culture. The child's clothes, furniture, the very spaces of the home reflect aspects of cultural institutions – social, economic, educational. In addition, the child is presented with artifacts specifically designed for children – toys, pictures, books – meant to impart cultural knowledge (i.e. to enculturate). In part, this is accomplished through the guided participation, play, and direct teaching activities of parents. But in part it is simply implicit in the furnishings and arrangements of the home and community. A home furnished with books and magazines not only provides the child with specific cultural experiences and opportunities but also establishes a particular status within the community at large. These furnishings provide the backdrop for parental teaching – implicit and explicit – of the child's role in the society, both as child and as future adult (Ochs & Schieffelin, 1984; Hodge & Kress, 1988).

Much of the parent–child activity in middle-class American homes involves deliberate attempts to orient the child to the symbolic world, and to teach the meaning of various symbols. Much of this teaching takes place through language, yet language is less the point than the tool. For example, children are taught to categorize and name colors and shapes, and are introduced to pictures of animals and of people in various roles (e.g., doctor, nurse). The child's dishes and clothes often display such pictures, and the child's attention is drawn to them. The child is lulled to sleep with songs and music. These examples show that parents do not simply guide children in activities, but also attempt to teach them symbolic forms beginning in the first year of life. The symbolic forms invoke cultural values, and the routines they are embedded in are representative of the larger culture. Social representations draw on cultural representations, just as individual representations draw on social representations. Thus the content and context of the child's representation of this experiential world must reflect the specific cultural, social, and physical world in which the child lives.

In this chapter early development is approached from the experiential perspective, assuming the cultural framework just described, the support of parents and others, and changing engagement with the physical and social world as the potentials of motoric and cognitive functions develop. The basic assumption is that children's knowledge begins in participation in events arranged by others. Developing knowledge of the object world and of social relations, communication, play, and beginning language is considered within this framework as background to the more extended role that language plays in later developments, which is the topic of the following chapter.

Making Sense of Events and Objects in Infancy

In the sense used here, an event can be said to consist of an organized sequence of actions through time and space that has a perceived goal or end point. This is an extremely open-ended definition, in that it does not provide any temporal boundaries; also, it does not exclude many human activities, most of which can be said to be purposeful or goal-oriented. Note, however, that it does imply extension through time, a series of actions. A single action, such as picking up or handing an object to someone, does not count as an event in these terms. The utility of this definition is simply to contrast events with objects and single individual actions. Chewing, for example, is no more an event than is food, but eating lunch is a prototypical event.

The assumption of event knowledge as a beginning point offers a perspective different from the usual orientations to cognitive development in infancy and early childhood. We have considerable knowledge at this point about infant knowledge of objects, and categories of objects. This is not surprising, given that object knowledge has always been the main focus of philosophical and psychological investigations, beginning with the Greeks, on the assumption that establishing object knowledge is epistemologically prerequisite to all knowledge structure. However, there are important differences between the assumptions of event schemas as basic representations and models of infant cognition focused on object relations. For example, when laboratory studies of object knowledge by infants are viewed from the perspective of events, a different picture emerges. For the infant, participation in a laboratory experiment is an event, similar in some ways to other events that have been experienced, but also novel in some ways. The challenge for the infant is to understand and ultimately to *classify* that event with respect to its functional significance and its perceptible characteristics.

Viewing the classic Piagetian observations of infant behavior in event rather than object terms, the behavior takes on entirely different meanings. Piaget claimed that children must learn that objects are independent of their own actions, and the demonstration of this is the classic series of object permanence tests in which the experimenter hides objects in different places, culminating in the series of invisible displacements, where the child cannot see whether the experimenter has left the object under the first, second, or third of a series of screens. When the child (between 18 and 24 months) has managed to solve this task, what does it indicate? To Piaget it indicated that the child has formulated a concept of the permanence of objects that consists of the knowledge that objects are substantial, persistent through time and space, and independent of the child's own actions. But from the event perspective, what the child learns is that people – in particular, adults – can dispose of objects in different ways, hiding them first in one place and then in another, and that there are search procedures that can be successful in uncovering them, regardless of whether one has seen where the adult has hidden them. If the child truly believed that objects move independently of any person's actions, as Piaget seemed to imply, then there would be no point in playing the game, because the object might be anywhere. Indeed, an important part of the child's acquisition of object knowledge must be the distinction among different types of objects, some of which move independently (e.g., insects), some of which don't; some of which change form (e.g., ice), some of which don't; some of which are not permanent (e.g., food), some of which are. In physics objects are permanent; in the infant's experiential world they are not necessarily so. Recent research demonstrating earlier understanding of object permanence than Piaget observed (e.g., Baillargeon, Spelke, & Wasserman, 1985) may even rest on the fact that these experiments have successfully disentangled social understanding from understanding the physical relations involved.[1]

It is only through experience with different types of objects in different events that the child can build up differentiated object knowledge of the type that indicates in the experiment of invisible displacements that this is the kind of object that adults can move about from place to place, and that this is the kind of event in which the child can expect to find the object where the adult has left it. There are other kinds of events in which this is not true. When the child picks up a bit of paper from the street and begins chewing on it, the adult takes it away and disposes of it where the child cannot retrieve it. To all intents and purposes, in this type of event the object has disappeared. Object permanence does not differ in the two situations, but event type does. The child is learning or constructing not laws of object relations, but rules of social interaction with objects *as they apply to the infant during that stage of the child's development.* The latter is a very important condition, because as the child grows and becomes capable of complex motor movements and locomotion, the possibility of acquiring much more detailed knowledge of both adult activities and spatial relations involving objects and people becomes possible. As a consequence, the child's world models will become expanded, more general, and more stable and reliable.

As soon as one begins to think in terms of events, rather than only in terms of objects, it becomes necessary to frame the discussion in terms of events situated in a social context, and within a temporally and spatially particular situation. When the focus is upon objects *qua* objects, it is possible to conceive of the object world in static, even abstract, terms.

But when the emphasis is upon events, this is not possible. Moreover, when the focus is upon objects, they can be conceived of as physical entities independent of all social and cultural meanings. Events, however, are always socially and culturally particular.

To have knowledge of an event is to have organized knowledge of the *sequence* of actions, that is, to represent the temporal order in which the components of the event take place, and of the causal relation among actions within an event. Only in recent years has research begun to document infants' understanding of dynamic displays and the context of events (Gibson & Spelke, 1983; Haith, 1992; Rovee-Collier & Hayne, 1987). But there are many indications from those concerned primarily with social-emotional development (Ainsworth, 1973; Campos & Stenberg, 1981; Stern, 1985) and early language use (Barrett, 1986; Dromi, 1987; Nelson, 1985) that at least from the last quarter of the first year the infant's organization of knowledge is based in routine events. Recent work by Bauer and her colleagues (e.g., Bauer & Thal, 1990; Bauer & Mandler, 1992) on action sequences, and by Meltzoff (1988) and his colleagues on early imitation, have demonstrated reliable temporal and causal sequence memory in 9- to 24-month-old-infants.

Evidence of structured knowledge of routine events such as lunch indicates that infants and young children have an *event category* of eating lunch, a category whose extension includes all the successive occasions of lunch, and whose intension includes the specification of necessary components – actions, objects, persons. What we don't know at this point is how the child forms such categories – what are the necessary similarities across events that make an event count as a repetition of a prior event rather than a novel experience? Is spatial consistency important? Are person roles critical? Are the objects within the event critical? Although we have ample evidence from many studies of generalization from one event to another, we do not know the basis for the generalization. These questions remain to be investigated. Nonetheless, the evidence is convincing that by the last quarter of the first year if not before infants have established basic event representations as anticipated in Donald's (1991) theory as well as by my previous work (Nelson, 1986).

The events experienced by young children are framed and carried through to a large extent by adults; children are first of all participants in other people's activities and secondarily actors on their own. They must therefore learn the parts played by others and how they relate to their own role in the activity. At the outset event knowledge *is* social knowledge and social knowledge *is* event knowledge. From the beginning of the child's life adults establish caretaking routines (feeding, bathing, dressing, putting to bed) and ritual games (e.g., "ride a cock horse," "patty-cake"). These routines are at first completely under the parent's control. But by the middle of the first year the child begins to respond to the reciprocal demands of the routine, playing an increasingly participatory role. Parents tend to institute signals, explicit and implicit, that provide guidance to the child's anticipation and participation. For example, a mother may routinely ask, "Do you want lunch now?" before heading to the kitchen, or, "How about a bath?" as the accustomed hour draws near. Babies toward the end of the first year respond to these verbal, and nonverbal, signs, typically following or even preceding the parent in the expected direction. Parents often find that their young children begin to demand a part in the action, even before they can successfully carry through; such demands are strong indicators that the child has internalized the social routine and knows the roles to be played. These observations are commonplace among parents and caretakers generally; their significance for the child's growing knowledge schemes cannot be overstressed. What the child has come to represent is not simply some equation between the word "bath" and the event BATH,[2] but a representation of an entire event sequence that incorporates the word as well as the props and the sequence of actions that constitute that event.

The social construction of these events, first under the sole production and direction of the adult, but gradually incorporating the child's active role, is evident. To apply the levels analysis introduced in Chapter 2, learning routines is an individual process, but it is socially guided, and the cultural knowledge that is conveyed thereby (e.g., how to use tools for eating, what foods are acceptable) is passed on from older members of the society to younger through explicit social signals (modeling, gesturing, vocalizing, bodily directing). From this perspective, the child has learned a great deal about how close conspecifics behave in familiar situations, and how to match her own actions to those of her parents in routine activities by the end of the first year. Social construction of activities by adults and event knowledge in infants are thus closely aligned. Together they provide the basis for the establishment of several mimetic-like activities.

Emergence of the Mimetic Mind: Play, Imitation, and Communication

Three strands of development emerge during the latter part of the first year that are recognized as indicators of a new level of functioning: play, imitation, and intentional communication through motoric gesture or vocalization. These have also been variously seen as important foundations or precursors of language. Each plays a role as well in the theory advanced by Donald in the phylogenetic transition to mimetic representations. Each of these is also tied to understandings of event structures.

Pretense and Play

Social play in the first year involves simple games such as peekaboo that adults at first initiate, and that infants learn to take a part in and eventually to control. Bruner (1975) pointed out the similarity of structure in simple social games to the turn-taking and reciprocal role requirements of communicative language. For example, peekaboo, which children will play endlessly if encouraged at about 1 year, involves a hider, a screen, and a peeker. Many things can serve as a screen, and either partner can play either role, thus modeling the kind of general structure of communicative roles that can be reversed between speaker and listener.[3]

Reciprocal action games are succeeded late in the first year and in the second by social symbolic play with objects, usually toys. Symbolic play – using objects in pretense to stand for something else – was recognized by Piaget (1962) as integrally related to the emergence of symbolic language. This proposal has been examined by a number of authors who have mostly found that stages of symbolic play are correlated with stages of early language development (e.g., McCune-Nicholich, 1981; McCune et al., 1994; Ogura, 1991; Shore, O'Connell, & Bates, 1984), concluding that a general symbolic function emerges or develops during the second year, as Piaget suggested. This finding also fits Donald's proposal of the prelinguistic symbolic function (mimesis), where symbolism is externalized in the play, game, or song worked out between people, or by a child playing alone.

Social play engages the child in joint construction of pretense, the suspension of real-world representations in favor of an unknown but possible world. In contemporary American homes parents typically engage their children in play of this kind, beginning in late infancy, using stuffed animals, for example, as pretend agents, threatening to bite, kiss, or hug the young child. Such playfulness on the part of parents may accelerate the child's own establishment of a pretense mode (Zukow, 1986).[4] In many societies of the world parents may not engage in this kind of activity with their children, presumably believing that play is what children do together or alone, not with adults. However, throughout the world peer play is common, typically in mixed age groups where older siblings, cousins, or playmates establish a pretense game and guide the participation of the younger (Harkness, 1990). The relation of such activity to the child's establishment of alternative possible realities has not, however, been the focus of research.

A major theoretical issue has arisen with respect to the level of internal representation that is necessary to this kind of pretense. Leslie (1987, 1988), maintains that to use, or to recognize another's use of, one object for another in play requires a level not only of mental representation but also of metarepresentation, conceived as the representation of a representation. For example, he claims that understanding that when mother puts a banana to her mouth and ear, in the gesture of a telephone, the banana is at once both a banana and a symbol of a telephone, requiring the simultaneous dual representation of the thing itself and of the thing symbolized. However, Lillard (1993) has examined this claim in the context of other issues involved in children's theory of mind (Chapter 10), and has provided evidence that young children take pretending to be acting in a certain way, but not necessarily to involve dual representations.

An alternative interpretation of the banana-telephone is that the pretense serves to break apart the holism and continuity of the experienced world (in which bananas are to eat) and is thus conducive to imagining alternative states of the world. This kind of operation is analogous to using words to refer to objects, separating the objects out from their roles in the real world to be considered as individuals with identities apart from the events they participate in. In support of this interpretation, it may be noted that the child's engagement in pretense with dolls and other toys is temporally associated with the use of combinatorial language suggesting that "children are coming to recognize the world in more differentiated terms" as Ogura (1991, p. 290) states.

Rather than supposing that this development requires a prior establishment of simultaneous representations of real and pretend objects, it is reasonable to suppose that action with objects in pretend sequences, such as telephoning or pouring tea, facilitates the child's holding in mind an imagined sequence. But the imagined sequence does not need to come first; it is in line with the general external to internal assumption that Donald's proposal rests on (like Vygotsky's), that the activity itself may give rise to the mental representation of the activity. Representing what is happening and has happened no doubt are developmentally prior to representing what could happen but has not. Thus when the toddler lies down on the floor with her blanket and "pretends" to sleep, we do not need to suppose that she has *first* imagined the floor to be a bed. Rather, it is reasonable to suppose that the action is recognized as pretense, *during* and *after* it is engaged, and that the child smiles with the recognition that this is not a real bed and not a real sleep.

Similarly, doll play for the 2-year-old involves projecting familiar activities onto simulated props. There is no need to assume that the child represents the doll as standing for herself or for another child (Huttenlocher & Higgins, 1978). Rather, the doll is a stand-in in the activity for the purpose of action itself, not for its object-quality or for its symbolism. The doll is useful to enact the play, but if that doll is not available another will do, or some other object will be brought in. A similar analysis may apply to the banana-telephone in that the child, unlike the adult, has only the vaguest notion of the real character of either banana or telephone; thus using the banana as a telephone may be no more strange than using a telephone as a telephone. What may be amusing is that the usual function of the banana is violated.

Harris and Kavanaugh (1993) have reported a series of studies of the ability of very young children (2-year-olds) to carry through pretend sequences, for example, wiping up imagined juice that has imaginedly spilled from a container. In these sequences children demonstrate considerable capacity for representing a non–real world and acting within it. Harris and Kavanaugh analyze these abilities, in a counter to Leslie's claims regarding metarepresentation, arguing that children flag *activities* as PRETEND and this does not require the simultaneous dual representation of objects as both real and pretend. This is close to the position outlined here: The child's early pretense is not so much based on symbolism as it is based in activity with objects, usually involving very familiar activities or scripts. The activity itself invokes a nonpresent reality that may include some peculiar features. Mental symbols of objects may be abstracted from these activities, but need not be the basis for them.

The interpretation of early play and pretense in terms of action, rather than objects, ties together early action games (peekaboo) that have little connection with "serious" activities and later pretense activities involving objects. It is the surrounding action – the event – that defines the role that the object is playing. The child's prior event representation enables the interpretation of the play object, and the pretense action.

Mental representations of events of all kinds – real as well as pretend – require the ability to hold in mind a sequence of actions that are only potential, not realized in the immediate scene. The child's MERs (e.g., of feeding, bathing, etc.) embed objects as well as actions on the representational level. Thus the move from acting on the basis of an established MER to acting on the basis of pretense requires only the instantiation of a variation on one's MER model and the carrying through of the implied actions. In a real sense objects are at the disposal of the child's MERs (similar to Piaget's claim!). It follows that representing objects in pretense does not require a more advanced stage of representation ability, but only a variation on an ability already well established.

The MER analysis of pretense just presented is supported by research findings with 18- to 36-month-olds indicating resistance to using objects in modeled action sequences that reverse the standard order (O'Connell & Gerard, 1985; Rothstein, 1991). These studies use toy props in pretense involving such familiar activities as bathing or feeding to elicit imitation from the child, thus to test the representational coherence of event sequences. Combining imitation and pretense to test the child's representation of reality underlines the real, close connection between these allegedly distinct theoretical entities.

Imitation

Piaget's description of sensorimotor intelligence, in children up to 18 months old, placed the beginnings of imitation late in the first year, and delayed imitation in the last half of the second as a major component of the emergence of symbolic functions (Piaget, 1962). Donald's idea of mimesis, an advanced form of imitation with a representational or symbolic component, appears consistent with this proposal. Meltzoff (1988) and his colleagues have challenged this sequence, demonstrating robust delayed imitation (social modeling) after one week in 9-month-olds, as well as older infants. In their studies, imitation is more successful if infants are able to reproduce the actions they have seen (self-practice). The idea of self-practice is consistent with the importance Donald attributes to auto-cueing and refinement of motor skills in mimesis. The early development of imitation – reproducing observed behaviors to produce a similar result – in human infancy, in contrast to nonhuman infants and adults, implies an ontogenetic equivalent of the mimetic phylogenetic stage projected by Donald's thesis. It also suggests that, despite his mistakes with respect to the timing of critical developments, Piaget was right to place imitation in a critical role with respect to the development of symbolic capacities. However, as Meltzoff implies, delayed imitation has social significance, related to its symbolic function. Piaget viewed early symbols as individual constructions (and as deficient for this reason), whereas the mimesis claim, consistent with other semiotic analyses, views symbolization as socially constituted, the significance of which an individual may only partially or fully share.

It goes without saying that acquiring language depends in total on the capacity for reproducing the sounds and signals of others (Bates, Thal, & Marchman, 1991). Of course, language acquisition requires more than "mere" imitation (which is why imitation has been given such short shrift in language research in recent years). But its critical role in human cognitive and communicative development in the early years should be widely recognized, not only for learning language but also for learning the ways and meanings of the culture, and thus furnishing the mind. In addition, Meltzoff (1990) argues that "imitative interactions provide infants with a unique vehicle for elaborating the similarity between self and other and for understanding that others, like the self, are sentient beings with thoughts, intentions, and emotions. In other words, imitation may be an important, primitive building block in the nascent development of a 'theory of mind' . . . in the child" (p. 141).

Tomasello and colleagues' (1993) theory of cultural learning proposes three forms, of which imitative learning is the first, and foundational to the others – instructed learning and collaborative learning. They claim that cultural learning is a form of social learning unique to humans (see discussion in Chapter 2) that allows fidelity of transmission of behaviors and thus provides the psychological foundation for cultural evolution.

Together these findings and analyses suggest the hypothesis that imitation, play with learned activities involving objects (tools for play), and skill practice with objects are all emergent characteristics of social intelligence that were characteristics of early humans and appear late in the first and in the second to third year of human childhood. All three – pretense, imitation, and skilled practice – decouple action from its immediate pragmatic function and require the maintainence of an MER that is unconnected to present reality.

Self–Other System

Stern (1985) proposed that the infant builds up a general *schema* of self and other during the infancy period, based on general representations of dyadic interactions ["working models," in Bretherton (1987) terms], a conception that fits well with the event representation model. The establishment of joint visual attention within this dyadic interaction system (Butterworth, 1990; Tomasello, in press) is an important development in the first and second year, leading up to shared symbolic communication. At first, up to 6 months of age, infants will often look in the direction of the mother's gaze, so long as the gaze is within the infant's perceptual field, and not behind. Butterworth (1990) calls this first mechanism of joint visual attention "ecological," enabling a " 'meeting of minds' in the self-same object. It is as if the change in the mother's gaze signals the direction in which to look to the infant and the object encountered completes the communicative link" (p. 226). Two further stages in the infant's gaze following are called "geometric," emerging at about 1 year, when the infant can follow the angle of the mother's head and eye movements and fixate correctly on the object indicated thereby, and "representational," established in the middle of the second year. At this later stage the infant extrapolates to objects outside of the immediate perceptual space to include those located "behind" the self. The child plays a significant part in the establishment and utilization of these activities through "social referencing," whereby the infant follows the direction of the adult's gaze and turns her own attention in that direction (Campos & Stenberg, 1981). The argument is that the mutual involvement and attunement implicated by this process establishes the basis for communication through symbolic means.

Infants also begin to comprehend the intention behind a communicative point at about 12 months. Intentional infant pointing emerges at about 13.5 months, completing the indicative circle. Butterworth claims that pointing is not learned (or shaped) but develops epigenetically as a biologically specified communicative signal. Early in infancy pointing may be associated with mouth movement or vocalization, but it is not reliably associated with object gaze. Later it may be associated with object interest but is not reliably directed toward the object. The social-communicative nature of pointing is indicated by the fact that by 15 months infants check that mothers are attending before they begin to point.

The general claim from these studies is that following the gaze of another, following a point, and producing a point are all processes of shared attention that are species-specific social-communicative adaptations that emerge in infancy and provide the basis for establishing the beginnings of symbolic communication. As communicative devices used to draw the attention of another to the object of one's own contemplation, they must potentiate the differentiation of self and other if they do not already incorporate it into the system. The "point-sharing" system may be viewed as a first stepping-stone toward the capacity for taking an "objective" view of self with respect to others of the social world, or a self among other selves, which constitutes a step beyond the primitive experiential self. It will be recalled that mimesis, as described by Donald, draws the individual into the social symbolic action scheme and also enables individual mental re-representation of the scheme. The use of pointing to establish the tripartite relation of self, object, and other in activities may mark them as separate participants in MER relations. Thus pointing may serve an important developmental function in the establishment of the self–other relationship.

Most of the experimental studies of the self-concept in ontogeny and phylogeny have focused on the point in evolution and development when self-recognition is established. Modeled on Gallup's (1970) studies with nonhuman primates, infants' recognition of self in a mirror is indicated when they attempt to rub a surreptitiously placed mark off their own forehead (rather than, say, pointing to the mark on the mirrored image). Prior to about 15 months children seem to react to the mirrored image in a social fashion, as though viewing another child. The mirror test requires recognition of the child's own features, and may depend on prior experience with mirrors. Butterworth (1990) argues that a more basic sense of self may be established in terms of *visual proprioception*, locating one's body with respect to the environment, relying on a perceptual-motor system that is evident in the newborn. This position puts the "experiencing organism" at the center of self-concept development, even before the self–other system of joint attention.

Meltzoff's (1990) ingenious series of studies of "social mirroring," or "social modeling," identifies further developments in the domain of self and other from the point of view of the experiencing infant. In this research adults mirrored 14-month-old infants' actions on objects, contrasted with control adults who engaged in other actions similar in their temporal patterning. Infants looked at and smiled at the imitating adult and engaged in test behaviors – apparently in the effort to discover whether adults were really following their own actions – significantly more than they did with the control adult. These results imply that at least by 14 months infants are aware of their own actions, that is, of *self as actor*. Like Butterworth, Meltzoff believes that "There are good theoretical reasons for thinking that *the first, psychologically primary notion of self concerns not one's featural peculiarities but rather one's movements, body postures, and powers*" (p. 142, emphasis in original).

This objective view of self and other becomes evident during the early stages of language, and is significantly advanced thereby. But awareness of self in this way proceeds jointly with awareness of others. As the object point evolves into a communicative signal used by infant as well as by mother it becomes a part of a social representation, that is, a signal to attend to something whose significance or relevance is shared between two (or more) people. The notion of social representation implies more than that the individual represents social relations and activities. It implies either (a) that social actors/agents are active in setting up or guiding the individual's representations in an interactive mode; or (b) that social agents actively construct external representations – symbols or signs – that are shared by and thus become part of the individual's representations.

Emergence of Language in an Event-mimetic Sociality

Language is, of course, the primary system for humans, and it enters into social exchanges between parent and child from the beginning of life. But early uses of language have different functions for both the infant and the adult than later uses do. The implication of Donald's model is that before language itself is established as a representational system, the prelinguistic systems – the nonsymbolic event system, and the symbolic mimetic system – must support the child's language learning. The representational levels hypothesis implies that language would begin to express meanings that are evident in the social situations that children participate in, incorporated into games and event routines. Further, it would predict that a layer of linguistic representations would begin to be established as language forms accumulated and would eventually constitute the matrix from which representations in language could be reconstituted and by means of which lexical concepts could be developed. But these would be emergent properties of the developing language system, and would not be the beginnings from which it was made. The extent to which these developmental implications of the evolutionary model are borne out can be seen in the preparation for, onset, and development of language in the first years of life.

The human infant is surrounded by talkers,[5] speech directed to the infant, or part of the ambient background, from birth. Although the child's experience in the first year varies considerably across social and cultural conditions, by 1 year (+/−3 months) almost all children understand some language and produce one or more words and/or phrases. This regularity suggests a system that is strongly buffered and canalized (Waddington, 1957). Over the second year, a great deal of individual variation is observed in both the speed and type of acquisition of language forms (Nelson, 1973b; Bates, Bretherton, & Snyder, 1988), yet by $2\frac{1}{2}$ years these differences have diminished again, and the linguistic system appears to have become established and relatively stable, although still developing. Between $2\frac{1}{2}$ and 4 years language subsystems become organized, and they in turn reorganize the child's conceptual systems, including systems of social knowledge. From about 12 months to about 36 months the language system is being developed within and in service to communicative contexts already established as social activities. Its early development within the event-mimetic context is the topic in this chapter. Its elaboration as a representational system is discussed in Chapter 5.

Language in the First Year

Human infants are exposed to the sound of language prenatally, but precisely what they hear is not clear. It has been shown that shortly after birth infants preferentially attend to the language of their community – that is, when it is contrasted with a nonnative language – and prefer their mother's voice to the voice of other women (Bahrick & Pickens, 1988; DeCasper & Fifer, 1980; Spence & DeCasper, 1987). These results imply that what is heard in the womb is influential in establishing familiarity with some aspects of a particular language. As for the sounds of language, it has been known for some decades that very young infants can discriminate categories of phonemes, and that they are sensitive to phonemic distinctions that adult speakers of their languages do not make and cannot discriminate (Mehler & Dupoux, 1994; Miller & Eimas, 1983). For example, Japanese infants will discriminate between /r/ and /l/ sounds, which adult Japanese speakers cannot distinguish. These various early capacities for processing linguistically relevant sounds of speech clearly implicate the fact that *human* infants are biologically prepared to acquire linguistic skills of speaking and hearing speech.[6]

Infants are especially tuned to the patterns that distinguish linguistic productions from other types of sounds, and they have an early sensitivity to the prosodic contours of the language they hear, contours that differ across languages (Hirsh-Pasek et al., 1987; Morgan, 1986). They have been shown to be sensitive to clause boundaries even during the stage in which they are producing only consonant–vowel babbling such as "ba-ba" and "ma-ma." Throughout this period the maturation of the CNS is proceeding rapidly. Lateralization of the hemispheres is observable at birth (Kinsbourne & Hiscock, 1983; Turkewitz, 1993), and linguistic processing begins to be established in the speech centers of the left hemisphere during the first year. These developments presumably result from the most recent, specifically human, evolution of the brain. It is not known how efficiently human infants process the rapid information-bearing speech sounds that are typical of human language. It is likely that processing at the requisite level of rapid native language speech requires both maturation and practice.

The infant's early vocal productions are greeted as "speech-like" by many adults and responded to as though they carry messages. At least in middle-class Western cultures, parents often carry on "proto-conversations" with their prelinguistic infants (Snow, 1986). When gurgling and cooing turn to babbling phonetic productions (at about 5 or 6 months), the adult responds with imitations and interpretations (e.g., "Mama?" "Can you say mama?") of the most word-like productions.[7] Parents also engage in characteristic patterns of prosody specific to infant-directed speech (IDS), with exaggerated intonation, high pitch, and emphasis on lexical items (Snow & Ferguson, 1977). These characteristics of infant-directed speech are observed cross-culturally, and appear to be universal, although they are given more emphasis in some cultures and languages than in others[8] (Fernald, 1992).

In summary, given normal endowment and a normal language-using environment, by 1 year the child has established the basis of both speech perception (phonemic processing, prosodic parsing) and production (babbling). Without normal language input these components of the system will not develop. Speech/language development within the first year depends on cognitive psychological and social communicative support. Even at this early stage "biology" does not proceed on its own, and "language" does not mature without support.

Language and Categories

Language is based on categorical structures – of phonemes, grammatical classes, and word meanings (Brown, 1958b). An infant/child who could not categorize phenomena would not be able to acquire language. For this reason the categorization capacities of infants and young children in and out of language have become of intense interest to researchers. Unlike simple discrimination learning, categorization involves grouping together items that can be discriminated on some basis (e.g., color) but that share some other critical attribute (e.g., shape). Human infants and young children spontaneously recognize a variety of shared attributes as a basis for categorization. This variety becomes manifest during the early stages of word learning, when children extend their early object terms to diverse items, each of which may share only a single feature with the prototype object initially associated with the name (Bowerman, 1976; Clark, 1973; Nelson, 1973b; Rescorla, 1980).

It was early found that at 13 months, children tend to group objects into sets of "kinds" when presented with a set of two contrasting types. For example, children's sequential touching and actions indicate that they distinguish between four-legged animals and cars (Nelson, 1973a; Sugarman, 1983). Ross (1980) showed that infants between 1 and 2 years differentiated between members of superordinate categories such as food and furniture. Subsequent research has traced the beginnings of these capacities for categorizing objects to the middle and latter part of the first year (Cohen & Younger, 1983; Reznick & Kagan, 1983; Bauer & Mandler, 1989b). Moreover, Mandler and McDonough (1993) have shown that infants as young as 7 months can make distinctions between what they term "global categories" of animals and vehicles before they distinguish conceptually between members of basic-level categories, such as dogs and fish.

Mandler (1988, 1992) has proposed a theoretical account of how the infant derives concepts from perceptual analysis. Infants direct visual attention to perceptual displays – in particular, to objects and relations, such as movements along a path – to engage in *examining*, a deliberate activity that goes beyond the automatic perception of viewing and see-ing. Through examining, the infant abstracts information, engaging in a *redescription* [in Karmiloff-Smith's (1992) terms] of the display. These ab-stractions result in "image schemas" of the kind proposed in cognitive semantics by Lakoff (1987). Image schemas represent abstractions such as containment, caused movement, self-movement, and so on, and in turn are used to compose complex concepts such as *animate*, and rich images that are used to symbolize specific and global concepts such as *car* and *animal*.

Mandler's theory avoids the trap of innate content, resting only on innate processing mechanisms. It assigns to the infant mind the capacity to represent aspects of the world, and suggests a mode that mediates between the sensory (or simply perceptual) and the conceptual base that is needed to support language. But it takes scant account of infant activ-ity and experience beyond examining, or the social conditions for these. Moreover, Mandler's solution to the origin of linguistic concepts runs aground on a point that Piaget (1962) explicated. According to Piaget's analysis, the child's original symbols, which he saw as imagery derived from imitation, are deficient specifically because they lack the conventional component of the linguistic sign. In Piaget's original theory (1962) the solution to this problem lay in further cognitive advance on the operative or logical level, enabling the child (only at the concrete operations stage) to achieve an understanding of the logical relations inherent in linguistic signs. This analysis can be faulted on the now generally conceded grounds that natural language categories do not rest on the rigorous logical base that Piaget then assumed, as well as on his neglect of the interpersonal plane.

Both Piaget and Vygotsky (1986) had the vision to see the central problem that has stymied contemporary developmental theorists, who have attempted to derive symbols, and more specifically natural language, from prelinguistic forms of thought. Piaget thought the solution lay in the move to a higher form of logic, while Vygotsky thought the solution lay in the move from social speech to inner speech. It is now obvious that neither solution is satisfactory, leaving open the prior questions of how logic emerges and how social speech evolves. It is important to recognize that the symbolic basis for language arises from collective symbolic activity, not from individual thought (Vygotsky, 1986; Wittgenstein, 1953). Of course, there must be a preparation on the individual level in order to make the interpersonal possible, and Mandler's theory is clearly designed to solve the problem of individual preparation through conceptualization. However, the preparation must also be seen as part of a social-communicative as well as cognitive system if the connection is to be made.

The questions left open by traditional analyses are for a preverbal child: Why this symbol and no other? Why this perceptual analysis and not some other? What is the consequence of forming this concept, as opposed to all the other infinitely many possible concepts that might be formed? Many theorists faced with these questions have concluded that the system must be innately programed to construct just these concepts, in preparation for learning language forms appropriate to them. The experiential alternative is that the concepts that infants form are those that have consequences for their own lives, as presently lived; or that the concepts they form are those that are salient in the social world defined through interactions with adults. These influences, of course, must operate in concert with biologically determined predispositions to attend to certain aspects of the environment, thus jointly to determine what the emerging conceptual system of the infant will contain. But the system is open, not constrained to particular parts or types. What then is the relation, sequential or developmental, between the child's event representations and concepts and categories of objects?

If event representations are basic and objects are viewed in terms of their roles in human activities, it seems logical that the infant's concepts of object kinds would include specifications of how they are used in such activities. This was essentially the proposal that was advanced as the "functional core concept hypothesis" (Nelson, 1974; see Chapter 8 in this volume). The claim was that infants would form concepts of objects that were functional in their own lives, and would therefore learn to name them easily and early. The object's function from the child's point of view (e.g., rolling a ball) would form the core of the concept, and its perceptual appearance would be added as a cue to the identification of instances. Later, we proposed (Nelson, 1982, 1983; Nelson & Lucariello, 1985) that object concepts were first embedded in event representations, accounting for some of the earliest uses of object words to refer to whole events (discussed in the next section).

In the human cultural world, objects of all kinds surround the child, and in modern complex societies infants and children are presented with many different toy objects to explore and play with. Thus most of the events that the child is engaged in involve artifacts of varying kinds, and much of the play that parents take part in with their babies involves objects. Not surprisingly then, most infants by 1 year of age have formed many rather global categories of objects on the basis of their exploration of the object world, reflecting their understanding of both perceptual and functional characteristics, prior to beginning to learn words for the categories. Concepts and words embedded in events must be abstracted from the contexts that initially bind them if they are to serve as generalized symbols. Thus experience with the way words are used by adults to indicate kinds of objects refines and reorganizes the child's initial categories, and results in the extraction of some event-embedded object categories from their first contextual binding (Nelson, 1985; Nelson & Lucariello, 1985). While some objects are bound by their embeddedness in the infant's event schemas, infants also form some categories of objects in their own right, and make categorical distinctions among them on both perceptual and conceptual bases (Lucariello, 1987; Mandler, 1992; Nelson, 1985).

Gopnik and her colleagues (Gopnik & Meltzoff, 1986; Gopnik & Choi, 1990) have proposed that object categorization is a specific prerequisite for the acquisition of linguistic symbols for objects, and have presented evidence from English speaking and Korean-speaking children that the developments are sequentially organized, with the Korean-speakers significantly delayed in both categorizing and object naming in comparison with English speakers. The object naming in their proposal is that associated with the vocabulary spurt in the middle to end of the second year, which typically is composed of object names. This proposal can be reconciled with other findings documented here by assuming that children's categorization and object naming are advanced through experience with the use of such names by parents to pick out significant types, as suggested previously. Indeed, Gopnik and Choi (in press) noted that Korean mothers do significantly less naming of objects in play with their children than do English-speaking mothers.

Categorization, of course, applies to many phenomena besides objects, and human beings use their abilities to form categories on the basis of shared attributes – overlooking possible distinctions – for many ontological categories, including people, events, locations, emotions, time, natural states of the world (e.g., snow), and so on. Social categories of familiar versus nonfamiliar, age (adult versus child), and gender (male versus female) are recognized by children within the first two years. For example, 2-year-olds differentiate between male activities and female activities and between male-type and female-type toys (Bauer, 1993). Indeed, the very idea of forming general event representations implies that somewhat disparate episodes are recognized as belonging to a single event category. For the infant's world, for example, those categories might consist, among others, of feedings, baths, walks, and bedtime. The properties identified for categorizing objects are not necessarily characteristic of those used to classify other kinds. For example, goals and locations are critical aspects of events.

Premack and Dasser (1991) have made an important observation relevant here. They emphasize the distinction between explicit and implicit knowledge and note that some distinctions that infants make in habituation paradigms (such as those used in the infant categorization research) are not explicitly accessible to children younger than 4 years of age. Therefore, it seems likely that categorization in infancy is implicit rather than explicit, and may require explicitation processes, including particularly externalized symbolization in language, to enter into a generalized explicit knowledge system on a par with the child's emerging event knowledge. What the experience of language referring to objects may achieve is the re-parsing of experience in the categories of the language, effectively re-representing experience in a new culturally shared representational mode.

Language from 1 to 3 Years

The early stages of productive speech have been extensively documented over the past 30 years (Brown, 1973; Bloom, 1973, 1993; Bruner, 1983; Nelson, 1973b, 1985; Bates, Bretherton, & Snyder, 1988; Barrett, 1986; Kuczaj & Barrett, 1986; Smith & Locke, 1988). The "typical" course of development may be characterized as follows: Toward the end of the first year, beginning at about 9 or 10 months, children begin to give evidence of responding to some specific language forms, including names of family members, signals for games (e.g., "patty-cake") and routines (e.g., "bath"), and so on. Somewhat later, a few consistent word-like forms may be produced, usually within a specific event or routine. By 15 months, children use an average of about 10 words consistently, but the variability among children is very great.[9] Some children have 100 words or more at this age, while others produce none or only one or two. Consistent with the mimetic proposal, children around 1 year of age use gestures instead of or in addition to words to convey meanings (Bates, 1979). At 16 months, about half of Italian children studied used more symbolic gestures than words, but thereafter vocal signs become dominant (Iverson, Capirci, & Caselli, 1994). It seems probable that the enveloping verbal environment encourages words rather than gesture, while both are consistent with early mimetic symbolization.

A typical pattern is reached between 18 and 20 months in terms of two related "milestones": a "vocabulary spurt" in which the number of new words learned increases markedly over the previous months, and the total vocabulary amounts to 50 to 100 words; and the onset of two-word constructions. Again, considerable variability in these milestones is the rule. Sometime between the middle and the end of the second year, usually after the child has experienced a vocabulary spurt, the child may begin to put together chunks of language – two words, or two short phrases, or a phrase and a word, thus launching into simple grammatical constructions. Children tend to be quite systematic in their productions at the two-word stage. For example, they may consistently order words in the sequence "Action–object acted on" [see Brown (1973) for description and discussion]. However, children's constructions appear to be based at first on lexical categories of varying size (Braine, 1976; Tomasello, 1992) rather than on general grammatical categories, such as noun or verb. The evidence on this point suggests that abstract grammatical categories such as NOUN are constructed from experience with the language and are not innate properties of the human mind.[10] By 2 years, most children have moved beyond two-word constructions to increasingly longer phrases and to the elaboration of basic constructions by way of prepositions, pronouns, tense forms, and auxiliaries.

Bates and her colleagues (1991) have presented evidence that the milestones in language observed over the first three years coincide with "cognitive milestones," many of which involve gestural, motoric, and social components of the kind expected on the basis of an ontogenetic analogy with Donald's proposal that mimetic symbolization preceded true language in hominid evolution. The consistency with which children move through the early stages of language and embark on patterned constructions of two words and longer toward the end of the second year has been generally taken to imply a specific biological imperative. The considerable variation in both the pace and the direction of these developments, however, supports the proposal that the biological imperative is of a very general kind that directs the child to attend to patterns of language (Bates and Carnavale, 1993). Of course, in the absence of a socially engaged language model these developments of the second and third years will not take place.

The wide variation in both the timing and organization of the emergence of productive language points to its construction as a system based on many underlying competencies (Van Geert, 1991) rather than a single module or a set of discrete modules. One variation consistently observed is an emphasis on extracting phrases for analysis (Lieven, Pine, & Dresner Barnes, 1992) in contrast to a focus on single words, and specifically on object nouns. Although it is often claimed that children begin learning to talk by learning names of objects, closer analysis of the data indicates that this is rarely the case. Even in group data, the earliest stage of vocabulary acquisition is characterized by words used in routines (Caselli et al., in press). As word learning proceeds, individual differences among children are found, with some children learning mainly object words and others concentrating on socially useful phrases. This difference in vocabulary composition has been associated with differences in social and cultural activity patterns among individual children and mother–child dyads (Hampson & Nelson, 1993). Indeed, the widely accepted claim that language is acquired in a universal stage sequence is a scientific myth belied by the empirical data. Rather, language is composed by individual children in different ways within the adult–child communicative system. A closer look at the process indicates how this takes place.

Establishing Shared Meaning.   Language as a meaning system evolves within the parent–child dyad beginning in the second year. This presents a central problem of language acquisition: How can the parent and child make sense to each other when one of the pair commands no part of the symbolic system – neither the symbolic forms nor the relevant interpretants? It is presumably through the system of intersubjectivity established earlier that the barriers imposed by differing conceptual systems can be breached. Certainly by the time that the child has begun to use words, the simple biologically determined development of speech has merged into the problem of establishing a system of shared meaning with a community of speakers. Then the particular language that is being acquired becomes a means to this end; its structure emerges from its function but is not its primary focus. This development must then be understood within the experiential-social-communicative system established between 6 and 18 months, described earlier. As the infant works into the language system during and after the second year, the social world establishes activity contexts and the talk that takes place therein, which the individual child represents in terms of event representations. Parents, as social partners, guiders, and directors, focus the child's attention on specific aspects of the context of the activity, by way of both verbal and nonverbal markers. Thereby, parents guide the child to extract aspects of the world that need to be given special status as concepts and categories of objects, people, scenes, actions, and events.

The problem of establishing shared meaning is solvable via the joint contributions of prior mutually established representations in routines, play, and communicative exchanges, and the principle of relevance emphasized by Sperber and Wilson [(1986); Nelson (1992); see also Bloom (1993b)]. Around the child's first birthday the mutual subjectivity system established in the preverbal period enables the parent to interpret a vocal production by the child as fitting into a shared event situation, and thus to credit the child with a word. The child may have been attempting to insert appropriate sounds (modeled on parent productions within the event) into the situation previously. The parent's acceptance and repetition of the sound provides the assurance that the child has succeeded in entering into the speech game.

The particular words that children learn in the first part of the second year are predictable in that they fit into the activities that children engage in, and that parents structure for them: they are also idiosyncratic in that each child's world is structured and interpreted differently, so that what is salient in one child's experience and thus worth mentioning is background for another child. What is consistent is that the use of words is dependent upon their fit to the child–adult communicative transactions. Therefore, words may be learned primarily for objects, because parent and child are focused on naming objects as a game or as a task; or they may be learned for directives and actions ("give it" or "turn") because the dyad has established these as understandable messages within their routines. For some middle-class children in Western societies most of the early words learned are names of objects; many writers have taken this to be a universal disposition, a privileged entry into language. But contrary to this widespread assumption, this is not universal across children, class, culture, or language.[11]

The event-bound basis for the production and interpretation of the child's early words has been demonstrated in many studies. Barrett (1986) provides an example of his son's word "duck."

> initially produced by Adam only while he was engaged in the process of hitting one of his toy yellow ducks off the edge of the bath (which is where they were normally kept). He was never observed producing this word in any other situation at this initial stage: he never produced it while he was playing with his toy ducks in other situations, or while he was looking at or feeding real ducks. This behavior therefore tends to suggest . . . that Adam had not yet learned that the word *duck* could be used to refer to either his toy ducks or real ducks. . . . [H]e had simply identified one particular event in the context of which it was appropriate for him to produce the word *duck*. (p. 40)

This restriction of words interpreted by adults to refer to categories of objects to single-event contexts is precisely what one would expect if the child were interpreting and using words in terms of her own MERs.[12] Soon after this point, Barrett's son Adam began extending the term "duck" to other instances of ducks in other contexts; that is, he began to use it to refer to members of an object category. This extension is based on the externalization of the word by producing it in the initial social context in which it was accepted, thereafter observing its use in other contexts and generalizing therefrom. An internal concept not externalized presumably would remain tied to its initial restricted context.

The close relation between activities, the experiential knowledge base, and early word use is further seen in a 16-month-old child's use of the word "Lardi" to refer to all kinds of fruits and vegetables (Rescorla, 1976). "Lardi" was a term used in a specific event context – the context of the produce man, Mr. Lardi, coming to deliver fresh produce to the child's house twice a week. From the mother's use of the phrases "Here comes Mr. Lardi" and "Look what Mr. Lardi brought us" the child extracted the word "Lardi" and applied it to the objects delivered. From one point of view this was an incorrect term for a correct generalization to a higher-order category of a type of food. But the child began by using "Lardi" to indicate the whole event, announcing the man's arrival, no doubt in imitation of the mother's use. Like most mothers, this mother did not correct the child's extension of the word from a restricted to an overgeneralized use – from the man to what he brought – but rather interpreted the child's use as being *relevant* to the *context*. The principle of relevance to word learning and use can be seen clearly here. Relevance interpretation runs both ways from the very beginning: Mothers interpret their children's words as relevant to the context even as children are making inferences about mothers' meanings on the same basis.

The early establishment of shared meaning thus involves an interaction of the child's preword interpretation of events and objects and the adult's use of those words, and acceptance of the child's uses within jointly constructed and mutually understood activities. Words and sentences can then be used and interpreted by partners in an activity, adult caretakers first, peers and unfamiliar adults later, as carrying communicative force, aiding in the ongoing action. During this phase of the child's communicative and cognitive development the important achievements are those that allow collective symbols to be established, practiced, refined, and extended, whether the symbols are objects used in play, actions, or words. The child practices on her own in symbolic play, private speech, and motoric skills, and the practice refines the symbols of the society – of action, object, and word. Thereby the private world of the child begins to integrate her own presymbolic understandings of experience with the meanings attributed to them by the social and cultural world of the adult.

Toward the Mediated Mind

The goal of this chapter has been to uncover evidence for emerging layers of representation in ontogeny analogous to those Donald identified in phylogeny in terms of episodic and mimetic mentalities and cultures that were hypothesized to be precedents of the linguistic or mythic culture. The discovery process has been successful in finding good evidence for both MERs and mimetic social structures apparent in play and games, imitative routines and skills, and triadic communicative relations. It appears, however, that the period from late infancy to early childhood (roughly 9 months to $2\frac{1}{2}$ years) is one in which MERs and mimetic structures develop contemporaneously and interactively.

Symbolic individual and social play, imitation, and nonverbal communication, as well as event routines, all emerge and become elaborated during the latter part of the first year and the end of the second. This period is marked also by evidence for objectification of self and other, as well as for skills in categorizing objects, events, and other entities, and beginning use of language. Thus rather than sequential development, as Donald (1991) hypothesized for the phylogenetic progression, it is apparent that in ontogeny the process is characterized by overlapping dynamic development of interrelated representational systems.

The present framework posits that the infant and young child move from an individually constructed model of the world in terms of events to a breaking apart of those global event structures and the marking of event components in their social and cultural presentations, as they are decomposed with the help of others. Through the process of decomposing, symbolic forms in language and play may be used to rearrange the components (even as the child resists rearranging the parts in real-world activities). It is hypothesized here that language enters into the represented event first as part of the event itself, and next as a marker of parts of the modeled world of events.

The more complex view revealed here is that potentiations of all the representational systems posited by Donald are visible in the developments taking place between 1 and 3 years of age: events, mimesis, language, and categorization, with the latter containing the potential for the theoretical structures of the fourth and final stage. However, as vaguely realized potentials, the latter types do not form fully realized representational systems; rather, they are incorporated into event and mimetic structures and processes, not as representational levels in their own right. The implication may be forecast at this point, to be explored in Chapter 11; that these developments provide a different interpretation of the levels of explicitation theorized by Karmiloff-Smith (1986a, 1992). A part of this process, which can be noted here, is that mimetic activities – play, imitation – provide the impetus for the development of self–other consciousness and thus for making what is implicit to self explicit.

In Chapter 3 and earlier in the present chapter it was noted that contemporary children are developing within a cultural world that encompasses all the representational systems of the adult hybrid mind and surrounds the child with signs and symbols of these systems. Thus the simultaneous appearance in development of aspects of these different representational modes may be a reflection of the access that the adult society makes possible. Additional constraints from cognitive maturation and learning processes prevent the full flowering of the more complex and culturally developed systems (narrative and theory), resulting in a kind of "cascading" of modes, appearing simultaneously but completing sequentially.[13]

Chapter 5 examines further the hypothesis that the first three years of life exhibit the exercise of human intelligence, aided by language, and incorporating the use of socially shared symbolic forms, but that knowledge is not yet represented *in* language. The years from 3 to 6 are viewed as the critical years during which language emerges as a representational system for the human child, transforming thinking from intelligent practical action to the inclusion of the potential for symbolic representations and processes. Whereas earlier language has marked out the components of experience that are significant within the social and cultural world of the child, the emerging capacity during the preschool years incorporates the possibility of constructing whole new structures not evident in the real world itself, but modeled and represented through language in the social world, and encouraged by it. Stories, categories, myths, and theories become realized therein.

A major challenge to developmental theory emerges from this process: the challenge of conceptual change and, in particular, reconciliation of a preexisting experientially based system with a semiotically mediated system. The discussion thus far has shown only how the beginning language system may be organized within the structure of event representations and the socially established mimetic activities. The latter structures reorganize the categories of the former, but much more radical change is expected when the categories of the language are imposed on the experientially derived conceptual structures. Chapter 5 examines the beginnings of this process in the development of complex discourse, succeeded by further exploration of memory and construction of narratives, concepts, and categories. Each of these has been seen in an early form in the overview in this chapter.

The conclusion thus far is that the progression from the unmediated to the mediated mind is not a matter of sudden or simple change. To some degree the human mind is "mediated" from birth, through the representation of cultural categories implicit in the furnishings, food, toys, and other artifactual arrangements of the infant's world, as well as through caretaking practices. But in another sense, the infant's mind is impenetrable by the representations of other minds until language as a representation exchange system becomes available. In this latter sense, language is the medium through which the mind becomes culturally mediated. And, while recognizing all the semiotic and culturally significant possibilities inherent in the social forms of dance, gesture, song, games, pictorial displays, artifacts, and so on, it is still true that the major forms of hybrid representational systems are established through language, both in informal folk psychological systems and in formal theoretical systems. Therefore, it is to language that we turn next.

5. The Emergence of Mediating Language

The mediating role of language involves its capacity to convey knowledge about the world, about other people, about social and cultural interpretations of situations and events, and about imagined possibilities, plans, mythologies and theories. In this role, language serves a different metafunction than that of regulating interactions between people. Halliday (1975) differentiated between the *mathetic* and *pragmatic* functions of language use in the early phases of acquiring conventional linguistic forms, a contrast that captures this distinction as it emerges in development.

A major point to be brought out here is that language must be well developed in order to serve the full range of its mediating functions. The child does not immediately make a leap from prelinguistic to linguistic, or from sensorimotor to representational, or any of the other stage changes that have been proposed as explanations of developments between 1 and 3 years. The transition is long and composed of a complexity of developments in different parts of the social-linguistic-cognitive system. At this point the transitions have been traced most completely in the linguistic system itself, documenting developments in an expanding meaning system, an expanding grammatical system, and an expanding pragmatic system. The connection of these with developments in social and cognitive competencies has been less well worked out. In this chapter some of the major developments that take place to establish language as a mediating system for an individual child are discussed. Succeeding chapters consider how language functions for the preschool child as a mediating system in different representational formats and in different knowledge domains.

Representation in Language

The unique contribution of human language is that it serves to communicate representations of states of affairs between individuals, transferring complex information from one mind to another, structured in such a way that its transference maintains to an important degree the intended form and content of the original.

The development of this dual function as both an internal (cognitive) and an external (communicative) representational system is a critical turning point in human history and in human ontogeny. This bidirectional function has two interrelated roles, that of speaker/messenger and that of listener/interpreter. That is to say, each participant in a communicative situation uses an external linguistic representation to relate to an internal mental representation. In the case of the speaker, the mental representation (MREP) must be transformed into a language format that imperfectly represents its intention (imperfectly because there is no one-to-one mapping between thought – or for that matter, the world – and language). In the case of the listener, the external linguistic representation (LREP) must be internalized, interpreted, and transformed into an MREP that again, and doubly, imperfectly represents the intention of the speaker. To the imperfection of the speaker's LREP is added the imperfection of the transformation of the linguistic format into the listener's knowledge or belief (MREP) system. Such is the fallible communication system that we rely on to transfer meaning from one person to another. If this is the situation for adults, what can children make of it?

Consider in this regard a well-worn example utterance:

(1) The cat is on the mat.

To interpret this utterance from, let us imagine, a parent, a child must understand at least the words "cat," meaning certain domestic animals of the child's acquaintance, and "mat," meaning a kind of fabric construction, usually found on the floor, perhaps in the bathroom, or in front of the front door; and probably the preposition "on" as indicating a location on top of and not beside, behind, in front of, or underneath. If the child is in view of a well-known cat that is in fact sitting on something understood to be a mat, this utterance may be interpreted to say what is obvious, perhaps to draw attention to it. But suppose this is not the case, and the utterance is spoken out of context. It might be imagined that the child would conjure up an image as many adults do, of a cat curled up in front of a fireplace resting on a bit of rug. This picture, however, requires a good bit more conventional cultural knowledge than our hypothetical 2-year-old possesses. Suppose the child does not share living space with a particular cat and is not viewing a book about cats, and her only acquaintance with mats is in the bathroom. Will she then go to the bathroom to look for the strange visitor? More likely she will judge that the sentence just uttered is one more of the many things said around her that are irrelevant to her pursuits, whatever they are.[1]

In general, 2- and 3-year-olds attend to language that informs them about their current activities, provides wanted information, or directs them in familiar actions, and not to random overheard utterances. Building up knowledge from what is said is a highly complex skill that calls on, not just syntax and lexicon, but modes of relating to the experiential knowledge base, and ways of adding to that base new information arriving in the form of discourse about an unfamiliar topic. The kind of representation that is involved takes language in the form of utterances in discourse, relates these to established knowledge about the world – derived from experience or from prior linguistic representations – and constructs a new mental model conforming to what is said and meant. This process can of course go awry in many directions for many reasons beyond those of inadequate linguistic knowledge, but linguistic competence is clearly a first step toward this achievement.

What Makes Language Different?

Language represents states of affairs in special ways. It is based on special kinds of categories (grammar), on linear sequences of items (words), on hierarchical orders of constituent parts, and on special ways of referring within and outside of text, among many other things. To represent something in linguistic form is to make choices about what aspects to represent and how to present them. Events do not simply present themselves as linguistically codable. Any event might be expressed in innumerable ways (e.g., "Muffy is sleeping on your favorite rug again," "That feline is shedding fur all over the mat I just vacuumed," etc.). The visible world does not appear (to the untutored eye) as separable animate objects undertaking discrete actions that eventuate in visibly different states, as the structure of sentences implies. Discrete units combined into linear propositions are special characteristics of spoken language, not of human thought in general. There is then a thought/language mapping problem for the child to solve.

The linear sequence of elements in language is necessary to representations presented in the oral medium. However, there is an important payoff for mental functioning from this system of discrete units linearly arranged: words and sentences slow down, break up, and objectify thoughts that might otherwise be fleeting and ineffable, chaotic or densely complexive. Linguistic forms and structures thus make it feasible to manipulate mentally the separate parts of a concept or idea that in its dynamic nonlinguistic form might be impenetrable. In the more individuated and structured form that language imposes, the idea becomes not only more manageable but more memorable. Thus the linguistic form of representation reveals new potentials not evident or accessible in prior forms of mental representation. For the child, then, acquiring language requires effort, but the achievement results in a continuously unfolding new perspective together with new cognitive and communicative potentialities.

Language Competence

The important question to ask then is, "When do these potentials become opened up in childhood?" To enter into the full potential offered by human language and culture the child must acquire the complexities of grammar that make extended discourse possible. It is not until the child is capable of following an extended dialogue and constructing parts of dialogue that mesh with those of the partner that the child can actually enter into the language/culture complex. A special problem for the beginning language user is the rapidity with which information in language is presented. Rapid-fire speech may simply pass the young language learner by, so that only the slow and short utterances are processed at all. "Motherese" – the special register used by adults speaking slowly and distinctly to young language learners – ensures that some messages get through.

We know, both from common observation and scholarly research, that typically by about 4 years of age most children have mastered basic structures of sentence grammar, have acquired a vocabulary of a few thousand words, speak sufficiently articulately to be understood by strangers, and have mastered some basic pragmatic structures such as how to ask questions and how to address adults and peers.[2] But there is much more to be learned. The most important outcome of language acquisition in childhood is mastery of language at a level sufficient to serve the varied cognitive and communicative representational functions possible for adult language users. These functions include telling stories, making plans, reading novels, gossiping, studying history, reading the newspaper, following written instructions, and formulating formal and informal arguments. These activities are possible because language, in its original oral and derived written forms, has become a functional mode of both cognitive and communicative representations for individual language users.

Language Functions

Different perspectives on these representational language functions in both developing and mature forms are found in the sociolinguistic and philosophical literatures. For example, Taylor (1985) proposes that language performs three critical and unique functions: (1) It explicates thoughts, bringing them into explicit awareness; (2) it puts matters into public space where a thought, an idea, a feeling can be shared between people; and (3) it formulates our ideas about important human concerns that are otherwise inaccessible, such as justice and truth. The first of these is recognizable as the explicitation function of language, a goal in formal discourse and often a by-product in informal discourse. As noted previously, language slows down and stabilizes what are sometimes fleeting thoughts, thus making them accessible to conscious reflection and reformulation. The conventional symbolic medium (common to mimetic symbolism as well) not only stabilizes, but enforces a (more or less) common understanding of what has been brought into awareness. This commonality makes the second function, sharing of ideas and feelings, possible. The possibility of such sharing emerges for the child only with the acquisition of language or some other symbolic form. The third function involves the actual construction in language of ideas that are not thinkable in other forms, including concepts of morality, mythology, religion, science, and the arts. Children begin to reach for these ideas in early childhood, as soon as they acquire the words, but full grasp of their meanings is a lifelong process.

Halliday's (1975) six basic functions of early speech map quite closely onto those outlined by Jakobson (1960) as basic linguistic functions (emotive, conative, phatic, referential, poetic, and metalingual). Halliday divided these functions into Pragmatic and Mathetic, and he proposed that children began with Pragmatic functions. Pragmatic functions include Instrumental, Regulatory, and Interactive, while Mathetic (functions related to knowing or learning) include Personal, Imaginative, and Heuristic. Examples of each and of the Informative function, which Halliday suggested emerges later – toward the end of the second year – are shown in Table 5.1, drawn from my study of crib dialogues and monologues from the child Emily during her second and third years (Nelson, 1989c, 1990).

Table 5.1. *Halliday's functions of beginning language*

Function	Example[a]
Pragmatic	
Instrumental	I need more juice (request)
Regulatory	Put blanket on (directing parent)
Interactive	Night-night (response to parent leaving)
Mathetic	
Personal	I standing up (describing own action)
Imaginative	Carl playing ring a rosie (comment on picture)
Heuristic	Mommy tired, mommy go nap (repeating parent explanation)
Informative	[Toy Mouse is] In Daddy's room (providing information from own memory)

[a]From Emily at 2 years (Nelson, 1990). Reprinted from J. Miller (ed.), *Research on Child Language Disorders*, with permission of the publisher.

Halliday suggested that early in development each utterance encodes only one function, but in mature language each utterance expresses both interpersonal (communicative) and ideational (cognitive) functions, as well as an intertextual function, relating the individual utterance to other elements of the discourse. He suggested further that the Pragmatic functions of early child language map onto (in some sense) the Interpersonal, whereas the Mathetic map onto the mature Ideational, although of course the specific functions addressed by an utterance are quite variable and more complex than those expressed by the beginning language learner. From this perspective the Informational function, which first appeared in his data from his own son at about 18 months of age, expresses both the Interpersonal – in that there is someone to whom information is being directed – and the Ideational, the information being conveyed.

Halliday's (1975) theory explicitly claims that the Informative function (using language to inform someone about something that that person does not already know) develops late, toward the end of the second year, and that it develops in conjunction with the development of grammar and entering into dialogue with others. Halliday puts the emphasis on dialogue and the structures that form a coherent text, highlighting the point when conversation between parent and child on a topic sustained over more than one turn becomes possible. This is an important entry point for the child into the full meaning potential of the culture.

What we lack is a description of how the child moves from this set of primitive functions to the mature set of complex uses of language. Between 3 and 5 years most children become much more adept at all the uses of extended discourse. By 5 years they can retell a story, maintaining its sequential and causal structure, although in skeletal form. Their memories for events are more elaborated, and they can begin to use language for planning and explaining to others, as well as to follow the directions, plans, and explanations that they are given. They use language creatively in setting up and carrying through narrative play themes (Sachs, Goldman, & Chaille, 1984). These capabilities indicate that they have developed basic skills in using linguistic presentations to build novel representations that are different from those they have constructed from their own direct experience, and that they are able to move back and forth between their own representations, the linguistic representation of those representations, and the linguistic representations of other people, whose representation of an event may differ from their own.

Halliday's theory is explicitly social-interactional. The functions he attributes to the child's early expressions are those that relate self to others. Vygotsky's (1986) interpretation of private speech (speech for self – what Piaget termed "egocentric speech") viewed the use of language in monologue as a development from social speech toward inner speech, thinking in speech, or what here has been termed "cognitive uses of LREPs." The private speech literature has been primarily concerned with the use of speech in the preschool period for self-regulation of action (Luria, 1961; Diaz & Berk, 1992; Kohlberg, Yaeger, & Hjelvtholm, 1968). But Vygotsky's description of inner speech clearly implies more than this single regulatory function. As the study of monologic presleep speech has revealed (Nelson, 1989c), talk to self in the early childhood years appears to serve a number of cognitive representational functions. It is interesting that the incorporation of other voices is among the earliest of these.[3] Thus the interiorization of speech-encoded representations appears to be, as Vygotsky suggested, an important process in moving toward the full functional complex of the language potential.

Beyond Basic Functions.   The achievement of mediating language functions requires the acquisition of skills for composing and interpreting extended discourse, and for retrieving from discourse presentations the representation of a previously unknown event, narrative, theory, or other knowledge form that the producer intended to impart. As everyone who has attempted, successfully or not, to learn a second (or later) language knows, this level of accomplishment takes extensive practice

with discourse genres – conversation, narrative, explanation – both written and oral, usually over several years of intensive exposure. Part of the
skill involves memory and conceptualization, which are also developing
during the early childhood years (see Chapters 6 and 8), but these must
be tuned to the language mode. Thinking in a language differs from
thinking in images (or in some neutral code), and differs from language
to language, as bilingual and multilingual individuals testify.[4]

It is this high level of cognitive and communicative functioning with
language that is the concern in this work. As is the case for those who
learn a second or third language to this degree of competence, its
achievement by first language learners takes years of practice in a community of like speakers. Although children learn their first language
with what is often characterized as amazing speed and efficiency, it is at
least two years after the beginnings of productive speech before most
children have acquired reasonably complex grammar at a level sufficient
to carry on a connected conversation (Bloom, 1991a). It is at least another
year before the average child can begin to represent complex states of
affairs in language and thus engage in extended discourse. Thus the
turning point for achievement of this milestone is tentatively set at about
4 years of age, and the skills involved continue to develop further for
many years.

To engage in the functions of language at the level of preliterate oral
competence with language attained by a reasonably competent 5-year-
old, ready for school lessons, involves many skills. On the cognitive
side, a level of conceptual knowledge encompassing aspects of the common culture, such as knowledge of plants and animals, tools and machines, numbers, space, and time is necessary, as well as the skill of
attending to verbal explanations and stories extending over at least several minutes, and remembering critical parts of these. Conversation with
peers and adults, respecting turn-taking conventions and topic extension, playing with others in fantasy dramas or games, participating in
formal and informal groups of different kinds are all important preparation. Specific linguistic skills include developing a vocabulary of about
6,000 words or more, mastering both sentence and discourse grammar,
and understanding the pragmatics of language necessary to interpret
most common usages of the child's social group and community.

Regrettably, there is little in the language literature that focuses directly on the issue of the achievement of these integrated skills, although
many of them have been considered separately. Much of the research on
language in the preschool years is focused on "preliterate" accomplish-

ments, concerned primarily with print. To set the stage for a more detailed consideration of some of these achievements, a proposed sequence of representational levels in language is sketched next.

Levels of Representing with Language

It is proposed here that language as a representational medium develops through a sequence of stages. Representation is used in the two senses that were introduced earlier: (external) representation for others and (internal) representation for self (Miller, 1990). The general thesis is that these two faces of representation stand in a dynamic dialogic relation such that development in one leads to development in the other in a continuous chaining process. The theoretical model is conceived as operating on four successive levels that make possible the use of language for cognitive functions in different increasingly complex ways. As before, the internal mental representation or mental models will be referred to as "MREPS," while the external linguistic representation (of self or others) will be referred to as "LREPS."[5]

Level 1: Undifferentiated

At this level (introduced in Chapter 4) the MREP is based solely on direct experience. Language forms experienced in specific situations are entered into the MREPs of those situations, thereby taking on meaning within them, and can be used productively within them. However, the form and content of the MREP is resistant to influence or input from any source but direct experience. This level is characteristic of the early stages of language acquisition, up to about 2 years, when grammar and dialogue begin to develop.

Language forms used within events that the child experiences may be learned and used to indicate any part of that event or the event as a whole. During this early period children begin to narrow their word meanings to the size and content implicated in the references used around them, extracting them from event contexts and generalizing to new instances of the same type, building on the connections that exist in the mental model, as examples in Chapter 4 demonstrated. Nonetheless, the words learned remain tied to their world models and do not form systems of their own. The models may incorporate Donald's social-mimetic representations, as well as basic personally organized event schemes. They are thus already social and symbolic but not truly linguistic.

Level 2: Transformation

This marks the beginning of the real communicative-cognitive exchange process. The child can transform some part or aspect of her own MREP – her mental model – into verbal form to convey information to others on the basis of her own experience.[6] Halliday (1975) recognized this as the emergence of the informative function of language, which he dated to the end of the second year (see previous section). But the MREP itself is still not open to input from any but direct experience. The ability to transform an underlying representation into a verbal message effectively improves over time, becoming more complex as the necessary language skills develop. This level makes possible the beginning of the use of language to exchange talk about the past, the anticipated future and the unreal (pretended), as well as the present ongoing activity. The child can interpret another's question or comment regarding her own present or past experience and respond contingently, but she does not adjust her MREP in response.

Level 3: Opening to Language

At this level the child can interpret another person's LREP in ongoing discourse and can enter parts of it into her own prior or present MREP of the same event, which is now composed of a mixture of event representations, social mimesis, and language forms embedded therein. It is possible that the LREP may become confused with her own MREP, and parts of another's presentation may thereby enter into her own at this point. But the *child will not or cannot maintain two simultaneous mental representations of the same situation*, that is, her own MREP and another's LREP. This constraint exists because the *basic* event representational system cannot support two versions of the same event at the same time. This restriction does not apply to the dual representation of a *component* of the event; for example, a child at this stage may remember that something that was present at the beginning of an event has disappeared.

The cognitive prerequisites for this level include the capacity for detailed and extended extraction of, and memory for, patterned information. The language prerequisites include the acquisition of grammatical forms and lexical items that make interpretation of connected discourse possible. These forms (e.g., temporal and causal language, intratextual reference) have been extensively studied and found to undergo a lengthy development, lasting well into the school years, indicating that their organization as an integrated system is a prolonged process, not completed in early childhood. The child must experience presentations of extended discourse in order to develop the system. Stories, memories, and in general talk about the child's own experience – past, present, and future – are the major ways that children are given practice with these functions, at home and in preschools and schools.

Level 4: Language Modeling

At this level, incorporating the verbal LREP of a novel reality from another person (something that the child has no representation of from her own experience) into a new MREP begins to become possible. This implies that the child now has the capacity to construct enduring *representations in language* in her own mind. Note the distinction between a temporary language representation in the "mental space" that enables an interpretation of a linguistic LREP in terms of the MREP (level 3), and the maintenance of an internal linguistically formulated LMREP (level 4). The difference is roughly that of short-term (operational) memory and long-term semantic memory. Gradual improvement in this ability, involving increasingly complex and lengthy constructions, can be expected. At this point, the child is aware of the difference between her own MREP and that of someone else and will not confuse the source of her MREP. Two contrasting MREPs or possible views of the same situation may be maintained simultaneously. At least one of these must be – and possibly both will be – in linguistic form. It is the existence of dual levels of representation – event/mimetic/imagic and verbal – that makes comparison possible.

At this point, then, children will have developed basic skills in using linguistic LREPs to build novel MREPs that are different from those they have constructed from their own direct experience, and they will be able to move back and forth between their own basic event MREPs, the linguistic LREPs of those representations, and the linguistic LREPs of other people, whose representation of an event may differ from their own. These developments have important implications for cognitive functioning during the preschool years, implications that will be further considered in later chapters.

Figure 5.1 represents the interactive progression of these representational skills in graphic form. On the right-hand side of this diagram is the parental figure [represented as a hybrid mind in Donald's (1991) sense] consisting of simultaneous MREPs in event, mimetic, and linguistic forms. On the left-hand side is the developing child mind, equipped first

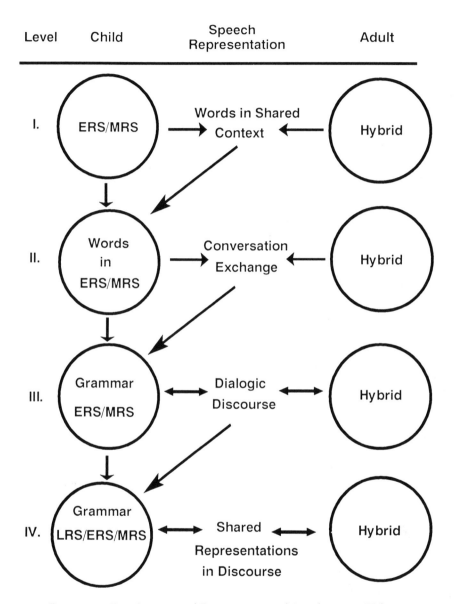

Figure 5.1. Development of Representational Levels. *Note:* ERS = event representation system; MRS = mimetic representation system; LRS = language representation system; Hybrid = mixed representation system in mature mind.

with event structures (ERS) and mimetic structures (MRS), as described in the previous chapters, which come to embed words within them. At the third stage words and grammar develop their own complex systems, functioning to support transformation from ERS and MRS MREPs into language LREPs, and at the fourth stage language becomes an inrepresenting medium. Movement between stages is supported by the increasingly elaborate and complex use of language in communicative exchanges, shown in the middle of the diagram.

Figure 5.1 incorporates the supposition that whereas at first children produce words and more complete utterances to express their prelinguistic MREPs and interpret parents' words within this system, parents produce and interpret from a different mental representational complex, including a long history of representing in as well as through language. Thus parent and child are operating with different mental representations of the same represented reality. In particular, the parent has a multilayered culturally and historically informed conception of whatever activity parent and child are engaged in, whereas the child's MREP in confined to the event as experienced. This asymmetry is in fact the key to the developments outlined. Figure 5.1 also conveys that grammar (language systems of all kinds) is not the language MREP itself, but is a necessary *tool* prerequisite for interpreting and mentally representing through language. As shown here, words, as the basic carriers of meaning, are the mediators between the more basic representation systems and the linguistic one.

Note that this scheme puts equal emphasis on the child's representations and expressions and on the social interactions that provide the context and the impetus for the move to the next level. This dialectic process is considered again in the last section of this chapter.[7]

Words and Meanings

The beginnings of the entry into language – acquisition of first words and early multiword constructions – were described in Chapter 4. The problem of word learning is sometimes discussed as though it begins and ends in the early years of life, but of course it is one component of the linguistic system that continues to develop, acquiring new forms and new meanings throughout life. It is in fact the key to the development of all cultural knowledge domains. Therefore, while recognizing the special problem of word meaning facing the beginning first language learner, we must also recognize that a theory of word meaning acquisition must span the limited cognitive, social, and linguistic capacities of infancy to the most sophisticated knowledge structures of mature adulthood. Implicit in many current proposals regarding word learning in early childhood is the assumption that different processes apply at that stage than at later stages. However, the present proposal is that we can best understand the acquisition of words and their meanings if we consider the problem as continuous across the lifespan.

This proposal grows out of the experiential system view on which the overall theoretical framework of this book is based. It is at odds with a view vigorously set out by a number of writers (e.g., Markman, 1987, 1991; Golinkoff, Mervis, & Hirsh-Pasek, 1994) that the young child is in special need of "constraints," "rules," or "principles" that can be applied in word-learning situations to decode the meaning of a novel word. These proposals are based in formal linguistic or cognitive theories that are in turn formulated in terms of rules and principles; thus the child is seen as needing to acquire the right rule to apply to a novel word. But as argued by many scholars (e.g., Anderson & Nagy, 1989; Johnson-Laird 1987; McNamara & Miller, 1989; Miller, 1990), word meanings are complex and multilayered, and are acquired partially and fallibly over time from experiencing their use in different contexts (Sternberg & Powell, 1983), a process consistent with the developmental view espoused here. This view has been interpreted as one that rests language acquisition on social interaction (Behrend, 1994), reducing a complex product to one source of causation in an either/or contrast (either the child has internal constraints or principles or the child relies on social learning). The dialogic system view is far more complex, relying on the child's cognitive, social, and knowledge structures, as well as her increasing command of the language and its lexical organization and her experience of words in their social discourse contexts. Indeed, it is this complexity that makes the achievement of meaning, even of some seemingly very simple words, so prolonged and uncertain, as the following discussion lays out in more detail.

From about 18 to 20 months of age children begin acquiring words at a rapid rate, so that by 6 years of age they have accumulated somewhere between 6,000 and 14,000 lexical items (depending on different estimates). These estimates yield a rate of about 4 to 10 new words a day, suggesting a powerful engine at work. In light of this impressive accomplishment, many researchers have searched for the mechanism and have identified a process of "fast mapping," which involves assigning words to evident referents on first encounter.[8] Such assignments may be off-track for various reasons, yet a striking characteristic of children's acquisition of words is that they tend to be used in appropriate sentential and extralinguistic contexts. This is not to say that children never misuse words – their errors often strike us as amusing. Nonetheless, on the whole both the grammar and the semantics/pragmatics tend to be in the right court.

Paradoxically, when children are tested for understanding of specific words, or when they are pressed by psychologist interviewers, the results often show that they lack an understanding of critical components of the meaning of common words. For example, preschool children often insist that "animal" refers to groups of different animals and not to any given instance of *animal*. Or they may respond similarly to both "before" and "after," to "same" and "different," or to "more" and "less." They may seem to treat "because" as though it means "so," and "tall" as though it means "big." Therefore, a major puzzle is how they can be so right in production and so fallible in comprehension. It appears that "fast mapping" may be a weak mechanism at best. Moreover, as an explanatory mechanism it stops short, providing only an association between a form and something encountered in the same context, leaving meaning to be constructed in some way as yet unknown.

A classical view of word learning based on Augustine (1950/397) is similar to the fast mapping proposal: "When they [my elders] named any thing, and as they spoke turned towards it, I saw and remembered that they called what they would point out, by the name they uttered" (p. 9). Many theorists since Augustine stated his case 1600 years ago have echoed, more or less, his description of how children learn to speak.[9] The process implies an "ostension" paradigm wherein the adult points to something and names it, causing the child to acquire the word (e.g., Brown 1958b; Quine 1960; Macnamara 1982; Markman 1987). Recently, however, psychologists, drawing on Quine (1960) and Wittgenstein (1953), have recognized the weakness of this paradigm. Quine (1960) drew attention to the problems in the following way: How can a linguist in an alien world who observes a native speaker uttering "gavagai" as a rabbit runs by be certain that "gavagai" means "rabbit"? There are numerous other referential possibilities that Quine and others have pointed out: "gavagai" might mean rabbit running (or just running), rabbit in grass, the color brown, rabbit ear (or ear in general) or, more exotically, "mere stages or brief temporal segments of rabbits" or "all and sundry undetached parts of rabbits" or "the fusion of all rabbits – that single though discontinuous portion of the spatiotemporal world that consists of rabbits" (pp. 51–52). It seems obvious that the ostension paradigm on its own cannot solve the word-learning problem.

The ostension paradigm works, if at all, for object labels, and traditionally it has been assumed that these are what the child begins with at least (see Chapter 4 for counterevidence to this assumption). Recent accounts explicitly assume that children beginning language learn primarily nouns and make the default assumption that "words refer to whole objects" (Markman, 1991). From the perspective taken here, however, the lexical acquisition problem viewed in the Quinean mode is misanalyzed, and the solutions proposed are inadequate to the real problems of word learning in early childhood, as well as in later life. The ostension paradigm on which the analysis is based is limited to a subset of words, to a limited period of developmental time, and to a single aspect of the multifaceted meaning of words (reference).

Emphasis on noun learning in the literature on lexical acquisition in early childhood leaves the superficial impression that the only words that parents and children use together during the preschool years, and thus the only words that children learn, are those referring to object kinds and object hierarchies (superordinate and subordinate). However, although nouns form the largest grammatical class of words acquired by young children – and of words used in the language – they are not the majority of words learned. Other word types include action verbs, and also adjectives, prepositions, pronouns, and a miscellaneous set of often unclassified words (such as "thank you" and "okay"). Equally important is the fact that not all nouns – including those learned by young children – refer to objects. English grammar makes a distinction between count nouns and mass nouns, the latter usually but not always referring to substances rather than discrete items. But both kinds of nouns can refer to a variety of other ontological types, for example, locations (e.g., "park," "kitchen"), events ("lunch," "party"), times ("morning," "week"), and natural phenomena ("rain," "sun"). (All these examples are from vocabularies of children under 2 years.)

In addition, words do not come identified as noun or verb; some words refer to actions as well as objects in the same form, and others denote actions in both verb and noun forms (Nelson, 1995). An instance of the former is the word "drink" which is often used to refer to an entity that may be interpreted as an object (e.g., a glass or bottle holding a liquid) or a substance, the liquid itself, and is also used to refer to the act of consuming the liquid. For example, a mother talking with her 20-month-old daughter says,

(2)　"D'you want *a drink?*"

and follows within a few minutes with the imperative,

(3)　"Allison *drink.*"

as Allison blows bubbles in the glass rather than drinking. "A drink" is actually ambiguous in most uses. It uses a count noun quantifier (*a*) to apply to what is presumed to be a substance, a liquid, requiring a mass noun quantifier. In this case the count noun is used in English to encompass the liquid in its container (the quantified).

An example of the action noun/verb problem is taken from a transcript of telephone play between child (C) at 18 months and mother (M): C picks up phone.

(4)　M: Make *a little phone call?*
　　　Who are you *gonna call?*

This sequence is typical of talk between mothers and their 20-month-old children in the context of the toy telephone, where the word is first used in a noun phrase (a little phone call) denoting an *event* and immediately thereafter as a verb denoting the *act* of speaking on the phone with someone.

The implications of these complexities of nouns and "dual-category" words for the child's semantic and grammatical category development have been generally ignored (Nelson, 1995; Nelson, Hampson, & Kessler Shaw, 1993). The Augustinian paradigm won't work for these words (or for many others), neither will the "whole object" or other alleged principles now in the literature (e.g., Golinkoff, Mervis, & Hirsh-Pasek, 1994). Rather, children must be working at both very abstract and very concrete levels simultaneously during language acquisition. They must be able to interpret the discourse context to assign *call* in the above example to the action of calling, and also to accept it in both its noun and verb roles. The strategies that children use to untangle these complexities have begun to be identified for both nouns and verbs (Tomasello & Olquin, 1993; Olquin & Tomasello, 1993), showing that their strategies rest importantly on the child's interpretation of the adult's discourse intention.

Of course vocabulary acquisition does not end at 2 or even 6 years of age, and the child's words are not confined indefinitely to a small range of contexts. Between 6 years and 18 years many children expand their vocabularies 10-fold from about 10,000 to about 100,000 words according to some estimates, which works out to about 20 new words a day, twice as many as the most generous estimates quoted for the preschool years. Most observers agree that the vast numbers of words learned during the school years must be learned from seeing or hearing them used in context. That is, they are not specifically taught in vocabulary drills. The theoretical question this poses is then just that faced by the toddler: How does a learner extract meaning from context? According to Sternberg and Powell's (1983) analysis, the answer depends upon finding a *relevant* fit of the novel word to one's *knowledge base*. Indeed, the general principle of relevance to the knowledge base has wide application.

Relevance

Sperber and Wilson's (1986) analysis (introduced in Chapter 4) of how any speaker and listener make sense to each other despite the vagaries of the language they use provides the theoretical framework for this interpretation. They claim that verbal communication between two or more people is made possible because participants assume that what is being communicated is *relevant* to ongoing discourse, to the current concerns and the *cognitive environments* of the communicators. It is suggested here that the general problem for the language-learning child is not greatly different from that of any speaker and listener – it is to interpret the utterance of another within the context of the activity, as represented within the listener's current cognitive environment. The application of this model to the problem of establishing a first meaning system then requires consideration of how the two participants may mutually interpret each other.[10]

Sperber and Wilson (1986) rest the assumption of relevance on *shared context*, but they do not conceive of context simply in terms of the moment-to-moment external environment within which two people are situated. Rather, they invoke the idea that relevance applies to the *cognitive environments* that the communicators share. They emphasize that people construct *different* mental representations of their environments based on the history of their different experiences with it. In a statement applicable to the developmental problem they write: People "have mastered different concepts; as a result, they can construct different representations and make different inferences . . . even if they all shared the same narrow physical environment . . . their *cognitive environments* would still differ" (p. 38). In spite of these differences, speakers and listeners are able to communicate by making assumptions about what is shared of their cognitive environments, what the listener knows about the speaker's context. The relevant point for the present purpose is that communication between people always rests on *inference* and *interpretation*. The cognitive environments of the communicators at least temporarily share sufficient common structures so that the relevance of a communication can be inferred. If not, the usual strategy of the child is to ignore it, although an adult, expecting intentionality, may pursue the matter by further inquiry as to the speaker's meaning.

An important part of the relevance assumption is that words may be interpreted differently depending upon their relevance in a particular cognitive environment. When attempting to communicate, a speaker makes assumptions about the cognitive environment of the listener, and the listener, to interpret the message, makes assumptions about the relevance of the words to the present situation, when the situation includes the prior discourse, the listener's cognitive environment, and the listener's assumptions about the speaker's cognitive environment.

This idea about shared cognitive environments is precisely equivalent to the notion of *cognitive context* that Nelson and Gruendel (1979) introduced as a proposal for how children might begin to learn to make sense to each other. We analyzed talk between 3- and 4-year-old peers playing together in a preschool, showing that their talk relied upon a background of shared understandings of such things as the school day, the structure of telephone conversations, and the content of meals (see the later section of this chapter entitled "Developing Discourse"). We suggested that sustained talk would be established within contexts – both present and those familiar to the child from previously established scripts – that provided supportive structure independent of the actual discourse. We tested this idea further with mothers and their 2-year-old children in conversational contexts that provided different degrees of scripted support (meals, play) and found, for example, that children answered questions more readily in the familiar scripted context, and that more complex language involving categorical language and talk about the past and the future was used in the familiar structure (Lucariello & Nelson, 1986). These findings support the model presented in Figure 5.1 indicating that at levels 2 and 3 the cognitive context is that of the mental event representation (MER).

Sperber and Wilson's (1986) position implies that words can be used in many different ways to convey messages, and that the listener must *actively interpret* what the speaker's *intention* may be. A person's lexicon may contain much relevant information about the complexities of possible uses of particular word forms, but no given instance of the word can be perfectly predicted outside of its context of use. The child who must somehow use the situation to interpret flexibly what is meant in that context is therefore only at a somewhat greater disadvantage than the adult. In contrast, if the child came to the language with highly constrained expectations about word meanings (e.g., Markman, 1987, 1991; Golinkoff, Mervis, & Hirsch-Pasek, 1994) she would be at a loss.

These claims imply that in order for the child to extract elements of meaning from the *discourse context*, the word must be made relevant to the child's *cognitive contexts*, conceived here as event knowledge. The child's cognitive contexts may vary in terms of the familiarity of situations, of speakers, of activities, and of ways of formulating messages. Some of the ways in which the child's cognitive context and the social context work together are evident in studies of the conditions under which children acquire nouns (Tomasello & Farrar, 1986) and verbs (Tomasello & Kruger, 1992), which have established that very specific conditions of making words relevant to the child's attentional focus within an activity – different for different types of words – determine whether the child will acquire the word. Further, the child may come to recognize how certain words are used in quite specific discourse contexts, and gradually accrue meaning to them. Again, it is the relevance of a new word to the child's interpretation of a communication within an established cognitive activity context that determines whether the word will be entered into that context and thereby derive meaning from it.

How and whether words and their meanings are acquired also depends on what words are already known, and on the state of the general knowledge base. Much recent work on children's category knowledge, and their ability to make inferences about properties of instances from hearing a category name, underscores the intricately tangled relation between general knowledge and lexical organization, in young children as well as in adults. For example, from hearing "This dax is a bird," a child might be able to infer properties such as flying and nest-building (Gelman & Markman, 1986; Taylor & Gelman, 1988). When children learn words, they not only call on old knowledge – general and specifically lexical – but also acquire new general knowledge.

Thus the general solution to the puzzle of how words are learned at any age lies in the fact that people – children as well as adults – use *discourse context* to interpret language. They make inferences about what is *relevant* within the context of the utterance. The context they use for this purpose is *cognitive context* – in the child's case, the dynamic model of the world of events, built up on the basis of present and previous experiences in similar event contexts, and updated within the particular discourse context of the situation of use. It is because of this basis that words may sound right in the child's first productive use: Children have assigned the word to the appropriate context; but because it is restricted to the contexts in which it has been encountered it will be found to lack aspects of a more general meaning that becomes apparent in testing situations.

Thus the claim here is that word learning is a matter of *inference* based on *contexted relevance* within discourse situations. Both the strengths – the rapid acquisition of vocabulary appropriate to the child's uses – and the weaknesses – context-restricted meanings – result from the same process. This process thus accounts for three common observations of children's word learning: *Fast mapping* is the entering of a novel word into its context of use. *Appropriate production* occurs because the word is used in contexts similar to those in which it was observed. *Restricted comprehension* is observed because accrual of meaning outside the context of first use is a slow and uncertain process.

'Cause: An Example of Developing Meaning in Discourse[11]

The model in Figure 5.1 places the burden of representational development as well as word meaning on discourse practices. The dialectical process involved at both levels can be seen through a detailed examination of gradually developing situated meanings. A longitudinal study in collaboration with Elena Levy (Levy, 1989; Nelson & Levy, 1987; Levy & Nelson, 1994) focused on the dialogic and monologic talk of a child, Emily, whose language in the crib was tape-recorded at frequent intervals between the ages of 21 months and 36 months (Nelson, 1989c). Pre-bed dialogue, mostly with Father, and talk to herself when alone enables a view of the use of the same term in both dyadic and individual function over several months.

Here the development of the term " 'cause," beginning in Emily's second year, is examined. Causal terms (e.g., "because" or " 'cause") are assumed to express intentions, goals, and cause–effect relations, and in general it is observed that children begin to use the terms "because" and "so" early in the preschool period (Hood & Bloom, 1979; Bloom et al., 1980) but do not achieve full understanding of their logical implications until much later (French & Nelson, 1985; French, 1988; Byrnes, 1991). Emily used the word " 'cause" in her monologues from the earliest observations when she was 21 months.

"Because" or " 'cause" was used by Emily's father at this time in passages such as the following:

(5)   F: everyone's asleep
        you know Tanta's asleep and Mormor's asleep
        everyone is going to *sleep because* you know what happens
            in the night-time? people go to sleep at night-time . . .
      E: Carl mommy sleeping
      F: yeah, Carl's mommy's sleeping too
        do you think Chris is sleeping?
        how about Chris? hmmm?
        and Annie and Jeannie?
        everybody's *asleep 'cause* it's . . . [E interrupts]
        . . . (???) *sleep because* he's a little baby   (1;10.30)

Note that in this example "because" follows "sleep" three times.

Before 2 years Emily's own monologic uses of " 'cause" tended to occur in specific patterns, such as with "sleep" or "baby," as the following examples illustrate:

(6)   Emmy went to sleep *'cause* M Mor   (1;9.8)
(7)   Emmy didn't go to sleep *'cause* in bed   (1;10.30)

This pattern "sleep . . . 'cause" is thus similar in form to segments of pre-sleep dialogues between Emily and her parents, concerned with negotiations over sleep. Another set of early uses of " 'cause" was followed by a clause containing "baby" or "bed." These instances coincided with Emily's move to a new room and a new bed in anticipation of the arrival of a new baby; no doubt her parents provided a justification for her room change, using similar discourse patterns.

The similarity between Emily's uses and her father's discourse patterns suggests that her use of " 'cause" was borrowed from her father's, not in the sense of verbatim imitation, but rather as internalized pattern: " 'cause" follows "sleep," linking it to a second utterance. Note that the pattern was embedded in talk when Emily was already in her crib, being urged to sleep. However, the talk itself (like Emily's own talk) was not specifically about the here and now situation but about rules and expectations surrounding the going-to-sleep event. Thus Emily's interpretation of this talk (to the extent that she interpreted it rather than simply accepting it as part of the going-to-bed- ritual) must be based on her MER of the sleep situation.

Emily's use of " 'cause" was then borrowed from the discourse patterns of adult speech in the going-to-bed/sleep context of discourse. This use of a term in a borrowed context requires little or no grasp of the semantics of the term or the full interpretation of parental explanation. It is simply a connector, linking "the baby," "sleep," or "bed" to another utterance, in the context of parental justification of an action or event, grounded in the child's representations of routine events. Many early instances of " 'cause" in fact were partly or fully inappropriate with respect to their larger discourse context, indicating that the semantic interpretation was missing, as in the following:

> (8)   Emmy went to sleep
>   *'cause* Mommy Mormor Emmy get up   (1;9.8)

The proportion of inappropriate uses in her monologues declined with time; 68% of the instances of " 'cause" in the early period were judged inappropriate, 47% of those in the middle period, and only 19% in the late period (between $2\frac{1}{2}$ and 3 years).

Later, " 'cause" began to co-occur with a coordinate clause introduced by "but," as in the following example:

> (9)   my won't go to sleep
>   *but* I later
>   *'cause* my hava cold   (2;0.9)

The co-occurrence of " 'cause" and "but" formed part of a pattern used in Emily's pre-sleep negotiations with her father. In these negotiations Emily attempted to attain a goal and her father attempted to block it.

> (10) (Emily requests a toy)
>   F: Okay you go get it
>   *but* be quick about it
>   *because* we have to go to sleep   (1;10.30)
> (11) E: Daddy (rock) me for a couple min . . .
>   *but* this is the last night
>   *because* then (?) . . .   (1;11.20)

"But" and " 'cause" together help create a compromise agreement: "but" offers an alternative to an absolute refusal and " 'cause" provides a justification. In these contexts " 'cause" expresses a relationship between an action (or blocking of an action) and a judgment, statement, or desire that expresses a motive for the action (cf. Bloom et al., 1980; Bloom & Capatides, 1987). Here " 'cause" is a connector used in the context of a second type of connector, "but." This discourse pattern includes a statement (often negative) followed by justification (" 'cause"), sometimes including a compromise ("but").

In the later months the logic of psychological justification became more complete. Most (73%) of the instances of " 'cause" were now fully interpretable, and sometimes the term occurred with "so" or with other forms, for example.

(12) *actually* it's Stephen's koala bear . . .
      'cause it's really Stephen's
      as a matter of fact it's Stephen's (2;9.12)

This usage suggests that Emily was extending her understanding of the semantics of " 'cause," and systematizing it with other terms that refer to causal and truth conditions.

Thus it is seen that, during the first two to three months of the study all uses of " 'cause" were apparently borrowed from parental uses, or were pragmatic generalizations based on distributional relationships observed in adult speech. During the later months ($2\frac{1}{2}$ to 3 years) uses reflected a better grasp of the format of psychological justification: desired action + negative contrast (*but*) + compromise (*so*) + explanation (*'cause/actually/really/as a matter of fact*). This organization of related terms into lexical domains or paradigmatic structures reflects a process of semantic systematization during the preschool years that has been studied in detail by Bowerman (1982) and Karmiloff-Smith (1979). It is indicative of the child's analysis of components of meaning of related words and a new recognition thereby of their relatedness.

General Course of Word Meaning Over Time

This analysis of Emily's uses of " 'cause" over the 16 months of this study sheds more light on the gradual acquisition of both grammatical and semantic components of language, and their relation to both the child's event representations and parental discourse. On the basis of this and similar analyses of other words (Levy & Nelson, 1994), a general process of the derivation of meaning from discourse context can be extracted, consistent with the preceding sections of this chapter, as follows:

1. New language forms are acquired, together with their distributional relations with other language forms, on the basis of the discourse con-

text, both extrasentential (broad discourse patterns) and intrasentential (syntactic).

2. Discourse patterns are interpreted in terms of the child's event knowledge system; extralinguistic context provides the conditions for instantiating relevant event representations. Recognition of patterns and forms may be first restricted to the particular activity contexts in which they were originally experienced (where experienced means noticed by the child). For the child, the relevant event context may be different from the immediate event observed by the adult; thus it is "cognitive context" that is at issue here, as discussed previously. Sentential context includes the co-occurrence of forms, for example, noun–verb; and/or a recurrent syntactic frame such as a particular prepositional phrase.

3. On the basis of adult uses of the form in identifiable contexts, the child may form a discourse notion regarding the use of the form and subsequently use it herself in closely constrained syntactic "formats" and in the context of specific topics.

4. Use of the form itself – especially in formally contrastive alternation with other forms – alerts the child to further uses by other speakers and leads to additional knowledge about the "meaning context" that it represents.

5. Comparison of the uses of the form by self and others may lead to a period of resystematization of the form and other forms that are semantically or syntactically closely related.

6. Subsequently the child's uses indicate at least partial control of the form in productive speech. However, comprehension tests of the form may reveal gaps in the child's knowledge, and productive uses may remain confined to well-understood event contexts.

7. Full control of some forms ("full meaning") may be delayed for years after the form is first acquired and readily used. Further reorganization of the meaning system may be required before adult-level understanding is achieved.

In its most general claims this description is expected to apply to the acquisition of all linguistic forms, but different types of forms may exhibit some of these developmental characteristics and not others. For example, the child may need to do very little refining of her use and understanding of names of common objects, whereas terms referring to abstract notions such as temporal perspective (Clark, 1971; French & Nelson, 1985; Weist, 1986) or quantification (Karmiloff-Smith, 1979) may be used for many years before their context-independent function is fully analyzed.

The patterns observed here illustrate the process of deriving lexical and grammatical knowledge from discourse; they indicate both that discourse is the source of knowledge of language forms, and that discourse is the context within which meaning and use of language forms is developed and elaborated. The use of words themselves contributes to a change in their function, implying an ongoing process of a dialectical exchange between the child and her social/linguistic environment, as outlined earlier.

Whereas Emily did appear to be quite sensitive to both the discourse and grammatical constraints on uses of " 'cause," her initial use revealed little or no realization of its semantic entailments. This is the reverse of the assumption of constraints models, which assume that the child works with a hierarchy of ontological principles to choose among hypotheses one that is likely to be correct. The alternative proposed here is that use of the term by self and others in well-understood event contexts furnishes the substantive data that eventually become organized as semantic knowledge.

Extracting meaning from discourse context requires that the child identify what the relevance of the word is within that context. Discourse cannot provide meaning, but only clues to meaning, as this example indicates. But as implied in the example, discourse also provides a way into structured meaning of complex sentences, and it provides the basis for extracting paradigms that underlie the internalized language system. Novel words occurring in discourse are related by the listener to the cognitive context and the particular utterance in which they occur. The process of *use before meaning* (within similar contexts) may be engaged by the child, from which *meaning from use* gradually accrues.

The process as described here is general, applying to all types of words and at all phases of development. The major differences in ease of acquisition for some words, such as object nouns, appear, not because of internal or external constraints, but because the relevance of some words to the discourse context is more apparent than it is in others. Seen in this way, shared meaning emerges from shared cognitive context and the mutual interpretation of relevance to that context by speakers and listeners, tutors and learners.

Developing Discourse: from Scaffolds to Frames

Thus far discourse has been considered as context supporting the acquisition of word forms and meanings. However, the inverse problem is how discourse itself is constructed from language forms and functions and how it develops over time. If words must be learned from discourse, the child must engage in discourse, but discourse requires that the child interpret words and sentences. How can this circle be breached?

Although there are many discourse forms, genres, styles, and registers in a language (Hymes, 1974; Bakhtin, 1986), the discourse context of the young child begins as simple conversational exchanges.[12] Most systematic analyses of conversational exchanges between parent and child have focused on the achievement of pragmatic competence. Bloom (1991a) assumed that "A major goal of language acquisition is for the child to be able to take something from what someone else says and form a contingent message that converts simple turn taking into discourse" (p. 435). Bloom's longitudinal research with children from 2 to 3 years indicated a developmental increase over this period from simple adjacency (a child utterance following a parent's) to greater contingency of topic. Younger children introduced new topics or changed the topic more than half the time, while older children's contributions shared the topic of the parent utterance, and added information. As Bloom (1991a) notes: "To participate in conversations, children must be able to use the information in a prior message to access something stored in memory, hold that representation in mind, and access the procedures of language for its expression" (p. 436). This formulation of the problem provides a perspective on the representational demands involved in dialogic discourse that accords with the view developed here. Bloom's characterization involves using a presentation in language to access something in one's own representation, which is then expressed in language form. Her study documents how long and hard is the progress toward ease in accomplishment of this level. A number of authors have emphasized the importance of "scaffolding" by the parent as the child learns to take a part in these exchanges. Bruner (1983) provides a theoretical account of this process and shows how a parent may "up the ante" over time, requiring more quantity and more complexity from a child as linguistic and cognitive development advance.

Engaging in a conversation on a single topic that extends to 3, 4, or more turns requires even greater representational capacity and skill than studied by Bloom and her colleagues in 2- and 3-year-olds, and necessitates kicking away some of the scaffolding previously depended upon. The grammatical requirements for this engagement go beyond those of simple and complex sentence structures, and involve deixis, that is, the establishment of relations of space, time, and person in relation to the speech context, and anaphoric reference, reference to elements previously introduced as topics. Analysis of conversations between parent and child that are focused on talk about the past (see Chapters 6, 7, and 9) indicates that the parent initially scaffolds the child's contributions to maintain coherence from one exchange to the next, resulting in extended discourse on a single topic. By 4 years of age, and earlier for some, the child is able to engage in fairly long conversations with an adult on a topic about something she has experienced (Hudson, 1993; Fivush, 1993) or is experiencing (Tessler, 1991), indicating that the child is able to share the adult's frame of the topic.

In contrast to talk with adults, preschool children's talk with peers has been stigmatized as egocentric since Piaget's (1926) report, characterizing children as talking past each other, talking for their own sakes and not for engaging others. More recent analysts (e.g., Garvey & Hogan, 1973; Garvey, 1990; Nelson & Gruendel, 1979) have emphasized the opposite: that children do engage in perspective-taking and shared topics. Nonetheless, as French, Boynton, and Hodges (1991) have pointed out, much of the communication between young peers (around 2 years) is limited to attention-getting and struggles over possession. Their analysis reveals that extended interactions lasting more than a few seconds between peers aged 2 to 5 years depends strongly on establishing shared background event knowledge and/or a shared familiar activity context, such as the housekeeping center in preschool. These provide the frame that serves simultaneously to support the play and the language in it. In play with props, as in the housekeeping corner, or with doctor props (Sachs, Goldman, & Chaille, 1984) the talk is incidental to the activity. Seidman's study (Seidman, Nelson, & Gruendel, 1986) following up the suggestions from Nelson and Gruendel (1979), showed as predicted that play and talk interactions were more sustained when the participants instantiated a shared script. The shared familiar context of the play, and the objects that help to instantiate it, provide the background event and mimetic context in which talk contributes to sustaining the pretense, but do not convey new representational material.

By 4 to 5 years many children can use shared cognitive contexts to sustain an extended conversation on a single topic that also introduces nonshared information, without the support of related props or pretense. One of the conversations between two 4-year-old girls reproduced from Nelson and Gruendel (1979) illustrates this more sophisticated level of exchange of representations and presentations of new knowledge.

(13)   A: At morning it's lunch time.
       B: But *first* comes snack, then comes lunch.
       A: Right . . . Just in school right?
       B: Yeah, right, just in school.
       A: Not at home.
       B: Well, sometimes we have snacks at home.

A: Sometimes

. . .

B: Because when special children come to visit us, we sometimes have snack. Like, like, hotdogs, or crackers, or
   cookies or or something like that.

A: Yeah, something. Maybe cake.

. . .

B: Or maybe hotdog.

A: Maybe hotdog.

B: But, but, but, Jill and Michael don't like hotdog. Don't
   you know, but, do you know Michael and Jill?

A: I know another Michael.

B: I know, I know another Michael.

A: No, I know just one Michael. I just know one Michael.

Note: Ellipses (. . .) indicate bits of repetitive talk.

At the outset these two children have agreed that "at morning it's lunchtime." They then go on to consider snack at school (shared event knowledge that they can agree on; thus there is no conflict in their representations presented by the conversation). This is followed by the information that sometimes there is snack at home, and that under particular circumstances (special children) different foods can appear. Both children contribute to and agree on this. But then the notion of hotdogs for snacks raises a conflict. Some children that B knows don't like hotdogs. How to deal with this raises the issue of whether A knows these children. Remarkably, they are able to agree that they know different Michaels. By wending their way through this shared information about snacks and friends they have apparently succeeded in conveying new information and modifying prior representations of their structures of these categories. This kind of achievement is not possible, even for the 3-year-old, who does not conceive of more than one reality, because representing different experiences through language has not yet become a possibility.

This level of exchange, which is not supported by external play activity or props, goes beyond talk about shared experience, present or past. In this exchange, the two girls first share knowledge based in the preschool routine, and then move to individual knowledge of their own nonpresent home routines, effectively asking questions and acknowledging differences. This level of interaction reflects an ability to represent and express one's own event knowledge, and to compare another's different event knowledge presented through language with one's own.

Of course, this sample is still replete with infelicities in comparison with adult exchanges, and it reveals a somewhat complexive and circular structure reminiscent of Vygotsky's conceptual complexes. Nonetheless, it is clearly a step along the way to competent dialogic discourse without the requirement of detailed scaffolding provided by adults.

The progression from very limited ability to engage on a sustained topic even when scaffolded by parents, to a reasonable level of ease in carrying on a conversation requiring the processing of nonshared information with a peer, takes a very long time. "Co-constructing" an account with an adult or exchanging information with peers does not yet indicate that the child can either (1) construct an account of an episode (remembered, anticipated, or imagined) with the necessary linguistic markers and structures for providing an understandable account to another person who has not experienced the episode herself; or (2) interpret the account of an unshared episode presented by another. But these earlier, less demanding forms are steps along the road toward the later achievements. As with any development, one must be careful not to confuse earlier precursor abilities (in this case, engaging in scaffolded conversations) with the full range of competence of the developed form.[13] Indeed, analyses of older children's conversations (Dorval & Eckerman, 1984; Dorval, 1990) indicate that it is many years before children acquire the skills that enable them to stay on topic and share perspectives. Second graders still produce many unrelated turns, and coherence continues to increase at least through the ninth grade. Dorval (1990) views these developments in terms of steps toward collaboration within a participation structure. These more developed conversational skills and structures lie beyond the abilities of the preschoolers that are the focus of the analyses here, and thus beyond the scope of this discussion.

Thinking in Language: How Culture Enters the Mind

As previously proposed, to enter into the potential offered by human language and culture the child needs to acquire the complexities of grammar that make extended discourse possible. It is not until the child is capable of following an extended dialogue, and constructing parts of a dialogue that mesh with those of the partner, that the child can actually enter into the language/culture complex. The developmental course implies a long period during which language is learned and used for communicative functions, and its mechanisms for constructing extended forms of discourse are acquired in these communicative contexts, prior to the point where they may be used for more advanced functions, so that the earlier levels provide a ratchet for movement to the next level.

The limited extent of cognitive functions of language during the early levels have been noted in the preceding sections, but these limitations should not negate the importance of those cognitive aspects that enter the mind within the language envelope from the very beginning. These include attention to the ways that language in general and a specific language in particular carves up the world into more discrete and conventional categories than those of the prelinguistic period (see Chapters 4 and 8). Beyond this very basic cognitive function lie many further cognitive reflections of communicative functions of language. The emphasis in this chapter on words and word meanings reflects the proposed ideas that language must first be *extracted* from its communicative functions and forms before it can serve to establish new representations. But this does not mean that in the early stages language use has no impact on mental representations. Learning the use of words of all types indicates how one's language partitions the world. Learning the use of "call," "help," and " 'cause" articulates notions of communicative, social supportive relations, and intentions that may not have existed in the implicit MER system. Later, learning the meaning of words like "know," "remember," "fair," and "wrong" signals entry into the cultural categories of knowledge and justice. Each move involves establishment of new vocabulary for new cultural concepts, each at a more complex and abstract level.

Learning words is thus learning to think in cultural forms. This proposition does not entail that particular words of a particular language carve up the world and its ways differently than any other language, although many such differences between language do exist. However, the claim does entail that to learn the language means learning to think culturally in addition to thinking individually or even socially. This is the true meaning of the Sapir–Whorf hypothesis (Lucy, 1992; Whorf, 1956): Language embodies the culture, thus thinking in language is thinking culturally. This meaning is implicit as well in Vygotsky's ideas of inner speech, although it was spelled out more completely in his discussion of scientific concepts. Wertsch (1990, 1991) has extended Vygotsky's account to encompass Bakhtin's (1981) conceptions of "voices in the mind" (heteroglossia). As suggested previously, children seem to be exceptionally open to a variety of different voices and are able to "reenvoice" them quite accurately from early in development (Dore, 1989). Thus it is not only the categories of the culture that enter the mind from language use, but the language users themselves also are represented there. As well, the individual knowing system remains and develops, not only in terms of other persons and linguistic cultural representations, but also in terms of the integration of all this within as well as without. The remainder of this book considers more fully these important issues of language, culture, and the developing mind.

Conclusion

In this chapter, the following topics have been broached that relate to the thesis of the book:

- Meaning – of words and other forms – is acquired through social discourse.
- Discourse reports external representations of affairs that may differ from a person's prior internal representation of such affairs.
- Participation in discourse requires extensive practice.
- Competence in interpreting discourse representations facilitates and may be necessary to establishing internal representations formulated in language.
- When internal language representations come into play, thinking in language emerges.

To these propositions we only need to add the recognition that language is a cultural system. Its forms and structures have a cultural history, and its meanings are culturally embedded; they are not the property of individuals, dyads, or small groups. It follows that when thinking in language emerges, culture enters the mind. Unlike the thinking of the 2-year-old, that of the 5-year-old – and much more the 10- or 20-year-old – is not only socially mediated but also, by virtue of sharing a common language, culturally mediated. Because most of the interesting knowledge organizations exist as cultural properties (not as childish individual constructions) this step is the most important one for bringing the child into the cognitive world of adults. This chapter has only begun the exploration of these revolutionary developments. Succeeding chapters tell more of the story, and show other ways in which language comes to be used representationally – both internally and externally – in the preschool years.

6. Memory in Early Childhood: The Emergence of the Historical Self

Memory is the primary form of all mental representation: Other forms such as concepts, categories, schemas, imagination, dreams, pretense, plans, conjectures, stories, even language all derive from memory in some way.[1] From this perspective, memory is a *cognitive function* or *set of functions*. Memory *systems* may reflect different functions [for example, Tulving's (1972, 1983, 1993) proposal of procedural, episodic, and semantic systems]. The functional approach allows us to ask what functions memory serves for the individual at different developmental periods, how these functions change, and how they bear on and are influenced by other aspects of neural, cognitive, and social development. The particular questions that arise within the levels theory outlined in Chapter 3 include: What effect do different representational systems have on memory? And the reverse – What effect does memory (e.g., capacity or system type) have on representational potential?

It is sometimes noted that human memory appears to be almost inexhaustible, based on extimates of 10^{11} neurons in the human brain, each with an average of 3,000 synaptic connections (Flanagan, 1992). Phenomenal memory feats by professional mnemonists (Luria, 1968; Hunt & Love, 1972) demonstrate that through the use of strategies of storing and retrieving words and images, what we think of as natural limits on memory, or ordinary memory constraints, can be expanded almost without limit and remain accessible almost indefinitely. In ancient Greece and Rome such mnemonic systems were extensively developed to aid in rhetoric practices, and were continued into medieval and early modern times.

In an extension of these observations, Carruthers (1990) reports on the functions of memory in medieval society, emphasizing the importance of trained memory for literate scholars of that period, who worked without ready access to the texts on which they relied. It is frequently assumed today that rote memory for text was primarily useful in oral societies, which necessarily relied on memorization rather than written materials. Individual memory is the repository of tradition, myth, and narrative in such societies. But Carruthers notes that retelling oral tales such as the Odyssey typically involves variation on the basic outline of the tale. In contrast, she emphasizes that in medieval society written texts were copied verbatim and were considered inviolate among literate people. The written text was seen as authoritative, and the interpretation of its meaning was an important scholarly occupation.

Therefore, in an age where a single copy of an authoritative text might be found in a remote monastery, the ability to memorize and recall critical passages from it was of supreme importance to a scholar. Carruthers reports that Thomas Acquinas was reputed to have an extraordinary capacity for recalling and integrating material from many different sources, a capability that enabled him to dictate commentaries from memory, and frequently to dictate two or more different texts to two or more scribes at one time. Such memory feats were viewed until the contemporary period as marks of great intelligence, and the training required to attain or approach them was highly valued by the educational system up to and into the present century, in spite of the widespread availability of printed books and reference libraries.[2] Rote memory for text of this kind underscores the vast potential of strictly linguistic representations.

In contrast to the presumptions derivable from this historical view, psychological views of memory are generally based on the widely accepted premise that memory is a limited *capacity* of the individual processor. Then variations in the constraints on capacity in development or between individuals at the same stage of development may explain differences in memory retention and recall, and strategies for organizing memory are seen as overcoming capacity limitations of the system. Improvements in memory with development are viewed as the result of either biologically determined increases in capacity or of learned strategies. Memory training is not antithetical to these assumptions; from the beginning of modern cognitive theory, the idea that information capacity could be expanded through chunking (Miller, 1956; Chase & Ericsson, 1982) has been part of the story. But in most discussions of memory in cognitive psychology, training has played a minor role.

Based on studies of differential disabilities in amnesias, there is increasing acceptance that a fundamental distinction exists between two types of basic memory systems, one of which – the explicit system – may be destroyed in amnesia, while the other – the implicit system –

remains intact (Squire, 1992; Schacter, 1992; Tulving, 1993). The primary disputes appear to be over how to characterize the two systems, and whether there are more than two basic systems. It has also been proposed (Schacter & Moscovitch, 1984) that the two memory systems develop at different rates in ontogeny, with the declarative (explicit) or late system emerging after the early or procedural (implicit). Tulving's (1993) proposal is that there are (at least) three basic systems: the procedural, semantic, and episodic. Episodic memory in his terms is distinguished from semantic memory, which is roughly equivalent to general knowledge and is free of specific context, undated, and unlocalized. Episodic memory, in contrast, is held to be located specifically in time and space and to consist of a sequence of activities that constitute an event. In his conception it is the episodic that is lost in the typical amnesia syndrome, making it impossible for the amnesiac to recall any specific event memory from even the recent past, while learning and retaining new semantic facts remains possible although difficult. The neural basis for these systematic effects has begun to be understood (Squire, 1992), tracing the circuits from the hippocampus to the frontal lobes that make the establishment of memory possible. Many further questions are raised by these claims, some of them directly relevant to the developmental issues of concern here.

The focus of the chapter, as with other chapters in this book, is on developments in the preschool years. To provide background for this discussion, memory in infancy is considered first, followed by a brief look at the disjunction between memory in the school years and in the preschool period. Developments in the preschool period are interpreted in terms of a theory of functional change in early childhood, based on representational change from prelinguistic to socially mediated linguistic forms, consistent with the story outlined in previous chapters.

Functions of Early Memory

How can memory in infancy be conceptualized from the perspective of the experiential model? Consider that the fundamental cognitive task of infancy is to cumulate knowledge of the particular world circumstances in which the infant has been born, as well as to exercise basic motoric and perceptual operations crucial to the whole developing individual. As emphasized throughout this work, the infant's knowledge base derives from particular experiences and is reflected in the representations of the memory system, the MERs. One important type of experience involves repetitive routines, both infant-centered caretaking and playful, gamelike routines, as well as non-infant-centered familial routines that the infant participates in or only observes. As outlined in Chapter 4, although these routines typically occur with variations, there is substantial regularity within them. For example, giving a bath may change almost imperceptibly over time in terms of the degree of active participation of the infant in the activity, the objects involved (such as toys allowed in the bath), the bathgiver (mother, father, or other caretaker), words used during the activity, the length of time allowed, and the ways in which the different parts of the event are marked (beginning, middle parts, and end). But the invariant skeletal structure of the bath remains the same on different occasions over time. Moreover, there is sufficient commonality across households so that children from different homes construct the same general script for the event, as demonstrated in several studies of children's event knowledge at age 2 (e.g., O'Connell & Gerard, 1985; Bauer & Shore, 1987; Rothstein, 1991). These routines are represented in the child's knowledge structures as general mental event representations (MERs), as discussed in Chapter 4.

Memory is of course basic to forming MERs. At least by the last half of the first year, memory for sequences of actions is secure (Meltzoff, 1988; Bauer & Mandler, 1989a; Bauer, Dow, & Hertsgaard, in press). Each specific experience of the event provides input into the structure of the general sequence, and, as noted, this structure is transformed over time as the experience itself evolves in concert with the rapid physical and mental growth of the infant. This fact – that rapid growth continuously changes subjective experience – may explain some of the functional characteristics of infant memory, in particular its failure of retention over the succeeding years. In order to maintain stability in the face of change, each experience of an event may be overwritten by the next. The general skeleton of the experience is then retained as general knowledge (semantic or generic memory), and within a given time period, variations may be notable. For example, a 1-year-old may note the presence or absence of a particular toy that has customarily – over the past several weeks – been present at bathtime. Yet, as toys come and go, and the bath routine itself evolves, that toy may cease to be noted and may vanish from the child's memory entirely in subsequent months. It is, in effect, overwritten by other toys and other variations in the routine.[3]

A different type of experience is the one-time or novel event, the kind of experience that adults tend to think of as particularly memorable.

Infants surely have many of these; in fact, in the beginning of life they must be the overwhelming majority of experiences, simply because the infant knows so little of the expected happenings in the world. Visiting a laboratory to participate in a memory experiment must be a novel and exciting experience (positive or negative) for the infant.[4] As Rovee-Collier and her colleagues have shown, memory for such experiences does persist for weeks, but if the experience is not reinstated within a period of weeks, it soon ceases to be aroused under standard cueing conditions (Rovee-Collier & Hayne, 1987). Even repeated experiences of this kind rarely persist over the long haul (Myers, Clifton, & Clarkson, 1987; Myers, Perris, & Speaker, 1994).

Memory in Infancy

Beginning in the 1960s researchers using novelty preference paradigms found that infants retained information about specific stimuli (e.g., faces) over extended periods of time, but by the nature of the evidence the claim was restricted only to recognition memory (Fagan, 1984; Olson & Strauss, 1984). Rovee-Collier and her colleagues (e.g., Rovee-Collier & Hayne, 1987) have provided extensive evidence of memory for specific aspects of events and context in infants as young as 4 months. Their basic paradigm presents an infant with a contingent response situation, specifically with a mobile that moves when the infant kicks (a ribbon is tied to the infant's foot and connected to the mobile). The object-action association is retained by infants of 2 to 3 months over delays of 6 to 8 days; older infants retain the memory for longer periods after its establishment. Among the important findings from this paradigm is that specific details of the mobile are lost before the general situation (i.e., in early tests kicking is observed only to exact copies of the mobile, but over time variations from the original are responded to). The suggestion here is that the general function of the response is retained while the specific (episodic) details are not, a suggestion that is consistent with the general outlines of the functional theory proposed here. In addition, they have shown that reinstatement of the memory (involving exposure to partial conditions of the original memory) within a definite time period after learning doubles the period of its retention [see Rovee-Collier (1995) for a thorough review and discussion of these effects]. It is of considerable importance that the effect of reinstatement on the duration of a memory is found across organisms (it was first described in animal models) and developmental periods, as later research with toddlers (Hudson, 1993) and preschoolers (Fivush & Hamond, 1989) has shown (discussed later in this chapter).

Recall in infancy has been difficult to assess because of the lack of viable measures in prelinguistic infants (and more generally nonlinguistic animals). However, on the basis of her review of evidence, Mandler (1984a, 1988, 1992) argues that it clearly indicates that recall is within the capacity of infants, and that recall is indicative of declarative (semantic or episodic) as opposed to procedural memory. For example, Meltzoff (1988) and his colleagues have demonstrated delayed recall for an observed event over a 24-hour period by 9-month-olds.

Infantile Amnesia

Despite the evidence that memory for objects, people, and actions is robust in infancy, such memory is not retained, or if retained is not accessible, for long. Infant memories, if they exist, cannot be recalled in later years. This failure to recall experience from the early years of life is referred to as infantile, or childhood, amnesia, first identified by Freud (1963). Memories for events from before about 3 to 4 years are not available to adult consciousness, although many memories from later childhood usually are easily called up. Most of the research on childhood amnesia has come from studies of adults' recall of childhood memories [see review by Dudycha & Dudycha (1941)]. Summarizing over a large number of such studies, Pillemer and White (1989) found that the earliest memory is reported on average at about $3\frac{1}{2}$ years. They note that there are actually two phases of childhood amnesia: the first a total blocking of memories, usually prior to about 3 years, and the second a significant lack of many accessible memories relative to later memories between 3 and 6 years. They also note that early memories are of two different types: fragmentary images and more complete reports of events.

Note that the amnesia period typically lasts for several years beyond infancy, until the fourth year of life on average (and for many individuals much later). Thus the Schacter and Moscovitch (1984) later memory system, hypothesized to emerge at 1 year, does not explain the continuing effects of infantile amnesia. Some recent studies by Myers and her colleagues (Myers, Clifton, & Clarkson, 1987; Myers et al., 1994; Perris, Myers, & Clifton, 1990) have provided evidence of memory in early childhood for events experienced before the age of 1 year, suggesting a long-term retention function by 1 year. However, the evidence reveals only a very weak, fragmented implicit memory for the event at best, characterizable in Schacter's (1992) or Tulving's (1993) terms as procedural. There is no evidence to date that any experience from the infancy period (before 1 year) is retained into later childhood (after 6 years) or adulthood (Nelson, 1994).[5] Thus, whereas long-term memories from infancy to early childhood are important in indicating that memory for a procedural experience does not simply or completely evaporate during this period, that is, that some portion of the experience is retained in memory for months and sometimes years, this evidence does not bear directly on the phenomenon of infantile amnesia as it is understood in the adult literature.

Although interest in the phenomenon has been surprisingly slow to develop, it is increasingly recognized that the discontinuity in memory function indicated by infantile amnesia is critical to understanding the development of memory in human childhood. Memory in early childhood differs from infant memory but is also not retained into the later years. The important question to ask is not "Why does forgetting occur?" but "What is the function of memory for a one-time experience?" Clearly, memory for routines is functional in providing the infant with the ability to anticipate the sequence and content of the routine event, and to take part and even exercise partial control over it. But memory for a novel experience does not have the same functional value, *unless it is repeated.* Therefore it is rational that it be discarded. The theoretical question this raises is "Why would a one-time experience ever be retained as such?" This question is addressed later in the chapter when a more complete theory is laid out.

At this point it can be observed that an intermediate set of experiences for the infant are neither one-time nor routine, but consist of infrequent events with the same overall structure. Visits to the doctor are prime examples of such events. Most parents are quite familiar with the negative reactions of their 6- or 8-month-old infants when entering the doctor's office, assuming that monthly visits have been the norm. The pediatrician is likely to announce in pleased tones that the infant's cry on seeing his or her face indicates that the infant is now capable of forming a memory. As research has clearly demonstrated, much younger infants form and retain memory for extended periods. Yet, some capacity for retaining the *meaning* of the visit to the doctor over a month's time must have emerged at the later age. Capacity for extending a memory over the period of a month, the effect of strong affective arousal (e.g., in response to getting a shot), and establishment of sufficient general event knowledge so that a novel disruptive experience is not immediately overwritten are all probably relevant. This latter possibility rests on the assumption that in the immature memory system much information is retained but is subject to rapid deletion through overwriting. Selection for retention is based on repetition: what is likely to be functional in future encounters. A corollary to this proposal is that if selection is for the value of predicting and controlling future encounters, negative experiences will be no more likely to survive into later memory than positive ones. These tentative suggestions have not been tested in research to date, but they are consistent with the functional model presented later.

That the infant remembers the experience of a previous visit or visits to the doctor suggests an emerging capacity for recall [see Mandler (1988, 1992); McDonough & Mandler (in press)] rather than simple cued recognition. However, the evidence that the infant remembers a *specific* visit is not at all clear. Further, evidence for episodic memory in Tulving's (1983) sense, including specifications of temporal and spatial location, is clearly lacking. On the other hand, episodic memory need not involve the specific dating that Tulving has specified. A memory may exist that an event happened "one time" without specific contextualization of time and space. This *semi-episodic memory* might characterize the infant's recognition of the doctor's office as a cue for recalling the unpleasant experience of having a shot. Indeed the requirement of locating episodes at specific times is too restrictive for the episodic memory; episodic memory clearly does emerge in early childhood, as evidence reviewed later in this chapter indicates, but temporally dated memory emerges later still, and is properly considered autobiographical.

One can summarize the outlook from the infant period of memory by saying that memory is alive and well during this period, but that memories of events – specific or general – do not survive for long. Some evidence of retention from the period around 1 year of age until 3 years has been forthcoming, but in general little is retained, and what is retained is fragmentary and not accessible to deliberate recall, evident only indirectly in behavioral responses and relearning.

Memory in Childhood

Traditional studies of memory in childhood were based on memory experiments with adults, in particular studies using lists of words to be recalled. This paradigm established many reliable findings for children as well as adults. For example, words that are high associates are likely to be recalled together, and words from the same semantic category are likely to cluster together in recall. Memory was basically considered a unitary faculty or resource. From this perspective children had either good or poor memory; preschoolers in particular, who had very poor list recall, were viewed as having a general memory deficiency. Given a list of 8 to 10 words to recall immediately after presentation, a 3-year-old might recall two, and a 5-year-old four or five, while an 8-year-old could recall about 8 (Nelson, 1969). The digit span test for short-term memory, a standard feature of IQ tests, revealed similar limitations, leading to the conclusion that young children have poor memory *because* their short-term-memory space (STM) is very limited.

Young children do not cluster together words from the same semantic category in their recall of lists of instances from different categories randomly presented. Nor do they impose any subjective organization on lists repeated over trials, as adults do (Nelson, 1969; see Chapter 7). For these reasons, organizational factors have been proposed to explain deficiencies in younger children's memory, and recent studies have implicated a complex interaction of memory strategies and categorical knowledge as determinants of memory performance in free recall studies (e.g., Bjorklund, 1985). Earlier studies of memory strategies showed that only in the early school years do children begin to engage in deliberate rehearsal of lists (Flavell, Beach, & Chinsky, 1966; Flavell, Friedrichs, & Hoyt, 1970), suggesting that younger children engage not in voluntary but only in involuntary memory processing. Flavell (1971) concluded that memory development from the preschool to the school years involved the use of metamemory, that is, deliberate attempts to engage in memory for its own sake. This requires the conscious awareness of memory as a process and deliberate manipulation of strategies, as well as organization of material, for accomplishing memory tasks.

The "novice–expert shift" in knowledge acquisition (e.g, Simon, 1972; Chi, 1978; Chi & Koeske, 1983) suggests that many apparently developmental changes in memory capacity or ability are actually effects of increased knowledge and its organization. The domain in which younger children are experts is the domain of knowledge about their own world of experience. But even in this domain, there is a disjunction of memory in terms of childhood amnesia, as already discussed. Children of 2, 3 and 4 years, as well as infants, retain little or no memory of their experiences into their later childhood and adult lives, whereas adults have many memories from the early and middle school years. This disjunction does not result from a knowledge difference, and memory for life events apparently does not depend on metamemory or deliberate strategic processing. Thus, the developmental question remains as to why there is this major change midway in the preschool years.

It is apparent that the kinds of memory studied in school age children and found to be deficient in preschoolers serve functions different from the basic memory function that is operative in infancy. Schoolchildren are expected to learn and remember facts in the knowledge domains valued and explicitly transmitted by the culture in verbal form. Language at this period, both oral and written, has taken on a major function of the explicit transmission of knowledge. It is hardly surprising, then, that school age children display more skill at using it for this function. Memory in the preschool period – the period between the basic memory of infancy and the linguistic/cultural memory of the school years – provides a critical link, and, as already sketched in the preceding chapters, the proposal here is that the link involves the integration of the event-mimetic system with the linguistic system of representation.

Memory in the Preschool Years

Today most studies of memory in the preschool years recognize that the function of memory for young children is closer to the "natural memory" of infancy than to the "cultural memory" of the school years, and therefore aim to study memory in its natural ecological niche. Memory in early childhood is not usually the result of explicit deliberate attempts to learn material for future retention and recall but includes memories formed incidentally to the process of achieving other goals. This distinction was the focus of a classic study by Istomina (1975) demonstrating that when preschoolers were motivated to remember items on a list by appropriate goal-orientation, their performance greatly improved. In particular, her studies contrasted children's requirement to remember items in a school context with remembering a list of items to buy at the store in order to prepare lunch. This situation presents not only a familiar understandable goal with social consequences, but a familiar, well-structured routine, and knowledge of familiar items, all important aspects of memory in natural settings. [See Rogoff (1990) for a replication and extension of these findings with American children.]

Recent studies converge on the conclusion that the memory abilities of preschool children had been severely underestimated in earlier work. It is now clear that preschool children can remember objects, locations, and events in experimental tasks when they have the knowledge and motivation to do so. Under appropriate conditions (e.g., interest in materials, familiarity of context, understandable goals) very young children can remember both specific and general information about scenes, events, stories, and items presented for remembering. Research has also demonstrated that children retain specific episodic memories for life experiences over 6 months to a year from at least the second year of life. Reviews of this research from a number of different laboratories can be found in Fivush and Hudson (1990).

Yet autobiographical memory – enduring chronologically sequenced memory for significant events from one's own life – has its onset only during the later preschool years, $3\frac{1}{2}$ to 4 years on average. The onset of autobiographical memory is the inverse of childhood amnesia. An obvious hypothesis to account for the lack of early autobiographical memory is that one of the basic types or systems of memory has not yet matured in the early preschool years. For example, younger children might have semantic memory only, or gist memory only (Brainerd & Reyna, 1990). In fact, early studies of children's generic and specific memories suggested that a reasonable explanation for infantile amnesia was that children do not preserve episodic memories, although they may remember bits of information from specific events in their schematic event memory. In early childhood, it was suggested (Nelson & Ross, 1980), all information retained from experience is absorbed by the generic memory system.[6] As discussed earlier, such a system is functional for building up general knowledge of the world, and quite likely is characteristic both of infant memory and nonhuman mammalian memory.

However, the hypothesis that young preschool children have generic memory only has not stood up to empirical test. Subsequent research found that very young children do remember novel events, within limits, and sometimes quite readily report episodes that they find interesting (Hudson, 1986; Ratner, 1980). When asked about routine events they simply give routine (script-like) answers, but when asked about novel events children as young as 2 or $2\frac{1}{2}$ years are sometimes able to respond with details. Although very young children often need extensive probing to elicit their memories, suggesting that they may retain only random and unschematized fragments, there is also evidence of specific episodic memories that have the same form as we might find in older children.

The study of a single child's spontaneous memory productions over the period from 21 to 36 months supports the proposal of a developmental progression in their organization. The data come from transcripts of Emily's pre-sleep monologues, which were introduced in Chapter 4 [Nelson (1989c) provides a full account of this study]. Monologues recorded when Emily was 21 to 22 months contained fragments of remembered experiences, such as the following concerned with Daddy's activities:

> (1) That Daddy brings down basement washing, I can hold Emmy, so, Daddy brings down the, washing on the basement, washing, so my can, so why, the, the, the, no-daddy brings washing.

Like other early monologues, this one seemed to be organized around familiar events, but it is questionable whether this is a fragment of a memory for a single episode. Certainly it has no coherent structure, albeit it has a clear topic. In some cases during this early period, long sequences of talk were focused on the same event, but the memory itself appeared to consist of a single fragment, as in the following excerpt from an early (21-month) monologue:

> (2) The broke, car broke, the . . . Emmy can't go in the car. Go in green car. No. Emmy go in the car. Broken. Broken. Their car broken, so Mommy Daddy go in their car, Emmy Daddy go in the car, Emmy Daddy Mommy go in the car, broke, Da . . . da, the car . . . their, their, car broken. [Continues]

However, by 2 years Emily was reporting her experiences in a more extensive and organized form, and at $2\frac{1}{2}$ she produced coherent accounts such as the following:

> (3) We *bought* a baby, cause, the well because, when she, well, we *thought* it was for Christmas, but *when* we went to the s-s-store we didn't have our jacket on, but I saw some dolly, and I *yelled* at my mother and said I want one of those dolly. So after we were finished with the store, we went over to the dolly and she *bought* me one. So I have one.

In this example, Emily was recounting to herself what apparently was a significant episode in her life. Although the episode was identified by her mother as one shared less than a week before, she had not rehearsed it with her parents (or presumably with others). This recount is clear and concise, well-organized as a narrative in a temporal and causal sequence.

Evidence from Emily's monologues, and from other event and memory studies, calls into question some traditional explanations for the phenomenon of childhood amnesia. For example, Schachtel in 1947 and Neisser in 1962 suggested that autobiographical memories are the out-

come of a reconstructive process based on schemata or frames of reference, along the lines suggested by Bartlett in 1932. Remembering in this
conception involves *reconstructing* past events using presently existing
schemata, and the claim is that adult schemata are not suitable recepta-
cles for early childhood experience because adults cannot think like children and thus cannot make use of whatever fragments of memories they
may retain. In this view, socialization and the impact of language forces a
drastic change in the child's schemata at age 6. However, Emily's monologues at 2 to 3 years do not suggest that the preschool child's schemata
are dramatically different from those of the older child and adult. Rather,
young children's free recall of salient episodic memories reported by
recent investigators (e.g., Engel, 1986; Hudson, 1990; Tessler, 1986) support the conclusion that the basic ways of structuring, representing, and
interpreting events are consistent from early childhood into adulthood.
As in the examples from Emily's monologues, children of 3 to 4 years
typically tell their experience-based stories in a sequence that accurately
reflects the sequence of the experience itself and with the same boundaries (beginnings and endings) that seem natural to adult listeners (Nelson, 1986; Nelson, 1989a). These findings are consistent with the proposal of MERs as basic representational structures.

Of course there may be other important differences between adult and
child memories, including what is noticed and remembered of an event.
Often, extensive cueing and probing are required to elicit details from a
young child, suggesting that adult and child may have different memories of the same event (Fivush & Hamond, 1990). An analysis of the
content of Emily's crib talk also suggests that adult and child may focus
on different aspects of the same event. Emily's memories were mostly
concerned with the quotidian, unremarkable routines of her life. They
were not concerned with the truly novel events of her life (from the
adult's point of view), such as the birth of her baby brother or her
airplane trips to visit relatives (Nelson, 1989a). Thus, interest in – and
therefore memory for – aspects of experience that seem unremarkable to
adults, and indifference to what adults find interesting, may account for
why young children sometimes seem to have organized their knowledge
in a different form or to have remembered only fragments from an
episode that the adult considers memorable.

The apparent idiosyncrasy of children's early memories may reflect
their focus on understanding and representing the consistencies of their
world. Specific novel events or parts of events may be remembered because they are variations or seeming violations of routines. Emily's verbal-

izations of episodes were mostly of routine or everyday experiences, the types of events that are absorbed into scripts in adult memory. Recounts were especially frequent at two periods of her life: after her baby brother was born, when many of her routines were therefore changing, and nine months later, when she entered a preschool program for the first time. Both time periods incorporated significant life changes, and her monologues are interpretable as attempts to incorporate the new experience into the ongoing representation of "what happens." Thus, although it might seem reasonable that her monologues provided rehearsals or reinstatement attempts of significant events, a plausible alternative interpretation is that they served as cognitive organizers of generic information about routine events. From this perspective, her verbalizations were in service of semantic or generic, not episodic, memory. The fact that she sometimes repeated a verbal account several times in one session, with variations, supports the supposition that she was attempting to solve a problem or get matters straight. Moreover, her monologues did not repeat memories from an earlier period that had been rehearsed. There is no evidence that she was savoring a particular episode with the result, intended or not, of retaining it for the future. Because her language was relatively sophisticated, it is plausible that her narratives might serve to reinstate a memory through the linguistic medium; but if so, there is no evidence that she later attempted to retrieve such a memory. Thus, what memories existed at that time were lost in later years, as evidenced by the results of a memory probe 4 years later, which revealed no specific recoverable memories from her third year.

In summary, recent research on episodic memory in early childhood indicates that children have at least some well-organized specific as well as general event memories, similar to those of adults. They do not seem to be victims of a rapid and inevitable overwrite mechanism. Nor does the suggestion that a schematic reorganization accounts for infantile amnesia appear to be supported. Rather, findings from the study of memory in early childhood are consistent with the expectation that memory preserves information about events that are routinely repeated or that are salient in the child's individual organization of experience, her world models.

Social Development of Memory

Memory talk – talk about the past – between parents and their young children has been the focus of a number of recent studies [see Hudson

(1990) for review]. Susan Engel (1986) recorded parent–child memory talk in the latter part of the second year, visiting four mother–child dyads over a six-month period when the children were between 18 and 24 months old, and including a cross-sectional study of 2-year-old children who were specifically prompted by their mothers to talk about three memories of recent experiences. Engel found that mothers varied in the amount of memory talk they engaged in, and in the kinds of questions they asked [see also Ratner (1984)]. But she also found that the dyads varied in the *kinds* of memories they focused on and in the *manner* in which they formulated their talk, identifying two styles of memory talk, *pragmatic* and *elaborative*. Pragmatic mother tended to talk about practical matters, such as where a child had left a toy, and when they talked about experiences they had shared, they tended to focus on the "who" and "what" rather than the "where," "when," "how," and "why." Elaborative mothers made stories of their experiences and invited their children to participate in them. In the most successful cases, even at 2 years children "co-constructed" the narrative with their mothers.

In the following example a 24-month-old boy and his mother have been recalling a visit from Aunt Judy, with no apparent relevance to what follows regarding an event from two months previous.

(4) C: Mommy, the Chrysler building
    M: The Chrysler building?
    C: The Chrysler building?
    M: Yeah, who works in the Chrysler building?
    C: Daddy
    M: Do you ever go there?
    C: Yes, I see the Chrysler building, picture of the Chrysler building
    M: I don't know if we have a picture of the Chrysler building. Do we?
    C: We went to . . . my Daddy went to work
    M: Remember when we went to visit Daddy? Went in the elevator, way way up in the building so we could look down from the big window?
    C: big window
    M: mmhm
    C: ( )
    When . . . we did go on the big building
    M: mmhm, the big building. Was that fun? Would you like to do it again?
    Sometime.

C: I want to go on the big building.
[Unpublished data from Engel (1986), used with permission]

In this excerpt, the child introduces the topic and provides some evidence of having a memory of going to visit Daddy, but the mother reconstructs the remembered episode, providing the action sequence of going up in the elevator and looking out the big window, as well as the evaluative comment that it was fun and the child might like to do it again.

Engel found that the children of elaborative mothers engaged in more episodes and more extensive episodes of memory talk at 2 years than did the children of pragmatic mothers, although at this young age most of the burden of reconstructing the event falls on the mother. Fivush and Fromhoff (1988) found a similar relation between mothers' talk and children's memory, distinguishing between elaborative and repetitive mothers. As in the example above from Engel's data, elaborative mothers provide a progressive story line, inviting the child to contribute bits to the story, while repetitive mothers focus on a single bit of information without providing further narrative framing. A telling example of repetitive mother's memory talk is the following, from a conversation between a mother and her $2\frac{1}{2}$-year-old child about their recent trip to Florida (Fivush & Hamond, 1990, pp. 230–231):

(5) M: And where did we eat breakfast? Where did we go for
         breakfast?
     C: What?
     M: Where did we go for breakfast? Remember we went out,
         Daddy, you and I? What restaurant did we go to?
     C: Gasoline.
     M: Gasoline? No, what restaurant did we go have breakfast
         at?
     C: Ummm . . .
     M: Do you remember? It was Burger . . . ?
     C: King!

In contrast to the mother in (4), who leads on from the child's comment to build a story organized around his contribution, here the mother is intent on extracting a single bit of information, but provides no additional cues for the child to build on, no little story about what happened at the restaurant, for example. Rather – perhaps because in the mother's view going to Burger King for breakfast is a novel and memorable event – she repetitively urges the child to produce the "correct" answer to the question, and finally provides the associative link that enables him to succeed on her terms. Whether her cue accesses any actual memory of the event on the part of the child cannot be established from this evidence, but there is no reason to believe that the child has produced anything more than a verbal association between Burger and King. In the Fivush and Fromhoff study, as in Engel's, children of elaborative mothers revealed better memory for episodes six months later. However, these kinds of data are inherently ambiguous. Mother–child dyads are mutually influentiable; therefore, attributing causal relations is not possible. For example, mothers might be led to tell more elaborate narratives with children who are more verbal, more responsive to the telling, more interested in the kinds of details such narratives contain. Moreover, mothers inclined to storytelling about the child's past experience may tend to have children who display the cognitive style that Wolf and Gardner (1979) called dramatist, being inherently inclined to engage in similar narrative constructions, thus encouraging the mother's efforts.

However, the suggestion of a causal relation remains viable when other factors (such as general language ability, number of memories discussed) are controlled at the first measurement, and when the lagged correlation (more memory displayed by children whose mothers provided more encouragement of a seemingly appropriate kind) is significant. Reese, Haden, and Fivush (1993) have reported such a longitudinal study in which they observed mother–child dyads talking about shared past experiences at four time points – when children were 40, 46, 58, and 70 months of age. Mothers were consistently classified as either elaborative or repetitive, although all mothers became more elaborative over time. Cross-lagged correlations revealed a relation between maternal elaboration at the early observations and children's memory at the later time points, although bidirectional influences were also observed at the older ages.

It should be emphasized that the effects found by Engel and those reported by Reese and colleagues were not simply that children remembered *more*. Rather, the narrative format of the memories was apparent in the kinds of information that children contributed and in the organization and language used to present it. As discussed more fully in Chapter 7, the narrative format organizes the memory as a coherent whole, representing the perspective of consciousness as well as the perspective of action.[7] As Hudson (1990) noted, children "are learning *how* to remember, not *what* to remember" (p. 194). But, as is apparent from other studies, some children have less experience with the narrative model that shows "how" to remember effectively than do others. It is important to emphasize that, as with other kinds of "style" differences in language and cognition (Nelson, 1981), parental style of memory talk is not an all or none issue, but rather one of points along a continuum, with extremes where some parents cast a great deal of talk about the past in narrative form and others talk about memories very little and provide little scaffolding for the child's contributions.

It is becoming clear that talk about the past provides a model for young children of how to organize and remember specific events. Additional evidence suggests that talk about *ongoing* events serves a similar memorial function. Minda Tessler (1986; Tessler & Nelson, 1994) studied the social construction of memory by examining the effects of adult framing of an event *while it was being experienced* by the child. In her first study she took 3½-year-old children and their mothers on a visit to the American Museum of Natural History in New York. Half the mothers were instructed not to provide any input regarding the visit beyond answering the child's questions, while the other half were encouraged to talk with their children as they usually would on such a visit. A week later the investigator returned and obtained children's memory for the museum trip in both a free recall and probed interview.

There was a striking difference between the children whose mothers provided a frame for the experience and those whose mothers did not in the number of items seen that children later recalled. Moreover, Tessler observed that, even among the mothers who were encouraged to act naturally, there was a difference in the style in which they interacted with their children about the experience. This style difference was very similar to that described by Engel (1986) for mothers talking about the past. Tessler formulated the two styles according to Bruner's (1986) distinction between *paradigmatic* and *narrative* cognitive modes. Some of the specific characteristics of the paradigmatic style include naming and a focus on object characteristics, whereas characteristics of the narrative style include the perspectives of time, intentionality, causality, and evaluation. Narrative mothers more frequently related what was on view to the child's own experience. Children of narrative mothers remembered significantly more than children of paradigmatic mothers, and most intriguing, no child remembered anything from the experience that had not been talked about between mother and child. It was not sufficient for the mother to talk about an object or for the child to draw the mother's attention to it; rather, there had to have been an interchange between the two for the topic to become memorable.

Tessler (1991; Tessler & Nelson, 1994) extended these findings in a second study in which she took 4-year-old children on a picture-taking expedition with their mothers in an unfamiliar neighborhood. She first divided mothers into groups on the basis of the way that they interacted with their children around a picture book containing urban scenes. Paradigmatic mothers were those who, in their talk about the book, displayed the characteristics that had been identified in the previous study. Narrative mothers were those who displayed the opposite style in that situation. The two styles were further verified by analyzing the dialogues they carried on with their children during the picture-taking event. At a subsequent session the investigator returned with the pictures and interviewed the child about his or her memory of the event. The interview was conducted in either a narrative or a paradigmatic style, based on the characteristics previously identified, crossed with the mother's style. Thus a child might be in a consistent (narrative-narrative or paradigmatic-paradigmatic) or inconsistent (narrative-paradigmatic or paradigmatic-narrative) questioning condition. The mother's style had consistent and significant effects on the child's style of recalling the event, regardless of the interviewer's manipulation. Moreover, children of narrative mothers recalled more of the pictures they had taken, and reported more from the event, although there were no differences between the groups in the number of pictures recognized.

These findings strongly suggest that style is a characteristic passed from mother to child and resistant to the efforts of an interlocutor to elicit a different style through a different mode of questioning. Further, they suggest that the narrative style of framing an event *while it is being experienced* is more effective in producing a subsequent memory of that event than is the paradigmatic style. Yet it also appears that this effect is specific to the effects of the narrative structure, including its coherence, sequencing, and evaluative details. The recognition results suggest that the underlying memory for the individual parts of the event represented by the pictures may not have differed.

In summary, these studies of mother–child talk about the past and the present provide strong evidence that during the preschool years children learn to talk about – and to remember – their experiences in specific ways. They learn, that is, to "narrativize" their experience.[8] What these studies have shown is important evidence for the impact of language on thought at the midpoint of early childhood, and specifically, as Donald (1991; Chapter 3) claims, in the formation of narrative representations.

That parental talk of the kinds studied is relevant to the establishment of autobiographical memory as an enduring system of personal memories is an obvious hypothesis. Recent research with adults supports this hypothesis. Mullen (1994) reported four questionnaire studies with adults designed to evaluate effects of early childhood experiences on the origins of autobiographical memory, specifically on the age of earliest memory. Across the four studies she found that older siblings had earlier memories than later siblings, that children with more siblings had later memories, and that girls tended to have earlier memories than boys. These findings are all in line with observed differences in prior research that indicate that mothers talk more with daughters than sons, and with older siblings than later siblings, and have more one-on-one talk with each child in one- or two-child families than in larger families. Assuming that some of the talk is organized around memories, these data support the supposition from the research with young children that early autobiographic memory is facilitated by talk with parents.[9]

Of even greater interest is that the strongest relation of age to early memory emerged as a difference between ethnic/cultural groups, specifically between students of Asian or Caucasian identity. Anthropological and psychological studies report differences in Asian and Caucasian concepts of self, specifically that Asians have a more interdependent view in comparison with the independent self-concept fostered in the West (Markus & Kitayama, 1991). On this basis it was hypothesized that Asian adults would have personal memory systems that were established later than those of Caucasians from similar social and educational backgrounds. The reasoning here is that American parents tend to encourage and reinforce independence and a strong self-image in young children, through discourse about their thoughts, feelings, and attitudes toward their experiences, and Asian parents are likely to focus less on the child's independent experience and more on the child's participation in the familial group. This hypothesized difference in the fostering of an individual self-concept would be expected to be reflected in the later establishment of a personal life story. Consistent with this hypothesis, Asian students in all four studies had later memories than did Caucasian. When the Asian sample was restricted to students who had spent their childhood years in Korea, and who responded to questions written in Korean, the difference between groups was 17 months (55.5 for the Korean group, 38.5 for the Caucasian), a highly significant result that could not be accounted for by differences in age dating or in other plausibly related variables.

An additional study reported by Mullen (Mullen & Yi, 1995) found differences in the talk between Korean mothers and their young children and that of Caucasian mothers and their young children. Caucasian (American) mothers in this research talked much more extensively about shared past experience and focused on the child's point of view, in comparison with the Korean mothers studied. The cultural difference found among Korean adults in comparison with Caucasian adults is consistent with the difference in discourse experiences of young children found in this study, as hypothesized.[10]

These studies have helped to pull together the findings and hypotheses from research with American preschool children, indicating that the social influences expressed through discourse about past and present experiences in early childhood transform episodic memory into autobiographical memory. To understand this process it is necessary to consider the varying functions of memory in more detail.

Social Construction and the Functions of Child Memory

A number of authors have suggested that autobiographical memory is the product of social construction in early childhood (Fivush, 1988; Hudson, 1990; Nelson, 1991b, 1993c; Pillemer & White, 1989). The proposal is that autobiographical memory is a distinct form of episodic memory, a form that comes into being as the child is inducted into the ways of talking about shared experiences and that comes to incorporate the adult values of talking about the experience. The perspective is drawn from Vygotsky's (1986) theory, as well as from Bakhtin (1981, 1986; Wertsch, 1991), and from other earlier theorists who focused on the social construction of mind and self (e.g., G.H. Mead, 1934). It is not suggested that learning to talk about the past is a simple matter of acquiring models transmitted from parent to child; rather, a dialectical process of collaborative construction of remembered events in linguistic form is involved.

The social-cultural proposal does not deny that the child herself brings distinctive episodic memories to the sharing. There is good evidence that children may remember episodes that their parents have forgotten (Fivush & Hamond, 1989). And, as noted earlier, Emily's memories were largely of events that were not remarked upon or were not known by her parents, and were not rehearsed with her parents, but rather were first recounted to herself as she prepared to sleep.

Basic general event knowledge is the basis for understanding and therefore remembering episodes. Without a good script, knowledge about what happens, based only on direct experience with the happenings, may be quite chaotic, as was seen in the examples from Emily's earliest monologues, (1) and (2). As we know from recent work by Bauer and Mandler (1992), reviewed in Chapter 3, children are able to reconstruct brief temporal action sequences late in the first and early in the second year. It seem likely, however, that, in contrast to reperforming action sequences (a mimetic skill), holding action sequences in mind *as explicit memories* requires more cognitive processing power, and therefore is a later development. As the fragment of Emily's monologue about Daddy washing (1) suggests, some of her earliest productions seemed to be attempts to bring into focus many different actions on the part of her father and mother as well as herself – rather than a sequence of actions from a single event – and these attempts resulted in strings of verbalization of actions related complexively (Applebee, 1978; Vygotsky, 1986). Sometime between 2 and 3 years of age, children typically become able to hold in mind not only brief overt action sequences, but also the representation of extended event sequences that they can externally represent in play (action) or in language. These externalizations are constituted from the basic event knowledge system that must also support the specific episodic memories that become evident about that time.

In summary, what the young child brings to the social construction process is the capacity for holding in mind a sequence of events, involving self and others, temporally and causally arranged. This capacity is applied both to generic scripts and to specific episodes. The social construction process then builds on these skeletal event sequences. Parents and others may talk about what is going to happen, what is happening, and what has happened in different ways. Parents seem to assume that the child will experience, is experiencing, or has experienced the same event in the same way as the parent, and that the child can interpret what the parent is telling her about it. Evidence from Emily and others indicates that children may try very hard to do this interpretive work and they may sometimes succeed, although they may also misinterpret or be confused by what parents tell them, either because they lack the requisite background knowledge or because they have not experienced the same event in the same way

The different ways that parents frame an event prior to, during, and after it is experienced will build on the child's basic event knowledge to construct memories together that may then enter into the child's autobiographical memory system. Parents also contribute evaluations and reinterpret the child's emotions (Fivush, 1994). Depending on the kinds of episodic accounts the child hears and contributes to, the system will tend to be more or less narrative-like, and will form the basis for constructing better or poorer narratives about experiences, as well as stories, dramatic play, and such activities as "show and tell" (see Chapter 7 for more on this topic). Because memories are socially constructed systems, one may expect social and cultural variation, as well as individual and family differences, in the kinds of memories developed.

Functional Memory Systems

The social-cultural model can be generalized as an extension of an evolutionary model of memory functions. In this perspective, all memory is considered as a functional system that has adaptational value. In general, any system of learning and memory conserves information about variable environmental conditions [Oakley (1983); Plotkin (1988); see Chapter 2]. It enables the organism to undertake action to meet goals under specific but variable conditions. Learning and memory are thus trade-offs for specific genetic behavior programs. The functional memory system supports action in the present and predicts future outcomes. That is to say, memory has value for the present and future because it predicts on the basis of past probabilities.

As suggested earlier, the kind of memory most useful for this purpose is memory for recurrent conditions and routine actions. Memory for a single, one-time occurrence of some event, if the event were not traumatic or life-threatening, would not be especially useful, given its low probability. Thus a memory system might be optimally designed to retain information about frequent and recurrent events – and to discard information about unrepeated events – and to integrate new information about variations in recurrent events into a general knowledge system. Such a system may be described in terms of schemas and scripts, or what have been referred to here as general, or mental, event representations (MERs) or generic memory [equivalent in many ways to Tulving's (1972) semantic memory]. This description can be recognized as essentially that of the infant memory system outlined in the first section of this chapter.

In the basic system, specific episodic memories as described become part of the generic memory system when a new situation is encountered, and it is apparent that a new script must be established. Presumably a new experience alerts the child to set up a new schema, which at first may function as an episodic memory but with further experience with events of the same kind increasingly assumes the function and characteristics of a script (Fivush, 1984; Hudson & Nelson, 1986; Linton, 1982).

The problem is that the system cannot know whether a novel event is the first of a recurrent series of events and should therefore be remembered (i.e. schematized for future reference), or whether it is an aberration that is of no functional significance for future action. The solution for a limited memory system is either to integrate the new information as part of the generic system or to keep the novel memory in a separate, temporary, episodic memory space for a given amount of time to determine if it is the first of a series of recurrent events and thus should become part of the generic system. If a similar event does not recur during that test period, the episode is dropped from memory as having no adaptive significance. In this primary functionally based system all event memory is either generic knowledge – script-like – or *temporarily* *episodic*. The basic episodic system is a holding pattern, not a permanent memory system. This system is in place, according to the evidence reviewed previously, at least by 1 year of age.

The type of memory system just described can explain both short-term episodic memories (perhaps lasting up to 6 months or so) and long-lasting generic memory. But what accounts for long-lasting episodic memories? As the developmental research has shown, although young children's episodic memories mostly come from recent experiences – within the past six months – some memories may last as long as $2\frac{1}{2}$ years (Fivush & Hamond, 1990). The concept of *reinstatement*, introduced in the section "memory in infancy" may explain these findings. In the infancy (and earlier animal) studies, reinstatement has been demonstrated for a learned response to a stimulus cue, which has also been demonstrated in preschoolers (Howe, Courage, & Bryant-Brown, 1993). The first question to ask is whether the effect holds for reenactment of a one-time experience, rather than that of a response learned to a criterion. There now exists evidence to this effect.

Fivush & Hamond (1989) studied 2-year-olds and found that specific memories that tend to be lost over a period of weeks can be retained if they are reinstated at least once within a specific period of time. In their study, children were brought to the laboratory and given a number of specific experiences with objects and activities in particular locations. Half of the children were brought back to the lab two weeks later and experienced the objects again. All children were brought back for a memory test three months later. Those whose memory had been "reinstated" remembered significantly more than those children who had not had this experience; in fact the youngest children (24 months) remembered twice as much. Equally important, the reinstated group remembered as

Table 6.1. *Comparison of first and second recall sessions in Tessler picture-taking study*

	Time 1	Time 2
Mean # pictures recalled	3.62	3.98
Mean # pictures recognized	7.43	8.48
Mean # information units/picture	12.58	23.10

much at three months as they had at two weeks; that is, there was no subsequent loss. Hudson (1993) reports similar results of the effectiveness of reenactment on a memory for an event in 18- to 24-month-olds. Sheffield, Sosa, & Hudson (1993) have carried out an extensive comparison of the effectiveness of the partial reenactment at different delays after the initial experience. It is clear from their study that immediate reenactment on the same day as the experience is ineffective, while a lag of two weeks between initial experience and reexposure does reinstate the memory, as evaluated by a later recall test.

Reinstatement has been considered thus far in terms of reinstating a behavioral response – an action in response to a stimulus object [also Howe, Courage, & Bryant-Brown, 1993]. Consistent with the theory proposed in this volume, it is suggested here that with the development of the representational function of language, talking about an experience may come to serve as a reinstating context (Hudson, 1990; Nelson, 1993b, 1993c). That is, one of the effects of remembering an experience with others is likely to be reinstatement and thus preservation of the memory. Tessler's (1991) experiment provided evidence for this effect: When revisited a second time, all children in her study recalled almost twice as many details (information units) as they had two weeks earlier. As shown in Table 6.1, they also recalled more pictures and recognized more of the pictures on the second visit. These results were unexpected, as the main interest was in the effect of different style of talk (as reported earlier). The effects of verbal reinstatement are being followed up in controlled laboratory studies by our research group. The first study in our series again reveals a significant effect of verbal reinstatement on later memory in comparison to a control group (Walkenfeld & Nelson, 1995).

Reinstatement is an effect of subsequent reexposure to part of an initial experience. It may result from reenactment – partial or complete – or through active strategic rehearsal of important parts of the experience to be remembered. Reinstatement is an important mechanism in explaining the development of autobiographical memory from the basic generic functional memory system. Reinstatement signals that the episode may not be a one-time occurrence and thus the memory should be retained for future reference. In effect, reinstatement might be expected to double the amount of time that a memory is held in the episodic system (Rovee-Collier, 1995). Verbal reinstatement as a mechanism for the retention of memory over time thus answers the "how" question: "How does memory persist?" But reinstatement does not answer the "why" question: "Why talk about experience?"

The Function of Autobiographical Memory: Why Remember?

The suggestion here is that, at least in its beginning and to an extent throughout life, the functional significance of autobiographical memory is that of sharing memory with others, a function that facility with the use of language in discourse makes possible. Thus the potential value of memory itself changes as language becomes a two-way representational system, as described in earlier chapters. Subsequently memories become valued in their own right, not only because they predict the future and guide present action but also because they are shareable with others and thus serve a social solidarity function. This is a universal human function, although one with variable culturally specific rules. In this respect shared memory is analogous to human language itself, uniquely and universally human but culturally – and individually – variable. Further, it is apparent that this social function of memory underlies all of our storytelling, history-making narrative activities, and thus ultimately all of our accumulated knowledge systems.[11]

Support for this claim can be summarized as follows. First, children learn to engage in talk about the past, guided initially by parents who construct a narrative around the bits and pieces contributed by the child. The timing of this learning is consistent with the age at which autobiographical memory begins to emerge, based on the adult data. Indeed, Fivush and Hamond (1990) found that $2\frac{1}{2}$-year-olds were relatively uninterested in talking about their experiences, whereas the same children at 4 were both interested and capable. Also, the variability in age of onset of autobiographical memory and its relation to sibling status, gender, and cultural background (Mullen, 1994) are consistent with possible variability in children's experiences in sharing memories of the right kind (narrative vs. paradigmatic) and the right degree, as the research by

Ratner (1980, 1984), Tessler (1986, 1991), Engel (1986), and Reese and Fivush (1993) has documented.[12]

Given that the child's initial functional system is one that values general knowledge useful in the pragmatic event contexts of everyday life, coordinating this system with the adult's narrative system involves more than just learning the verbal forms. The major cognitive problem that the child faces in taking on new memory forms and functions is to coordinate earlier memory functions with those that the adult displays, incorporating adult values about what is important to remember, and the narrative formats for remembering, into her own existing functional system, the system based in event and mimetic representations. This problem is recognizable as a subproblem of the general representational change that must take place in early childhood as language takes on its representational potential. The child must learn to tell a coherent story – to tell the truth; get the facts right; remember specific important details of when, where, and why (components not significant in the generic system); and emphasize some parts, those considered interesting by others as well as oneself, and not other parts, which may be of only idiosyncratic significance. In doing all this, the child must become reasonably adept at taking the perspective of another and of viewing events from a somewhat detached, metarepresentational distance. This kind of decentering has been recognized as a significant achievement of the preschool years, in both Piaget's (1926) theory and in more recent studies of children's theories of mind and metarepresentational change (see Chapter 10).

This is then the functional part of the claim, suggesting that sharing memories with others serves a significant social-cultural function; the acquisition of such sharing means that the child can enter into the social and cultural history of the family and community. However, identifying this function, and some of the mechanisms that support it, does not in itself explain why personal autobiographical memories continue to persist over long periods of time. Language again enters as an important mechanism in this development.

Reinstatement through language requires a good degree of facility with language, and especially the ability to use the verbal representation of another person to set up a representation in one's own mental representation system, thus recognizing the verbal account as a reinstatement of one's prior experience. Some of the examples that we have seen from children cued to remember specific details [e.g., (5), the Burger King example] do not have the appearance of instantiating the same memory for the child as for the adult. Moreover, it is plausible, as argued previously, that most of the verbal recounting that Emily engaged in at 2 years, for example, was not effective as reinstatement of a memory, but only as a knowledge-organizing activity. Using another person's verbal representation of an event as a partial reinstatement of one's own representation (memory) depends on the achievement of language as a mental representational system in its own right, and not simply as either an organizing tool or a communication tool. In line with the argument put forth throughout this book, this achievement is an important cognitive-linguistic development of the late preschool years (Nelson, 1990), and the evidence for the overcoming of infantile amnesia and the establishment of autobiographical memory at this age supports this claim.

In summary, the theoretical claim here is that sharing memory narratives is necessary to establish the new social function of autobiographical memory as well as to make reinstatement through language possible. Following Vygotsky's (1978) model of internalization, after overt recounting becomes established, covert recounting or reexperiencing to oneself may take place, and thus take on the function of reinstatement of a personal memory system, including memories not shared with others. Autobiographical memory need not be verbal, however. Most people report a large component of imagery in such memory (Brewer, 1986). But it can be organized and reformulated in verbal narrative terms. Once an autobiographical memory system is established, it takes on a personal as well as a social value in defining the self, as others have argued (Brewer, 1986; Fivush, 1988; Pillemer, 1992). Thus replaying a memory through imaging, even without talking about it specifically, overtly or covertly, might well reinstate it and cause it to persist, once the autobiographical system is set in motion. This proposal differs from the claim that Schachtel (1947) and Neisser (1962) made that the schemas of the language community fundamentally change memory. Rather, the claim here is that language opens up possibilities for sharing and retaining memories for both personal and social functions. Among the most important of these functions is the establishment of a self-history that serves as a source for self-understanding and an enduring self-concept. The succeeding chapters provide additional observations on the emergence of the self through the reflections of the social world.

Other Memory Functions

Autobiographical or personal memory can thus be seen as one form of episodic memory, but it constitutes only one function of memory. An important question to raise is: "Does social construction apply to the development of memory in general after the infancy period?" For example, do children who experience more narrative talk and thus remember more from their personal experiences also prove to be better at other memory tasks, such as those encountered in school? Weinert (1991) has reported considerable dissociation between tasks such as story memory and memory for word lists in the early school years. This finding is not surprising if memory constitutes a set of cognitive functions, rather than a general capacity or ability; it will enter into different activities in different ways. In particular, the kinds of personal memories discussed here may form the foundation for understanding stories, dramatic play, and even histories. Narrative formats are important to all of these, and familiarity with narrative forms makes memory and understanding in these kinds of activities easier. It is unlikely, however, that these formats support learning the multiplication table or other mechanical or rote forms of memory, or that they necessarily support memory for facts in school domains.

However, it is plausible that these other forms of memory are also social collaborative constructions dependent upon linguistic form. Consider those children who experience primarily paradigmatic memory talk with parents. Are they doomed to have no autobiographical memories? Probably not. Recall that the paradigmatic children in Tessler's (1991) study recognized almost as many of the pictures that they had taken on their walk as did the narrative children, although they spontaneously recalled fewer and talked about the experience and the pictures in less elaborate ways. The recognition results suggest that they may remember similar parts of the experience, but that their ways of verbalizing that underlying knowledge have not been honed in the same way as that of the narrative children, who have learned to bring the information to recall and to organize it in narrative fashion.

It is worth recalling that Bruner (1986) emphasized the narrative mode of cognitive organization to contrast with the paradigmatic, which he believed had been up to that point the primary – if not the only – focus of studies in cognitive psychology. But the emergent recognition of the narrative mode of thought should not deny the significance of the paradigmatic, which after all retains its preeminence in what Vygotsky (1986) referred to as scientific (or academic) thought and Donald (1991) as theoretical, and which is much valued by educational systems. As Mullen's (1994) study indicated, parents in other cultures, such as in Korea, may emphasize different aspects of the child's experience and knowledge.

Certainly there is no evidence that Korean children are less capable in memory tasks such as those encountered in school. Indeed, quite the reverse may be the case, according to international educational evaluations. The point here is that memory functions from preschool to the school years and later are fostered by the social-cultural conditions and values of the society. The effect is especially notable and dramatic in the evolution of the personal memory system, but it is not confined to that system.

Recall that Donald's (1991) thesis emphasizes that memory comes to rely on external memory aids, a proposal that was a central part of Vygotsky's theory as well (1978; Van der Veer & Valsiner, 1991). These aids, from the use of knots to the use of written notes, mathematical formulas, graphs, and libraries, make possible the construction of culturally shared as well as individually understood memory systems and formal thinking. Very few of these aids are either available to or used by children in the preschool years. By the end of the preschool period children's memory has become socialized through discourse practices at home and school. However, in important ways it remains an individual and experiential memory system. Memory may be cued from external sources, and may be shared with others, but children do not yet have access to all the memory resources of the society through written and graphic materials, electronic media, and institutions such as schools and museums. Moreover, the content held in memory during these years tends to consist of what is of personal interest to the child, whether fleeting or enduring. Use of memory for engaging cultural knowledge systems under the demands of pedagogical goals, aided and directed by the artifacts and procedures of society's schools, still lies ahead. Through these means the child's memory escapes from the confining boundaries of personal experience into the broad historically situated cultural world at large.

In summary, it may be concluded that narrative models and influences in early childhood help to transform the episodic memory system into a long-lasting autobiographical memory for significant events in one's own life, and thus a self-history, determinant to a large extent of one's self-concept (Nelson, 1993a). Categorical models and influences from language, in discourse with parents and teachers, help to transform generic or semantic memory into a long-lasting general knowledge system organized in terms of the theoretical knowledge domains of the society, particularly as transmitted in school. In the case of "narrativized" personal memory, the system provides the model and some of the content transformable into all the historical, mythological, literary, and metaphorical or analogical forms of discourse and argument. In the case of socialized categorical memory, the system is open to transformation through all the theoretical schemes of the society and scientific or logical forms of argument, Donald's "theoretical mind." As Bruner (1986) has persuasively argued, narrative and paradigmatic (or categorical) are different forms of thought, and, as discussed in Chapters 7 and 8, they have different developmental histories in the functional memory systems. As will also be made evident, however, they are intertwined in development, and as some have argued (e.g., Polkinghorne, 1988) they are intertwined as well in adult human thought at the highest levels.

7. Emergence of the Storied Mind

Socially constructed narratives as organizers of children's nascent auto-biographical memory were a central focus of the previous chapter. According to the account sketched there, narrative constructions develop in collaboration with adults and serve to structure the child's memory for personally meaningful experience. Such a theory encompasses two major functions of narrative: narrative as a discourse genre, organizing conversational interchanges; and narrative as a form of thinking. As noted previously, both Bruner (1986) and Donald (1991) claim that narrative serves a broader, social and cultural function of myth-making, establishing shared narratives that convey culturally significant messages. In a similar vein, Miller (1994) and her colleagues have suggested that narrative is a socializing form, conveying through narratives of personal experience the ways of being and behaving within a particular social-cultural group.

These varying functions of narrative in human society and in children's lives, and the claims surrounding them, raise important issues of relevance to cognitive development. If, as Bruner (1986) proposes, narrative is a universal mode of human language, is it a universal mode of thought, as Donald's theory as well as Bruner's proposes? Is it then also an innately determined mode of thought? Or does it develop in response to cultural models, as suggested in Chapter 6? If the latter, what is the course of development, and what role does narrative play at different developmental points in the child's construction of mental models? These questions, related to how narrative is acquired, developed, and used, are themes of this chapter.

Stories, tales, and myths are told in all human societies. It may be that narrative forms are universal because they are natural to the way that humans interpret events, and are essential to the temporal perspective of social-cultural life. Carrithers (1991) proposes that *narrativity* is "a

distinct capacity . . . a property of the human species which differentiates it from other species. . . . It is narrativity which allows humans to
grasp a longer past and a more intricately conceived future, as well as a
more variegated social environment" (p. 306). Carrithers emphasizes the
complexity of social relationships within any society (kin and status
relationships, for example) as well as their definition through events that
take place over long periods of time (for example, marital relations,
career achievements). The types of such relationships "are constituted
by, and are only conceivable within, a wider social and temporal setting:
a church, a community, a university" (p. 309). Narrative is essential in
providing the framework for articulating these complexities.

The Schank and Abelson's (1995) claim is simpler: Stories constitute social
intercourse; they are what social communication is all about. In consequence, in their view human cognition is basically formulated in terms
of stories, and logic, classification, and rational inference are all in some
sense derivative from storytelling. These claims fit well with Donald's
(1991) general thesis, that narrative is the "natural product" of language;
it precedes and is the source of theoretical thinking.[1]

Whereas Carrithers views narrativity and its associated "mindreading"[2] from a phylogenetic and sociological (rather than an ontogenetic and psychological) point of view, he rightly suggests that the
broader conception has implications for the narrower. To put it in the
framework here, the child lives and grows in a social and cultural world.
Language is used for social and cultural purposes, and the child comes
to share in those purposes, often quite directly through experience with
linguistic forms and functions. The functions that narrative serves for
adults and within the social community are reflected onto the child,
who, in play, in taking on pretend roles, and in negotiations with peers
and adults, enters into the social complexities of the world shared with
adults.

The question here is: "What is the course of development?" On the one
hand the claim (Bruner's, Schank & Abelson's, Carrithers's) appears to be
that narrative thinking directs narrative discourse – we tell stories because that is the way we think of the world. On the other hand, evidence
indicates that narrative forms vary culturally (Bartlett, 1932; Gee, 1991;
Heath, 1982; John-Steiner & Panofsky, 1992) and developmentally (Applebee, 1978; McCabe & Peterson, 1991; Peterson & McCabe, 1983), suggesting that narrative discourse develops as a product of cognitive organization, social interaction, and cultural models provided through linguistic
forms. From this perspective, we learn to tell the kind of stories that our

social world values, and our storied thoughts come to conform to the models of our society. These different proposals can be evaluated only if what counts as narrative is first clarified.

What Is Narrative?

It is quite clear from recent writing that for most authors "narrative" is one of those Humpty Dumpty words that may mean whatever one wishes it to. Although the skeletal scripts that 3-year-old children provide are far from what adults think of as mature narratives, they nonetheless reflect at least one very basic characteristic of narrative: the sequencing of events through time. Indeed, Labov and Waletsky's (1967) basic definition of narrative goes no further; they define a narrative as "any sequence of clauses which contains at least one temporal juncture" (p. 28). One of the 3-year-olds in our early study of scripts provided the following account when asked to tell "what happens when you go to a restaurant":

(1)   You eat and then you go home.[3]

Except that it is in the present tense, this meets Labov and Waletsky's minimal definition.

   Dictionaries tend either to be circular, as in *Webster's New World Dictionary of the American Language* (Guralnik, 1974), which defines "narrative" as "Of or having the nature of, narration," and "narration" as "The act or process of narrating"; or to equate narrative with story, as in "narrate": "To tell (a story) . . . to give an account of (happenings, etc.)" and "narrative": "A story; account; tale." Narrative is often further delimited to fictional tales, but again broadened to encompass history, one's life story, and so on.

   As Labov's definition implies, temporal organization is basic to narrative. McCabe and Peterson (1991) relied on this facet of meaning in providing the following definition for their authors, who were charged with discussing narrative development: "The oral sequencing of temporally successive events, real or imaginary." Yet Gee (1991), author of the first chapter in their collection, explicitly contradicts the idea that temporality is the central characteristic of narrative, emphasizing instead its thematic structure. His point is certainly well taken, in that a simple temporal sequencing of actions, as in (1), seems to most people to be an impoverished narrative at best. Good stories seem to need more than temporal structures.

Polkinghorne (1988) takes the broad view, considering narrative to be "the primary form by which human experience is made meaningful. Narrative meaning is a cognitive process that organizes human experiences into temporally meaningful episodes" (p. 1). This definition embodies three crucial concepts concerning narrative: (1) it is cognitive; (2) it is temporally organized; and (3) it consists of episodes, which are meaningful and also, by implication, discrete. "Episode" is another undefined but intuitively understood term; for the present it is sufficient to note that episodes constitute parts of the whole of narrative.

Bruner's (1986) conception of narrative goes beyond the temporal perspective of action to incorporate what he calls the "landscape of consciousness," that is, the interpretation that humans put on actions and events in terms of goals, motivations, intentions, beliefs, affect, and values. Emerging here is the idea that an action sequence on its own is meaningless, providing only the skeleton but not the flesh of an event; similarly, a meaningful narrative involves not only temporal organization but also thematic content. Going further, Carrithers (1991) considers the distinction that Bruner made between the "landscape of action" and the "landscape of consciousness" as a false one, claiming, "In our evolutionary past, as in our later history, the landscapes of action *and* of consciousness have been part of one real and determining flow of deeds and mortal consequences" (p. 306). Therefore, from the developmental point of view we may inquire as to whether and when children incorporate the landscape of consciousness into the landscape of action. Are these ever separate in ontogeny, or do they constitute from the beginning a single "flow"?

Narrative Structure

Implicit in virtually all definitions of narrative and of narrative structure is the unfolding of actions through time; thus time and temporal and causal relations are central to the concept of narrativity. Time of events may be ordered in two ways. One way is locative, and is essentially deictic, the location of time with respect to the present. For this purpose it is necessary to specify whether an event took place in the past, is an ongoing experience, is anticipated in the future, is a generic representation of a type of event, or is in "irreal" time, a fantasy, counterfactual, or a possibility. These different event perspectives are captured in linguistic form in terms of tense, locating an event in some time-space. This location can be contrasted with the alternative temporal perspective realized in terms of sequencing actions and states within an event that is itself located in time. These may be thought of as extra- and intranarrative perspectives of time. In general, tense indexes the extra perspective, and aspect and relativizing terms index the intra perspective.

Story grammars (Mandler & Johnson, 1977; Stein & Glenn, 1979) were developed to model the sequence of actions in constituent episodes, organized around problems and the resolution of problems. The organization of prototypical classical children's stories is the usual focus of story grammars, aimed at explaining the mechanisms by which people, including young children, can comprehend and interpret the meaning of stories. Story grammars incorporate goals to be reached by protagonists, and obstacles that are overcome to attain goals. These analyses have revealed that memory for story components is affected by the role played by each component in the structure of the story, for example, the relation of each episode to the main goal (Stein & Trabasso, 1981; Trabasso & Van den Broek, 1985). In story grammars, the structure is hierarchical and recursive, so that the complicating actions may build up indefinitely. Many stories, songs, and chants for young children reflect this kind of recursive structure, as in "The House that Jack Built" or the "Story of Epaminondas" (Mandler & Johnson, 1977).

"High-point" analysis (Labov & Waletsky, 1967; Peterson & McCabe, 1983) rests on the assumption that a story – whether a narrative of some personal experience in the past or a fictional narrative – has a "point" toward which the beginning parts orient, and away from which the ending parts carry it to a conclusion. The high point is not necessarily related to a goal; rather, it typically incorporates some surprising element that blocks the narrator's expected outcome, and that therefore must be resolved in some way. The parts of a good, complete narrative from this perspective include an orienting statement providing context, complicating action detailing the trouble that is the point of the story, an evaluation of the happening, a resolution, and perhaps a coda or formal ending (e.g., "And they lived happily ever after"). In the high-point scheme, the complicating actions are the major "on-line" components, the actions that take place in a sequence along a time line. Narrative clauses may be distinguished in terms of being "on-line" event clauses and "off-the-line" clauses, the latter providing context, description, and evaluation of the mainline events being recounted.

Another very general approach to structure was described by Bruner (1986; Bruner & Lucariello, 1989) in terms originally set forth by Kenneth Burke (1945). Good stories, according to this analysis, involve *"characters* in *action* with intentions or *goals* in *settings* using particular *means*. Drama is generated . . . when there is an imbalance in the 'ratio' of these constituents. . . . [A] character . . . is in an inappropriate setting, or an action does not warrant the goal to which it is leading a character" (Bruner, 1986, p. 20). In this analysis, the who, what, where, when, why, and how form the basis of the narrative structure. Thus, lying behind any story is the implicit assumption of the canonical event, which unfolds unproblematically in terms of expected actors, actions, times, places, motives, and instruments; the point of the story comes from deviations in these constituents. The canonical event that for Bruner assumes central importance is precisely Schank and Abelson's (1977) script (or the general event representation) in disguise, the default assumption for any culturally recognizable event.

Like stories, scripts[4] are temporally organized structures composed of sequences of actions leading to a goal within a specified temporal and spatial location; they incorporate as well expected actors, props, and the objects of actions. These elements are specified in terms of "default values," the components that are assumed if no specific items are mentioned or encountered in a particular instantiation of the script. Some scripts determined by cultural convention (such as birthday parties) have little causal structure; others incorporate both weak (enabling relations) and strong causal relations among actions and states. Thus scripts may well form the basis for constructing and understanding more specific narratives, as Schank and Abelson (1977) claimed, and as research with young children has supported (Nelson, 1986). In the Burkian scheme explicated by Bruner, a narrative (or a "good story") is constructed around deviations from the canonical event, deviations that then need to be explained or resolved. As Bruner and Lucariello (1989) note, "trouble" is what drives a narrative. "Actions do not reach goals, scenes and agents do not match, instruments and goals are out of kilter, and so on. The narrative is a vehicle for characterizing, exploring, preventing, brooding about, redressing, or recounting the consequences of 'trouble'" (pp. 76–77). These mental states provide the "landscape of consciousness," which complements the "landscape of action." Thus it is the intentionality of the actors that provides the consciousness, and ultimately the meaning, to the story.

Structure may be considered in terms of the temporally organized constituents that form the plot of a narrative, but it may also be thought of in terms of basic *themes*, which stand outside of time as reflections of universal human experiences and conditions, instantiated in narratives in varying forms. Whereas in most story analyses the sequence of events is the core of the construction, the narrative includes more than the bare temporal sequence. It is these other parts that provide the *meaning* of the narrative. More provocative, Gee (1991) stakes the claim that space, not time, is basic to narrative, and it follows that theme, not plot, is central. Basic themes recur in culturally significant stories, whether generated by schoolchildren or enshrined in sacred texts. Such a claim is basic also to Propp (1968) and the Russian Formalists, who view the *fabula*, universal recurring themes, as what the story is about – "ambition thwarted by vanity, self-defeating greed, lost love" (Bruner & Lucariello, 1989, p. 77). In this formulation, the *sjuzet* is the particular instantiation of the *fabula* in story form.

These claims do not exhaust the views of narrative that we might consider from a developmental perspective, but they are sufficient to suggest that narrative structure has two essential dimensions: temporality (its syntax), theme or meaning (its semantics). If we take the simple chain of actions in time as the basic stuff around which narrative is woven, the weaving constructs a meaning out of the added strands that project the narrator's attitude toward the events, and the perspectives, intentions, motives, and attitudes of the actors within it. Whereas the temporal structure of the narrative seems (at first glance) rather straightforward and readily subject to developmental analysis, the meaning dimension is more elusive (as meaning always is).

In summary, narrative is the unfolding of events through time as told from a particular perspective of time, person, and situation, involving a departure from the expected canonical happening of events that requires reflection and explanation; and it may explicitly or implicitly recapitulate recurrent enduring, perhaps universal, themes of cultural significance. The microstructure of a narrative emerges from macrostructure as the parts from the whole, bound together through the narrative devices of discourse grammars. As with any form, however, there may be partial realizations of the ideal, proto-narratives or incomplete or distorted forms of varying kinds.

Narrative Development

To what extent are young children capable of understanding or producing narratives of the kind proposed in these analyses? How do their narrative structures originate and develop? The construction of narrative rests on an underlying conception of the event narrated – both its canonical and deviated forms. It has been amply demonstrated that mental event representations (MERs) are basic forms of cognition available in early childhood that may therefore support narrative development. It is of particular interest to narrative development that (contrary to original expectations based on Piaget's theory) very young children are extremely accurate in remembering temporal sequence, and especially sequences that have causal components. Such action sequences, of course, are central components of narrative structure. From the point of view of the skeletal definition of narrative as two or more actions temporally related, sequential processing ability would be a sufficient cognitive base for the interpretation and production of narrative. However, the more complex characterizations outlined here show scripts to be diluted narrative forms, typically lacking a landscape of consciousness, and not exhibiting problems and resolutions or universal themes. In addition, important questions arise in terms of how the cognitive representation is realized in linguistic form, and how that form may reflect back on and transform the underlying representation.

Narrative constructions in thought and discourse must therefore involve a complex of structures and related skills. On the basis of the discussion thus far, narrative development must include the following dimensions:

- The ability verbally to project events in time, including the temporal and causal relations among events.
- The ability to formulate connected discourse using cohesive linguistic devices and to understand discourse so connected.
- The ability to differentiate the canonical from the noncanonical and to mark events in terms of necessity, probability, and uncertainty.
- The ability to take the perspective of different actors and of different temporal and spatial locations.
- The ability to resolve deviations from the expected course of events in humanly and culturally understandable terms.
- The capacity to recognize and reformulate enduring culturally significant themes.

These different abilities may be expected to be revealed in children's own narratives, whether based on experience or fantasy. They may also be expected to enter into children's comprehension of narratives told by others. One important fact must be kept in mind in these considerations: Extended discourse, whether narrative or paradigmatic in form, requires the cognitive and linguistic capacity to set up and *hold in mind* a *representation of a complex reality formulated in language.* Certainly, as argued in Chapter 5, narrative discourse is not possible until complex language is learned;

it depends upon the manipulation of extended language forms, which requires a reasonably complex level of language competence. Therefore, we need to consider in more detail here what the grammar of narrative requires, as well as the other components identified previously.

Narrative Displays

To understand the development of narrative, it is important to ask: "What is the role that narrative plays in children's lives?" Narrative can be displayed in many nonverbal forms – in dramatic play, in dance, in mime, through pictures or silent film. Indeed, Donald's (1991) thesis (Chapter 3) that mimesis preceded language as a symbolic form implies the priority of these forms of narrative. Yet, as Donald also claims, the natural product of language is narrative; certainly language seems the natural vehicle of narrative, and it is in language that narrative has been primarily examined by scholars. On the other hand, the existence of narrative in nonverbal forms suggests the possibility that as a form it may develop independently of language, or at least that there may be other contributions to its development. Children not only hear stories read from books but also watch narrations on television and in films, and construct narratives in play.

Miller (1994) emphasizes that children from a very young age are exposed to varying kinds of personal narratives, stories from real life told by adults. Many such stories are told to other adults, in the presence of children, and are thus formulated in adult terms for adult interests; when these stories are overheard by children, who may attend or not, they may take in in passing the general structure and dramatic form of such narratives. Other stories are told by adults to other people about the child, thus inviting the child's interest and attention. In addition, adults collaborate with the child in telling a tale about something that has happened, whether previously shared with the adult or not, for example, in drawing out from the child something that has happened in preschool. The latter collaborative narratives have been the focus of most of the research attention on parent–child constructions of the past, as described in Chapter 6. However, Miller emphasizes that the frequency of exposure to adult tales, and the interest that children express in them, have been underestimated as an influence on the child's own developing narrative competence. Indeed, in her research with working-class parents, collaborative telling was less frequent than the tales told in the presence of the child to other adults, although cultural differences are to be expected with regard to such practices.

On the basis of her studies of parents and their children in natural settings where other adults are also present, Miller (1994) has found that personal storytelling is extremely common, and she claims that it is "a pervasive, orderly, and culturally-organized feature of social life in every culture" (p. 159). She sees storytelling as a major mechanism of socialization. It is an important part of the "flow of social and moral messages [which] is relentless in the myriad small encounters of everyday life" (p.159). Her claims grow out of the theory of discourse socialization, namely, that "Young children are socialized into systems of meaning through recurring interactions with family members which are mediated by particular types of discourse" (p. 160).

Applied to socialization in general, this view sets the consequences for the child, which include both the acquisition of narrative skills and self-construction (other consequences may emerge as well) in a broader framework where the outcome is a by-product of practices that serve other social functions. That the outcome is a by-product rather than a focal goal does not render it less important, but this may have implications for how we study it, and the assumptions we bring to the study. For example, if the "past talk" that has been the focus of much parent–child discourse research in recent years is not designed to teach children how to construct the past or how to remember, but rather serves other social functions, it might be important to search for context features that determine when such talk is effective in providing models. Or, a matter that Miller (1994) and her colleagues emphasize, the exchange of stories by adults takes place only when more than one adult is present, but our current research paradigms tend to isolate one parent and one child for analysis, thus screening out opportunities to observe the full range of discourse that children may be attending to, including the range of personal storytelling, which may provide the most important models for the child of how to tell a dramatic tale.

The kinds of personal narratives that Miller (1994) and her colleagues have collected include content that is violent, fearful, and dramatic, such as verbal and physical threats and assaults, as well as natural processes such as childbirth. Content was skewed in the negative direction, but humor and modes of dealing with threatening events were emphasized and provided the opportunity for the child to learn behavior appropriate to such situations, as well as discourse patterns.[5] Some of the stories that adults exchange involve reports of the child's doings, and the children naturally attend to and enter into such stories, but the aim of the telling is similar to that of the adult reports – to make a good, that is, a dramatic story out of the happening. This is no doubt where the child learns to focus on the "point" and to bring out the meaning. But the meaning in these oral tales resides as much in the emphasis that prosody, phrasing, and nonverbal gesture provide as it does in the words that are used.

Miller and Moore (1989) have suggested some of the lessons that children may be learning from these stories. The first task, they suggest, is for the child to pick out stories from the rest of the ongoing talk, one clue to which is the "affectively tinged" nature of the narratives. "Even before the child can fully understand the spoken language in the story, he or she may pay attention to the paralinguistic and nonverbal features that are abundantly available in storytelling – the rhythmic contour of the story, the shifting voice quality of the narrator, the exclamations of the listener, and the accompanying gestures, facial expressions, and postural changes" (p. 441). It is notable that a highly salient characteristic of Emily's first crib monologues at 21 months (Nelson, 1989c) was her use of an appropriated "story voice" to mark her nascent narratives, with raised pitch and extended contours, easily differentiated from the "play voice" that she used in discourse with and around her toys. By 2 years she incorporated other voices (e.g., her mother's and father's) into her monologues, differentiating quotations from these sources from the ongoing tale. These observations support the supposition put forth by Miller that prosody and other metalinguistic markers set narrative off from other types of discourse for the child. Emily's monologues indicate that they are not only set off, but also used as models incorporating these characteristics.

Once the child has achieved a level of verbal competence sufficient to follow the linguistic line, she or he may begin to respond verbally, to try to tell part of the story, and then to listen actively for stories. Among the provocative observations coming out of this program of research is that young children occasionally "appropriate" others' stories (Miller et al., 1990). Examples are cited from children in a preschool class reformulating what they have heard from others in the first person (thus appropriated to self), and from a child who converted his mother's story of falling when she was a child into his self-narrative. Miller and colleagues conclude that narratives in these cases may "be functioning as a means by which the child vicariously relives another's experience" (p. 304).

A different interpretation of such appropriations, plausible within the framework presented here, is that the dual representational potential of the verbal form at first obscures for the young child the source of the representation – whether internal or external. This possibility is related to the observed heightened suggestibility of 3- and 4-year-old children's memory for events (Ceci & Bruck, 1993; Doris, 1991). This interpretation is nonetheless consistent with the comments of Miller and colleagues (1990): "When a child appropriates another's experience as his own or allows another's story to call forth a related experience from his own past, he has extended personhood beyond the skin. The line between the child's experience and the other's is blurred" (p. 304).

As discussed in Chapter 6, much recent research has documented that parents talk with their children about episodes they have shared in the past, as well as commentary on the child's present experience. Parents also spend considerable time talking about events anticipated in the future. References to future events were most prevalent in Emily's parents' pre-bed talk [see also Benson (1994)]. The narrative model of talking about the future is quite similar to that for talking about the past, and tends to be based on scripted formulations – scripted for the adult, that is, but often novel for the child. In contrast to the vicarious participation that Miller (1994) and her colleagues emphasize, in these studies the narrative is told for the child's benefit, and in Emily's case, at least, it is often told and retold as the child requests. Consider the following excerpt, from an exchange between Emily and her father when Emily was almost 28 months, talking about what will happen on the weekend:

(2)　F: Well after, then we're going to come back and have lunch and then you're going to have a nap, and then after your nap we're going to have a hot dog at the ocean, with the S's, and Mr. and Mrs. S., and, and their kids, and a bunch of other kids are going to have hot dogs at the ocean, and then we're going to come back . . .

　　　E: And we can sit in the ocean!

　　　F: Yeah, we can sit in the ocean, yeah, if it's a warm day, in the sand you can sit in it, we'll be, take your bathing suit . . . it's like your pool, only it's much bigger, and there's sand.

　　　E: And I can splash!

　　　F: And you can splash, you bet!

　　　E: And I can . . . [kicking]

　　　F: Yes you can. Well, we're going to have a lot of fun, but you know, you've got to be rested, so, in order for us to have all that fun . . .

E: I want you to tell me about the [picnic]
F: Tell you about the what?
E: [picnic]
F: Picnic? Well, that's on Sunday . . .

   . . .

F: . . . we're going to get up and have breakfast and mow
the lawn, and go to an antique store and have a nap and
go to the ocean and have some hot dogs.

Emily very frequently picked up on these accounts and elaborated them to herself after her parents left the room, for example:

(3) [we are going] . . .
at the ocean. .
ocean is a little far away,
baw, baw-buh-buh (x2) . . .
far away . . .
I think it's couple blocks away . . .
maybe it's down downtown and across the ocean and down
  the river
and maybe it's in
the hot dogs will be in a fridge
and the fridge will be in the [water] over by a shore
and then we could go in
and get a hot dog
and bring it out to the river
and then [Ss?] go in the river and [bite] me,
in the ocean,
we go to the ocean,
and ocean be over by I think a couple of blocks away,
but we could be,
and we could find any hot dogs,
um, the hot dogs gonna be for for the beach,
then the [bridge? fridge?]
we'll have to go in the green car
cause that's where the car seats are.
I can be in the red car
but see I be in the green car,
but you know who's going to be in the green car.
Both children,
I'm going to be in the green car in my car seat,
Stephen going to be in the green . . .

This example illustrates that the child has picked out a few pieces of the parent's narrative, and has woven them together with her own knowledge base of events, such as what car will be used for the trip. This appears to be a variant "appropriation" of the parent's account, in that pieces (but not the whole) become part of her imagined future. One should not underestimate the complex reasoning that is involved in this construction, but it must be recognized as well that there is little evidence here of comprehension of the narrative given as a whole piece, in spite of Emily's advanced linguistic uses.

These various kinds of narratives – past, present, future, self, and other – and the contexts in which they are experienced – dyadic sharing and collaboration, group participation – provide models for the child's own construction of personal narratives, considered next.

Children's Personal Narratives

The relation between event knowledge, narrative discourse, and narrative thinking is seen in emergent form in Emily's crib monologues, as in the example just given (see Chapters 5 and 6 for the source of the data). Consider next the following excerpt from a pre-sleep monologue at 32 months:

(4) Tomorrow when we wake up from bed, first me and Daddy and Mommy, you . . . eat breakfast eat breakfast, like we *usually* do, and then we're going p-l-a-y, and then soon as Daddy comes, Carl's going to come over, and then we're going to play a little while. And then Carl and Emily are both going down the car with somebody, and we're going to ride to nursery school, and then we when we *get* there, we're *all* going to get *out* of the car, go *into* nursery and then we will say good*bye*, then he's going to work, and we're going to play at *nur*sery school. Won't that be funny? Because sometimes I go to *nur*sery school cause its a nursery school day. Sometimes I stay with Tanta all week. And sometimes we play mom and dad. But usually, sometimes, I um, oh go to nursery school.

The monologue then repeats the day's sequence, with variation.

This long account of what will happen tomorrow, incorporating the event script of her everyday experience, demonstrates that Emily at $2\frac{1}{2}$ years is capable of constructing extended connected discourse about events. But unlike the affectively tinged personal narratives that Miller has emphasized, this is an unremarkable but cheerful anticipation of the future, no doubt modeled on the parental pattern. Still, it demands a functional explanation that goes beyond the parental model. Such an account is not a memory, although as noted previously some of Emily's narratives were of specific memories. In Chapter 6 it was pointed out that Emily's memories had the quality of being *representative* of everyday experience, and this anticipatory fragment is clearly a *representation* of some importance to her. Consistent with this observation, it appears that the first and primary function of the narrative form in Emily's mono-logues was to establish the canonical events of the child's world from which other narrative types emerged. We can understand this best as the search for stability in the dynamic of experience.[6]

Bruner and Lucariello (1989) suggested that the "timeless" recounts that Emily produced [such as (4) above] were close to the "gist" or the "fabula" that underlies all instances of actual stories. An alternative inter-pretation views the theme or "fabula" as emerging from the "breach" in the canonical event. The *fabula*, according to their account [based on Propp (1968)] lies beneath the actual recounting of a happening, where the recounting is a representation of an event that is basically canonical (and therefore meaningless) with one or more deviations. It is the devia-tions, not the canonical form, that enable the theme to emerge and pro-vide the meaning. There is a possible conflation here of two kinds of timeless structures – the canonical form of the event (what happens usu-ally during the everyday) – and the underlying theme that speaks to the "trouble" in the event. Emily's canonical retellings (what happens when her parents take her to nursery school, what one needs to take to the airport) do not recapitulate themes such as loss, triumph, fear of the unknown, love, jealousy, and so on. Rather, they express her understand-ing of the quotidian, the banal, the expected. It is therefore the unex-pected, the deviation from the usual, where one would expect to find greater perspective-taking reflecting the "landscape of consciousness." That is where enduring themes might be expected to emerge through specific stories or *sjuzets*.

However, Bruner and Lucariello's (1989) analysis found that the forms that indicate temporal and personal perspective appeared more fre-quently in Emily's timeless monologues than in the specific episodes. This observation is consistent with previous analyses (e.g., French & Nelson, 1985) showing that temporal terms, among other abstract rela-tional words, appear earlier in children's accounts of well-known scripts than they do in production or comprehension of novel stories. Later, when the forms are well under control, they can be used to structure the novel as well as the familiar. Such a progression was illustrated by the form " 'cause" in Chapter 5. The suggestion here is that Bruner and Lucariello's observations were appropriate to the linguistic stage of Emily's development, but their theory is appropriate to a later stage of lexical and discourse structure. Thus the apparent contradiction can be understood in terms of related developments in both linguistic forms and narrative structures.

The canonical event does not always unfold as expected, and as Bruner claims, it is the trouble – the breach in the canonical form – that impels the narrative to emerge to resolve the problem. Emily's monologues were indeed replete with problems and attempts at resolution. Consider the following – (5) is from the early period at 2 years, and (6) is from the later period at $2\frac{1}{2}$ years:

> (5) maybe Carl turn, or maybe Emmy turn, or maybe Stephen turn, or maybe Lance turn or Danny turn. I don't, I don't know what boy bring book tomorrow. Maybe Lance. I don't know (whether), which boy bring book today. Maybe Danny or maybe Carl, maybe my, maybe Lance, maybe (too-wee). How about Lance bring book . . . Carl bring book . . . one . . . boy's (Jewish) . . . and bring (?) what if (for) doing. What if (for) Carl bring Dr. Seuss book for my. Maybe my get Dr. Seuss book from Carl, maybe . . . the bear . . . the book. Maybe . . . boy book it . . . maybe . . .   (24 mo.)
>
> (6) Today Daddy went, trying to get into the race but the people said no so he, he has to watch it on television. I don't know why that is, maybe cause there's too many people. I think that's why, why he couldn't go in it. . . . So he has to watch it on television . . . on Halloween day, then he can run a race and I can watch him. I wish I could watch him. But they said no no no. Daddy Daddy Daddy! . . . No no, no no. Have to have to watch on television. But on Halloween Day he can run, run a race. Tomorrow (he'll) run (???) He says yes. Hoorary! My mom and dad and a man says "you can run in the footrace," and I said "that's nice of you. I want to." So next week I'm going to . . . run to the footrace and, and run in the footrace cause they said I could.   (32 mo.)

In (5) the trouble is in the unspecified slot-fillers – who brings the book and what book will be brought to the baby-sitter's. The canonical event is clear enough, and serves as background to the problem. However, the "trouble" does not have a clear resolution – no one and no thing is settled on, although many are considered. The problem remains a problem rather than a narrative (cf. Feldman, 1989).

In (6) the canonical event is unstated and less clear but the problem is well specified: Daddy cannot run in a race that he wanted to run in. Here Emily creates a resolution that includes not only Daddy but herself ("I'm going to run to the footrace cause they said I could"). We could speculate in each case as to how much of the content of these examples comes directly from discourse with parents; the point is that the structure of the problem-resolution narrative is emerging here against the background of Emily's clear mastery of temporal and causal structure of events. It is in fact an important finding that Emily gained control over the temporal-causal structures of narrative, and the linguistic forms important to their construction, as she formulated her own model of herself in her social world, which, as Carrithers (1991) has emphasized, is a world of temporality [see Nelson (1989b), and Chapter 9]. On this evidence, the initial use of personal narrative for the child alone is as a structuring of the mental model of the world, and this mental model in the form of MERs provides the basis for further uses of narrative in fantasy construction, alone or with others. From this stronghold Emily could move on to speculate and even to fantasize about events that might happen or imaginary characters that could engage in possible events, events made possible by her own sturdy understandings of real life – the mental model of EMILY'S REAL LIFE WORLD.

Structure of Personal Narratives.   The social construction of personal narratives by young children in family contexts, for example, at the dinner table (Blum-Kulka & Snow, 1992), reveals that there are both familial and cultural differences in the amount and kind of such experiences. The function of "telling one's day," a common practice in these settings, is rather different from the function that Emily's monologues served. Rather than focusing on the representative and canonical, it requires focusing on points of interest to the group, deviations from the expected. Telling about events that others have not experienced, common in middle-class American homes, requires the child to practice skills that go beyond those needed to participate in retelling of shared experiences, where the narrative may be scaffolded by the adult. These practices are relevant to those used in school, where personal narratives are elicited, at least in the United States and Britain, in the common practice of "sharing time" or "show and tell," in which preschool and young school-age children are encouraged to recount for the benefit of the group some experience they have recently had.[7]

Many studies of children's productions of personal narratives have attempted to trace developmental trends in the structure imposed. Peterson and McCabe (1983) studied a large collection of personal narratives from children aged 4 to 9 years. Children were asked (informally) to recount some personal experiences, they were given little in the way of scaffolding, and it was assumed that their productions were reflective of individual narrative abilities. Peterson and McCabe traced the complexity of children's accounts in terms of length and of inclusion of the components identified in Labov's and Waletsy's (1967) high-point theory (discussed earlier). They concluded that children by the age of 6 years have developed an adult pattern of narrative for these kinds of accounts. The youngest children, however, tend to jump from one event to another within what is presumably a single episode, and 5-year-olds tend to end at the high point, without a conclusion.

As implied in Miller's studies of adult narratives, emotion is an important organizing component of stories, children's as well as adults'. Hudson and her colleagues (1992) studied 4-year-old children's narratives about events that involved different emotional states – happy, mad, and scared. They found structural as well as content differences among the different types. Negative emotions (scared and mad) tended most frequently to be organized around a plot in which actions were causally structured with a climax involving the emotion, and with an identifiable theme such as success, escape, or trickery. In contrast, happy stories tended to be either simple chronologies or "moment-in-time" stories, that is, stories dwelling on a specific situation rather than a sequence of actions. Hudson and colleagues suggest that children acquire "emotion genres," and they consider several possible sources (e.g., implicit modeling, cultural forms, inherent in the emotional experience). They stress that different emotions are embedded in different kinds of narrative structures, and that the classical plot story found for these young children's stories of anger is not necessarily a marker of sophisticated development; its absence from children's accounts may reflect their emotional content, not their narrative ability. In a related vein, Stein, Trabasso, and their colleagues (e.g., Stein, Trabasso, & Liwag, 1993; Trabasso et al., 1992; Trabasso & Stein, in press) have emphasized the relation of emotions and their expression in children's narratives to the goals and plan structure of the narrative.

The Discourse Grammar of Personal Narrative. Reporting an event in sequence is a very complicated cognitive maneuver, requiring the child to hold in mind the present time, then to move back (or forward) to the beginning of a prior event, move forward again through the event and reach the end, then move forward to the present. It is not a simple referencing of something from the past. It is not surprising that children might need help in reconstructing events from the past at a time when they already are quite competent at reporting how things generally are. The latter script-type knowledge is assumed to be the basis for all their active understanding of how things are in the world, who does what, and so on. They are very practiced at and have firm control of this kind of knowledge. But to reconstruct a specific instance of what happened is a different matter.

Narration graphs were constructed for some of Emily's monologues to show how the sequence of action unfolded in the narrative. These graphs [reproduced from Nelson (1989a)] were based on Chafe's (1986) unit of analysis, the intonation unit (IU). Here each IU was graphed against each proposition as it was produced over time. A narrative that unfolds simply from beginning to end will then produce a straight line at a 45-degree downward-sloping angle; one that is repetitive will circle back on itself more than once. One narrative is reproduced here (Figure 7.1) to show the circular production of an early monologue (from 21 months) that focused on a single event [(2) in Chapter 6]. The second graph shows the straightforward construction of the account of an episode at 33 months [(3) in Chapter 6; reproduced below as (7)]. The graphs were constructed to reveal the cognitive units entering into the child's construction of narratives, following Chafe's (1986) hypothesis that narratives are structured in terms of intonation units, which map onto memory units and are formed into wholes that represent a larger cognitive unit, or chunk. It can be seen from these graphs that one aspect of development may be that of learning how to move a narrative forward rather than recycling. Sequencers such as *so* and *and* are often used to introduce phrases or clauses, and they are shown in the graphs in Figures 7.1 and 7.2 for this purpose.

It may be that connectives relate intonation units to one another to form a structured whole. This speculation is related to the questions of how the child's mastery of the forms of linguistic narrative is affected by the forms of thought, and how the latter are influenced by the former. The relation between narrative development and language development

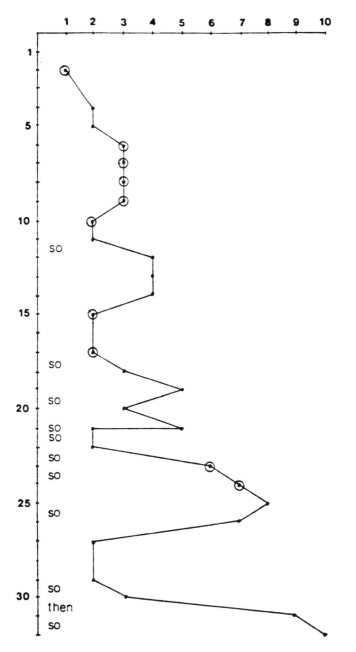

Figure 7.1. Narrative graph of monologue (2), Chapter 6. *Note:* Event sequence on horizontal axis; proposition sequence on vertical axis. Circles indicate full stops. *Source:* K. Nelson, *Narratives from the Crib* (1989c). Permission to reprint from Harvard University Press.

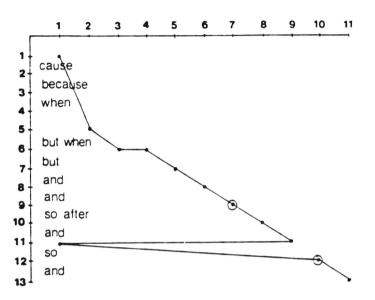

Figure 7.2. Narrative graph of monologue (3), Chapter 6. See source note to Figure 7.1.

may be reciprocal: To tell and to understand narratives, children must acquire particular linguistic forms; but the experience of hearing and telling narratives provides practice with specific linguistic devices that are in fact central to the competent use of language.

The microstructure of narrative is concerned with how the parts are made to hang together to compose the whole, the issue of cohesion in text. Narrative cohesion goes beyond much of what has traditionally been considered in the discussion of child language development, which has focused on the units of phoneme, word, and sentence. Cohesion relies on relative clauses, causal connectives, anaphoric pronominal reference, and, most especially, temporal relationships. The development of these aspects of complex syntax cannot be studied in abstraction from their discourse functions. That such components function in larger discourse structures – and may thereby be influenced by the larger structure – has generally been considered of secondary interest and importance. Indeed, Karmiloff-Smith (1986b) concluded that children do not have a "discourse grammar" adequate to the task of cohesive discourse, including especially narrative, until after age 5. Before that time children are assumed to have a "sentence grammar" useful for pragmatic purposes. But more recent evidence indicates that this conclusion was premature.

Three aspects of relations in the text have been considered within the developmental literature, as well as in the adult literature: (1) use of temporal expressions, especially tense and aspect, to convey actions, states, and relations among them within the narrative and to place the narrative itself in time; (2) use of relational terms, including temporal, causal, and conjunctive terms, to relate actions and express relations among them; (3) use of pronouns to express relations among actors within the narrative.

Consider, for example, the narrative produced by Emily at 33 months (shown also in Chapter 6 and graphed in Figure 7.2):

(7)   We *bought* a baby.
      [*False starts:* cause, the, well because, when she, well]
      we thought it was for Christmas,
      but when we went to the store we didn't have our jacket on,
      but I saw some dolly,
      and I yelled at *my mother and* said
      I want one of those dolly.
      So after we *were finished* with the store,
      we *went* over to the dolly and *she* bought me *one*.
      So I have *one*.

This narrative illustrates each of the textual relations noted above: (1) manipulation of tense (perfective – *were finished* – as well as simple past) and temporal adverbs (*when, after*); (b) connectives (*but, and, so*); (c) cohesive pronouns (*she, one*). Thus there is evidence from this example at $2\frac{3}{4}$ years that Emily has acquired a number of the devices that are thought to be critical to the construction of narrative texts. This evidence strongly suggests that sentence grammar and discourse grammar develop as interdependent systems rather than the latter waiting in the wings while sentence grammars are finalized. Analysis of Emily's monologues revealed that some of the devices needed can be found only in connected discourse (Levy, 1989; Levy & Nelson, 1994). Most analysis of children's grammar use only single sentences as evidence, thus failing to find evidence for cohesive forms connecting two or more sentences. Moreover, in most psycholinguistic studies children are not observed in circumstances where they produce extended discourse, so their knowledge of cohesive devices is not relevant and is not revealed.

Anaphoric reference is one of the major cohesive structures that hold a text together. It involves the use of pronominal forms to refer to entities previously introduced in the discourse. Adults use anaphoric pronouns to differentiate major and minor characters in a narrative, but research with young children has shown that preschoolers do not use anaphoric pronouns systematically to refer to characters previously introduced (Karmiloff-Smith, 1986b). But evidence for this claim comes from asking children to tell or retell a story with pictures, where children can easily use the pictures as a prop and do not need to use pronouns cohesively.

In contrast, Levy (1989) analyzed 2-year-old Emily's use of the cohesive pronouns *it* and *that,* revealing gradual changes in the function of the forms. Although these pronouns were used in appropriate contexts from the beginning of the study, they were at first used without full control of their adult coreferential function, that is, as referential indices[8] (Silverstein, 1985). Rather, similar to the findings reported in Chapter 5 for " 'cause," these forms were acquired to fit discourse patterns borrowed from adult speech, in particular, appending *did that* or *did it* to the end of a series of clauses, as in the following examples:

(8)   when my slep
        and and Mormor came
        then Mommy coming
        then get up
        time to go home
        time to go home
        drink p-water[9]
        yesterday did *that*   (1;11.8)
(9)   Mommy Daddy Mommy put my in bed in my regular bed
        actually actually Mommy did *it*   (1;11.8)

Later developments showed that the forms gradually were freed from specific discourse patterns and were used to refer in extended narratives to long sequences of talk or text.

These uses first for well-developed script topics, followed by application to novel formulations, are consistent with the use of other forms in children's script productions (French & Nelson, 1985). Even the youngest children's scripts included temporal and causal linking terms ("so," "when," "then," "because"), conditionals ("if . . . then"), disjunctions ("or") and adversatives ("but"). We concluded that children's event knowledge supports their ability to produce scripts, as well as the cognitive "slot-making" into which to insert the relational terms appropriate to forming a coherent sequence. Thus basic event knowledge not only appears to provide an important part of the macrostructure, but also supports the development of the microstructure of narrative. Just as our script studies showed that children used more advanced linguistic forms when they were forced to verbalize their knowledge about events without pictures or props, additional studies are needed to investigate children's use of cohesive pronouns when no pictures or props are available.

Children begin to use connectives to hook the parts of the narrative to one another very early, as the examples presented thus far have illustrated. Sequencers are used to connect two clauses that express events on a time line, and *and* sequencers (including *and then*) are the most frequently used (Peterson & McCabe, 1991). *So* and *because* are used to mark causality (see Chapter 5), *but* to mark contrastive relations, although all these connectives are also used in nonsemantic, pragmatic ways to mark beginnings, for example.

It has been assumed that connectives provide the glue that holds the events in the story together. However, a striking finding in Peterson and McCabe's (1991) study was that when they eliminated all the connectives from children's narratives, the lack did not interfere with adults' interpretations or judgments of the stories. That is, the connectives were used by children in appropriate contexts to glue clauses together within the story, but the glue was unnecessary for the listener to make sense of the story. What then was the function of the connectives – might they help the child speaker to keep the sequence straight? Of course, children's narratives are often transparent in terms of sequence – events follow each other in the order in which they occur, or if they are misplaced it is evident to adults that this is the case. Temporal relations in adult narratives may be much more complex, and connectives might be much more vital to their comprehension. Indeed, even in stories for children, relations can be much more complex than they are in children's own productions. Children might then pick up the use of connectives in a nonsemantic but discourse-pragmatic appropriate formal way prior to understanding their actual functional use, as was apparent for Emily's use of *so* and the pronouns *that* and *it* described earlier [see Levy & Nelson (1994) for a generalization of this argument].

Given the importance of time in the structure of narrative, a major issue for narrative development is the child's understanding of and ability to manipulate the expressions of time in linguistic form. As noted at the outset, there are two temporal dimensions to be mastered: the location of the narrated event in some time frame, and the sequencing of actions within the event. Tense and aspect are the grammatical forms critical to these functions, and their acquisition begins usually around the end of the second year, followed by the first temporal adverbs and prepositions used to locate events in time (Weist, 1986). Further consideration of these developments is deferred to Chapter 9, which is specifically focused on time concepts.

In summary, on the basis of children's productions of personal narratives, it is clear that preschool children have the basic temporal structure of narrative well under control. Their personal narratives reflect different types of narrative structure, appropriate to different kinds of emotional content. Between $2\frac{1}{2}$ and 5 years they gain in fluency and elaboration, but even the youngest children display a sense of the drama inherent in deviations from the expected or safe and the language forms appropriate to their expression.

Fantasy Narratives for and by Children

In addition to talk about personal experiences, reading stories to young children is a common practice in Western society, especially in middle-class homes and schools. Story listening is a major exposure to narrative forms, and the structure of stories written for children would seem to be ripe for analysis. However, little such analysis from a psychological process point of view has been undertaken. Heath (1982, 1983) led the way by pointing out different ways of reading stories, and the different expectations that are set up for the children who hear them, as well as the possible cognitive consequences.

Story understanding at 2 years has not been extensively studied, although it is widely observed that children hear books "read" to them by parents from as early as 12 months. But what can and do 2-year-olds make of stories? Most analyses of book reading with children of this age have focused on mother–child exchanges about the topic of the pictures and the child's acquisition of topic-relevant words (e.g., Evans & Schmidt, 1991; Snow & Goldfield, 1983). For these young children mothers often simply describe what is in the pictures of a storybook rather than produce a connected story line (Trabasso et al., 1992). Mothers do not seem to expect very young children to attend to more than one pictured situation at a time; they do not expect their children to attend to an extended story line and do not produce one. This is hardly surprising if children have not yet acquired the skills of attending to connected discourse and building a representation from it.

An analysis of Emily's "reading" of a storybook to herself ("Dandelion") that had been read to her by her parents when she was 26 months showed that she had gleaned bits and pieces of the story but not the connected story line (Nelson, 1991a). Although she was looking at the

Table 7.1. *Emily's story recount (25;18) (based on* Dandelion *by Dan Freeman)*

Emily's monologue	Page: Text
I am Dande . . . lion (?)	27: I'm Dandelion he roared
and (it's) it's raining outside	31: It began to rain in torrents
and you better come outside with me/	
I am Dandelion.	
I wanna play with you.	
(???)	
(and she)	
I want to	
and then (it was) raining	
and she said	
Why don't you take uh nothing,	
it's sunshine out here	34: and the warm sunshine came bearing down
I (??) Dandelion likes it	
(mother?) you cannot keep it	
(??) don't you	
(other mother?)	
(mommy?)	
Dandelion	
I am coming to your party. now	24: I've come to your party, he answered
I came already	
It was good the (handsomely?)	
One all alone.	
(???)	
Dandelion . . .	
and I know you had a letter.	3: There was a letter . . .
A little outfit	
Outfit I have it	
I Dandelion woke up	1: On a sunny Saturday morning D woke up
and outside	3: He put on his sweater and went outside . . .
and he's a . . .	
and then he's a	
he will have a happy	
what then	
then he went alone at home	
for a *friend*	
I'm mother.	
No hat mother	30: And his snappy cap blew off
I am not wearing a hat	
I got fancy clotheses mother	18: What a dapper dandy he had suddenly become

Table 7.1. (*cont.*)

Emily's monologue	Page: Text
I am coming to your party for goodness sake. And that's something. I am coming very soon. and that's when, pretty soon.	24: I've come to your party
I am Dandelion I am just a lion And ??? everything	27: I'm Dandelion he roared
(??) flower.	36: he spied 3 dandelion flowers

Source: Table reproduced from *Journal of Narrative and Life History 1*, 2 & 3, 1991, p. 121, with permission of the publisher, Lawrence Erlbaum Associates.

book and turning the pages to follow the pictures, the parts that she reproduced were not in sequence, and were frequently distorted in the direction of her own life experience. Emily was a highly verbal child who had been listening to stories for many months at this time and apparently greatly enjoyed them. Table 7.1 [reproduced from Nelson (1991a)] shows that she may have internalized very little of the structure of what she was presented with. In this table Emily's monologue accompanying her turning of the pages of the book is shown on the left, while related passages from the book, together with their page numbers, are shown on the right. It can be seen that Emily's "pieces" of text are filled out with imagined bits from her own experience, that the sequence of the story is not maintained, and that a whole does not emerge from the parts.

If this evidence correctly represents her memory and comprehension of this story, it suggests that children younger than 3 may be getting something from stories but not what the author or adult reader expects or intends. For example, it was striking that Emily had acquired not only a "reading voice" or "storytelling voice" (elevated pitch, extended intonation pattern), but also the ability to imitate characters speaking in different voices. A recent study of private speech in fantasy play (Mitchell, 1991) supports the suggestion that one of the most important elements that children may acquire from stories is the variety of voices and roles that characters may play. This is an aspect of development that has been little studied, however.

Further evidence is available in the fascinating account (Wolf & Heath, 1992) of one child's absorption of the language and themes of fairy tales into her own life and fantasy from an early age, mainly beginning at about $3\frac{1}{2}$ years (although there are examples from as early as her second year as well). A related account is provided by Miller (Miller et al., 1993) of her son's repeated reinterpretation of the story of Peter Rabbit in terms of his own life and emotional states. These scattered examples suggest that children may begin story understanding in terms of bits and pieces that appear relevant to their own experience, and reconstitute the "story" in ways meaningful to their own lives. Much more systematic analysis on this topic over the years from 2 to 6 is needed.

The suggestion that children appropriate stories to their own lives raises the question as to whether children differentiate between fantasy and real-world stories. According to Applebee (1978), children do not recognize that the stories they hear are make-believe: "As long as stories are seen as true, or at least. . . . simply an inversion of the true, they can only present the child with the world as it is . . . " (p. 41). Applebee concluded that 6- and 9-year-old children may cling to the idea that favorite characters belong to the real world after they have begun to accept that stories do not necessarily have to be about real things. For example, one 6-year-old was interviewed as follows (child's responses italicized):

> Is Cinderella a real person – *No* – Was she ever a real person? – *Nope, she died.* – Did she used to be alive? – *Yes.* – When did she live? – *A long time ago, when I was one years old.* – Are stories always about things that really happened? – *Yes.* (Applebee, 1978, p. 44)

In Applebee's study about half the 6-year-olds maintained some convictions that fictional stories are about the real world, and 9% of 9-year-olds did as well.[10] These findings, which have not been widely cited or replicated, may have important implications for understanding how children interpret stories in the preschool years, and for their difficulties with differentiating stories from personal narratives and scripts. If from the child's point of view stories are real events of other people's lives, then one's own accounts of real-life events must also be stories in the child's view. This implication may help to explain the findings from story production studies showing that children produce script-like "stories" when asked to tell a story (see discussion in the following section).

That story understanding may grow in a nonlinear pattern is suggested by study of story memory by 3- and 4-year-olds (Zazanis, 1991). Children were presented with a story about familiar activities that reported either a simple, highly predictable script (going to the grocery store) or a less predictable arbitrarily sequenced episode (a visit to a park); the story either was presented only verbally or was accompanied by illustrations. We expected that the 3-year-olds would depend more upon the pictures to follow the story than the 4-year-olds, and that this would be more true in the arbitrary than the routine story. Unexpectedly, we found that the 3-year-olds gave longer reports and used more temporal and causal language when they heard the arbitrary story without pictures than in any of the other conditions, although they made more sequencing errors, and their recounts were typically very short. This pattern of results suggests that the 3-year-olds were actually distracted by the pictures, and that they were not able to coordinate and integrate the information that was being simultaneously presented in both pictorial and verbal modes. They were, however, able to retain the contents (but not the sequence) of the story when it was presented only verbally. Again, this study suggests that children may use different strategies to grasp parts of a story, depending on background knowledge and story presentation conditions.

Studies of language development have found that children employ both global and analytic strategies in mastering sentence structure, sometimes focusing on whole phrases and sometimes analyzing into parts and reconstituting the parts into new wholes (Nelson, 1981; Bates, Bretherton, & Snyder, 1988; Pine and Lieven, 1990). Something similar may be the case for the understanding of narratives. Script structures may help children to grasp the whole when a familiar script is relevant to the story; isolating bits and pieces that relate somehow to aspects of the child's own life – particularly affectively laden aspects – from less clearly understood wholes may be an alternative strategy for beginning to grasp meaning. These suppositions are clearly only speculative at present and rest on too fragile a database.

Developing Story Structure

The analysis of children's own story productions has a considerable history in child study. Applebee (1978) reanalyzed stories from children 2 to 17 that Pitcher and Prelinger (1963) originally gathered from children who were simply asked on various occasions: "Tell me a story." Applebee's basic analysis used terms introduced by Vygotsky (1986) for the analysis of children's conceptual development, characterizing stories from less to more developed in terms of heaps, sequences, primitive narratives, unfocused chains, focused chains, and finally narratives. An example from Applebee of the least developed story (although quite long by the standards of most studies with preschool children) is the following, from a boy aged two years and eleven months:

> (10) The daddy works in the bank. And Mommy cooks break-
> fast. Then we get up and get dressed. And the baby eats
> breakfast and honey. We go to the school and we get
> dressed like that. I put coat on and I go in the car.// And the
> lion in the cage. The bear went so fast and he's going to
> bring the bear back, in the cage. (p. 59)

Applebee's examples of the various types of story productions do not clearly distinguish among the intermediate kinds. But the final stage of narrative, produced by some of the older preschool children, is more or less equivalent to the problem-resolution narratives identified by other researchers (Mandler & Johnson, 1977; Stein & Glenn, 1979; Gruendel, 1980). An example from Applebee is the following, from a boy aged four years and ten months:

> (11) Once there was a doggy and a little boy. This doggy was
> pretty silly. He ran away from the little boy and went far-
> ther and farther away. The little boy caught the doggy. He
> reached out and caught the little doggy with his hands. He
> put the doggy down. The doggy ran away again. He came
> near a railroad track. He stepped on it and the train ran over
> him. But he was still alive. This was a big white bull dog
> and he wanted to go back to his home. When the little boy
> went back home he found the doggy. He was happy. His
> doggy was still alive. (p. 66)

These stories are considerably longer than the averages reported in the recent literature for children of 3 and 4 years. For example, Hudson and Shapiro (1991) found that preschoolers in their study produced a mean of fewer than 6 propositions per story (about the same as for personal narratives and scripts). We cannot be certain what the difference between the studies was that might account for the difference in length. It might be that the children in the Pitcher and Prelinger study were used to telling stories in school and thus were practiced and encouraged in the art. Or Pitcher and Prelinger might have selected among the productions those that were most interesting. And in both the Hudson and Shapiro study and the earlier study by Gruendel (1980), children were given topics to tell stories about, which might have diminished their inventiveness and thus their length.

Gruendel (1980; Seidman, Nelson, & Gruendel, 1986), who was interested in the issue of how stories might be differentiated from scripts, gave children of 4, 6, and 8 years themes to organize a story around, for example, "building a campfire" or "planting a garden." She reported that the majority (63%) of stories told by 4-year-olds in her study were classifiable by structural and content characteristics as simple scripts and most of the rest (30%) as personal episodes. Stories told by 6-year-olds were either scripts (60%) or simple transformations or elaborations on scripts, with only 6% problem resolutions. For example a garden might be said to grow lollipops. Even the 8-year-old children produced 43% scripts and only 7% accounts that could be classified as stories, with the remainder story variants – elaborations, transformations, or problem resolutions (14%). Stein (1988) also gave children (kindergartners and third and fifth graders) topics to make stories from and, consistent with Gruendel's findings, reported that only 11% of the kindergartners' stories were goal-based with obstacles to be overcome. Almost half were non–goal-based.[11]

Hudson and Shapiro's (1991) study with preschoolers and children in the first and third grades that compared the structure and content of scripts, stories, and personal reports found similar results. Using previous theories, Hudson and Shapiro looked for the following elements of a well-structured story in children's productions: (1) a formal beginning and orientation introducing setting and character; (2) initiating events, goal-directed actions; (3) a problem preventing the achievement of the goal; (4) a resolution of the problem; (5) a formal ending device. The preschoolers in this study produced stories that were reported in the present tense, characteristic of scripts. They "were very capable in reporting what they knew or could remember about the events, but could not restructure that knowledge into a story format" (p. 123). First graders used more fictional characters, but only a little more than a third of their stories included a problem-resolution structure. Although third graders included setting statements, problems, resolutions, and endings in more than half their stories, they still lacked explicit reference to internal states, goals, and reactions.

Consistencies among these studies of children's story productions implicate scripts as the source of young children's stories. Note that the first story presented by Applebee (1978) as an example of a heap (10) also contains as a major part an "early-day script" in which the activities of the different family members on a typical morning are recounted. Note also that this part of the story is told in the present tense, appropriate to the script form, and typically used by children in preference to the past tense when reporting familiar events. The latter part (not differentiated by Applebee) differs from the first in not only the apparent shift in time and space, and in characters (bear, lion), but also in the shift to the past tense. In contrast, the story told by the older child (11) displays not only plot and theme (loss and recovery) but also both characterization ("silly doggy") and perspective of the characters ("the dog wanted to go home, the boy was happy to see him"). It is appropriately told in the past tense throughout. Thus by late in the fifth year this child has moved beyond the script format to the complexities of plot and of the "landscape of consciousness."

Stein and her colleagues [see Stein (1988); Trabasso & Stein (in press)] analyzed children's productions; the children were given a story stem for completion (e.g., "Once there was a girl named Alice. Alice lived by the seashore."). They found that the youngest children (3-year-olds) produced descriptive sequences with no temporal order; older children developed action sequences (without causal order) and reactive sequences (including causal relations and emotional reactions). From 5 to 9 years, children constructed incomplete episodes, and later more complete episodes. They emphasize that by 5 years children tell stories and narrate events organized in terms of goals and plans, indicating that they use this structure to interpret novel events. This may enable them to move beyond the script in their story productions.

Analyses of younger children's story productions have uncovered little evidence of the semantics or meaning of Bruner's "landscape of consciousness." In pursuit of this dimension, Lucariello (1990) studied kindergarten children's attempts to resolve the discrepancy from the expected unfolding of a familiar event (a birthday party). She hypothesized that children would invoke a character's intentions when there was a breach in the canonical form of the story. For example, in a story of a birthday party the action "threw water on the candles" was substituted for the canonical "blew out the candles." Children were asked to suggest reasons for the action, or in the case of affect, for the affective reaction. In comparison with the canonical version, children provided more explanations of the character's intentional states (the "landscape of consciousness") when responding to breach versions of the story, supporting the hypothesis that imbalance in the story structure components evokes the move into the subjective plane of the minds of the actors. This suggests that at least by kindergarten age, children are sensitive to this dimension even if they often fail to incorporate it into their own productions.

What about the universal themes that organize culturally significant narratives? Under some circumstances, the fantasy narratives of young children may be quite revealing of children's concerns and understanding of the world they live in (Paley, 1990), even though they tend to be quite short and simple in structure. For example, two stories from Paley's kindergartners:

>   (12)   A little girls is losted. The mother finded her.   (p. 71)
>   (13)   There was a lion. And he saw a bad guy but first he didn't see him because the bad guy was in a tree but he heard something strange. Then he saw the bad guy so he asked him "Why are you in a tree?" "Because someone said I was bad." So the lion told him he wasn't bad. So he came down. The end.   (p. 67)

As these stories exemplify, the tales that these children constructed often incorporated those "enduring themes" of loss and recovery, moral transgression and remorse, and so on, although the literary resources for incorporating them into coherent narrative structures are not yet sufficient to make "good sense" from an adult's point of view. The storytellers' peers, however, apparently accepted these tales as satisfactory on their own terms.

Taken together, evidence from children's own personal narratives and fantasy stories indicates that these productions incorporate significant features of narrative structure, theme and plot, and become more complex and complete toward the end of the preschool and into the early school years. It is not surprising that even by 6 or 7 years of age, children are not yet skilled storytellers. But they apparently know a good story when they hear one by that age. They have the canonical event well under control but have not differentiated the discrepancies from the canonical sufficiently to construct a good story, and they have not focused on motives and intentions sufficiently to provide a rich landscape of consciousness. Overall, the results of these studies of children's story productions indicate that when children produce stories in response to an experimenter's request, the products reveal little of the complexity or rich motivational understanding that is found in stories in children's literature sources, books or magazines, much less that of adult literature. Do children see the events they participate in in this simplistic, straightforward, two-dimensional way? Or is the rich context simply hidden from our view? Do the enduring cultural themes found in folktales and fairy stories resonate in children's own thinking about the world? Unfortunately, on these issues we have more speculation than reliable research at this point.

What Develops

Earlier in this chapter six abilities were suggested as necessary to the development of narrative competence. It is now possible to summarize what this review reveals about children's developing understandings and attempts to produce narrative and what must develop further in the school years or later.

The ability to project events in time verbally, including temporal and causal relations, is well-documented in children 2 or 3 years of age, reflecting the underlying cognitive ability to order events that has been established in infancy as mental event representations (MERs). The ability to formulate connected discourse using cohesive linguistic devices is evident in script productions at 3 to 4 years, and was found in Emily's monologues by $2\frac{1}{2}$ to 3 years. Less certain is children's ability to use the devices in connected discourse to interpret episodic accounts from other people, whether in story or other narrative form.

On the other hand, the ability to take the perspective of different actors and in different times and places appears uncertain at best during the early years, given the suggestive evidence that children assimilate stories to their own life experience. As will be seen in Chapter 10, children's understanding of others' perspectives develops slowly over the preschool years. And Applebee's (1978) study of children's understanding of the reality of story characters implies a very weak grasp of broadscale temporal and spatial perspective.

Preschool children have a firm grasp of the canonical nature of routine events, and mark the noncanonical as uncertain and contingent. They use this base for engaging in fantasy play, and for constructing stories when asked. They incorporate bits of stories that they hear into their own fantasy life as well. They do not seem to differentiate the routine from the "troubled," however. Thus they do not produce problem-oriented stories or provide resolutions for disruptions of canonical events.

Do young children recognize the enduring cultural themes that are incorporated into folktales and fairy stories? There is no evidence on this point that I know of. Logically, it would seem that a child would need to be capable of comprehending the story line (the *sjuzet*) before internalizing the *fabula*, and it seems probable that much experience with listening to stories during the childhood years is required before a story line becomes comprehensible.[12] The advantage of the recursive story lines of a tale such as Epaminondas lies in its structural repetition. Similarly, the repeated requests for the same story by preschool children suggests that it may take many tellings before a full and coherent tale is understood. On the other hand, pieces of the story may be identified as relevant to one's own life and incorporated into the child's own personal story.

Representational Development and Narrative Competence

In line with the suggested development outlined in Chapter 5, a sequence in terms of the capacity to utilize event representations as a basis for developing narrative competence can be constructed, as follows.

The first phase involves the capacity for "reading off" an MER in verbal mode. Children as young as $2\frac{1}{2}$ are able to do this, in skeletal form. At a similar age a child may be able to "read off" an MER of a one-time (nonscripted) experience.

Next, a child might be able to listen to an account (a story, a memory, a plan) of another person and match it to some story of her own, a script or memory. Schank and Abelson (1995) suggest that this is what normally goes on in adult conversations. The child might contribute bits of her own story to that of the adult, as Miller's (1994) studies show.

Much more complicated is the situation where the child is presented with a story that does not match one of her own and must then construct the others' stories from scenes that she has available in MERs. If she does not have appropriate scenes, she may use whatever is available from her own experience, transforming the tale of Peter Rabbit into the tale of her own flower garden, for example (Miller et al., 1993), or transforming Rapunzel into herself (Wolf & Heath, 1992). Because this process is complicated and fault-ridden, it is likely to result in many misunderstandings and fragments. Children may request that a story be told over and over while they work on this construction.

Eventually, a child may be able to construct a new story of her own from available scenes in MER, producing a "made-up story." Not all children are likely to find this a worthwhile or enjoyable pursuit, but by 6 to 8 years many are able to do so, and when an encouraging context is provided, as in Paley's (1990) classroom, or in the groups that provided

Applebee's (1978) corpus, many transformations of reality into fantasy occur, from children aged 3 to 5 years.

Understanding or constructing a coherent whole story from disparate scenes on one-time hearing or telling is no doubt a late development. Practice in this skill is provided in activities in preschool as well as in homes as children are exposed to story-reading and to requests for "sharing" time accounts. In the process, children not only learn how to engage in coherent narrative discourse but also are exposed to the particular forms and "fabulas" of their culture. Far from being a natural unproblematic form of thinking, however, as some suggest, storytelling and story understanding require practice. Nonetheless, because stories reflect the shared human concerns of everyone in the social world, they seem to fit very well into our ways of understanding the world, of "making sense." Thus, with practice, narrative takes over a large part of our thinking, taking the basic script knowledge that we begin with and overlaying it with more complex understandings of the world and its people. The narrative mode is established as both internal and external representations, carrying with it the universal and specific values of the social and cultural world within which the individual lives.

As Miller (1994) has emphasized, narratives are the source of socialization into the ways of the social-cultural world, a proposal that fits very well with Donald's (1991) and Carrithers's (1991) speculations about the role of narrative in cultural construction. What can we expect children to learn from narratives? A few of the domains that are displayed in the personal narratives and fantasy stories that they hear in the early years include ideas about time, space, geography, religion, gender roles, biology and the natural world,[13] socioeconomic groups, and moral reasoning and actions. Certainly narratives are important for children's developing understanding of the actions and intentionality of other people and reflections on the self. Narratives are an important source for deriving abstract concepts about emotions, attitudes, character (e.g., the importance of striving for goals and resisting evil), and *fabula* – the enduring myths and fables of one's culture, and the proverbs and moral lessons that these convey. Narrative can support these developments because it provides the organization of the whole that makes the content memorable. Yet during the years when narrative is becoming an important cognitive organization, its very attraction appears to fuse fantasy and reality. Animals behave like people; monsters and ghosts, princesses and frogs all share the world of vicarious experience. The experiential world of the child is enormously enlarged through narrative, but at the same time the world represented in stories may become a confusion of real and irreal, as well as a confusion of yours (or theirs) and mine, raising the question: "Whose story is it, anyway?"

If all these kinds of knowledge derive from narrative experience, and narrative understanding is a developmental achievement, one may expect an interaction of narrative development and understanding in these social-cultural domains of dramatic quality during the late preshcool and early school years. Much of psychological development during these years may take place in the telling, retelling, transforming, and reconstructing of stories for oneself and for others.

.

III. Developing Conceptual Systems

8. The Emergence of the Paradigmatic Mind

Are hierarchical category structures natural products of human cognition independent of language? Or do they depend on language for their development? As discussed in Chapters 4 and 5, language is based on categories of various kinds, from phonemes to sentences to word classes and lexical referents. Moreover, as reviewed in Chapter 4, research has documented that infants categorize objects at varying levels of generality from global to specific. Perceptual categorization is characteristic, not only of human infants but of all complex organisms that must distinguish between food and not-food, species members and others, for example. Thus categorization is basic to cognitive functioning of all kinds, and certainly to the construction of event representations, mimetic symbols, basic and complex language, and narrative.

However, hierarchical categorization or taxonomic classification goes beyond this basic level. It operates on basic categories and sets them into new order relationships with other categories at the same level and at higher and lower levels. These operations are engaged in by people in all cultures (Berlin, 1978), who form "folk taxonomies" of plants and animals, for example. The questions as to when children are capable of engaging in these kinds of ordered relations, and what cognitive competencies are required (for example, what logic), have long been topics of study in developmental psychology. As with the assumption of basic numerical and grammatical principles, there is now an implicit assumption on the part of many researchers that infants and young children have basic taxonomic principles that are displayed under conditions of learning the appropriate language, or being given appropriate materials (e.g., MacNamara, 1982; Waxman & Gelman, 1986). This assumption is bolstered by the observation that natural language (e.g., English) incorporates hierarchical category structures, with superordinate and subordinate branchings, and that children learn and use the terms applicable to the different levels in ways that appear to reflect the level distinctions. For example, they learn to apply the term "animal" to groups of diverse animals, and "dog" to members of the *dog* class. However, as outlined below, it has been argued against this observation that children's uses do not reflect the same understanding of the categorical relations that adults' uses do. The issue of levels of categorical thinking by young children has been the focus of intensive study by Piaget, Vygotsky, and many other developmental psychologists. Although young children and adults use the same language terms to refer to categorical structures, children may associate concepts with their category labels that are different from the concepts of adults, in terms of both intension and extension, as both classic and contemporary studies have revealed. How these concepts, and word meanings, evolve into their adult counterparts is a fundamental developmental problem.

The assumption defended here is that, although children do possess certain cognitive skills that enable them to form categories and hierarchies, acquisition of the taxonomies of a given cultural and linguistic community is a result of exposure to and experience with the language used to formulate them. Taxonomic principles of inclusion and asymmetry emerge from these acquisitions and are not prior or prerequisite to them. These assumptions are based in turn on the observation that hierarchical categories of even the most concrete kind, such as "food" and "animals," much less abstractions, such as kinship relations, are formulated in language and exist as cultural abstractions, not as concrete realities. There is certainly a reality to hierarchies, but it is a symbolic cultural reality, not a material reality. Therefore, the questions addressed here include: "What are the cognitive skills and organizations underlying the process of forming categorical hierarchies?" "How do they relate to the representations already in place?" "How are they applied to the representations in language that the child meets in the course of everyday discourse?"

Concepts and Categories in Developmental Psychology

Research and theorizing on concepts and categories, from the earliest perceptual categories to highly abstract theoretical structures, has proliferated in all branches of psychology over the past 30 years (Smith & Medin, 1981; Harnad, 1987). The vast majority of this research has been focused exclusively on object categories to the neglect of less obvious, more dynamic, more general and abstract categories. Therefore, in what follows, "category" should be assumed to refer to "object category" unless otherwise noted.

The classic theory of concept structure held that concepts are composed of the logical combination of separately necessary and jointly sufficient features. Although this conception has been largely abandoned in philosophy and psychology over the past 20 years, it was the basis for the classical work in the development of concepts and categories, including that of both Piaget and Vygotsky. Piaget (1962; Inhelder & Piaget, 1958) held that young children, being logically deficient, are incapable of forming true concepts. They are necessarily limited to preconcepts: concepts that rest on prototypes, that confuse the whole with the part, and that do not coordinate intension and extension. Piaget's early research concerned the reference of words by very young children, including what to a logician is the oddity of referring to one's grandmother's house as "Lausanne," the name of the town (confusing part with whole); or referring to each individual slug as "the slug" (confusing intension with extension). Later, Inhelder and Piaget (1958) studied the composition of categories in a well-known series of class inclusion tasks. The class inclusion task requires a subject to answer questions of the following kind: "Here are four daisies [pointing to a group] and six roses [again pointing to pictured flowers]; are there more roses or more flowers?" As has now been well established in further studies, children aged 7 or younger reply that there are more roses.[1] To Piaget this indicated that young children cannot coordinate intension and extension, and that they cannot maintain the parts and whole separately to set up the equation $A + A' = B$.

Vygotsky, like Piaget, accepted a classical logical definition of concept, and, based on his work with a concept formation task similar to one used by Inhelder and Piaget, he also concluded that younger children were preconceptual (Vygotsky, 1986). He found that children move through a sequence of preconceptual stages of heaps, chain-concepts, collections, and pseudoconcepts. True logical concepts, he maintained, are not achieved until adolescence, with the construction of taxonomic hierarchies. Vygotsky saw the problem of conceptual change in childhood in terms of the difference between spontaneous and scientific concepts. He summed up the issue as follows:

> The two processes – the development of spontaneous and of nonspontaneous concepts – are related and constantly influence each other. They are parts of a single process: the development of concept formation, which is affected by varying external and inter-

nal conditions but is essentially a unitary process, not a conflict of antagonistic, mutually exclusive forms of thinking. (p. 157)

For Vygotsky (unlike Piaget) the move from spontaneous concepts to "scientific" concepts rested essentially on uses of language. In his view the most important characteristics of mature thought are (1) generality and (2) systematicity, and he held that these characteristics are absent from the concepts of preschool children, and that scientific concepts are acquired through formal instruction.

Luria, Vygotsky's close colleague in the 1930s, ventured to test these ideas through studies of peasants and workers on newly collectivized farms in the Soviet Union. These studies, published in English in 1976, presented category choice problems, such as the following: Of hammer, wood, ax, and saw, which does not belong? The results of these studies indicated that uneducated adults group items thematically rather than categorically. For example, they said that the wood goes with the other items, because you use the ax and the saw to cut wood. Tulviste (1991) reexamined these studies and others in the light of Vygotsky's theory and Leontiev's (1978) extension of it in terms of activity theory. He argues that Vygotsky's ideas about the difference between scientific and spontaneous concepts reflects a basic difference between the use of words and categories in different activities. The claim is that scientific thinking often uses the same linguistic terms used in everyday activities, but that everyday language does not reflect the same logical structures, which are a product of schooling. This conclusion implies that young children's thinking does not employ categories in the same way or of the same type as adults' thinking.

In contrast, the contemporary understanding of young children's thought and concepts, as it has emerged over the past decades, is that they are similar to those of adults, although with a much restricted knowledge base. An important influence in this direction was Rosch's (1975) work, which introduced the idea of the *basic* level of a natural language semantic hierarchy, the level at which members of a category are most similar to each other in terms of shape and motoric actions and most differentiated from members of other categories at the same level. According to this proposal, basic level categories have higher *cue validity* in comparison with subordinate categories (which share more features with other categories at their level) and superordinate categories (in which members share fewer features). Rosch and her colleagues established that categories at the basic level have psychological salience for both adults and children. They observed that children tend first to learn names for object classes at the basic level, for example, "dog" and "car," rather than at a higher superordinate (e.g., "animal") or lower subordinate (e.g., "collie") level (Anglin, 1977; Rosch et al., 1976).[2] Prior to Rosch's work, Brown (1958a) suggested that parents tend to label things on the basis of the greatest functional utility for the child, and that, in general, words are used at the level of greatest utility within a particular context (an important and still little recognized principle).

Rosch's work on the internal structure of categories suggested parallels between the Piagetian and Vygotskian view of conceptual "deficiency" in the younger child and the way that adult categories are composed. Rosch (1973, 1975, 1978) proposed that the internal structure of natural language categories is organized around prototypes; that categories have graded structure, with more central and more peripheral members; and that categories are structured in terms of family resemblances (Wittgenstein, 1953), that is, overlapping features, none of which are either necessary or sufficient. Rosch also emphasized that attributes of objects are not randomly distributed in the world, but form patterns of correlated attributes. For example, having feathers is associated with having wings and with flying, whereas having fur is associated with different attributes, such as having four legs. Rosch's results implied that young children are not different from older children and adults in their basic conceptual structure. Rather, human concepts at all ages are formed around central exemplars or abstracted prototypical features (these are two different kinds of prototype models). And although children's concepts lack consistent logical structure (as Piaget claimed), so do adults' concepts.

Certainly one of the major effects of this line of work was to highlight the real conceptual and categorical competencies of very young children and even infants (e.g., Mervis, 1987; Bauer & Mandler, 1989b). This research has opened up issues about the basis for children's initial conceptual structures, and the developmental course of categorical organization. These developments relate to the basic proposals outlined here in terms of mental event representations (MERs), relations that began to be explicated in terms of the functional core hypothesis, introduced briefly in Chapter 4.

The Functional Core Hypothesis

Nelson (1974) proposed that the child's interactions with the world determine the child's view of the functions of objects, which in turn motivates the basis for the formation of concepts and the learning of early words. The functional core hypothesis (FCH) claimed that children form concepts of objects based on object function and form, with function as the core of the concept and form its probabilistic periphery, used to identify instances of the concept. The child's concept becomes the basis for word meaning, with the first words mapped onto already formed concepts. The word is then extended to other objects sharing form and function features, thus recognized as instances of the child's concept. This hypothesis argued against a model of the abstraction of perceptual features as the basis for concept formation and word meaning on the following grounds: Given that any object or set of objects can be described in terms of an indefinite number of features, and related to one another on the basis of similarity along an indefinite number of dimensions, forming concepts by abstracting features from encounters with the world assumes that there is already some motivating factor that makes some properties relevant and others not.[3] The child's experience with objects was assumed as the motivating factor. Evidence in favor of the model came primarily from an analysis of the words that children learned for objects that they could do things with. Additional evidence was sought in experiments that posed form against function as the basis for forming concepts.

During the 1970s a number of contradictory studies were reported that aimed to test the predictions of the functional core hypothesis by pitting function against perception. However, this became recognized as a false issue (Nelson, 1978b, 1979) on the following grounds. First, the FCH did not claim that children do not notice or rely on perceptual features, but rather that child-experience-based functional characteristics are more central to their concepts of objects. Second, function can be conceptualized in a number of ways. *Intrinsic* function – what something does – can be a perceptual feature as well (for example, characteristic movement or noise). Therefore, in these cases there is no difference between functional and perceptual features of an object, and the argument reduces to the claim that some features are more important than others, a claim empirical tests did not in fact support (e.g., Bowerman, 1976).

Extrinsic function, however, relates an object to something else, primarily to the people who interact with it. Although all interaction involves perception, the relation of person to object cannot be said to be a perceptual feature of the object; rather, it is a matter of perspective, intention, or stance. Moreover, extrinsic function may (but need not) involve the conventional uses of objects, for example, that telephones are used to communicate over long distances. Because of restrictions on the knowledge base of young children, their concepts of objects often do not incorporate such functions. Yet some studies of children's reliance on function in acquiring concepts and word meanings tested conventional functions rather than those based on child interactions, and thus their reports of no effect are not surprising (e.g., Andersen, 1975).

The FCH was designed to explain infants' spontaneously formed object concepts, which might lie behind their earliest naming practices, and it was extended to a hypothesis about the formulation of any new concept. Now I would recognize more strongly the collaborative nature of the child's conceptual processes, even in the infancy period, which might lead to concepts based on attributes other than function, as well as those with a functional core. Still, although function is not the only basis for forming concepts of objects, it has become more widely recognized as a critical component of conceptual structure for both adults and young children in recent years (e.g., Barsalou, 1991; Kemler Nelson, 1995).[4] Moreover, the idea of a core of conceptual properties supplemented with probabilistic features has also gained wide acceptance (Medin, 1989). The perspective of event cognition emerging from Gibsonian theory (Shaw & Hazelett, 1986) puts these issues into an adaptive perspective that is consonant with the evolutionary perspective presented in Chapters 2 and 3. In this perspective, action and perception are two sides of a single schematizing system, in which concepts emerge from the experience of invariances that exist in the world of events. Function and structure are then indissolvable abstractions from adaptive interactions.

Function may play different roles in different levels of a semantic hierarchy. Basic level concepts may have a functional core, correlated with perceptual features that are determined by function, as some of the early research (Nelson, 1979) supported. By contrast, superordinate categories are defined almost entirely in terms of function (Nelson, 1979, 1985; Scribner, 1974), and subordinate categories are frequently distinguished from basic level categories primarily in terms of distinctive perceptual features. For example, children as well as adults learn to distinguish among subtypes of cars, cereals, and shirts on the basis of perceptual features rather than function. This proposal accords with the developmental sequence that is usually assumed, namely, that basic level concepts (combining function and form) are acquired first, with some subsets acquired when perceptual features distinguish among instances, and with superordinate categories acquired only later when functions themselves become categorized across objects and events (Mervis & Crisafi, 1982; Horton & Markman, 1980).

Hierarchical Category Organization and Alternatives

Although not all researchers are as conservative as Vygotsky and Piaget, the majority have affirmed that the hierarchical structure represented in terms of coordinates, subordinates, and superordinates is inadequately grasped by children below the age of about 5 years. Rosch et al. (1976) showed that preschool children can classify at the basic level but do not succeed at higher levels; this finding has generally held. In language studies, a long tradition of empirical research has demonstrated the younger child's inability to form inclusive category structures of the kind represented by "X is a *kind* of Y," where X is a *hyponym* of Y (e.g., "a robin is a kind of bird"). These relationships require the understanding of inclusivity (robins are included in the class of birds), asymmetry (robins are birds, but birds are not robins), and transitivity – attributes of a higher class apply to the lower, but attributes of a lower category on the hierarchy cannot be assumed to apply to the higher. In this type of structure, when x is a member of y and y is a member of z, then logically it follows that x is a member of z. The logic of inclusion relations is not evident in classifications in the real world; it is an abstraction realized in symbolic form.

Grasping the implications of these relations is traditionally found to be a developmental achievement of the early or later school years (Winer, 1980). Greene (1994) found that kindergartners understand transitivity but not asymmetry, but even this conclusion is constrained by the fact that the artificial categories used in this study were equivalent to the basic level and lower branches, not to abstract superordinates. Greene concludes that critical developments in categorical understanding take place between years 4 and 7. Benelli (1988) reported three studies that provided evidence that superordinate categorization is essentially a matter of linguistic acquisition, that is, that children come to an understanding of semantic organization around the age of 7 years. This proposal is consistent with the conceptual and language integration hypothesis discussed in the latter sections of this chapter.

The logical relations of classes do not necessarily hold for part–whole or collective structures. For example, a child is a member of a school class, and the class is a part of the school, but the child is not a member of the school, and the attributes of the school (e.g., teachers, books) do not apply to the child. Whereas Vygotsky (1986) considered the collection to be a primitive conceptual structure, Markman's (1981) interpretation indicated that collections represent a pervasive alternative to inclusive categories for adults as well as children. Among other things, she showed that superordinate category terms in different languages often reference collections, in which members play differentiated roles [e.g., *army*, (school) *class*, *forest*] rather than true categories in which all members have equivalent status.[5] Markman also demonstrated that young children use collections more readily than categories in cognitive tasks such as class inclusion. Markman's hypothesis is that collections, as part–whole structures, are based on a more natural kind of organizing principle than that of hierarchical classification, based on inclusion relations, and that young children may be able to use this principle before they grasp the inclusive principle of true categories. Therefore, collections may precede and serve as a foundation from which children can construct true categories. By this hypothesis, categories (classes) might emerge from collections.

In a related vein Mandler (1979) proposed that there is a schematic to categorical shift in development such that younger children display knowledge organized in terms of schemas and older children and adults display knowledge organized in terms of categories. This hypothesis seemed to accord with evidence from memory experiments with young children, which revealed deficiencies in the use of category structures but proficiency in the use of information about scripts and scenes. Schemas include scenes, scripts for events, and stories that organize material in terms of part–whole configurations [see Mandler (1983, 1984b); Chapters 4, 6, and 7]. Schemas are based on functional organizing principles; for example, things belong together in a particular scene (such as a kitchen) because they have a function in that scene, and they are related to each other as parts within a functional whole. Thus they may be related to the development of categorical structures from functionally based concepts.

Since putting forth the schematic to categorical hypothesis, Mandler has revised her proposal, and now holds that categorical and schematic structures develop together (Mandler, 1983). She has carried out a series of experiments, finding that some of the categories infants and toddlers recognize are general or global, of the extension that is appropriate for superordinate categories in the adult world (Bauer & Mandler, 1989b; Mandler & McDonough, 1993; see Chapter 4).[6] But this raises an important issue: Are the categorical processes in infancy similar to or the same as those that underlie the formation of taxonomic hierarchies? Given the explicit inclusive asymmetry and transitivity of the latter, and evidence of the difficulty that even young schoolchildren have with these relations, the answer must be no, but then some way of relating the two types developmentally must be found.

Vygotsky's theory of conceptual development based on the contrast between spontaneous and scientific concepts addressed the problem of integrating spontaneously developed conceptual knowledge with "scientific" or "theoretical" cultural systems mediated through language. This problem, central to the thesis of this book, is this: how to reconcile individually and informally – often implicitly – constructed knowledge systems with culturally derived, formally organized, explicit systems of knowledge, when the two incorporate different concepts and conceptual relations but refer to the same domain of knowledge.

The problem in its essential form is pervasive from the beginning of the child's acquisition of language; the language that the child learns initially implicitly incorporates cultural knowledge systems that are only partially and imperfectly represented – and in important cases not represented at all – in the child's prelinguistic experientially based knowledge system. The problem is acute for words that denote superordinate categories. Because superordinate categories do not exist as such in the real world, but only in the language used to talk about them, the child cannot have a prelinguistic concept that is the equivalent of the adult superordinate concept. The child's problem then is to find a way of forming word meanings for superordinate classes that map the adult meaning system appropriately. Event representations provide a basis for such meanings.

Event Representations and Categories:
The Syntagmatic-Paradigmatic System

As is now well documented, young children have organized knowledge of familiar reliably structured events, such as having lunch (Chapter 4). Thus they have an *event category* of eating lunch, a category whose extension includes all the successive occasions of lunch, and whose intension includes the specification of necessary components – actions, objects, persons. Events incorporate two types of hierarchies. First, events can be said to be organized hierarchically, in that they may be composed of smaller event units. For example, the "eating lunch" event may be composed of subevents of preparation, eating the main meal, eating dessert, and clearing away. Each of these in turn can be considered an event in its own right, with different subgoals subordinate to the main goal of eating lunch. Moreover, the "eating lunch" event is part of a larger event sequence representing a typical day. This type of organization can be seen as a part–whole hierarchical structure.

A second type of hierarchy involves the combination of two or more events into a more general category. For example, lunch can be considered an instance of the meal category, which includes as well dinner, breakfast, British tea, late-night snack, and so on. In turn, dinner might be differentiated into the subtypes family, party, restaurant, formal, and so on. Rifkin (Lucariello & Rifkin, 1986) has demonstrated that such inclusive hierarchies of event categories reflect the same kind of psychological reality as object categories for adults. In addition, event categories provide the functional basis for construction of higher-order object categories, and it is this relation that is most significant to the developmental issues in focus here.

In brief, the claim is that children begin with functionally derived categories at the basic level, and that these categories are recombined into larger groups that enter into open slots in events, thus forming "slot-filler" categories. These categories are not true taxonomic hierarchical structures, but form the basis for the formation of such structures, which are constructed in collaboration with adult instruction and experience with the categorical structure of the adult language.

Syntagmatics and Paradigmatics of the Conceptual System:
Slot-filler Categories

The syntagmatic-paradigmatic axis is one of the three major organizing principles of language in Saussure's (1959/1915) theory. According to this principle, language is structured by: (1) combinatory principles, what can be sequentially combined with what in a given structure; and (2) substitutability principles, indicating which forms are alternatives within a particular slot in the structure to be filled. The former principle is known as the *syntagmatic* relation, the latter as the *paradigmatic*. Paradigmatic structures, according to Saussure, are abstractions from experience, whereas syntagmatic structures are evident in spoken utterances. The two types are interdependent in that the combinatory structures are defined in terms of the paradigmatic categories.[7]

Different lexical organization principles derive from syntagmatic and paradigmatic relations and are reflected in changes in children's responses on word association (WA) tasks from early to middle childhood (Nelson, 1977b). In the word association task the subject is presented with a list of words one at a time and asked to respond to each one with the first word that comes to mind. In this task adults respond most of the time with words from the same grammatical class, that is, with paradigmatic responses. Very young children respond primarily with syntagmatic associations, that is, words that come from a different form class. Such responses diminish as children advance in the school years – the syntagmatic-paradigmatic shift.[8] Many theories have been put forth to explain this shift [see Nelson (1977b) for review]. The perspective of event knowledge implies that the finding can best be interpreted in the broader context of the development of categorical structures.

A similar syntagmatic-paradigmatic analysis can be applied to event representations. Within a real-world event – for example, the event of eating lunch – there is a more or less fixed sequence of actions and a less fixed set of alternative slot-fillers of possible foods. Thus basic level concepts of foods are represented in terms of the meal events in which particular foods appear (such as sandwiches at lunch). Hierarchical SLOT-FILLER categories then may be formed by combining representations of food in different events under a single dominating term, the slot-header term, FOOD. This context-defined conception of slot-filler categories contrasts with the logical conception of food as an abstract superordinate concept whose intension is roughly "anything that can be eaten" and whose extension is all possible foods. The latter is an abstract notion of a functionally based and context-free higher-order category. The claim here is that this conception is a late achievement of categorical development but is based in the earlier achievement of an understanding of slot-filler hierarchies.

Many familiar object categories exist in relation to event categories as *slot-filler categories*, that is, items that can fill a particular slot in a particular type of event, for example, foods that can be eaten at lunch. Objects in events may also be related in terms of contiguity when they occur in the same event but not in the same slot. For example, plates and cups occur in the lunch event but not in the EAT x slot. The relation between plate and, say, spaghetti, is a *complementary* or *thematic* relation. In the developmental literature on category formation, a contrast is often made between thematic constructions and categorical (or taxonomic) constructions, with the latter assumed to be more advanced than the former, as Mandler's schematic to taxonomic (1979) hypothesis proposed. A thematic associate to *dog* would be a *bone* the dog was chewing on; a taxonomic associate would be *horse*, a member of the same taxonomic category. Thematic relations have typically been found to be highly salient to young children. Slot-filler categories are not the same as thematic associates; rather, slot-filler items are grouped together on the basis of similar functional roles, not on the basis of complementary roles.

The exclusive focus on objects and object taxonomies in psychology has led to the assumption that the thematic relation is primitive and that the preschooler must overcome it in order to achieve the taxonomic organization. In contrast, the event knowledge perspective on conceptual representations incorporates complementary (or thematic) as well as categorical (or taxonomic) relations, and demonstrates both how they are related and why they may be called on in different tasks. The view here is that both complementary and categorical configurations are based in the same conceptual organization but display different relations within that organization. Thus the relation between individual experientially based event knowledge and the construction of abstract category knowledge is a dynamic, constructive one that results in interacting planes of knowledge organization.

Substitutability. The slot-filler category proposal points to an empirical and rational basis for concept formation that has been neglected in both classical and contemporary studies. *Substitutability* is not included in the traditional accounts of the basis for category formation or associations – which include similarity and contiguity – and it has been little discussed in any literature. Substitutability, unlike contiguity, is not apparent in any single real-world context; items that substitute for one another in an event are not necessarily present in the same context at the same time. Moreover, such items need bear little similarity to one another; for example, bananas, cookies, and pudding may be alternative lunch dessert slot-fillers for a child but are not similar in appearance, texture, or taste. The traditional bases for associations of similarity and contiguity do not explain the basis for slot-filler categories. Substitutability, a paradigmatic relation, does.

Consider again the schematic to categorical shift proposed by Mandler (1979). From the perspective of the syntagmatic-paradigmatic basis for category formation, this move can be seen as the emergence of one structural type from the analysis of another, not as a substitution of one type for another. In this form of the proposal categorical structures are assumed not to replace the schematic structures, but to complement them. Schematic structures continue to be relied on by older children and adults, even for many purposes where categorical structures are generally assumed to be more efficient. Hierarchical category structures are ideal for the logical classification schemes demanded by scholarly work, and particularly by science. They exist in nonscientific cultures as folk taxonomies (Atran, 1990), and as semantic organizations in ordinary language use.

Paradigmatic conceptual structures thus parallel linguistic structures. The child's conceptual system appears designed, not simply to analyze patterns that are apparent in perceptual arrays, but also to analyze the resulting representations for structural characteristics. Among these characteristics is the alternation of items within specific locations in a sequence, and the extraction of possible items into a category. Given the evidence that this process is a general strategy of conceptual analysis, could it not be applied equally well to language categories in terms of paradigmatic alternatives? The analysis and developmental construction of grammar may well be similar to the analysis and developmental construction of conceptual representations. Might such a principle of category formation lie behind or generate the structure of language, rather than arising from it as a unique solution? This question is raised, not to point to an answer, but to emphasize the bidirectionality of the concept–language relation at its core.

From Event-based Slot-filler Categories to Semantic Categories

In time the child must somehow acquire a system of shared word meanings; that is, the child's ideas about what a word can refer to must come to coincide in critical ways with the way the word is used by others in her linguistic community. Experience with parental uses of category terms is a first step in this direction. Achievement of an abstract category language depends upon the further development of a differentiated – or abstracted – level of semantic representation in which linguistic terms are related to one another directly and are not embedded in the particular experientially based event representation and its derivatives.

In previous research it has been found that parents use basic level category terms with their beginning talkers, and that children acquire these terms more or less exclusively in their early vocabularies (e.g., Anglin, 1977). Lucariello and Nelson (1986) analyzed the category terms displayed in maternal talk with 2-year-old children in three different contexts in a study showing how natural language categories are related to event structures in discourse contexts. This analysis of the talk between 10 mothers and their 24-month-old children found that, although basic level terms predominated as others have found, there was also use of both superordinate and subordinate terms by both mothers and children. The non–basic level terms tended to appear most frequently in the context of familiar events, such as eating lunch or getting dressed. Mothers provided clues to the use of the hierarchical terms, such as, "What kind of a drink do you want?" following with alternative possibilities in the drink category. Another discourse clue was provided by using basic level items in the same syntactic frame as the higher-level category term, such as the following: "Let's put on your clothes. Put on your shirt, put on your socks." In this context the term "clothes" can be extracted as a general slot-filler term for items that are "put on."

The development over time of the construction of these relations between events and object categories can be seen in transcripts of the pre-bed talk between 2-year-old Emily and her father [see Chapter 4; Nelson (1989c)]. Alternative *slot-fillers* were found in Emily's talk about food, typically embedded in talk about breakfast. An early example from $22\frac{1}{2}$ months is the following monologue:

(1) Emmy like cornbread and toast.
     I don't like [?] apples and [?]
     I like toast and muffins.
     Food I like and [muffins] too.
     I don't like anything . . . cept for that, that bread daddy
     has . . .

Here we see that already Emily is using the general term "food" as an alternative to the basic level terms of specific items.

In the pre-bed dialogues with Emily's father there are many discussions of what she would like to eat for breakfast. For example, when Emily was not quite 2 the following discussion took place:

(2) E: What we have on breakfast day? What we have? ·
     F: What will we have for breakfast? You know, tomorrow
        morning, you're going to have yogurt, and bananas and
        wheat germ, like mommy gave you this morning, re-
        member that? Instead of an egg tomorrow we're going
        to have yogurt and bananas and wheat germ . . .

Later, Emily enters into the dialogue more actively, specifying what she wants, as in the following dialogue from almost 27 months:

(3) F: We'll get up . . . and we'll go down and have breakfast,
        you can choose what type of egg you want,

E: I want . . . a boiled egg.

F: Okay. And you can choose what type of cereal you want, you can have either shredded wheat or Cheerios.

E: Shredded *wheat!*

A month and a half later, Emily is entering her own suggestions:

(4)   E: And, so now tell me about today!

F: Well, today you had a Tanta day also.

E: I *want* . . . yogurt.

F: And you want yogurt. I know and I think I'll have some raspberries for you tomorrow.

E: And I . . . cereal!

F: Today you had strawberries, tomorrow I think you'll have raspberries.

E: Cereal! Cereal!

F: You'll have cereal? Okay. Cereal and yogurt? You want bananas in yogurt, or raspberries in your cereal?

E: Yeah.

F: Okay. That'll be good.

E: And strawberries in my cereal.

In these discussions, Emily's breakfast food category was highly constrained to the particular situation and did not stray from the alternatives specified by this particular family (e.g., yogurt, cereal, fruit, eggs). It did not wander into domains of pizza, hamburgers, or other items appropriate for dinner. That is, her category of alternatives for breakfast was specific to that event – it constituted a slot-filler category of breakfast foods.

These examples highlight the critical relation of language to the conceptualization of objects and events. Emily's monologues reveal that her event representations are not independent of linguistic formulations and of particular linguistic input from her parents. Thus even when Emily is 2 years of age we cannot speak of a conceptual system that is independent of language; rather, the two evolve together interdependently. Note, however, that the language that simultaneously expresses and shapes Emily's representations is not the abstract language of categories but the concrete language of experience. To be sure, her language includes category terms, but these are particularized to specific experience.

The coordination of the child's language of categories with that of the adult takes place in everyday activities and the discourse surrounding them. The child's MERs reflect the systematization of her experience in

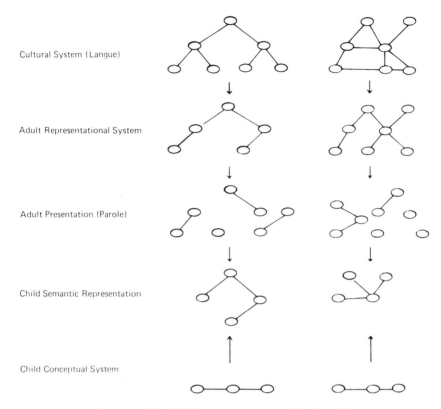

Cultural System (Langue)

Adult Representational System

Adult Presentation (Parole)

Child Semantic Representation

Child Conceptual System

Figure 8.1. Mediation of the child's semantic system by the adult's partial representation and presentation system and the child's conceptual system. *Source:* K. Nelson, *Making sense: The acquisition of shared meaning* (1985). Permission to reprint from Academic Press.

the world, but this system is not the system that organizes the relevant cultural categories. The conventional cultural system is displayed to the child, not systematically as in a school text, but in bits and pieces through adult–child talk. The child acquires a partial system mediated by both the adult's partial system and the child's conceptual system.

Figure 8.1 illustrates this process. The important points to be noted are (1) that the adult's representation is an incomplete structure in comparison with the cultural system as a whole, (2) that its display in speech is a partial and disconnected representation of the adult system as a whole, and (3) that what the child gets from this display is an incomplete, error-prone construction based on both prior (nonhierarchical) concepts and language use. The adult's talk about a category displays certain relations, implying a hierarchical relation, and provides a few of the submembers in the hierarchy. The child may recognize these as related members within her event scheme, and may form a bond between them. But event talk about the category is inevitably fragmentary and unsystematic (as the example from Emily's talk with her father illustrates), sampling bits and pieces from the cultural construction of the category, so that the child's mapping may be distorted and full of holes.

Achievement of an abstract category language depends upon the further development of a differentiated – or abstracted – level of semantic representation in which linguistic terms and their related concepts are not embedded in the experientially derived event representation system but constitute a semantic system of abstract relations. The development of that level makes possible the representation of a true semantic hierarchy – a taxonomy that is based on hierarchical inclusion relations and not simply on combinations of event-contexted slots. Its construction, in collaboration with adult informants, is a major development of the preschool and early school years.

Slot-filler, Thematic, and Taxonomic Categories: Evidence

If, as claimed here, children derive their first category hierarchies from event structures, we should be able to observe evidence of these structures in category membership, in what items are closely associated in memory, and in the use of categories in tasks such as sorting objects and pictures, remembering lists of category items, and forming new categories. These tasks have all been used to evaluate the proposal that slot-fillers form higher-order categories intermediate between the basic level and conventional superordinates; the evidence is summarized here.

Category Production. Three studies of children's category item productions have been carried out (Lucariello, Kyratzis, & Nelson, 1992; Nelson & Nelson, 1990; Yu & Nelson, 1993). In the study by Lucariello and colleagues, 4-year-olds, 7-year-olds, and adults were asked to provide category items for five superordinate categories: food, clothes, animals, furniture, and tools. The results were analyzed in a cluster analysis, and the resulting clusters were examined for their content, specifically for slot-filler or conventional subcategory clusters. Furniture and tools emerged as poorly organized categories for subjects of all ages. Four-year-olds produced very few items in these categories, and included a

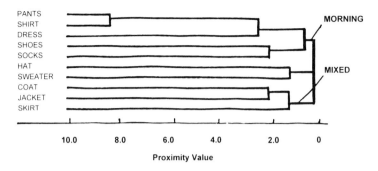

Figure 8.2. Clothing category clusters generated by 4-year-olds. *Source:* J. Lucariello, A. Kyratzis, and K. Nelson, "Taxonomic knowledge: What kind and when?" (1992). Permission to reprint from *Child Development*, University of Chicago Press.

relatively high number of nonmembers. Therefore, these categories did not seem to have a slot-filler basis. Furniture may be organized more in terms of collections in certain spatial configurations (bedroom, living room, for example); tools may remain at a more particular, local functional level. These categories warrant further investigation. It should be noted that although the thesis here is that slot-fillers in MERs form an important basis for the construction of higher-order semantic categories, they are not the only basis.

In contrast, food, clothes, and animals, which were assumed to have a slot-filler structure, were organized in terms of single-event contexts by the youngest children; by multiple slot-filler subcategories for the 7-year-olds; and by a combination of slot-filler and conventional subcategory by the adults. This evidence indicates that preschoolers organize categories in terms of single events, young schoolchildren combine slot-fillers from different event contexts under the single-category term, and adults organize these categories in multiple ways, relying on both event-based slot-fillers and conventional subcategories. Figures 8.2–8.4 illustrate the clusters for the clothes category at the three age levels.

In two studies with children not from mainstream American groups, Nelson and Nelson (1990) and Yu and Nelson (1993) reported findings similar to those above. Nelson and Nelson (1990) asked low-income inner-city African American children to provide category members in three categories: food, clothes, and animals. In one condition children were asked to provide items in two different event contexts (e.g., breakfast foods and snack foods); in the other condition they were asked to

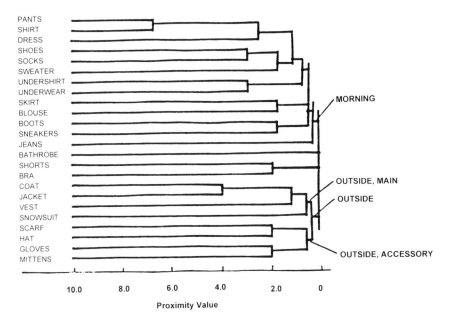

Figure 8.3. Clothing category clusters generated by 7-year-olds. *Source:* J. Lucariello, A. Kyratzis, and K. Nelson, "Taxonomic knowledge: What kind and when?" (1992). Permission to reprint from *Child Development*, University of Chicago Press.

respond to the general category term, "food." An interaction of age with condition was found, with 5-year-olds providing more category members under the event context condition, and 7-year-olds providing more instances under the general instructions. Again, examination of the content of clusters indicated that under general instructions items were clustered by event at both ages, and for the younger children one event context predominated. Further, of the 5-year-olds, those who had had preschool experience produced more category members under both conditions than those without such experience.

The results of this experiment, shown in Table 8.1, indicate that younger children may have difficulty accessing more than one slot-filler category at a time, and that they have not yet begun to combine categories into larger general conventional structures, as 7-year-olds have. The difference between the 5-year-old groups indicates that specific cultural experiences, such as preschool, influence the construction of conventional categories. This is to be expected under the hypothesis that category construction is culturally and linguistically determined. Preschool

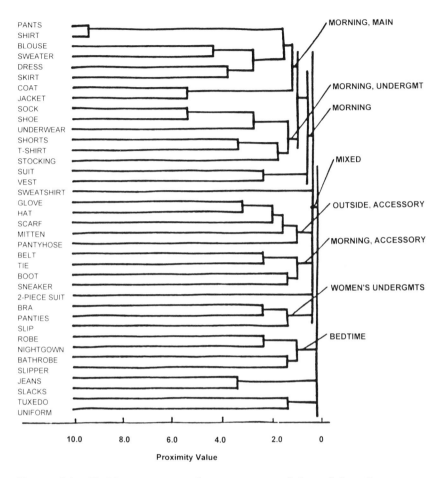

Figure 8.4. Clothing category clusters generated by adults. *Source:* J. Lucariello, A. Kyratzis, and K. Nelson, "Taxonomic knowledge: What kind and when?" (1992). Permission to reprint from *Child Development,* University of Chicago Press.

and kindergarten teachers specifically teach children the discourse forms for category inclusion (Watson, 1985; Wertsch, 1991).

In a cross-cultural and cross-linguistic study using the same paradigm, Yu and Nelson (1993) asked Korean-speaking children in Korea to produce category members in the same three categories used with American children, and the results were essentially similar to those found with English-speaking children, although with specific cultural variations. Thus the category production results indicate that slot-filler organization is common among young children across cultures and

Table 8.1. *Mean number of items produced by group, condition, and category*

| Group/Condition | N | Category | | | |
		Animals	Clothing	Food	Mean
K1					
Taxonomic	8	5.88	4.00	7.88	5.92
Slot-filler	8	6.25	9.12	10.87	8.75
K2					
Taxonomic	7	8.86	7.57	9.43	8.62
Slot-filler	7	11.29	12.43	19.00	14.24
Grade 2					
Taxonomic	8	17.25	13.00	27.63	19.29
Slot-filler	8	14.00	10.62	12.25	12.29

Source: Nelson & Nelson (1990), table 1, p. 435. Used with permission of the publisher.

does not disappear as conventional taxonomic categories are integrated with it, but can still be seen in the productions of adults for familiar everyday categories.

Word Associations. The word association paradigm was used with 4- and 7-year-olds by Lucariello, Kyratzis, and Nelson (1992), who presented slot-filler category items from the categories of food, clothes, and animals. The responses were analyzed in terms of the relation between stimulus word and response word. Relations could be categorical (conventional or slot-filler) or thematic or event-based (event, function, complementary). Older children produced significantly more categorical associates than younger children, but the great majority of these were slot-filler associates. Younger children, in contrast, produced three times as many thematic associates as categorical, and significantly more thematic associates than did the older children. Of these thematic associates, twice as many were functional responses (e.g., cookie–eat) than complementary (e.g., cereal–spoon). These results indicate that younger children's words are still spontaneously organized in terms of the events in which they are relevant, rather than in terms of categories, whether slot-filler or conventional; however, as the category production task showed, they are capable of production of slot-filler category items. By 7 years of age, children have begun to organize their words more in terms of categorical relations (means of 13 for categorical and 5.5 for thematic). But most of their categorical response associates are still slot-fillers. These results help to explain the well-established syntagmatic-paradigmtic shift in word associations found in the early school years, in that most thematic responses were from different word classes (e.g., noun–verb), and most categorical responses were from the same word class (noun–noun). Four-year-olds provide mostly thematic responses; 7-year-olds provide mostly categorical responses.

Sell (1992) reported a word association task with preschool, kindergarten, and fourth-grade children, categorizing responses as event-based, which indicated an object's function or purpose, slot-filler or taxonomic. There was a progression with age in this task: preschoolers provided primarily event-based associations, kindergartners provided slot-fillers as well, and schoolchildren were able to provide taxonomic associations in addition to slot-fillers. Thus Sell's research replicates and extends the findings from Lucariello and colleagues (1992).

List Recall.   A standard test of the establishment of categorical organization in semantic memory is the recall of categorized word lists. In general it has been found that young children do not recall more from lists containing members of the same category than from random lists, and they do not cluster category members together in recall (e.g., Nelson, 1969). Several experiments have been carried out using this paradigm to test the psychological reality of slot-filler categories. Two recall experiments (Lucariello & Nelson, 1985) presented 4-year-old children with three kinds of lists – conventional category, slot-filler category, and thematic – under free recall and cued recall, with either slot-filler or superordinate cues. Briefly, these young children recalled significantly more from the slot-filler list than from either of the other lists, and the best recall was found with the slot-filler list and script cues. Clustering was significantly better with the slot-filler list as well.

These results have been replicated with Korean children (Yu & Nelson, 1993; Yu, 1993). In Yu's studies it was found that 7-year-olds performed as well with the taxonomic list as with the slot-filler list, suggesting that they had integrated the slot-filler categories into a hierarchically composed taxonomic category. In her last two experiments (Yu, 1993), the same results emerged under different study conditions. Four-year-olds did consistently better with the slot-filler list, and they were able to use strategy instructions with this list but not with the taxonomic list, whereas 7-year-olds used strategies with the taxonomic list as well as the slot-filler list.

Other Studies. Slot-filler superiority over taxonomic (or coordinate) lists in different memory paradigms has also been reported from other laboratories by Rosner and Smick (1989), Krackow and Blewitt (1989), and Blewitt and Toppino (1991). Failure to find slot-filler superiority has been reported by Boyer and Rollins (1991) and by Krackow and Gordon (1992). (In both these studies slot-fillers produced higher means than taxonomic, but the effects were not significant.)

Without going into detail, it may be noted that often the items that are identified in conflicting studies as "slot-fillers" do not come from any recognizable script that young children might be engaged in. For example, it is a stretch of the imagination to suppose that any group of "land vehicles" constitutes slot-fillers in a child's script. Each vehicle (bicycle, car, bus, taxi, etc.) might be expected to enter into a different unique script as an invariant, not alternative, prop. "Land vehicles" is a legitimate subcategory of an adult superordinate "vehicles"; therefore, it is a taxonomic, not a slot-filler category. Also, some of the lists used in conflicting experiments have not been constructed around scripts that are familiar to young children (thus that might plausibly lead to slot-filler conceptualizations), or with items that children might plausibly have experienced in a slot-filler context. In one study "familiar slot-filler categories" were compared with "unfamiliar" ones. The idea of an "unfamiliar slot-filler category" is incoherent in that slot-fillers are abstracted from scripts with which the child is familiar enough to have experienced alternative objects in the same slot on different occasions. Slot-fillers are experientially derived, thus items must reflect that experience. It is conceivable for example, that anchovies might be a lunch food slot-filler for some child, perhaps a low associate, low typical food, but for most children it would not be in the domain at all. Individual differences of this kind can lead to very noisy data, especially when nontypical items are sought.

Moreover, conflicting tests of the slot-filler claims often seem to miss the point in more than one way. It has never been claimed that all familiar everyday categories have a basis in slot-fillers; rather, those that do are acquired earlier and provide a boot-strapping mechanism to the structure of more abstract hierarchically organized categories.[9] As already noted, in the category production task (Lucariello, Kyratzis, &

Nelson, 1992) the tool and furniture categories were so poorly structured for preschoolers that no significant clusters emerged. However, when a craft project task was designed to include tools as slot-filler items, kindergarten children readily formed such a category (Kyratzis, 1989).

In some studies an effort has been made to explain the slot-filler effect by reducing it to something more "basic" such as association in semantic memory between superordinate terms and slot-filler terms, or to strong associativity and high typicality. These efforts again seem to misread the slot-filler claims, which are based in the hypothesis that semantic memory associates and typical members of categories derive from the presemantic conceptual relations based on event scripts (and other schematic or part–whole relations). Associativity and typicality are themselves effects to be explained; the proposal of slot-filler organization is designed to explain these effects, not to be an alternative explanation to them. To be explicit: We would expect slot-filler items to be highly associated in memory and to form the most typical members of many categories, at least for young children. Because associativity and typicality effects are at least in part the result of slot-filler organization, they cannot negate slot-filler claims.

One line of research reported in Lucariello and colleagues (1992) was an exception to the finding from the category production and list memory studies of slot-filler superiority to thematic organization. This task was a forced-choice picture task in which 4- and 7-year-old children were presented with triads of line drawings and asked to pick which of two pictures "goes with" the target picture. Each choice pair consisted of two of the following: a related category member from the same script (a slot-filler), a category member from a different script (taxonomic), or a thematic associate. When the two category associates were paired, slot-filler choices predominated over taxonomic, as expected. But when thematic associates were included as choices, they were chosen significantly more frequently by children of both ages in comparison to both other types. Sell (1992) reported a similar finding with a similar picture-choice task, indicating that fourth-grade children make event-based choices more frequently than they make categorical choices. Why do 7- and 9-year-olds choose thematic associates in this task?

To address this question, it is of interest to consider a different line of research initiated by Markman and Hutchinson (1984) and continued by Markman and her colleagues and others in the years since. These researchers have used triads of pictures, one of which is the target picture.

Children are asked to find another of the same kind as the target picture from the remaining two choice pictures. In the first experiments, which have defined the paradigm, children were given choices between a member of the same category (e.g., a cat when the target is a dog) and a thematic associate (e.g., a bone). They found, similar to the results from the study by Lucariello and colleagues (1992), that when preschool children were asked to choose "another one" they chose thematic associates predominantly. However, when children were told that the target had a nonsense name (e.g., this is a "dax") and asked to find another of the same name (e.g., find another "dax") they chose the category associate. From these results researchers have concluded that children obey a "taxonomic constraint" on word meanings; that is, they assume that words refer to taxonomic categories and not to groups of thematically related items. Therefore, when they are given a name for the item, they override a natural propensity to group things thematically and instead group them categorically. The extension of this explanation to the picture-choice task used in the experiments by Lucariello and colleagues and Sell (1992) suggests that in the latter tasks children were relying on their natural tendency to see the world in thematic terms, unrelated to lexical knowledge, which is categorically (taxonomically) organized.

It is obvious that the thematic–taxonomic contrast is related to the event–category development projected here. However, the proposal of slot-filler categories based in event representations that become integrated into larger taxonomic structures has the advantage of providing a more detailed and deeply developmental explanation of the results of these experiments. It also is consistent with Donald's (1991) evolutionary hypothesis about the development of the hybrid representational systems of the human mind. It goes beyond the naming effect proposed by Markman and her associates to suggest that these effects are part of the emergence of the semantic representational system and the conventionalization through language of children's categories.

Our experiments (Lucariello et al., 1992) have shown that preschool children's conceptual organization displays both event (thematic) and category (slot-filler) bases, and that these persist throughout development. Thematic relations appear to be especially compelling when pictures are used in cognitive tasks, perhaps because pictures appear to represent parts of events.[10] What changes is the integration of spontaneous category structures into conventional, linguistically constructed categories as the child experiences these in school or through other instructional contexts.

Language and Conceptual Change

On the basis of the research reported here, it appears that a change in semantic memory organization leads to a conceptual shift in children between 4 and 7 years of age that has broad implications for many different cognitive tasks. How slot-filler categories become transformed into conventional categories provides important clues to what might be taking place at a deeper cognitive level during the preschool years. Briefly, development is hypothesized to proceed as follows.

As delineated here, the first assumption is that slot-filler categories are abstractions spontaneously derived from event structures, the latter based on experience with routine events. Because of the way that adults use category labels and functional statements relating basic and subordinate terms to superordinate terms, children learn to apply the general superordinate term to their slot-filler categories. This enables them to respond with slot-filler items to the request to produce category members. Slot-fillers then come to be headed by a conventional category label and, as the label is used in different script contexts, to be combined into more general categorical structures mirroring those of the conventional semantic category. This process was examined in an experiment (Kyratzis, 1989) in which children were taught the names and categories of tools used in a craft project. Five-year-old children had no problem acquiring these categories but did have problems with the inclusion relation connecting terms at the basic level to a term at the superordinate level.

The process of connecting terms and categories begins early and proceeds at a different pace for different categories varying on familiarity and complexity. During the preschool and early school years both parents [Adams & Bullock (1986); Callanan (1985); Lucariello & Nelson (1986); see previous examples] and teachers (Watson, 1985; Wertsch, 1991) engage in labeling practices that emphasize the inclusive structure of hierarchies. Yet until quite late in the game, young children do not easily take advantage of these inclusion statements (Horton & Markman, 1980; Kyratzis, 1989). It seems reasonable to conclude that although category construction begins and proceeds at a moderate pace during the preschool years, the hierarchical inclusion structures of categories are not well established, stable, and relatively autonomous within the semantic system until at least the early school years. This change – reorganization – in semantic memory is then observable in terms of age differences in performance on episodic memory tasks that involve semantic categories, such as the list recall task, as previously documented.

The contribution of linguistic experience in the construction of these conventional natural language hierarchies is important because, as previously noted, items such as different foods, animals, and clothes do not sort themselves into neat hierarchically inclusive structures in the real world. Rather, language itself imposes ways of categorizing items, categories that may vary from culture to culture and language to language. It is *necessary* for the child to be exposed to the particular ways that a language categorizes items in order to learn the compositional structure of the categories. Put simply, hierarchies are in the language (and in conceptual systems), not in the physical or material world [see also Wierzbicka (1994)].

Early in the preschool period (2 to 3 years) the child is still acquiring basic competence in using a first language for communicative purposes (Chapter 5). It is only after this point that one may expect more abstract organizations such as semantic categories to emerge as pragmatic structures from language in use. This shift in functioning emerges at about the same time that other language-dependent structures such as personal narratives and autobiographical memory do. Language uses of the community pull the child toward the organizations inherent in the linguistic structures of the culture. On their own, children might construct quite complex semantic organizations, but they do not need to because they have available linguistic models. Furthermore, in order to speak the language of the community they need to acquire the categories and organizations that that language incorporates. What they must do is to integrate the models of the language with their own emerging knowledge organizations.

Although children may gain a great deal of knowledge about cultural categories simply from interacting with adults around relevant activities, schooling advances the process explicitly, as the evidence from the Nelson and Nelson (1990) category production study suggested. Wertsch (1991) provides examples from school sessions that illustrate the process that takes place. In the following excerpt a teacher is involved in an exercise with six first-grade students of "finding the one that doesn't belong" among four pictures [similar to the categorization tests carried out by Luria (1976) and Tulviste (1991)]:

(5)   T: Why doesn't the key belong with the ham and a tomato
        and a banana, Mikey?
      C: Because the key isn't a fruit.
      T: Well, a ham isn't a fruit. What are all those things? Things
        you can . . .

C: Eat.
T: Eat. Things you can eat . . .
    . . .
T: Which one are we going to put an X on, Jessica?
C: The plant.
T: The plant. Why? Annie.
C: Because it's not clothes.
T: It's not clothes. Good . . .
    . . .
T: Patrick, which one are you going to *eliminate* in the last
    one?
C: Ummm . . . The goose.
T: Why?
C: Because it's not something you can sit on or sleep on.
T: Very good. It's not furniture, right? We can call that furni-
    ture.
    . . . (p. 133)

As Wertsch points out, this excerpt not only reveals the explicit teaching of everyday category vocabulary that does on in the school, but also illustrates the mixture of experience language and formal language. In the first exchange, the teacher not only accepts but also elicits the formulation "you eat" instead of the category term "food," but in the last exchange she switches to the formal verb "eliminate" and substitutes the category term (or linguistic object) "furniture" for the informal functional category. This excerpt illustrates the implied process of integration of everyday knowledge with the structures of cultural categories.

The inclusion relation that is critical to hierarchical categories is used to relate scientific concepts in taxonomic structures and has also infiltrated the common language to a greater or lesser extent. Children can learn the superordinate language that incorporates the inclusion relation without yet understanding its implications (e.g., the transitivity and asymmetry of its relations). The question that has not yet been adequately addressed is how children may come to understand these relations, and how the instructional efforts in school advance this understanding. The issue here is how conceptual reorganization and restructuring proceeds with examples that are simply displayed in cultural talk and through explicit instruction that formally lays out how systems such as taxonomic categories are structured. Conceptual restructuring on the basis of both implicit and explicit demands from the culture is likely to be characteristic of a great deal of knowledge acquisition and conceptual change from early childhood and on throughout life.

The research discussed in this chapter documents developmental changes in children's categories. However, it must also be emphasized that the fundamental conceptual processes are assumed to be the same throughout development. These processes include the formation of categories based on perceptual similarity and functional substitutability, of part–whole schemas constituted of causal, spatial, and temporal contiguity, analytical processes that differentiate and integrate experientially derived representations. They also include attention to relevant and salient aspects of the environment based on current cognitive models, and especially to the social and communicative contexts of activities and messages. What changes is the increasing content and organizational complexity of the knowledge base, the acquisition of the potential of the linguistic symbolic representational system, and the associated possibility of re-representation of existing knowledge within that system, and the differing perspective on the world and encountered knowledge systems as the child's place in the world changes over time. Changes are found as the child moves from primarily individual cognitive resources to the incorporation of more social resources, thence to specifically semantic resources, and finally to drawing on cultural knowledge systems.

Hierarchies and Theories

Researchers in recent years have questioned whether hierarchical semantic categories adequately explain conceptual organization. Lakoff (1987) has described a variety of more loosely and flexibly organized conceptual structures that are claimed to be more representative of human thought. Many theorists of concepts and categories now contend that the structure and content of concepts can be explained only in terms of the mental models or theories within which they are embedded (e.g., Murphy & Medin, 1985; Neisser, 1987). The central idea here is that concepts do not exist as singular items, but as part of a person's model of reality, a model that has many constituent domains. This way of thinking about concepts as unfixed elements within larger cognitive constructions suggests many possibilities and has been widely adopted in developmental psychology (e.g., Carey, 1985; Keil, 1991; Wellman & Gelman, 1992). Young children's thinking is now viewed by many as based on organization of concepts within theories of specific domains of knowledge [e.g., the biological – see Hirschfeld & Gelman (1994b)].

Carey (1985) introduced the idea that children's conceptual knowledge is organized in terms of theories that guide the acquisition and structure of learning in an area, a claim based in the philosophy and history of science. Theories apply within and not across domains of knowledge; physics theories differ from chemical theories, which differ from biological theories, and so on. Thus the theory proposal effectively partitions the mind into different domains of knowledge, at least some of which are claimed to be specified innately; in Carey's view these are basic naive theories of the physical and the psychological worlds.

Since Carey's work, it has been argued that children also construct biological theories applicable specifically to the world of plants and animals, as well as to such biological processes as birth, death, illness, and digestion. These claims seem particularly relevant to children's organization of knowledge in domains such as *animals* and *food*, but as we have seen, this organization tends to be in terms of experience: zoo animals, farm animals, pets; breakfast foods, dinner foods, snacks.[11]

The idea of theories as representational structures alternative to the traditionally accepted hierarchies of categories has been given weight by recent research indicating that children have deeper knowledge of category members than the surface similarities implicated in perceptually based categories. Keil (1989) has explicated this in terms of a "characteristic to defining shift," proposing that young children's categories of both "natural kind" terms and artifact terms are organized in terms of characteristic properties, whereas older children's categories rest on deeper, essential properties. For example, younger children might define "island" in terms of sun and palm trees, whereas older children will define it in terms of land surrounded by water. S. Gelman's research program (e.g., Gelman & Markman, 1986; Gelman & Coley, 1991), in contrast, has been designed to show that even very young children recognize that natural kind terms such as "bird" imply unobservable properties and that terms such as "bird" may be used to infer characteristics such as "fly," "builds nests," and "lays eggs."

There is general agreement now that children are not simply prisoners of their perceptual systems, but are engaged in organizing knowledge at a deeper level and making connections among originally somewhat disparate concepts. The source of such deep knowledge, however, remains in question. Some is directly taught and learned, some is constructed through inference. Even universal knowledge constructs such as that birds build nests and lay eggs are not usually the discovery of young children but rather are directly taught as properties of birds. Thus if we are to take the theory claims seriously, we need to ask where the theories come from: On what basis does a child construct a theory? By the time a child is in grade school it seems quite reasonable to believe that she has constructed from various sources, including verbally conveyed knowledge, mini- or proto-theories that serve to organize and explain common phenomena. However, it also seems reasonable that since theories are about phenomena in the real world, presumably, they must be constructed on the basis of pretheoretical knowledge about the real world, just as scientific theories are based on pretheoretical knowledge. Pretheoretical knowledge is gained in the ubiquitous process of making sense.

Theory building begins with a descriptive knowledge base in any field. The distinction between descriptive theory and explanatory theory has been made in different ways by both Chomsky (1965) and Mayr (1982). A descriptive theory is concerned with *how* things are in the world; an explanatory theory is concerned with *why* they are the way they are. For the individual child, as for science, description necessarily precedes explanation, and small-scale explanation precedes general theory. This is not to deny the validity of the claim that all observation and description are in some sense biased by one's interests (and in science by one's theory). But, simply put, to ask for an explanation of something is already to have knowledge of that something. If we are not to revert recursively to innate knowledge we must account for its initial acquisition.

Thus the attribution of theory structures to the knowledge that young children possess in certain domains is, from the present view, a questionable practice, especially when theorists equate a child's theories directly with scientists' theories (Gopnik, 1993b, p. 100), even though the child's theories are held to be implicit, not explicit, as are the scientists'. Theories in science are constructed according to well-understood, systematically organized knowledge domains, in accordance with formal principles of theory construction, including some form of hypothetico-deductive logic. Scientific theories define a set of concepts and order these within an explanatory system of causal relations. They are the property of a community of scientists and are in principle testable against newly discovered facts. A new theoretical advance may be originated by an individual, but it remains a hypothetical proposal until or unless it is accepted as valid by the community. The child's implicit "theory" has no such validation procedure, and the implicit theory by definition remains individual and unshared. Any testing that is done must be done in a single mind, and acceptance of validating or invalidating facts is then completely subjective.

In response to such objections, some "theory theorists" claim that children's implicit theories are the equivalent of "folk theories," not scientific theories. They are the construals of the world that the "folk" hold in common. But there are problems here, too. First, adult folk can articulate their theories, or at least the propositions that derive from them. Second, young children do not seem to share many of the folk theories of the adult community; therefore, they must be "little folk" theories, but unshared. Yet if these theories are unshared, what guarantees that children arrive at a single common theory; why not many different idiosyncratic theories?

Listening closely to young children in their everyday lives does not suggest systematic organized knowledge within well-delineated domains. Consider the following exchange between a 4-year-old child and her mother from a maternal diary study [Callanan and Oakes (1992, pp. 221–222)]:

(6) Situation: Bedtime
Child: Why does Daddy, James (big brother), and me have blue eyes and you have green eyes?
Parent: (Told her she got her eyes from Daddy. Then said goodnight and left the room.)
Child: (child calls mother back 5 minutes later) I like Pee Wee Herman and I have blue eyes. Daddy likes Pee Wee Herman and he has blue eyes. James likes Pee Wee Herman and he has blue eyes. If you liked Pee Wee Herman you could get blue eyes too.
Parent: (I told her it would take more than my liking Pee Wee Herman to make my eyes blue. I realized that she didn't understand me, so I explained that God gave me this color and that they couldn't be changed.)
Child: Could you try to like Pee Wee Herman so we could see if your eyes turn blue?
Parent: (I said I would think about it, but if my eyes stayed green it was ok.)

Although this example indicates creative causal thinking, it violates in the most extreme way the boundary between basic biological and symbolic cultural domains, and does not suggest the possession of systematically organized, causally related knowledge in either domain.

Theories have an important place in the construction of adult thought at Donald's (1991) fourth level. As outlined in Chapter 3, theoretical thinking is held to be a product of literate societies. Tulviste (1991) argues in a similar vein that hierarchical taxonomic categorical structures are cultural developments useful in scientific activities, but are not inherent aspects of human thinking. For example:

> If thinking appropriate to certain types of human activity were hereditary, we would undoubtedly have to expect a basic similarity in the thinking of peoples of any cultures and epochs. . . . But there is no basis for assuming that such specific types of thinking, as for example, formal operations (according to Piaget) or thinking in scientific concepts (according to Vygotsky) would have to arise during phylogenesis or anthropogenesis, and then be transmitted hereditarily. It is difficult to understand why these types of thinking would have to be formed in anthropogenesis if most of humanity that has nothing to do with schooling and scientific information even today gets along very well without them. (p. 70)

I think we should take theories seriously, but not attribute them to infants and young children without good cause. The attribution of theoretical knowledge to the young child is deeply misleading, I believe, in obscuring the differences between types of human knowledge systems and thus problems faced in conceptual change and development. In particular, the attribution of "theories" to the preschooler obscures the problems of integrating an experientially derived organization with a cultural system of knowledge. Theories rest on the prior systematization of knowledge that is culturally organized. Individual representations of theoretically based knowledge may be imperfectly represented (as Figure 8.1 suggests), especially if that knowledge is conveyed only implicitly through informal discourse. But partial representations may be a long way from fully established theories.

Making Theoretical Sense

A basic assumption here is that the child is engaged in the process of *making sense,* a process with many subprocesses that begins with the dawning of mind. The following scheme reviews the developments covered thus far in terms of a sequence of developmental tasks prerequisite to theory construction.

- *Data gathering:* From the first days of life the infant is intent on gathering data about the world she inhabits, including especially the people attending her and her surroundings. Data gathering initially proceeds along biologically well-established paths that determine what kinds of data are attended to and how they are ordered in memory. Toward this end, the child is equipped with ways of parsing the world, and capacities for interpreting and interrelating the pieces. For example, exploring spaces and objects appears to be as universal and as much a part of an epigenetic program as eating, sleeping, and smiling.

- *Model building:* From very early the infant appears to construct and to rely on models of relations in the world – what happens when, where, and in what way – that is, event or situation models. By 3 years of age, children demonstrate detailed command of the situational structures of their worlds, including expected people roles, objects, and action sequences, and can transform these in play.
- Small-scale *explanation seeking:* When children believe that they understand how things *are* they begin to seek explanations for why they are. They ask questions of adults about the how and why and they project explanations themselves, beginning at about 3 years. The 3- and 4-year-old's persistent "why" may be precipitated by a dawning of the notion that what *is* must have a reason for so being. But anyone who attends closely to the child's questions must be struck by the limited nature of her understanding of the world and its causal mechanisms at this age [see example (6)]. At first her own explanations often reveal a quite fragmentary and distorted picture of the world and how it works, and a readiness to cross ontological boundaries in seeking explanations, as example (6) illustrated.

Once some small-scale explanations in a domain have been proposed and accepted, and entered into the child's initial explanatory model, the child may begin to order them and generate new hypotheses on their basis, which can then be articulated and tested for acceptability by others. The process of minitheory construction may begin at around age 6 as children are inducted into cultural categories and cultural knowledge systems and as they integrate these with their prior experientially based knowledge. This proposal leaves open the recognition that children *construct* their own knowledge while at the same time recognizing the *social-cultural origins* of that knowledge.

The later steps in this progression are largely dependent on the use of language, and on social-cultural constructions made available to the child through language. The construction of a theory even in childhood is thus viewed as fundamentally a social act, based on culturally shared understanding of the phenomena in a domain [see Freyd (1983)]. Once a child can use language as a sense-making system she can begin to use cultural sources to reconstruct on the individual level what is already established and revealed on the social-cultural level. This proposal is consistent with Vygotsky's insight that systematic "scientific" concepts are learned through transactions with, including direct instruction from, the social world, and must be coordinated with the "spontaneous" concepts of the individual child.

Through the construction of cognitive models of her world, the human infant and young child re-creates in mind experiences in the world and thus can understand – in the sense of predicting – how things go. These are descriptive models, not explanatory models. The establishment of stable world models in infancy and early childhood is thus a necessary first and basic step toward the establishment of more abstract explanatory knowledge. As the child begins to seek explanations for why these relations are as they are, the models themselves may contain clues that are used to frame the deeper questions. The child's descriptive model of how things are supports the construction and understanding of reasons for why they are that way.

The process of projecting explanations and receiving them from others is among the new possibilities inherent in the use of language as a representational medium. The causal explanations of the young child may be based on what others have told her or they may emerge from her own inferencing processes. They emanate not from general theories in a well-defined domain but rather from small-scale observations. They can be seen as a step in the direction of the construction of larger, more systematic explanatory structures.

As the discussion in this chapter has emphasized, recognition of knowledge acquisition that is not available in perceptual displays does not necessarily imply theoretically organized knowledge. Rather than impose our scientifically derived notions of theories on the minds of young children, it seems wiser to remain open to different alternative possibilities when studying the organization of their knowledge. In this chapter the organization of events, and knowledge derived from and organized in terms of events, has been shown to be at least one very salient basis for organization in the young child's knowledge system. This basis bears little resemblance to the scientists' theories; it is more plausibly related to the narratively structured knowledge that was outlined in the previous chapter. Indeed, it appears that the syntagmatic structure of narrative forms the basis for the paradigmatic structure of categories and the theories – folk or scientific – within which these categories take their place.

9. The Emergence of the Temporal Mind

"What then is time? If no one asks me, I know; if I wish to explain it to him who asks me, I do not know." Augustine, *Confessions*

Time provides a good case study for the thesis of this book precisely because a sense of time is universal and to some extent present at least from birth, but the biological given is overlaid by the social, cultural, and linguistic systems through which time is measured and ordered, as well as by the theoretical systems by which scientists and philosophers conceptualize it.[1] Time is also organized according to domain-specific principles; it is neither narrative nor taxonomic, yet its organization varies culturally and linguistically. Therefore, it is not a heritable, encapsulated module. Development of time knowledge requires a different explanation.

Time is central to developmental processes and is a basic dimension of action, activity, and event structure. Coordinating the experiential dimension of time with its cultural and social conception presents a significant problem for the child. Yet in the past, developmental psychologists have viewed concepts of time primarily as a logical system of mathematical relations. In contrast, social and cognitive psychologists, linguists, and philosophers have recognized many more of the facets of time that are waiting to challenge a child coming to understand the workings of the social, cultural, and physical world.

The cultural definition of time in Western societies in many ways departs from its biological sense as well as its basis in natural cycles, to provide an essentially arbitrary system of time measurement ranging from picoseconds to epochs of millenia. Indeed, modern societies have engaged in increasingly abstract manipulations of time concepts, of which the Einsteinian view of space-time as relative, so seemingly remote from our daily experience, is only the most extreme abstract form. Temporal abstractions emerged from Greek antiquity, were reconceptualized in Christian terms of progress toward the teleological end point of salvation, and were again reconceptualized in the objective time conceived by Newtonian science. Peculiarly, it is the latter sense that has occupied developmental psychologists ever since Piaget (1969) defined the child's conceptual task in the realm of time to be that of differentiating time from speed and distance. Much experimental effort has gone into determining when and under what conditions children can make this differentiation. However, viewing this relation as *the* concept of time (as many developmental psychologists do) is roughly equivalent to viewing the formula for deriving the area of a triangle as *the* concept of space.

The basic sense out of which the child's concepts of time might emerge have been the focus of much less attention in developmental work. Remarkably, the number of publications devoted to time in developmental journals is minuscule in comparison to those devoted to concepts of objects, space, or other aspects of the natural world.[2] This chapter considers the many and various basic concepts and relations encompassed under the domain of Time, along with their linguistic and symbolic realizations and implementations, in order to suggest how the child may begin to understand them. First discussed are natural indications of time, experiential time, social constructions of time, and linguistic representations. Next, the way these are embedded in and differentiated from the child's event representations and use in discourse is considered. Finally, the problems of coordinating and integrating levels in this domain, and their relation to cultural models, are considered.

Kinds of Time

Natural Time

Natural time may be thought of in terms of basic biological rhythms as well as the cycles of the natural world by which humans have attempted to track time. Response to time is not confined to humans, or to mammals. All living organisms respond to temporal change. For example, oysters are sensitive to the rhythm of the tides and adjust the opening of their shells to take in food according to the daily changes in the hours of the tides. When transported to a new environment sheltered from direct exposure to the new and different tide times, oysters nonetheless – through some as yet unknown mechanism – adjust to the new, expected but not directly experienced, times of the tides (Aveni, 1989). As for humans, the functions of our bodies oscillate daily in over a hundred different ways, from brain waves to cardiac and respiratory rhythms to daily temperature cycles. These biorhythms have become more obvious to many people in the age of jet travel when shifts in the circadian rhythms of the daily sleep–wake cycle disrupt their functions. Our biological systems contain longer cycles as well, including the female 28-day menstrual pattern and sensitivities to seasonal changes.

We – children as well as adults – live in time with our biorhythms, although we are seldom consciously aware of them. Natural biorhythms are, however, also subject to the influence of social and cultural patterns. The sleep–wake cycles of infants are entrained over the course of several years to the patterns of the households they live in, whatever these may be. When individuals are removed from all temporal signs, including day–night cues, they become disentrained over the course of weeks, losing all track of time, and behaving as though their "pacemakers" had become totally disoriented. Thus, although humans, like all other organisms, are naturally tuned in time, their basic sense of time is interdependent with their environment, including the social environment, which determines specific times for eating, sleeping, working, and playing.

Thus the time to which our human biorhythms are tuned is part of both the natural world as well as the socially constructed world. The day–night and yearly cycles are determined by the relation of earth to sun, the monthly cycle by the moon's phases, which are reflected in the shifting tides. These natural cycles appear as obvious constants of human existence, but different societies experience them differently, depending among other things on distance from the equator, distance from large bodies of water, and geographical altitude. Because of the different orientations of these natural phases in different parts of the world, they have been used in different ways by societies to organize daily or seasonal time, both of which are nonetheless quintessentially "natural." The changing patterns of planets and stars are also traditionally and historically used to track celestial time, and in many societies they have been thought to influence human events, as in the zodiac of astrology.[3] Ways of marking time necessarily involve symbolic systems. Raeithel (1994) has even speculated that language itself evolved as its function in tracking seasons and cycles of days became important. Others have claimed that the first external symbol systems, such as tally marks on stone, were used for marking the passage of days.

Personal Experiential Time: Time in Events

Time is usually described in terms of two basic dimensions: *sequence* and *duration*. These relations exist within and between events and thus are basic to the child's experience. But, unlike aspects of space that can be

Table 9.1. *Basic temporal concepts*

Concept	Subtype	Conventional Examples
Perspective	Tense Generic	past, present, future
Location	Indefinite Definite	pretty soon, later lunchtime, yesterday, morning, Monday, 5 o'clock
Sequence	Simultaneous Order Causal	while, during first, before, after so, because
Duration	Within event Between events	until, long time since, many years
Boundaries		begin, start, end, no longer
Frequency	Frequency Probability Recurrence Cyclicity	always, never, sometimes probably, maybe again, next time day after day
Speed		fast, slow, quickly
Transactional	Age History Nature Cultural Memory	birthday, 6 years old modern, 100 years ago winter, sunset New Year's, school day remember
Units		day, hour, minute, second, month, week, year, decade, century

pointed to or explained through gestures (for example size, shape, and location), time concepts must be abstracted from experience or constructed. (In this respect time is like number.) Time may be represented in imagery or symbolic form, but it cannot be directly sensed; it is not a "thing" that is there for the child to discover. The two basic dimensions of sequence and duration embed other time concepts that are also based in experience with events. *Location* in time derives from sequence, *speed* derives from duration, and time *perspective* (now vs. past and future) derives from both duration and sequence. Other temporal properties of events involve *boundaries* (beginnings and endings) and *frequency*. These dimensions are shown in Table 9.1, together with some of the linguistic terms used to mark them in English. Expressions of these relations may be definite (e.g., "at 9 o'clock," "after breakfast," "for 5 minutes," "over 6 years") or indefinite (e.g., "pretty soon," "a long time").

All these concepts can be seen to have a fairly direct relation to the everyday experience of and memory for events. *Locations* are often referenced in terms of events (e.g., *bedtime, lunchtime, snacktime*). Events can be *sequenced* in relation to each other (e.g., getting dressed before breakfast), and the actions that compose the events themselves are ordered through time (e.g., put on socks before shoes). *Duration* may similarly refer to the duration of an event (e.g., how long breakfast takes) or to the interval between events (e.g., the time between coming home from school and dinner). Event *boundaries* are also temporally marked (e.g., "time to get up," "when we finish dinner"). *Speed* is related to the duration of an event (e.g., if you eat quickly, breakfast will be over sooner). The *frequency* with which an event has been experienced relates similar experiences to each other along the time axis. Thus, on the assumption that children's implicit and explicit understanding of time concepts and temporal relations derives from their understanding of events, and given the well-established event knowledge of young children, these concepts might be expected to be achieved relatively easily in early childhood.

Of course, children's understanding of events also depends upon their implicit understanding of temporal relations, that is, that one event component precedes and succeeds others, forming an inviolable sequence. Causally related events and highly routine events are more successfully sequenced than unfamiliar, arbitrarily related events (Bauer & Shore, 1987; Bauer & Mandler, 1989a; Slackman, 1985), but temporal sequence is a basic dimension of all event representations. There is good evidence that both duration and frequency are also basic dimensions for parsing and representing experience (Friedman, 1990a; Hasher & Zacks, 1979; Pouthas, 1985; Richie & Bickhard, 1988). As has been argued throughout this book, events are functional in the life of the child; it is important to know how routines proceed: when to expect lunch, the sequence of actions in the bath routine, what comes first in getting dressed, and so on. Therefore a functional representation system needs to represent sequence, duration, and frequency. Because these relations are not only perceived but also represented in the child's developing experientially based knowledge system, they may form a basis for learning the linguistic forms that express them.

Yet implicit aspects of experience are not easily transformed into concepts codable in language.[4] Event markers such as "bedtime" are based in the child's own experience; implicit in such markers is the idea that there are specific times during the day when certain events take place and not others. The regularity of bedtime, and other event times within the structure of the day, may facilitate associating clocktimes with them, and thus provide a meaning for times such as "9 o'clock." Some of the units people use for marking time are based in human social events (e.g., *lunchtime*), and others are based more or less directly on natural cycles (e.g., *morning, day, night*); however, most of those conventionally used (see Table 9.1) are arbitrary divisions (e.g., *minutes, hours, weeks, months*). There is in fact an element of conventionality even to the most "natural" units. Lunchtime and bedtime vary across households and cultures, as does the division of the day and night. (When does "afternoon" begin? Or "evening"? Does "night" begin at the same time in the summer as in the winter?)

In summary, many of the basic concepts of time derived from sequence and duration involve relations within and among events; children's event knowledge may implicitly embed them, thus making their "explicitation" through language relatively easy. However, time measurement, and comprehension of times at a distance from the living present, do not have this kind of support and thus may be delayed.

Social-cultural Time

> Time is not conceived in the same way by all human minds, nor is it reckoned by all peoples of the world in precisely the same manner. . . . In many parts of the world both past and present, for example, there is an overwhelming tendency to think of time in the form of recurring cycles, a continuous sequence of events with neither beginning nor end, the past forever repeating itself. (Aveni, 1989, p. 327)

The standard Western view of time is one-dimensional and linear, a time line along which either time moves from the future to the past, or the self moves from the past through present into the future. These two perspectives on time provide different metaphors with different implications [e.g., "Christmas is coming" vs. "we're approaching the end of the year": H. Clark (1973); Lakoff & Johnson (1980)]. The standard view emphasizes the temporal dynamic, in which the present is always moving into the past, a view that necessitates defining the boundaries of a stable but ever-changing "specious present" (James, 1950/1890). "Now" as distinguished from past and future is a concept that children must come to understand very early, but most observers believe that "now" is not an unlearned concept. As Valsiner (1993, p. 21) states, "The notion of present itself is a mental construction of our minds" dependent upon the capacity to reflect on the event that is currently in progress. Fraser (1987) claims that nonlinguistic creatures (human infants as well as nonhuman animals) live in an eternal present; this is reminiscent of Donald's (1991) claim that apes are confined to the present [see also Tulving (1983); Raeithel (1994)]. This view implies that the distinction between present, past, and future must be acquired in human childhood, presumably as the language of time is acquired (Nelson, 1989b).

We live in a strictly time-ordered society (particularly in North America), dependent to an extraordinary extent on clocks and calendars. In a very concrete sense our days are numbered. But this obsession with the passage of time, and mechanisms for marking and measuring it, is relatively recent in Western history and not universally spread among the cultures of the world even today. Simple agricultural societies generally mark times of the year for planting, harvesting, and other human activities, and usually relate these to celestial events of sun, stars and moon. The fifth-century B.C. Greek song-of-the-year (Hesiod's *Works and Days*) is representative of such a traditional "calendar." Aveni's (1989) analysis of this song cycle indicates that natural activities such as the coming of birds, appearance of certain plants, and changes in the weather were related to celestial activities on the one hand and to human activities (plowing, harvesting, sailing) on the other. Time was thus seen as a sequence of orderly events in tune with the natural world.

Most people – and certainly most children – in modern urban societies have little opportunity to understand time marking in this natural way. The Western concept of four seasons equal in length is actually quite arbitrary, derived from a solar-based calendar. Summer weather does not begin on June 21 at the solstice, and autumn does not begin on September 21 at the equinox, as Western calendars tell us. Indeed the entire concept of spring and autumn as separate seasons is questionable in most parts of the world; they are rather blurred transitions between the more distinct summer and winter seasons. In contrast, most agricultural societies have distinguished primarily between a wet and a dry season, sometimes with the result that large portions of the year are left out of their traditional calendars.

The construction of calendars in the literate world was undertaken by rulers of a society as a means of maintaining order, whether by the emperors of China (where clocks and calendars were held in great secrecy) or Rome, or later by Christian Popes. The Western calendar is a complex construction that has emerged over millenia from efforts to incorporate into one system the cycles of both moon and sun.[5] The Western year contains 52 weeks (plus 1 or 2 days) of 7 days. The week does not mesh with the division into months, and it is the most apparently arbitrary division of time units (why 7 and not 10, or 12, or 5?). Most societies have had some roughly equivalent division of days, apparently reflecting the rhythm of human work activity rather than any biological or extrahuman natural cycle. Within the week each day has its name, as well as its number within the month. Days progress linearly within the month, but cyclically by weeks, as Sunday comes around every eighth day. This is representative of the complex of line and cycle in the Western system of time reckoning, and typically in systems devised in other cultures.

The evolution of the clock and the standardization of clock time is as complex as the varied constructions of calendars. The division of the day into 2 cycles of 12 hours each is no more natural or logical than the division of the year into weeks of 7 days. The hour does not relate to any biological unit or rhythm; its 60 minutes could as well be 12 or 100. Clocks have existed in various forms in the West since Roman times at least (even earlier in China). The mechanical clock was invented and dispersed during the late Middle Ages; subsequently, the village clock tower came to rival the church in ordering the lives and activities of the community. However, until the late nineteenth century each village and town maintained its own time, which might differ from the next town down the road. It was the necessity of constructing train schedules and timetables that made the adoption of standard times and time zones necessary. Additional standardization has been imposed by radio and television schedules, and legislatures have imposed various forms of daylight saving time for summer months, requiring a biyearly adjustment of the clock and associated biorhythms.

To conclude, there is no firm basis in nature for the existing social-cultural systems of time. Yet children must somehow coordinate these with their own experiential temporal understandings. Furthermore, there is no single conception or system of time within either the natural or the social-cultural framework. Individuals must come to operate with many systems for different, and sometimes the same, purposes. The perspective that McGrath and Kelly (1986) refer to as "transactional" time is out of synchrony with the arbitrary systems of time measurement discussed here. In this perspective, "Time is divisible but differentiated, with certain points in time serving as 'critical values' (e.g., birth, metamorphosis, cell division, etc.) . . . an experiential time . . . phasic in passage, and irreversible . . . developmental in its flow, spiral in form rather than strictly recurrent" (p. 33). This perspective permeates an alternative "time frame" that is prominent in Western thinking but differs from the physical science perspective represented in clock time. Both children and adults in Western society come to understand, at least implicitly, both time frames.[6] As McGrath and Kelly (1986) put it: "We tend to *think about time* as if it were abstract, unidirectional, uniform in passage, divisible, and homogeneous; but we tend to *use time* as if it were concrete, phasic, and epochal" (p. 36).

Transactional social time is concerned with the passage of time in human lives, and as part of that concern, birth, death, and age since birth. These time concepts are those most frequently presented to young children by early childhood educators, for example, through the study of plants and the celebration of birthdays. Thus it is this perspective that children first encounter explicitly as a supplement to their implicit notions of time derived from events and from linguistic expressions. Not all peoples of the world calculate age, and those that do vary in the methods they use. For example, Koreans traditionally all count from the same day of the year, and the Chinese count from the first year, not the second as Westerners do. But all people recognize age in the sense of distinct periods of life, and mark progress along the age range, especially the move into adulthood.

Cultural celebrations of various kinds, associated with religion or secular affairs, are also marked at definite times of the year. Our American year is punctuated by at least 10 generally recognized major holidays plus minor occasions, such as Halloween, that are important especially for children. Societies also all construct some kind of history, at least tracing events back for a few generations, and universally produce mythological explanations of their origins. Of course, the modern sense of history, which now stretches into the remote past to the origins of the universe, and into the infinite future, is a recent construction of the scientific community as much as a reconstruction of human events. Thus the two perspectives intersect in the scientific, if not in the folk, conception of time.

The coexistence of these competing frames of reference may pose a challenge to the child who is coming to reorganize an experientially based conceptual system to accord with the culturally defined concepts exhibited through language and other symbolic forms. In a sense, the notion of time as uniform and homogeneous must be laid on top of the experiential sense of time as phasic and epochal. Language provides a way of thinking about and talking about both frames. Ultimately children must learn to work with many different temporal systems, together or separately, whether explicitly taught or individually constructed.

Educated Time

The preceding discussion refers to the many different systems that humans have constructed around time. These systems define categories and units through which to organize concepts of temporal location, sequence, duration (within and between events), and frequency. Conventional units of time are measured numerically (e.g., 6 weeks hence; 100 years ago) and additively, as in days of the month (e.g., January 6) and year (e.g., 1950). However, units of time are neither like apples and oranges, nor like sticks and stones that can be laid out in a line to be counted. Clocks and calendars mark out symbolic spaces that visually represent temporal units; these can be counted, but their relation to the passage of time is ambiguous and not readily apparent even with direct instruction. Distance in time enters into and cross-cuts all time concepts and relations: how close or how far in time from the present an event or a period is. The ability to conceptualize far-off time (past or future) is distinctly human (Fraser, 1987); that it depends on linguistic expression is a strong probability.[7] A grasp of historical time is achieved relatively late in development. The time scale of geological time was a late development in history (Gould, 1987), and is an abstraction that is difficult for most adults to grasp. At the other end, the measurement of time in units smaller than seconds lies also beyond the conceptual grasp of many adults, much less young children.

In addition to these cultural constructions of time, science has provided us with "objective" time – nonpurposeful and impersonal. It includes Newton's laws of time, speed, and distance, Einstein's relativity, and the picoseconds of electron movement. The dominant modern Western time perspective is permeated by classical physical conceptions of time as atomistic and divisible but homogeneous (all units are equal), its units flowing in linear succession, abstract and objective, unidirectional (not reversible). This objective classical scientific time contrasts with numerous other possible conceptions of time, including those of not only Eastern philosophy but also Einsteinian physics, in which time is relative and reversible. For humans time is irreversible, thus Newtonian time is more intuitive than is Einsteinian. Yet as Piaget's research demonstrated, Newtonian concepts are also late developments, and plausibly depend on formal education. Many cultural concepts of educated time, however, are displayed informally in everyday language, such as those of speed.

Time Language: What Is Coded?

The thesis of this chapter, in line with the overall thesis of the book, is that time concepts are initially mastered informally through experience with language forms related to temporal concepts in situations when such concepts are relevant to ongoing or otherwise contexted activities. Languages encode temporal relations in two ways: lexically and grammatically. Grammar includes the use of tense and aspect as well as complex syntactic constructions for invoking temporal perspective. Grammatical expressions of time have been much more intensively studied by developmental psycholinguists than have lexical expressions. The following sections consider some of the complexities that children encounter in acquiring both kinds of expressions.

Obligatory Grammaticization: Tense and Aspect

Almost all languages have some system of tense (Comrie, 1985; Traugott, 1978), the grammaticized expression of location in time.[8] English distinguishes past, present, and future, which can be conceptualized as existing as relative points along a time line. Tense is thus a *deictic* notion, one that depends upon the establishment of a "deictic center" in relation to which other points can be located. In the case of time this center is "now" or speech time (ST). Tense is distinguished from aspect, which expresses the internal temporal contour of a situation. For example, the distinction between *John is singing* and *John was singing* is one of tense (present vs. past), while the distinction between *John was singing* and *John sang* is one of aspect (continuative vs. completive).

Children typically begin to acquire the system of past, present, and future forms, and of progressive aspect (*-ing*) around 2 years of age. Although this does not imply that the relevant concepts are available independent of the language system [and different languages grammaticize different aspects of temporal perspective – see Slobin (1982); Berman & Slobin (1994)] it suggests that obligatory coding in the language at least makes these dimensions salient. There is some evidence that children first use the past tense to refer to the immediate rather than the remote past (Weist, 1986). However, when utterances are sampled in a context that supports reference to events from the non-immediate situation, children may use past tense to refer to the more remote past [and similarly for the future–Nelson (1989b)].

A dispute centers on the question of whether children first use tense to express aspectual notions (e.g., the completion of an action) rather than deictic ones (action in the past) as claimed by Antinucci and Miller [(1976); also, Bloom et al. (1980)]. Other studies (Weist et al., 1984; Weist, 1986) have indicated that children are sensitive to the deictic meaning of tense forms from very early in grammatical development [but see Bloom & Harner (1989)]. Evidence suggests that the specific past/present contrast represented in tense forms may be constructed in response to linguistic coding rather than being itself a base from which that coding is learned. For example, Bloom and colleagues (1980) argue that children are first sensitive to the form of action (aspect), restricting past forms to uses in reference to completed actions before generalizing to any activity or state prior to the present time.

In contrast to both these claims, Gerhardt (1989) argued that Emily distinguished only between what was happening *now* versus usual events that take place in the *not now* (that, as we would say, have taken place or will take place). Her first temporal perspective was thus said to be not a distinction between past and present, but between present and not present. This suggestion is consistent with a memory system in which representations of "not now" events are not coded for a specific time in the past or future, but only as general experience [mental event representations (MERs)]: as "this is what happens." If this is true, children must acquire an understanding of the specific past and specific future in contrast to the present as they acquire the grammatical tense system. Obviously more evidence is needed to shore up this speculation, but it accords with the general rather than specific basic memory system outlined in Chapter 6 [see Nelson (1989b) for further discussion].

Note that the acquisition of the past-present-future reference system proceeds differently for those children described as following an aspect before tense course (Antinucci & Miller, 1976) and for Emily, who seemed to first develop a now–not now contrast. But both proceed from what are assumed to be salient and functional nonlinguistic dimensions of events and event knowledge toward an understanding of events within a culturally conventional, linguistically coded system. Unlike other aspects of language learning, in which the child may begin with conceptual (semantic) relations that are subsequently grammaticized [see discussions in Levy, Schlesinger, & Braine (1988)], in this case it appears that grammatical coding precedes and leads to semantic conceptualizations (Nelson, 1989b).

Optional Lexicalization: Relations, Pseudo-objects

In addition to tense and aspect, there are numerous terms in the language that may be used to reference time: generally adverbs, prepositions, and conjunctions, but also nouns that refer to pseudo-objects (*yesterday*, for example may be used as either an adverb or a noun). As shown in Table 9.1, such terms may express definite location in time, sequence, and duration or interval. There are many other lexical items that encode relative temporal concepts (e.g., *while, during, already, since*), which have been little studied in the psychological literature. Languages also encode the definite arbitrary concepts tied to conventional temporal systems, such as those for months, days, years, hours.

As discussed in the previous sections, human concepts of time have a basis in the representation of events experienced through time. By 3 years of age children not only participate in, demonstrating predictive control of, familiar routines, but also verbalize the temporal sequence of actions within these activities, and they sequence events within a day (Carbery, 1989; Friedman, 1990b). Friedman (1990a) has also demonstrated that by 3 years children have some initial relative conception of the duration of familiar events.

The language of time must be coordinated with these understandings, and as the previous discussion has indicated, this is not a straightforward mapping process, in which language terms map onto preexisting concepts. Most temporal terms (including parts of the day – "morning," "afternoon," "night" – and the deictic terms for "yesterday," "today," and "tomorrow") denote abstract objects that cannot be mapped onto preexisting schemas or concepts derived directly from experienced events. Relative terms for sequence ("before," "after") duration ("while," "yet"), and frequency ("always," "never"), although bearing some relation to the knowledge implicit in event representations, nonetheless must be extracted from discourse about events and the relations marked by them made explicit.

Learning Temporal Language

Lexical terms for temporal concepts and relations are not usually acquired until after the basic forms of tense and aspect. Temporal adverbs such as *today* and *last night* and adverbial clauses beginning with *when* are among the first to be used, enabling the child to express relations such as "Today we went to the park" and "When Daddy comes home I can watch TV." Harner's (1975) studies of children's comprehension of "yesterday" and "tomorrow" concluded that at first children understood the terms as meaning "not today"; "yesterday" was understood as referring to sometime in the past before "tomorrow" was understood as referring to sometime in the future.[9]

An example from a 3-year-old child suggests how terms like "yesterday" may become understood in relation to the child's organization of event knowledge. In this example, mother and Steven are driving to nursery school:

(1) S: This . . . remember the water was here . . . the old pud-
         dle was here when it rained tonight?
     M: When it rained . . . the other day.
     S: No, it rained yesterday.
     M: No, it rained the day before yesterday.
     S: No, it was the day before . . . yest . . . yesterday. It was
         now yesterday!
     M: It was now yesterday?
     S: No, when we were . . . when it was night then . . . night-
         time then it was yesterday. When we waked up . . .
         when we had some supper . . . then we went to bed,
         then it was nighttime, then the sun was out, then it
         was nighttime, then it rained, then we waked up, then
         we . . . then we goed, then we went in that puddle.
         (Nelson, 1977a, pp. 226–227)

In this example it appears that Steven is trying to go backward in time to when it rained (the day before yesterday), even while constrained to ordering events in a forward sequence (i.e., supper, bed, sun, night-time). Coordinating the forward sequence, necessary to ordering activities in real time, with the backward sequence, necessary when representing events in the past, is obviously a formidable task. It appears to be solvable by Steven in terms of a hierarchy of temporal units, with the day sequence retaining its forward order while the sequence of days is reversed. This effort can also be seen as reflecting the difficulty of coordinating cycles and sequences, as Friedman (1982) noted. All this manipulation takes place on a mental/linguistic representation level with no concrete props to aid in the construction. This seemingly very simple reconstruction is a difficult task for the 3-year-old mind, and it is most unlikely that it could have been achieved without the use of the external-ized language representation, as the obvious struggle to articulate the relation suggests. Thus it involves significant cognitive work on the part of the individual child.

The acquisition of the temporal prepositions "before" and "after" and the use of these terms to introduce subordinate clauses is typically de-layed for a year or more after the first use of temporal adverbs (Weist, 1986). When these uses are mastered, the child is able to express rela-tions such as "Before we had our pizza, we ate the salad."[10] French and Nelson (1985) analyzed the use of temporal terms by preschool children who described scripts for familiar events, and found that in that context 3- and 4-year-olds used temporal language to express more complex relations than is reported in experimental studies with children of this age. In particular, the expression of relative time ("and then"), as well as the sequencing of events using "before," "first," and "after" appeared in the scripts of the youngest children, in contrast to findings from the experimental literature.

Concepts of seasons, holidays, and birthdays, and language terms referring to them are typically expected of young children, and are dis-cussed with them explicitly. Lexical terms for the conventional units of days, months, and years tend to be used in discourse but not directly taught until the early school years. Thus their forms may become famil-iar to young children although their reference remains obscure, and they may be found in the talk of 3-year-olds reflecting "use without meaning" (see Chapter 5). Language referring to arbitrary conventional measures of time is rarely observed in use by preschool children, and when it is, it is inaccurately used (e.g., in reporting a "making cookies" script: "the cookies have to bake for 5 hours").

Use before Meaning for Temporal Terms

Given that expressions for many temporal relations and concepts are not directly taught to the child and cannot be inferred from concrete refer-ence, how are they learned? Several clues from the study of Emily's crib monologues suggest a probable course of development. As documented in the previous chapters, Emily used her monologues to reconstruct events from the past, to forecast events in the future (based on what her parents told her and her own past experience), and to construct a gen-eral account of how things go (Nelson, 1989a). Within these narratives she produced many temporal terms although, as the earlier examples showed, there was often a misfit between the actual event parameters and her linguistic expressions relating to them. Still, divorced from the context of the real-world constraints, her use of the terms "sounds right." That is, they were appropriately used in terms of both syntax and narrative discourse. Thus it appears that she had acquired notions of what syntactic and discourse contexts the terms were useful in (e.g., "yesterday" indicates that talk is about the past; "so" connects two related clauses) without yet attaching any specific meaning to the terms. Levy and Nelson (1994) hypothesized that she was following a strategy for acquiring words in discourse contexts characterized as "use before meaning" (as explicated in Chapter 5). Use before meaning contrasts with other possible formulations to describe the course of learning, including attributing incorrect meaning or incomplete meaning to the child. Use before meaning implies that the use of a term will at first be tightly constrained to particular discourse and syntactic contexts in which it has been observed in use by others, and later extended to other contexts after the acquisition of some meaning derived from attending to its use by other speakers.

The working assumption here is that the terms Emily used in this "meaningless" way had been used by parents or other adults in conversation about events that Emily found interpretable on other grounds, on the basis of her general event knowledge and specific past experience. Then in talking about the same or similar events herself she could insert the appropriate words into more or less appropriate slots in her narratives. In the absence of negative feedback, the form might be used again in similar contexts. In the course of using and hearing it used the child could attend more and more to the conditions of use implied by adult uses, and eventually emerge with a meaning constructed from use that matched that of the adult language. The process then gradually builds up a system of related concepts reflecting in part those of the adult conventional system (analogous to Figure 8.1).

Parent and Child Time Language

From this perspective it is relevant to learn what kind of time language children hear and in what kinds of contexts. Lucariello and Nelson (1987) found that mothers tended to talk with their children about past and future events at times when the ongoing activity did not absorb their attention, that is, when there was extra "processing space" that could be given to matters beyond the here and now. During routine caretaking activities such as having lunch, mothers might talk about what had happened that morning or what would happen that afternoon. They used terms with their 2-year-old children such as "today" and "last night," locating events in the past, as well as relative time markers such as "later," "after," "when," especially in reference to anticipated future events. Parents embed these terms in remembering and planning narratives.

Emily's parents' bedtime talk was very largely concerned with talk about anticipated future events, and contained references to "tomorrow morning," "Saturday," "after your nap," and so on, as well as references to the present and the immediate future. For example, when Emily was 26 months, her father used the phrase "just a minute" only for limiting his assent to her request to be rocked in her crib ("I will rock you for just a minute"). In a following monologue Emily stated that "Daddy came in just a minute and rocked me." This particular expression had not been previously observed and it was used at that time only in the specific context in which it was used by the parent. The assumption here is that her representation of the event of Daddy rocking her had come to include the specification "just a minute." There was no indication that Emily attached any particular meaning to the phrase, however; "just a minute" did not specify a particular duration of time over which the rocking took place.

A tabulation of the varieties of uses of temporal language by Emily's parents during the course of pre-bed conversations with her at 26 months, and her own uses to express similar concepts in her monologues, is shown in Table 9.2, in the basic concept terms introduced in Table 9.1. This table reveals the many complex expressions to which a child may be exposed, as well as the several but still limited ways in which her own language (if not her concepts) match those of her parents.

A more detailed analysis of the data shows more precisely the restrictions on her uses of these terms and their possible generalizations over time (Levy & Nelson, 1994). Emily had already begun to use words for temporal concepts at 1 year and 9 months when taping began; her use over the entire 16-month observation of the conventional time adverbials "afternoon," "pretty soon," "tomorrow," "today," and "yesterday" was traced in detail, with a focus on changes in their use. As already noted, prior research indicated that the latter three words – "tomorrow," "today," and "yesterday" – are not generally understood in their conventional meanings by children younger than 3 years (Harner, 1982), and their meanings in discourse are often quite obscure. Many of the early instances of these time words occurred in discourse

Table 9.2. *Temporal terms used by Emily and her parents*

Concept	Parent		Emily
Location	afternoon earlier goodnight's (sleep) morning nighttime now right now Saturday	sometime Sunday time togotobed today tomorrow tonight weekend when	in the morning in the night in the nighttime now right now when yesterday
Sequence	after afterward because	so then while (simul)	and then if cause so when
Duration	a little bit a little early in the meantime in another month just a minute	not quite yet not yet pretty soon until yet	just a minute
Frequency	again already betcha	maybe probably sometimes	again already maybe
Other	any more birthday day (fun, nice, busy, mommy & daddy, Tanta) Good night	grow just starting til times (fun) tomorrow (topic)	any more day (fun) long time (topic) Good night tomorrow (topic)

Note: Includes all temporal references in the dialogues and monologues when Emily was 26 months (7 sessions: 231 parent utterances, and 101 child utterances).

contexts that appeared to be borrowed from adult speech patterns, as in the following example:

(2) *afternoon* Emmy wake up
then Mormor come
now Emmy
afternoon Emmy sleep
afternoon Daddy coming
pretty soon Emmy go sleep
then Mormor come   (1;9.13)

As this example illustrates, "afternoon," "pretty soon," and "tomorrow" tended to recur with the same expressions: *Emmy/my wake up, Emmy sleep,* and *Mommy/Daddy/Mormor come.* In fact, until 24 months all instances of these expressions occurred with the verbs *wake/get up, (go) sleep,* and *come.* The only instances of "today" that appeared before 2 years occurred with the related verbs, *go nap* and *come.* Other temporal relativizers, such as "now" and "then," were used with these terms as well. At this age Emily had not yet mastered the tense and aspect system of verb morphology; therefore, her grammar did not express temporal perspective, although her discourse structures did.

Emily's uses of these temporal expressions during these months was similar to that of her father as he negotiated with her about going to sleep. For example, the following passage begins with *(when you) wake/ get up* and continues with a list of anticipated activities. Note the proximity of the time word "tomorrow" to the verbs *wake up* and *get up.*

(3)   F: *When you wake up* we are going to Tanta's first of all. I'll tell
       you what we're going to do *tomorrow.* Let Daddy ex-
       plain. *When you wake up* you say "good morning Daddy,
       good morning Mommy." . . .
       Did you want me to explain what we're going to do *tomor-
       row* again? . . . You're going to *get up* and you say "good
       morning Daddy, good morning Mommy." . . .
       When we get up tomorrow morning. Now you listen to
       Daddy. Now you listen. We're going to have waf-
       fles . . .

The similarity of Emily's uses to her father's discourse patterns suggests that during this period her use of time words was borrowed quite directly from her father's speech. She appears to have internalized distributionally based generalizations that specify that "afternoon," "pretty soon," and "tomorrow" are connectors that occur with a small set of expressions, the generalizations taking the following form:

time connector + noun/verb combinations

Emmy/my wake up

Emmy/my sleep

Daddy/Mommy/Mormor coming

Daddy/Mormor get my up

This pattern indicates the grounding of the temporal connectors in event representations – in particular in Emily's routines surrounding naptime and bedtime. Whether or not at this point she connected the terms and the descriptions of activities with her prior and projected event experiences is unknown. We can only suggest that her father's descriptions and her repetitions of patterns of co-occurring expressions provided the opportunity for such an analysis, and thus for attaching some temporal significance to the use of the temporal terms.

At first most instances of time words occurred with other time words, such as "now." This suggests that the time words were beginning to be systematized with respect to each other, whether or not their temporal component was yet recognized. Different time words occur in similar clausal contexts, as the following example indicates:

(4)   *pretty soon* my daddy mommy come get
       this afternoon Mormor comes
       and Mommy Daddy comes
       Mommy Daddy come and get up my
       afternoon Mormor come   (1;9.9)

At this point there was no evidence that semantic differences had been worked out. Semantic differences may have emerged through associating particular time words with particular event sequences; for example, *afternoon* came, through continued repetition, to be associated with specific routine events.

After this initial period of formulaic uses, these temporal terms dropped from Emily's narrative monologues almost completely for about 6 months (from 2;1 to 2;7). Those that did occur were not used in connection with her daily routines, as previously. The virtual disappearance of time words from Emily's crib monologues coincided with the establishment of the tense and aspect system of verb morphology in her grammar [see Gerhardt (1989); Nelson (1989b)]. This coincidence is intriguing and leads to the following speculation: As the tense-aspect system came into play Emily became alerted to temporal perspective and to the temporal component of terms that had previously been viewed as neutral connectors. Because these connectors were no longer neutral, it was necessary to work out their semantic entailments through attention to the discourse uses of other speakers. As this process progressed, some of the words would be expected to reappear with a firmer semantic grounding, which indeed was observed in the later months of the study.

Between $2\frac{1}{2}$ and 3 years "tomorrow" and "today" began to represent time slots, different time slots for each term. Time now appeared as segmented into units, with activities occupying these units. It is proposed that activities created time units for the child, providing a functional basis for the use of borrowed time expressions, as the following examples illustrate:

(5)   *tomorrow* when we wake up from bed
      first me and Daddy and Mommy you eat breakfast
      eat breakfast like we usually do . . .
      but *today* I'm going to nursery school in the morning   (2;8.0)
(6)   *today* Daddy went trying to get into the race . . .
      tomorrow he'll run run run in the race   (2;8.8)

Tracing the process of acquiring lexical items in the terms that were laid out in Chapter 5, it may be noted that appropriate grammatical placement in sentence structures was observed for every temporal form acquired, although there was no evidence of specific control of grammatical function. Use in discourse was achieved and extended over the period to contexts where appropriate, from restricted generalizations based on adult discourse patterns to semantic flexibility, at least for the terms "today" and "tomorrow." Although some denotational meaning – temporal specification associated with activities – was achieved by the end of the period when Emily was just 3 years old, unrestricted use for interpreting and constructing temporal relations was not yet in evidence.

These observations provide strong evidence that construction of meaning from use may take a long time. As already noted, many children do not understand the specific reference of "yesterday" and "tomorrow" before the age of 4 or 5 years, although they hear them frequently and may use them themselves. And, as Carni and French (1984) showed, 3-year-olds tend not to understand the terms "before" and "after" outside of familiar well-structured events, although they produce them in appropriate familiar contexts. In some cases a child may check her explicit understanding of a term after having used it implicitly for some time. For example, Steven's attempt to reconstruct *yesterday* in dialogue (1) seems to involve a kind of explicit checking of his understanding of this relation.

In the present view, then, the child gradually develops knowledge about temporal expressions as they are used by others and as she uses them herself. The terms analyzed by Levy and Nelson are but a tiny sample of those listed in Tables 9.1 and 9.2, and do not include the formal system terms involving minutes, hours, days, weeks, and months that are also presented informally by parents. However, these may also begin to be acquired in similar ways. For example, following the model of Daddy's "I will rock you for just a minute" (cited earlier), the next time

Emily wants to be rocked, she is likely to include the phrase and ask Daddy to rock her for just a minute; his related use (e.g., "no that's enough for now, it's more than just a minute") can lead the child to adjust her understanding of the appropriate use of the phrase. As observations of its use in other contexts are accumulated the phrase may become generalized to novel situations. The child may notice that "in a minute" is a closely related phrase, and the two may be used interchangeably. (Indeed, in the use quoted the two are conflated.) Of course, in everyday speech these terms do not actually reference minutes as these are measured in clock time. Eventually the child has to adjust her understanding of "minute" to accord with the clock and to know that "5 minutes" is a definite period of time, whereas "just a minute" and "in a minute" are used to indicate "not very long at all." Thus constant adjustment of both her representation of reality and her representation of the possible meanings of words and phrases is necessary as the child proceeds through the preschool and into the school years.

The child's construction of meanings on the basis of event knowledge is only a part of the story, however. The other essential part is experience with language in discourse concerned with time, as the previous analyses have documented. Moreover, all the cultural constructions of clock and calendar time units must be acquired through direct instruction, whether at home or in school. The relevance of how adults incorporate their temporal models in discourse with children is evident in research showing that children who do not experience such talk are seriously delayed in achieving knowledge of temporal concepts. Two studies of children in poverty in the United States, both homeless and housed (Flores, 1993; Norton, 1990), documented this relation. Flores (1993) hypothesized that children whose environments were chaotic through overcrowding or homelessness would have impoverished MERs, reflected in poor performance on sequencing tasks and temporal knowledge. These hypotheses were confirmed for Headstart children from both homeless and housed poverty homes. Norton documented that children in poverty who did not hear temporal language from parents performed more poorly in school than those who did. Such deficiencies in comparison with expected child acquisitions emphasize the importance of social-linguistic experiences in this domain. Acquiring temporal concepts is never simply a matter of individual cognitive achievements or theory-building. But what is the relation of cognitive development to conceptual acquisition in this domain?

Cognitive Development and the Acquisition of Temporal Perspective in Language

Based on his analysis of the use of temporal language – tense, aspect, and temporal terms – by two of Brown's (1973) subjects, Cromer (1968) proposed a developmental scheme derived from Piaget's theory, in particular the notion that the young child is centered on the here and now, and needs to develop the capacity to "decenter." Prior to decentering, the child was held to be unable to take a perspective other than that of the present, thus delaying the achievement of complex temporal expressions. In particular, the use of the "timeless" verb form (the simple present to express the normative or general case) was thought to be a late achievement, a claim later contradicted by script research (Nelson & Gruendel, 1981). In reconsidering the "cognition hypothesis," however, Cromer (1989) took an interactionist view in which language is held to be composed of a number of subsystems, some of which may be dependent upon cognitive achievements and some of which are independent of general cognition. He also accepted that some time concepts may be derived from language use.

A related decentration suggestion is based on suggestions by Miller (1978), Weist (1986), and Smith (1980), who described the development of tense in terms – introduced by Reichenbach (1947) – of the establishment of relations between speech time (ST), reference time (RT), and event time (ET). Briefly, Weist's (1986) claim is that children progress "through a sequence of four temporal systems during the development of the capacity to express increasingly complex configurations of temporal concepts" (p. 357). At first there is a "here and now" system in which ET and RT are frozen at ST (as in the child's first tenseless statements). Next, the child differentiates ET from ST through the use of tense (at about $1\frac{1}{2}$ to 2 years), but RT is stuck at ST (speech time – now – is the only reference time). In the third system (at about 3 years), RT may be differentiated from ST but if so, ET is restricted to the RT context. At this point the child may locate events with adverbials such as "yesterday." Finally (around 4 years), RT may be established separately from ST and ET may be separated from both RT and ST, through the use of *before* and *after* clauses, and complex tenses such as the perfective.

However, there is reason to doubt that the developmental course of the expression of ST-ET-RT relations is as constrained by cognitive development as Weist claimed. Even at the very beginning of the development of the tense and aspect system (at 22 to 23 months) Emily was capable of expressing RT, ET, and ST independently. The following monologue [reported in Chapter 7, monologue (8)] can be analyzed to reveal this clearly:

(7)	My sleep	ET1 = RT1
	Mommy came	ET2 = RT1
	And Mommy "get up, get up time go home."	ET3
	When my slep and	RT1 = ET1
	And mormor came	RT1?
	Then mommy coming	ET2 = RT1
	Then "get up, time to go hoome."	ET3
	Time to go home.	ET3
	Drink p-water. [Perrier]	ET4
	Yesterday did that.	RT1 = ET{1,2,3,4}
	Now Emmy sleeping in regular bed.	ST = RT2 = ET5 > RT1

Here ET1 = the first event in the activity sequence, ET2 the second, and so on, while RT1 = the reference time of the first event.

My gloss on this narrative is straightforward, although not without its ambiguities: Yesterday (actually earlier the same day) Emily was sleeping at Tanta's (or perhaps Mormor's) when Mommy (or Mormor) came and told her to get up because it was time to go home. They went home and she drank "p-water" (Perrier).

Emily displays several characteristics of Weist's stage 2 (restricted RT): She uses both temporal adverbs ("yesterday," "now") and adverbial clauses (*when my slep*) to establish reference time separately from ST. This puts her considerably in advance of the age norms Weist projected. Even more interesting, this indicates that she can manipulate these relations with minimal mastery of the tense system itself. Note the inconsistent use of tenses in this segment: Mommy *came*, mommy *coming*; my *sleep*, my *slept* (and in another version, *my sleeping*). Yet from another perspective, she appears to be attempting to contrast tenses to set up temporal relations.[11] For example, in the first two lines: my *sleep* (RT) followed by Mommy *came* (ET); lines 5 and 7: my *slep* (RT), then mommy *coming* (ET). The last 3 lines here also contrast in an interesting way: *drink* (ET3), *did that* (RT = ET{1,2,3,4}), *sleeping* (ST = ET5). Present is used for the event in the narrative, past to indicate reference time for the narrative, and progressive to indicate now, speech time.

From the point of view of sentence structure, then, this segment represents an imperfect attempt at restricted reference time. But when viewed in terms of extended discourse, namely, as an attempt to construct a narrative of an experienced event, the effort is much more impressive. In the narrative, the speaker must go beyond sentential relations to relate events to each other over time. In this simple segment, what Emily has accomplished is to set up a reference time, not for one event but for a sequence of actions that are ordered in relation to each other. We can envision this in terms of positions along a time line, as follows:

$$\text{RT} = \text{ET1} \longrightarrow \text{ET2} \longrightarrow \text{ET3} \longrightarrow \text{ET4} \longrightarrow \text{ST}$$
$$\text{Time}$$
$$\longrightarrow$$

Given these relations, the narrator must first refer back in time to establish the beginning point (my sleeping) and then move forward toward the present in the order of the actions (events 1, 2, 3, and 4), finally moving to the present to reestablish ST in relation to the totality of the events recounted (yesterday did *that*). When viewed in this way it is clear that Emily is not restricted to an RT = ET system, but rather is able to use different events as references for subsequent ones. That is, "mommy coming" serves as the RT for the ET of mommy saying "get up," which serves in turn as the RT for the ET of "drink p-water." The RT system may not yet be entirely free, but it is already at not yet 2 years quite complex, at least when based on the child's own event representations.

The major point to be emphasized here, quite aside from the issue of specific ages, is that the ability to manipulate time relations appears in connected discourse prior to its appearance in single sentences. Therefore, conclusions about cognitive constraints drawn from sentence grammars or the use of lexical terms can be misleading. Moreover, the evident ability of this child to set up stable representations and then to manipulate order relations within them is consistent with evidence from other, albeit somewhat older children. The complexity of thought implied by this ability is impressive. At present there is little evidence for general cognitive constraints on the expression of temporal order relations. Thus, as discussed also in Chapters 5 and 7, discourse grammar may in cases of complex relations actually precede sentence grammar. Extended discourse may provide further evidence regarding the cognitive basis for the expression of temporal concepts and relations and the general course and conditions of their development around 3 to 4 years of age.

Coordination of Event Knowledge and Language

The hypothesis that the child uses knowledge of event structure as a framework for acquiring and eventually interpreting words coding temporal relations can be viewed in terms of the coordination of two relational structures: speech and event representations. Consider the representation of event A *while* event B [e.g., Mother cooked (A) while child watched TV (B)], each represented along a time line.

$$A \longrightarrow$$
MER B——————→ (now)

————————————

SR   A while B   ST
————————→
Time

(MER = event representation; SR = speech representation; ST = speech time. The horizontal arrows indicate indefinite continuation of activity in the past.) The SR presents the events sequentially; the ER, simultaneously. Coordination of the two requires that *while* is recognized as an indicator of simultaneous action. Other representations of this kind for some of the temporal terms that children come to understand are illustrated in Figure 9.1. The significance of learning to use terms within familiar structured events is brought out by this analysis: Without a prior understanding of the event structure the terminology of the SR cannot be interpreted.

The diagrams in Figure 9.1 suggest that the one-element terms (6–9: "already," "still," "soon," "yet") may be simpler than the two-element terms shown in 1–5 ("when," "before," "after," "until," "since," and "while"). Moreover, "before" and "after" represent the same event structures and may therefore be harder for the child to differentiate and assign correctly, an outcome that is verified by the research indicating their late mastery (e.g., Clark, 1971, 1983).[12]

In summary, then, the present proposal is that the child relies on event knowledge based on prior experience first to acquire and eventually to interpret the meaning of words that refer to basic temporal concepts and relations. Those relations that directly reflect the relations represented in event knowledge (relations of sequence, frequency, and some notions of duration) would be expected to take on meaning for the child relatively early and to be extended to novel contexts of use relatively easily. Those concepts and relations not implicit in the child's representations of events (e.g., definite conventionally determined locations in time, tem-

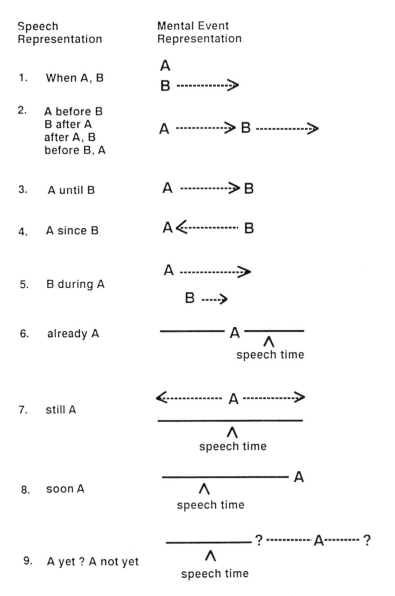

Figure 9.1. Coordination of mental event representations of time concepts with speech representations

poral measuring units) would be expected to be understood later and with more difficulty and to be used incorrectly rather frequently. As the data from Emily presented here indicate, terms such as "today," "afternoon," and "tomorrow" may also be understood in terms of their relation to familiar events, and thus may provide a bootstrapping mechanism for acquiring other conventional terms. Data do not exist at the present time that would allow a systematic test of these hypotheses, but research in progress is addressed to them.

Educated Time

Whereas many temporal terms and temporal concepts are incorporated into the child's representational system by way of their use in events, as described in the previous section, much of the cultural system of time is directly taught, beginning in the preschool years. Preschools represent time in many ways, implicitly through scheduling routines, and explicitly through daily plans, calendars, clocks, and books about temporality, especially seasons and holidays, as well as the passage of time of the day, week, and year. That these are difficult conceptual systems for children to grasp is evident in surveys of their knowledge (Ames, 1946; Harner et al., 1992). When asked when different routines take place ("When do you wake up?" "When does school start?" "When do you go to bed?"), preschool children 3 to 5 years old typically respond in terms of events ("when mommy comes to get me") rather than in terms of locatives ("in the morning") or clock time ("at 7"). Older preschoolers may mention numerical times, but inaccurately. Many 7-year-olds are unable to provide the correct hour of their daily routines. This progression indicates a movement from time based in events to conventional notions expressed in language terms to the acquisition of the conventional temporal measurements. In general in American homes and schools, children come to learn about their age and birthday first, then the days of the week associated with their weekly routines, and the seasons of the year, usually taught in the preschool years. Months of the year are acquired later through instruction of the calendar; finally, clock knowledge is taught formally in second grade but is learned earlier at home by many children.

These systems may be learned without much deeper understanding of their basis, however, as suggested by children's responses to questions such as "What happens to the clock while you're sleeping?" (Arlin, 1990) and "Is it the same time at home as at school?" (Harner et al., 1992). Preschool children claim that the clock does not move while they sleep, and that it is not the same time at home as at school. Children also have difficulty in dealing with the cyclical nature of time (Friedman, 1982). Preschool children can order the sequence of daily activities from morning to night (a linear order), but cannot start at different points in the cycle (e.g., begin at night and carry on to the next morning). The use of clocks and calendars provides the mechanisms by which people can track the passage of time, forward and backward. It is not surprising that children cannot do this on their own until they learn the skills involved in using these artifacts.

Cultural differences (Hall, 1983; Whorf, 1956) may be reflected in children's acquisition of time systems over generations and across societies that share conventional systems. Such differences were found in the comparison of the survey from 1946 (Ames) and the similar survey from 1992, indicating that today's children are more cognizant of clock times, but less advanced than the earlier sample in understanding conventional terms for weeks and months. Although the populations surveyed were not strictly comparable, differences in societal arrangements at different periods are most striking: working families dependent on strict daily regimes; widespread preschool experience; the omnipresence of television, with its rigid clock-time scheduling – all might serve to bring hourly measurements to the attention of young children today, in contrast to 50 years ago. Moreover, comparison with contemporary children in Hungary indicates that the particular emphasis in preschools may affect the order of acquisition of concepts. More event-related answers to "when" questions were provided by the younger children in the Hungarian sample, whereas the American children had greater familiarity with conventional time units and measurements. According to Korintus (1992), Hungarian society is much less clock-oriented than American society today, therefore Hungarian children are exposed to less talk about clock times in early childhood, although their routines are equally predictable. These cultural differences underscore the social source and dependency of concepts in this knowledge domain.

As noted at the beginning of this chapter, developmental psychologists have given much attention to how children come to understand time as distinct from speed and distance, a concept that has generally been assumed to be an independent cognitive construction, emerging at the outset of Piaget's concrete operations stage. Recognition of cultural constructions of time places this claim in a different perspective: Many dimensions are involved in understanding different temporal concepts and their relation to temporal expressions and temporal artifacts. Carbery (1992) demonstrated that the traditional Piagetian assessment of the child's concept can be considerably advanced by the use of a timing mechanism such as a clock. She trained 4-, 5-, and 7-year-old children to use a stopwatch-type clock as an aid in performing three types of "logical" time tasks used in prior research. In the first training task children estimated or timed differences in the duration of sleeping time for dolls, who began and ended sleeping at different times. Even 4-year-olds succeeded on this task with the aid of the clock. The second task compared durations of two activities – heaping beans into a container with a spoon or a scoop. Again, the clock enabled young children to succeed. In the traditional time, speed, and distance task in which two vehicles start and end at different times and places, and go at different speeds, the 7-year-olds and some of the 5-year-olds were able to succeed using the clock to measure time; however, they were unable to coordinate beginning and ending times with place and speed without the clock, which is the usual finding on this task, until the age of 8 or 9 years.

This study is not simply another demonstration that Piaget misjudged the sophistication of the young child's concepts (indeed, 4-year-olds were not able to use the clock in these tasks effectively). Rather, it demonstrates that our conceptions of time are in fact dependent upon the artifacts our culture has produced for measuring it. Without clocks to measure time the relation between time, speed, and distance would never have emerged as a physical science concept.[13] In this domain, as in others, to ignore the cultural constructions that surround the child growing up in the modern world is to misjudge the nature and problems of cognitive development. Cultural constructions are not simply add-ons to independent cognition; they are what children's cognitive systems must come to know and use in constructing their own conceptual understandings.

Time as a Bio-Cognitive-Social-Cultural-Linguistic Construction

To recapitulate, the child alone cannot *discover* time, because (unlike concrete objects) it is not an entity that exists to be discovered. Rather, conceptions of process and change have led different societies to conceptualize time in different ways, and those ways are conveyed to children through language forms.[14] The child's *knowledge of time concepts*, therefore, even those that are not directly taught, is *knowledge mediated through language and cultural artifacts*. Conventional time models, as discussed in the beginning sections of this chapter, represent knowledge that is constituted *in* language; that is, this knowledge is not simply a reflection of reality, but a cultural construction of reality. As such, conventional time models exemplify a large part of what children come to know of the world. The analysis of time concepts leads to the conclusion that issues of cognitive development cannot be considered without taking the many roles of language into account. From this perspective, we need to know how general cognition, knowledge representations, and the developing grasp of language terms and structures mutually affect one another in the developing child's MERs and what and how the child adds to knowledge about the world and about the language through transactions with others within the social and cultural milieu.

A very basic function of language in human cognition is the stabilizing property of words, noted previously. This property is important in the process of extracting time concepts from and coordinating them with event knowledge. We make time stand still by our talk about it. Valsiner (1993) emphasizes this aspect in his discussion of time constructions, for example: "We can distinguish the notions of the past, future, and present by way of superimposing upon the flow of our personal experiences a language-aided scheme of relative stability" (p. 22). More generally, "All our conceptualizations of time are the result of a semiotic construction process that is at first one of human psychological mediating devices . . . that organize our ongoing development in real time" (p. 24). As emphasized in the preceding section, oral language is supplemented with artifacts – clocks and calendars – that make counting and measurement of the stable linguistic units by which we mark time possible. Beyond this basic stabilizing function, in considering the case of systems of time concepts and time language we have observed three quite different relations between language and cognition, and the roles of language as a mediator of knowledge.

First, language may make salient a type of relation that was not previously apparent in the child's nonlinguistic conceptual representations. Present evidence suggests that this may be the case for the tense system, bringing out the distinction between past, present, and future. Prior to acquiring this system children may distinguish only now and not-now, or attend only to action relations in the here and now, the living present. In this case, the relation that must be expressed grammatically attunes the child to a relation to which she had previously been indifferent.[15]

Second, nonlinguistic experientially derived conceptual representations of events support the acquisition of language forms that appropriately express the relations implicit in those representations. This is the relation hypothesized to hold between the child's event representations and expressions of relative sequence, duration, and frequency (as represented in Table 9.1 and Figure 9.1). Here cognition, in the form of knowledge representations, supports and influences what language forms are acquired. Terms for relations implicit in events and expressed in parental talk about sequence, duration, and frequency can be learned implicitly through contextual use followed by generalization to other contexts, updating semantic knowledge to accord with speech use. In this case, language makes explicit knowledge that was previously implicit.

Third, language makes possible the *construction* of abstract concepts and complex representations that cannot be acquired solely from unmediated direct experience because they are culturally constituted through language. Concepts of specific location (*bedtime, Saturday*), measurement (*hours, days, years*), and of complex temporal systems such as calendars, and the meaning of terms referencing these, depend upon explicit knowledge mediated through language. In this case, cultural concepts constructed in language are conveyed to the young explicitly through talk about the concepts. As argued in Chapter 5 and throughout the book, the child cannot take advantage of talk about cultural constructions until the ability to use the representational function of language to acquire new knowledge is achieved. As exemplified in Steven's talk about "yesterday" in dialogue (1) and the analysis of Emily's talk about *afternoon* and *tomorrow,* these concepts become accessible around 3 to 4 years for children who have the requisite level of language mastery and experience. Broader surveys of children (Harner, 1975, 1982; Harner et al., 1992) indicate that systems of conventional terminology for clock and calendar reference begin to be acquired in the late preschool and early school years, providing entree to cultural systems of ordering and measuring time.

The perspective presented throughout this book, and particularly throughout this chapter, can be interpreted as one of radical linguistic and cultural relativity of the kind attributed to Whorf (1956). However, the view of cultural constructions presented here is simply that not all cultural knowledge systems are identical, and that children must be adapted to learning any knowledge systems that they might encounter. This view does not imply that human cognition in one culture is fundamentally different from that in another culture. Cross-cultural research shows that basic human cognition and language systems are similar throughout the world. But how cultures and languages represent the world is often quite different, as the discussion earlier in this chapter indicates.[16] It seems probable that these differences imply that individuals think differently about concepts in different domains of knowledge, depending upon how a culture has organized that knowledge. This conclusion is a natural correlate of the demonstration that experts in physics or chess think differently about their domain than do novices (e.g., Chi, 1978, 1992; Simon, 1972; Simon & Simon, 1978).

However time is represented within a culture, the representation imposes a symbolic overlay on the natural order. Aveni (1989) states: "Human culture emerges as the great processor of time" (p. 336). Moreover, the material embodiment of time, as in clocks and calendars, has "the effect of making past and future concrete and official" (p. 336). Cultures have always tried to find temporal order in the human and the natural world and to relate the two, but the systems they have devised for doing so have differed, and the differences are evident in the languages used to talk about time. Even if all cultures developed exactly the same models, they would still be cultural conceptions, and not individual conceptions. Thus children are faced with the problem of discovering, not time, but how their culture talks about it, and how that talk reflects ordered systems.

As Aveni (1989) states, contemporary cultures, by manipulating, developing, enhancing, processing, compressing, and packaging time "into a crazy-quilt patchwork to conform to our perceived needs" (p. 337), have changed the orderly biorhythms of the natural world. As cultures, and particularly economies with their attending bureaucracies, have become larger and more complex, time systems as well have become more complex and ornate. Then, "Paradoxically, our mechanical way of repatterning time has led to a way of knowing it that is totally divorced from the real world" (p. 338). It is this complexity of cultural systems that young children are embedded in today, and it is these complex, arbitrary, cultural/linguistic packages that children must integrate with their everyday, dynamic experiential knowledge of ongoing time.

10. The Emergence of the Projective Mind

To know and to interact with other people requires predicting their actions, their reactions to one's own actions, and their interactions with other social beings, including oneself. The focus of this chapter is on the psychosocial knowledge required for successful interactions. Social beings are complex and their behavior is not entirely predictable; so also are some physical phenomena. But in coming to understand nonsocial objects, predictions about the behavior of those objects may be made without concern for how those predictions may themselves alter the behavior of the objects. For example, predicting the weather is inherently fallible, because the system is so complex that very minor perturbations can have major unanticipated effects. But the predictions of weather scientists are not part of the system, and actions emanating from them do not affect the behavior of the system in any way. In contrast, a person within a social group of two or more people acts always with the knowledge that her own action may influence the actions of others in ways that she must be able to predict if she is to act intelligently.[1]

As outlined in Chapter 4, implicit knowledge of other people in relation to oneself begins in early infancy, as the child takes her place in the social world. Intelligent action, affective responsiveness, and communicative signals in response to others can be traced throughout the first two years. Beginning in the second year, acquiring conventional language provides the child with a sharper tool for dealing with the contingencies of the peopled world.

Much of the current interest in cognition of the social world focuses on young preschool children's understanding of other people's mental states – now referred to as "theory of mind." Because so many critical issues are incorporated in this research, this chapter opens with a summary of the basic research and theories surrounding it. These statements incorporate most of the major contemporary developmental theories;

thus they represent the state of the field as a whole, and provide a good ground for discussion of basic issues, and for bringing out contrasts with the theory of the mediated mind developed in this book.

People Knowledge: The Child's Theory of Mind

How does the child come to interpret what others think, believe, or know and thus to predict their actions based on these interpretations? This is part of the problem that has been the focus of philosophical analyses of *intentionality* (Searle, 1983), and of ethological and developmental studies of "theory of mind." In common parlance, "intentionality" indicates a person's intention to carry out an action. However, philosophers have adopted the term to cover what they call "aboutness." Beliefs, wishes, thoughts, knowledge, expectations are examples of intentional states; they are "about" other states (or, in semantic terms, they are about propositions). To account for the attribution of such states, philosophers speak of people as having a "folk theory" or "folk psychology"[2] of mental states; these states can be simple feelings of being in a particular state of happiness, thoughtfulness, and so on, or they can be about something, and that something may be either an object (thinking of ice cream) or a proposition (thinking that it may rain). The intentional states that people (and some animals) entertain affect their actions, and the problem of other minds is to interpret intentions on the basis of their verbal and nonverbal communications, or by inference from their behavior or what one knows of their perceptual access to information. The question is: "When and how do children come to have knowledge of other people's beliefs, of their own beliefs, and of differences between the two and between beliefs and states of the real world?"

This problem was actually brought to the fore in psychology through research with chimpanzees. In 1978 Premack and Woodruff asked the question: "Does the chimpanzee have a theory of mind?" Subsequent research with both nonhuman primates and human children has been concerned with this question and with the related questions of stages of acquisition of understanding of others' beliefs in problematic situations, in particular in situations where others might hold false beliefs because of faulty knowledge, and where their beliefs might differ from one's own. The popularity of this work in developmental psychology, ethology, and philosophy is based on its presumed significance for the individual's understanding and interpretation of others' behaviors and knowledge states, critically important in a complex social world.

The social world connoted in these studies is often not the familiar, benign world of the loving and attentive caretaker, but the alien Machiavellian world of the manipulator. The emphasis is on what other (unfamiliar) people may know about the existence and locations of desired objects and events. Although such problems may represent critical tests of children's representational and inferential capacities, they are far from representative of the vast numbers of everyday problems that children face in dealing with their own familiar, peopled worlds (Dunn, 1988). This is a point to be borne in mind in the discussion to follow, and one returned to in the concluding sections of this chapter. Further, one might ask: "Should we be exploring what children know about others' mental states or what they know about others' motives, goals, and actional dispositions within situations?" This kind of formulation reflects a more traditional psychological view of human action that does not require the psychologist to settle philosophical issues, or to presuppose one philosophical position in preference to another (Russell, 1992). This quibble will be set aside while considering the research that frames the issues today.[3]

Wimmer and Perner (1983) first adapted the problem of other minds to the human case, asking the question, "Do children have a theory of mind?" – in the sense set forth by Premack and Woodruff (1978), and by philosophers such as Dennett (1978). The first empirical investigations of children's understanding of others' mental states were carried out in a relatively neutral mode. Subsequent empirical work has been devoted increasingly to the testing of theories of how to explain the results of these first forays. A provocative outcome of the body of research is the finding that there is a fairly dramatic change in children's understanding at about the age of 4 years, or certainly between the age of $2\frac{1}{2}$ and 5 years. What is involved in this change and what explains it are the primary issues in all the work undertaken thus far. The particular age range pinpointed here may be seen as of more than passing interest, considering the discussions (in Chapters 5 through 9) of the developments taking place in linguistic representations over this age span. The possibility that language is involved in the development of mental state knowledge has been considered by some researchers, although its implications have not yet been fully explored. This topic is returned to later in this chapter.

Research Paradigms

Two lines of research initiated the explosion of interest in this area: those involving appearance–reality tasks (Flavell, Green, & Flavell, 1986) and those involving false belief tasks (Wimmer & Perner, 1983). Appearance–reality tasks were not originally conceived in the same light as false belief tasks; the former focused on issues of perspective-taking with respect to physical – not social – realities in an extension of Piaget's cognitive theory. Researchers later recognized that the representational demands of the tasks are similar, that the age range in which children gain success in the different tasks is also similar, and therefore that the same cognitive difficulties might be involved.

In an appearance–reality task the child is shown, for example, a sponge designed to look like a rock and is asked what it is, with the typical answer being "a rock." Then the child is allowed to explore the object manually, and its sponge qualities are demonstrated. Following this the child is asked, "Is it really a rock or really a sponge?" (There are many controls and explicit attempts to ensure that the child understands the "really" question.) Three-year-olds typically reply that it is really and truly X and looks like X (whether "rock" or "sponge" varies across children); the important finding is that the child maintains that it is what it looks like and looks like what it is. The standard conclusion is that 3-year-olds cannot maintain two representations of the same object, while 4-year-olds allow that the sponge may be a sponge although it looks like a rock. In Flavell's (1988) view, younger children have an understanding that there are cognitive connections to the world – we see things, think about things, want things, etc. – but they do not understand that the things thought about are representations of those things and not the things themselves. That is, they do not have a theory of mental representations. This is why they do not allow that something can look like one thing and be a different thing.[4]

The false belief task has several variants. One – the unexpected transfer task – was first designed by Wimmer and Perner (1983). The child watches the following scene: A boy (Maxi) puts some chocolate in a particular place in a cupboard, then leaves the room, and while he is out someone else moves the chocolate to a different cupboard. When Maxi returns he looks for the chocolate; where will he look first? We understand that Maxi believes the chocolate to be where it was first hidden, but this belief is now false. Three-year-olds predict that Maxi will look where the chocolate is (the realism error), not where he saw it hidden, but 4-year-olds predict correctly that he will look in accordance with his false belief in the original hiding place.

Another much-used task is the representational change (deceptive box) task. The child is shown a box appearing to contain candy ("smarties" –

well-known to European children) and asked to say what is inside (i.e., candy). Next the box is opened and shown to contain pencils. The child may then be asked what her friend who has not seen the pencils will think is inside (other false belief), and also what she herself thought was inside when she first saw the box (own false belief). In both cases the 3-year-old typically answers that the uninformed child will think (or she herself did think) that the box contains (or contained) what it really contains, namely pencils, and not what it purports to contain, namely candy. Four-year-olds report correctly that the uninformed viewer (including the child herself before seeing the open box) will expect (or did expect) to find candy.

As with the results of many of Piaget's experiments, there is something very startling about these findings. We expect young children to be able to think and reason about the world in pretty much the same way we do, given that they have the knowledge to do so, and taking into account limitations of language ability and information-processing constraints. None of these seems obviously to be a problem. Rather, young children seem to be handicapped by a different limitation. What do we possess that they do not? What is the knowledge domain, or the operational constraint, that makes the difference between the 3-year-old and the 4-year-old? The 4-year-old, of course, is actually not adult-like in all relevant ways, and 3-year-olds possess some relevant knowledge, as other research makes clear. However, for the purposes of this discussion we will focus on the shift from 3 to 4 because this is where most of the controversy turns; other research findings will be discussed when relevant.

Theories of the Child's Theory of Mind

As previously noted, the various theories that have been put forth to explain both the capabilities and the limitations on children's understanding of their own and others' mental states are representative of the major theoretical views of the field of cognitive development in general. In the discussion to follow, "theory of mind" is accepted as the common terminology for the understandings involved, without an implication that any particular theorist necessarily adheres to the claim that the child has a "theory," as some do not. In some contexts the abbreviation ToM will be used for the general concept.

Innate Modules.   Leslie (1988) has extended the concept of the innate structure of the human mind as containing encapsulated information-processing modules (Fodor, 1983) to the theory of mind domain. "The theory postulates a domain-specific, processing theory-of-mind mechanism (called ToMM) which uses a specialized system for representing propositional attitude concepts" (Leslie, German, & Happe, 1993, p. 57). The system expresses four kinds of information, including an agent, an attitude, an aspect of reality, and a fictional state of affairs. Leslie sees the child's early capacity to engage in pretense, and to interpret the pretense of others (as in the example discussed in Chapter 4 of a mother who holds a banana to her ear and pretends it is a telephone) to be an early manifestation of this capacity, wherein the child's ToMM enables him to assign the attitude "pretend" to this fictional state of affairs. In Leslie's view children with the normal capacity endowed by the ToMM, which is in place by 2 years (and presumably matures), operate with essentially the same theory thereafter but develop increased facility with a "selection processor" that enables them to solve the standard false belief paradigm problem more effectively at age 4 than at age 3. Like all theories that rest on innate modules, this is essentially a nondevelopmental and thoroughly mechanistic theory in which both the child's mind and others' minds are viewed as operating as autonomous units unconnected to bodies, actions, and social relationships.[5] Fodor's conception of innate modules applied to input information-processing systems – specifically, to perception and language – and not to general knowledge. The extension of the module idea to the ToM and other knowledge domains assumes detailed innate knowledge structures, a controversial assumption (Hirschfeld & Gelman, 1994b).

The Strong Theory Theory. The strongest "theory theory" position has been set forth by Gopnik (1993a). This approach is similar to others that view the knowledge of children and adults as formulated in theories within bounded domains (Carey, 1985; Spelke, 1991). Gopnik has formulated her position in terms that turn a philosophical dispute about the construct of intentionality into an empirical question. As she posed the issue, there are three distinct positions to be tested: (1) The theory theory account holds that intentionality is a theoretical notion constructed from evidence. (2) It contrasts with intentionality as a kind of "stance" developed by a process of enculturation. (3) Another contrast is seen in intentionality as "a fairly direct first-person apprehension of a particular brute fact about human beings" (Gopnik, 1993a, p. 3); knowing about other minds from this perspective requires attributing the same first-person insights to other people.

Gopnik's most challenging claim is that children construct theories of mind as a necessary condition for understanding their own belief states as well as those of other people. She bases this claim on evidence that 3-year-olds have as much difficulty reporting their own prior false beliefs (e.g., that they thought there was candy in the box before they found out that it contained pencils) as they do other people's false beliefs.[6] She asserts that 3-year-olds have a theory of mind, but it is the wrong theory, and that it is changed in the face of evidence, just as a scientific theory undergoes change. According to this account, 3-year-olds believe that "Objects or events are directly apprehended by the mind" (p. 5) or, as Gopnik (1993a) put it, quoting Chandler (1988), "Objects are bullets that leave an indelible trace on any mind that is in their path" (Gopnik, 1993a, p. 5). Others have similar conceptions of the 3-year-old's notion, as with Flavell's cognitive connections, already mentioned.

Gopnik suggests that 3-year-olds believe there are two kinds of psychological states – "silly states" that include images, dreams, and pretenses – and "serious states" including perceptions, desires, and beliefs. For the 3-year-old serious states directly and accurately reflect the real world. The 4-year-old, however, develops a representational model of mind, in which mental states are representations of reality and not direct relations to reality. Most important in this position is the claim that the construction of this model is necessary for accounting for one's own changes in mental state as well as for the varying states of other minds. What is meant by the term "theory" in theory of mind, and in other domains of development, is critical to the claims made by Gopnik and other theory theorists, and will be considered later in this chapter.

Wellman's Belief-Desire Theory.   Wellman also believes that children construct a theory of mind. Although Wellman and Gopnik have written jointly, defending the strong theory theory (Gopnik & Wellman, 1994), Wellman differs from Gopnik in details and emphasis, proposing that children first understand desire as a representational state, and only later come to understand the role of belief. Wellman, like Gopnik, perceives the child as coming to understand her own mental states in the same terms as, and at the same time as, she understands the mental states of others. The 3-year-old's understanding that mental states are different from physical states (as with dreams, imaginings), and that wants represent wanted things and not necessarily real physical things, all help the child to construct the proper theory, which predicts that wanting X implies believing that X exists, which in turn implies acting to achieve X [see Wellman (1990) for details of research supporting his claims].

Perner's Representational Change Theory. Perner (1991) formulates his position in terms of levels of representation, similar in many ways to Karmiloff-Smith's (1992) theory of representational change (see Chapter 1). The base level of representation present in infancy is that of "direct knowledge." Perner posits two further levels of representation: representation and meta-representation. At the re-presentation level, reached in the second year, the child is capable of considering two conflicting representations, for example, of past and future in relation to the present, and of pretend as well as the actual case. At the metarepresentation level, reached at 4 years, the child knows that what others and self represent are representations. Perner sees subsequent theory-building as a process in its own right, reflecting a higher level of understanding knowledge, based on criteria of distinguishing theories from pretheoretical generalizations. These criteria include distinguishing essential or necessary conditions from incidental or typical conditions, and "being in the grip of a theory." Persons in the grip of a theory are puzzled by incompatible evidence and might even deny its existence. Thus, although Perner adopts the "theory of mind" language for the stage reached after the age of 4 years, he sees it as a construction from a nontheoretical understanding. Rather than theory change, he sees theory achievement. This is a more obviously developmental view than others considered thus far, but it does not address the mechanism of developing from one level to the next.

Harris's Simulation Theory. Harris (1992) sees the child essentially as a "situation theorist," someone who views the world in terms of situations, a position most compatible with that presented here. Harris argues, contrary to Gopnik, that children *do* have direct access to their own experience of feelings, desires, beliefs, and so on. To understand other people's minds they *simulate* what they would feel, know, want, or believe if they had the same experiences (were in the same position, had access to the same knowledge, etc.) as the other.

Harris interprets the 3-year-old's failure on the false belief task as resulting from a failure to overwrite current information and thus a failure of the simulation procedure. He claims, in contrast to most of the other theorists cited, that the false belief task is poor evidence for a representational theory of mind. Although this task shows that children understand that information may be contrary to fact, it does not show that children believe in representations in the head [see also Chandler & Hala (1994)]. Even more strongly, Harris would deny the necessity for a constructed *theory* of other minds on the part of either children or adults (those who are not philosophers or psychologists), except in challenging cases that go beyond the "normal" such as cases of mental illness. Rather than theory, imagination does the work – we imagine (represent to ourselves) the mental states of others. There is nothing in this conception that requires the child to have a concept of metarepresentation, much less a theory of intentionality. Because children's knowledge of other minds accumulates slowly, and because they have limitations on the complexity of the information that can be simulated, developmental changes of the kind found can be expected.

The Case against Theory Theory

As discussed in Chapter 8, many developmentalists, not only those concerned with knowledge of mind, have adopted the framework of theories as explaining the organization of knowledge in specific bounded domains. The implications of this framework have been brought out most forcefully in discussions of theory of mind. Wellman (1988) set forth the criteria defining the theory stance on conceptual change: "Subscribers to a theory share three things: a basic conception of what phenomena are encompassed by the theory; a sense of how these phenomena and propositions about them are mutually interdependent; and consequently, what counts as a relevant and informative explanation of changes and relationships among the various phenomena" (p. 66). Wellman stresses thereby the ontological distinctions, coherence among the included concepts, and their causal-explanatory efficacy. Notice that Wellman's definition includes "sharing" as a characteristic of theories. It seems obvious that people must share the same theory of mind if they are to make sense to each other over decades of interaction. An important issue for theory theorists to address is: "What guarantees that a child constructing such a theory alone will arrive at one that is shareable?"

Both Gopnik and Wellman (separately and together) have vociferously defended the theory theory as it applies to understanding the mind. Harris (1994) has been the strongest critic of this stance, arguing that children are not like little scientists constructing theories.[7] He questions the assumption of domain specificity in children's thinking, noting that there is ample evidence that children (as well as people in nonscientific societies) do not respect the boundaries as theory requires, but extend psychological explanations across domains to the nonbiological movements of rivers, clouds, and so forth, as well as to physical objects such as dolls in pretend play [see note 1; see also example (6) in Chapter 8]. Moreover, domain specificity appears to require the integration of domain-specific minitheories in order to explain everyday situations. For example, to participate in a game of ball-throwing one would have to invoke an animate agent theory, a social game reciprocity theory, as well as a mechanistic inanimate object theory. The problem of how children might integrate several minitheories (i.e., those applying to people's mental states, causation in the physical world, properties of the biological world) in explaining a single situation, including those presented in ToM research paradigms, is never addressed. Theory of mind theorists claim that the theories in questions are implicit, not explicit; therefore, presumably implicit processes operate to combine them in action. But there is a serious question as to what is bought with the notion of an implicit theory, which is accessible neither to the theory-holder nor to others who presumably share it.

Harris suggests instead that *working models* of situations do the integration implicitly: "By not carving nature up into disciplinary domains, [working models] avoid the problem of coordination that would ensue" (p. 309). This notion of working models is quite compatible with the view of children's knowledge construction presented in this work. Moreover, Harris claims that adults, including scientists, also operate in their everyday and scientific activities with working models, rather than with theories. He argues that scientists do not usually carry out their scientific activities "in the grip of a theory" (as Perner suggests) but rather in terms of a concrete puzzle solution employing models or examples. He suggests that the concrete and psychological notion of paradigm (Kuhn, 1970) is close to children's thinking: "The child assimilates a new situation to a previously encountered instance or to a prototypical model of those instances" (p. 303). In other words, "Children and scientists think alike because in neither case does theory guide their thinking" (Harris, 1994, p. 303).

Harris also points out that theory theorists provide no account of the source of children's allegedly new theoretical ideas, and that 3- to 4-year-old children give no indication that they have confronted intellectual problems. In contrast, scientists openly confront their conceptual inconsistencies and make them explicit. Moreover, scientists work collectively to bring about theory change, whereas "Children are mostly left to get on with their own cognitive development" (p. 307). Children neither face theoretical crises nor invent new theories, according to Harris (1994).

> In summary, when we compare children's everyday thinking and the day-to-day thinking of a working scientist, we do find some similarities. Each of them engages in paradigm-based thinking, and each may encounter anomalous situations that provoke vacillation and inconsistency. Nonetheless, there are important differences. The anomaly for the child is a tacit, inarticulate uncertainty, a tendency toward contradiction. The anomaly for the scientist is engineered and amplified by the institutional machinery of the scientific establishment . . . [L]ikening children's cognitive development to theoretical change in science . . . is misleading because it likens a psychological change to one that is ultimately sociological. (p. 307).

In addition to the points made by Harris, it may be noted that science employs externalized symbolic systems to bring out the implications and inconsistencies in theories, and to bring them to the attention of others in the community, practices not available to 4-year-olds. It is also worth noting that most working scientists resist revolutionary theory change, and those who construct original theories of any kind tend to defend them against any empirical counterevidence. The claim that children might readily change from one theory to another in the face of evidence implies that their cognitive processes must be much more flexible that those of adults, so flexible, indeed, that maintaining any stable theory would seem improbable. Russell (1992) points out that children are not like scientists constructing theoretical systems to make Nature intelligible; rather, children are in the position of *adapting to human cultural systems*.[8] This is not a simple matter of enculturation, as Gopnik (1993a) characterized it. It depends on constructive processing, but as Russell points out it is simply implausible that all children heroically construct the system by themselves.

In summary, theory theories rest on two implicit but questionable assumptions about the human mind: (1) It is constructed and develops in terms of abstract principles rationally and coherently organized; and (2) it develops individually under its own creative power, responding to encounters in the world with new constructions derived somehow from universal principles. In contrast, the situational or experiential view sees minds as both embodied and encultured, developing working models of the world in which children live, not abstract theories of artificially partitioned realities. The latter is the work of theoretical scientists, not children.

Summary

Most of the major players in the game of theories of theory of mind agree that an important development takes place between the age of $2\frac{1}{2}$ and 5 years in children's interpretations, predictions, and explanations of other people's actions, based on the attributions of particular mental states, particularly beliefs. The basic phenomenon that has drawn most attention empirically and theoretically is the response shift in the classic false belief tasks between 3 and 4 years. This shift can be pushed downward or upward by changes in task configurations (e.g., Clements & Perner, 1994; Lewis, Freeman & Hagestadt, 1994; Lewis & Osborne, 1991; Sheffield, Sosa, & Hudson, 1993; Plesa, Goldman, & Edmondson, 1995), but something clearly seems to be changing in the child's understanding of the world or the task itself over this transitional period. None of the theories offered so far has explained or solved all the conceptual problems.

The Missing Link: Social Construction

Missing from the group discussed so far is any theory based on *social* construction, such as a Vygotskian theorist would propose, invoking the mechanism of semiotic mediation. Gopnik (1993a) specifically discounts such a possibility, comparing an enculturation account to the act of learning how to set the table. This omission seems especially peculiar in a domain that is centered on social relationships and interactions, where a theory based on social construction would seem to be most applicable. Indeed most of the evidence that has accrued on these issues has a fairly nonsocial appearance – problems are typically posed about what someone might think is in a box, or where some object is hidden. They are not about predictions of others' behaviors with respect to the self, for example. An exception is Olson (1988), who proposed a progression toward a theory of mind based on social-cultural construction, with an important role assigned to language, suggesting that when children "begin to see their utterances as expressions of belief, for example, they begin to distinguish their beliefs from their utterances, to distinguish beliefs from reality, to store their beliefs as episodic representations of events rather than simply update their model of the world . . ." (pp. 421–422).

Several of the authors who supplied chapters to the Lewis and Mitchell (1994) volume address the social and linguistic contributions to understanding more comprehensively (see the chapters by Baldwin and Moses; Dunn, Shatz, Robinson, Siegal, and Peterson; and Lewis); they have begun to provide a more humanly understandable course of development in this domain. Central to all of these discussions are the various roles of language.

Language for Understanding Minds

Children begin to acquire language at about 1 year, and by the age of 2 years they have acquired a good deal of fairly abstract terminology for talking about their world, as outlined in Chapter 5. If it is language that enables children to solve difficult problems of the interpretations of others' actions, why is it not then effective for this purpose at least by 2 years? Why are there important changes between ages 3 and 4? In the preceding chapters language has been revealed as many-faceted and multifunctioned; in particular, the representational potential of interpretative discourse about complex events has been emphasized as an important influence on the child's developing understanding of the social world. It would appear that such discourse would be of considerable significance to the child's understanding of other people's intentions and actions [see Dunn (1994); Shatz (1994); and Robinson (1994) for concurring views]. From another angle, Plaut and Karmiloff-Smith (1993) propose that the theory of mind research can be "understood in terms of progressive refinement and elaboration of the representations that underlie intentional states" (p. 70). They believe, "The developmental results are best interpreted in terms of increasing capability in using and generating symbolic representations that are sufficiently well elaborated to override the otherwise compelling interpretations generated by direct experience" (p. 70). Thus they emphasize the utility of a different mode of representation, the linguistic, as providing the symbolic "scaffolding" necessary to maintain a dual view of reality and false belief. These relatively advanced language functions are not achieved for several years after the onset of language learning.

The various developments within language that may contribute to the theory of mind problem may be summarized as follows:

- *Words:* Without words for the mental states (e.g., know, think) children cannot demonstrate their knowledge in tasks, and cannot exchange information with others about their feelings, desires, beliefs, and so on.

- *Meanings:* Meanings of words are implicitly contained within their usage in social exchanges, as discussed in Chapters 5, 8, and 9. Only gradually do the differentiated meanings that distinguish psychological states, social intentions, and cultural codings become accessible to the young child, who begins inevitably with his or her own interpretation of actions and activities in the social world.
- *Interactions:* Interactions in social discourse embed both implicit and explicit statements about the feelings, desires, beliefs of other people in different situations. Such evidence becomes available to the child for constructing more complex concepts of her own as well as others' mental states.
- *Direct instruction:* With language, more knowledgeable others (adults) can articulate inexplicit expressions by young children and can explain why people take some actions, make some decisions, have certain feelings, and so on. Concepts such as lying and intention can be clarified. Relations between terms such as "know" and "think" can be pointed out, providing a more coherent system for the child's semantic structures in the domain of mental terms.
- *Representational space:* Language becomes available for representing reality and nonreality to self and others, thus providing for shareability as well as for modifiability of the child's representations, and opening up the further possibilities of representing one's representations.

All these effects may be involved in what is usually referred to as "enculturation" or "social construction." But it should be noted that even the most direct instructional form, and certainly the first three effects listed, require cognitive construction by the child, based on social experiences; they are appropriately termed "collaborative construction."

Research that first related language to theory of mind problems focused on children's acquisition of mental state verbs. That research provides the background against which the general influence of language on shifts in performance on theory of mind tasks may be considered.

Word Meaning

If children do not properly understand what other people mean by such mental terms as "think," "see," "know," and "remember" they will not be able to answer questions framed in these terms. When do children use and understand the critical words? Bretherton and Beeghley (1982) reported that at only 2 years of age, children use "want" and "think"; they related their findings to the proposal that children at this young age have a theory of mind. Shatz, Wellman, and Silber (1983) studied transcripts from one child between the ages of $2\frac{1}{2}$ and 4 years to identify uses of the terms "think," "know," and "remember" as referring to mental states rather than as simple "conversational devices" (such as "know what?"). They concluded that mental verbs first appear in pragmatic conversational contexts as early as 2 years 4 months, and do not appear as true mental references until 4 months later. Contrastive uses, where the child contrasts two mental states or a mental state and reality (e.g., "I thought there was a snake on the ground, but there wasn't really a snake") were observed soon after, at 2 years and nine months [see also Shatz (1994)].

A follow-up to these analyses was undertaken by Bartsch and Wellman (1995; Wellman & Bartsch, 1994), in which they distinguished between talk about desires and beliefs, and reference to self or other, in transcripts from 10 children ranging in age from 18 months to 5 years. On the basis of these analyses they report three phases. The first is one in which children talk about *wants* and *likes*, distinguishing between desires and the actions or objects desired. Children beginning at about age 3 years were observed to talk about beliefs and thoughts, as well as desires. Bartsch and Wellman observed that children at about age 4 years talked about beliefs as explaining people's actions, constituting the third phase. Countering the simulation position taken by Harris (1994), they emphasized that children did not refer to their own beliefs or desires before they referred to others'. The data are presented as strong confirming evidence for a desire-action theory of mind followed by a belief-action theory at age 4, theories that apply equally to the child's own mental states as to the mental states of others.[9]

Bartsch and Wellman specifically excluded from their analyses all uses of mental terms that did not clearly specify mental states, and they noted that such uses typically preceded the "genuine" ones. This observation is significant within a theory of how children come to understand such terms, and it needs to be informed also by an analysis of how adults use the terms with children (such analyses are currently under way by Kessler Shaw). Bartsch and Wellman are, of course, aware of the problem of overinterpretation, and they have attempted to guard against it. But whether a child means what an adult would mean in the same situation often cannot be judged with assurance.

Studies of children's comprehension of the critical mental state words have found that differential understanding lags behind productive use, just as with other abstract terms considered in previous chapters. Johnson and Maratsos (1977) used a story comprehension task with 3- and 4-year-olds, contrasting the verbs "know" and "think." They reported that 3-year-olds provided little evidence of differentiated understanding of the terms, while 4-year-olds succeeded on their task, providing evidence that they understand both that "thinking may be false and that knowing must be true." Moore, Bryant, and Furrow (1989) confirmed this conclusion for the terms "know," "think," and "guess." Three-year-olds showed no distinction among the terms, while 4-year-olds reliably distinguished between "know" and "think" or "guess," but there was no improvement on the "think–guess" distinction up to 8 years. A subsequent study by Moore, Pure, and Furrow (1990) indicated that performance on the language tasks was significantly correlated with success on own and other false belief and appearance–reality tasks.

The discrepancy between children's productive command of words referring to abstract entities and relations and their comprehension of the terms in experimental contexts is not unique to this domain, and it has been found repeatedly for terms expressing time and causality [see French & Nelson (1985); see Chapters 5 and 9). The explanation for the discrepancy is plausibly that children learn to use these words in contexts where they are first used by other people. Through using and interpreting the words within their representations of the situation, children come to some preliminary understandings of the sense of the word – its meaning. But it may be months or even years before children's grasp of the meaning accords with the conventional meaning of the term in the adult language [see Chapter 5; Levy & Nelson (1994)]. As with all words that do not refer to concrete objects and specific actions, meanings gradually accrue as their use across different situations and experiences enters into a conceptual complex that eventually becomes stable and matches that of the communal use of the word sufficiently well that no further change or addition is necessary for communicative purposes. The gradual process is evident in children's failures on comprehension tasks. Thus the conclusion reached by studies of children's productions of terms, even when judged to be used appropriately, must be interpreted cautiously.

Many cognitive psychologists seem to believe that when children use these terms apparently in reference to mental states, the terms can be interpreted as expressing the *same meanings* that adults attach to them; that is, when a child uses a term like "think," she is referring to a mental process *of the same kind* as the adult who uses the term. There is no guarantee that this is the case, and the comprehension evidence suggests that it is not. Indeed, Booth and Hall (1995) trace changes in the verb "know" up to age 10 to 12 years. Although the Bartsch and Wellman (1995) data indicate that 3-year-olds use most of the mental terms in question in natural contexts to refer to mental states, we do not

know the extent to which their uses reflect reasonably deep understanding or relatively superficial knowledge of conversational and situational
appropriateness. The latter is not, of course, to be denigrated; it is the
source of deeper meaning, when reflected upon and integrated with
prior and ongoing conceptual understanding.

Importantly, the concepts referenced by the mental state words may
not exist as such for the young child until they are constructed in response to reflections on the use of the terms by others to refer to oneself.
For example, the distinction between thinking, knowing, and guessing
may need to be differentiated out of a global concept (or tacit impression)
of *believing* that is unarticulated and unnamed. It may be in fact that the
data from Bartsch and Wellman actually indicate that the coincidence of
children's contrastive uses – which are found at about the same age as
when they are capable of solving the false belief task – may be attribut-
able to their new understanding of what adults mean by the terms.

To perform correctly in false belief tasks the child must comprehend
"think" as a mental state that can vary from reality. If the child begins
with the default assumption that perception provides a true picture of
the world, and that everyone perceives the same reality, *thinking* as
distinct from *knowing* and from *what is* may not be available as a concept.
Thus "think" would be interpreted as referring to the real situation.
However, if a character actually *states* that she thinks something contrary
to fact, the child might well believe that that thought will cause her to
carry out an action in a mistaken direction. Confirming this, Sheffield,
Sosa, & Hudson (1993) showed that 87% of $2\frac{1}{2}$-year-olds solved a simpli-
fied false belief task, predicting correctly where a puppet would look
when the puppet said he thought his cookie was in a box although the
child knew that the box was empty. Experience with such expressions
and their consequences may lead the child eventually to make the relevant distinctions among knowledge states referred to by different
words. But Robinson (1994) reports that when a (real) adult stated explicitly that he thought something contrary to children's known reality, 3-
year-olds reported, nonetheless, that the adult's thoughts conformed to
that reality. Word meaning and use of the term "think" is obviously
unclear for young children.

From this perspective on the language-concept relation, it is not so
puzzling that the child sometimes misrepresents her own prior knowledge state, as well as that of others, in false belief tasks. The child may
misinterpret the words used, from the adult's point of view, and when
asked, "What did you think was in the box?" respond as though the

question was, "What was in the box?" Indeed, there is some evidence that providing a more explicit statement enables the younger child to handle the task appropriately (Lewis & Osborne, 1991). In a recent study using a modified procedure that followed the question using the word "think" with one using the word "say," 84% of 3-year-olds reported correctly what they had thought/said (raisins) prior to opening the box in comparison to 45% who were correct in the standard condition (Plesa, Goldman, & Edmondson, 1995). The theory of word learning applicable to opaque and abstract terms like "think" and "know" implies that the child might use these terms to mean something equivalent to *perceive reality to be*; then if apparent reality changes, it is reasonable to claim that one perceived it correctly all along.

The important point is that the language data need to be incorporated into a theory of word learning, as well as into a theory of social understanding that goes beyond the private expression of representations and takes into account the role of language and social interaction in the establishment of knowledge in the social cognition domain.

Language and Social Understanding

Dunn (1988) reported three studies that focused particularly on the natural interactions of mothers and siblings with children between 24 and 36 months of age in family settings at home. Her studies have important implications for how children learn about themselves and the social world during this age range. Even younger children are reported to interpret the feelings of others and to try to adjust their own behavior to the social rules and roles worked out within the family. Dunn summarizes her observations as follows:

> Children from 18 months on understand how to hurt, comfort, or exacerbate another's pain; they understand the consequences of their hurtful actions for others and something of what is allowed or disapproved behavior in their family world; they anticipate the response of adults to their own and to others' misdeeds; they differentiate between transgressions of various kinds. They comment and ask about the causes of others' actions and feelings. (p. 169)

She adds: "What our observations show is that children even in their second and third years have a far subtler comprehension of their social world than we have given them credit for" (p. 171). Children's understanding and intelligent action in the social world grows in the "familiar and emotional exchanges between family members, especially those in which their own interests are at stake. . . . Children have a practical grasp of some of the causes of states of distress, anger, and happiness in other family members, and of certain rules and roles in that family world, from early in their second year" (pp. 171–172).

Dunn stresses that while this understanding is vividly apparent in the everyday exchanges with parents and siblings, one would not expect the same understanding in unfamiliar surroundings, or in settings with different rules and roles, or where their own self-interest is not aroused. It is evident that the child's concept of self is at stake in many familial settings, that children learn about the social world in order to manage their own concerns within it. Social discourse is important for this understanding.

Of particular interest to the topics covered in this chapter is the evidence about children's own curiosity expressed in questions and narrative conversations. Children of around 2 years tend to ask questions about actions, and particularly about odd and unexpected behavior. Their questions are often quite disinterested – not attempts to satisfy their own desires, but "active attempts to make sense of the world rather than to meet immediate needs" (p. 133). Two examples illustrate that they show interest in others' goals and needs:

Child of 26 Months:

> (1) M: If I don't iron some of Daddy's shirts I shall be in a row
>   tomorrow.
>   C: Why do?
>   M: –
>   C: Why you iron?
>   M: Take the creases out.
>   C: Oh.

Child of 28 months when observer commented she forgot her pen:

> (2) C: To observer: You forgot your pen. Forgot your pen . . .
>   could – the other pen. Did you couldn't find your pen
>   at home?   (p. 133)

Children at this age also comment on their own behavior and the consequences for their own and others' states of mind:

> (3)   Mother who sees child (36 months) engaging in a disap-
>   proved activity:

> Look you know what D says about that, J. She says that
> she doesn't like you doing that.
> C: I know she doesn't!

And a child (36 months) who dislikes wearing a particular item of clothing hides it:

> (4)   C: Mummy won't find my vest now (laughs). I put it under –
> And now she won't find it.

The children Dunn observed at home appear to have considerable knowledge about others' mental states – their feelings, intentions, desires, and sources of beliefs. What explains their inability to demonstrate this kind of knowledge in systematic laboratory tests of theory of mind? Dunn provided several clues: Their understanding is implicit in their actions and reactions with others. "With development, children's understanding becomes increasingly explicit, and they are able to make use of their capabilities in an increasingly wide range of situations" (Dunn, 1988, p. 171).

Dunn and her colleagues (1991) reported findings relating family discourse about feelings and causality specifically with children's performance on perspective-taking and false belief tasks. The results support the view that discourse about the social world mediates the key conceptual advances found in the social cognition tasks. Other recent studies have reported relationships between parental and sibling use of mental state language and children's subsequent uses. Furrow and colleagues (1992) found consistencies in the frequency of maternal uses of these words and children's uses at age 3 years. "Think" and "know" were the most common words used by mothers and children alike, and mothers' uses when the children were 2 years old predicted children's uses at age 3 years. They conclude: "Our data suggest the possibility that the development of mental state language, and thus presumably a theory of mind, is fostered by the tendency of mothers to focus their children's attention on mental processes by talking about such processes and, more importantly, by using utterance types which conceivably direct the children to reflect on their own mental states" (p. 630). Two other studies provide suggestive support for these conclusions. Perner, Ruffman, and Leekam (1994) found that children from larger families performed successfully on false belief tasks at an earlier age than those from smaller families. Jenkins and Astington (in press) reported that language ability and memory capacity were both associated with performance on false belief tasks.

Becoming a Language User

The complexity of the process of the child's construction of a world model – using the raw materials of language to rerepresent understandings that were first established on the level of direct experience, and supported by familiar and predictable settings, people, and activities – was discussed in Chapters 5, 6, 7, and 8. New representations appear, fostered by experience with language representations of others, which incorporate implicit social and cultural models, providing the basis for reconstructions by the child, within the linguistic medium itself. The linguistic medium reveals relationships that were not apparent in the prior model. This general claim applies to the domain of social knowledge (knowledge of self and other minds) as well as to that of categories, narratives, and memories, as discussed earlier.

It is only through language, moreover, that the cultural frames for interpreting the actions of others become apparent. Primitive access to the social-cultural world is available through participation in its routines, but access to the ways in which the world semiotically structures concepts, ideas, frames, and theories is available only through language. Use of language in and of itself conveys many of the values, categories, and mythologies of the culture. Of equal importance, language constitutes a medium through which such categories and structures can be directly and explicitly imparted, as Dunn's work and that of others has shown.

Thus the cultural system reflected in adult ideas about others' mental states becomes more visible to children as they participate as language users in culturally constituted activities (games, routines, work, commerce, storytelling). Certainly the stories of the society contain a storehouse of lore about what different characters think, want, know, and remember, or don't remember, know, etc., and the consequences this has for the outcome of their actions. Similarly, narratives about the past and the future in the child's experience incorporate talk about feelings and beliefs (see Chapter 7). More studies of the way in which parents and teachers incorporate talk about mental states in their discourse with children are needed to illuminate this process. From the opposite perspective, Lewis (1994) has demonstrated the close connection between children's understanding of narrative, and facility with narrative forms, and their performance in theory of mind assessments.

Becoming a language user in communicative contexts implicates a powerful potential for understanding motives, goals, and causes of other people's actions, which are at best clouded and often beyond the reach of the intellect of the observer without the benefit of language explanations and interpretations provided by the other people themselves. Thinking is a state that is highly opaque to the outside observer. When a person states that she thinks A, this may have implications for action: It may predict (not cause) that she will act on object B. Note, however, that the simple attribution of thinking has no necessary implication with respect to the cause of the thought. When Cookie Monster enters a room and says that he thinks the cookie is in the blue box but does not say why he thinks so (Sheffield, Sosa, & Hudson, 1993), there is no way of knowing the cause, and for the child much thinking must be like that. That is, thinking may come from anywhere; it is free-floating like dreams or fantasy. Note that only when thinking is attached to a cause (e.g., "because I saw it put there") can the child engage in the kind of simulation that Harris's theory demands with respect to other people's beliefs. Before that, the simulation is as free-floating as the thought, and might take any form. Thus it is not "simply" that the child might have an incorrect or incomplete understanding of terms such as "think" and "know" but that that understanding is an essential part of the scheme of understanding other people's perspectives on reality and the ways in which and reasons for which they may differ from one's own. Until these conceptions are differentiated, the child's response regarding her own knowledge state may be as confused as it is regarding that of others'.

If indeed children elaborate their knowledge of themselves as persons in response to their interactions with others [as Mead (1934), among others, asserted], then knowing how to attribute the appropriate terms to oneself would not be expected in advance of knowing how to attribute them to others. Contrary to the claims of theory theorists, such an observation does not implicate the construction of a *theory of mind* applicable to both self and other. For example, Harris's (1992) simulation theory does not require that the child have concept and word appropriately sorted out and applied to self before applied to other, but only that personal experience of knowledge states be projected onto others. There is no implication in the simulation account that the child has a complete and correct understanding of her own mind before projecting it onto others. Rather, the claim is that what understanding of self the child does have may serve to interpret the actions of others. And, as the preceding discussion has indicated, understanding of self may be significantly aided by understanding the language that others use to refer to oneself and others.

The complexities of abstract concept–word relations may be realized first with respect to one's own knowledge state, but in response to the expressions of others' about self or other. Gradual building up of self-knowledge takes place as knowledge of others' feelings, thoughts, and attitudes in relation to the self come to be appropriately interpreted. The two are intricately interconnected. But simple exposure to the language of mental states in relevant situations is not sufficient for a child to come to an understanding of this domain of knowledge. The child must take the raw materials – observation of actions and interactions, feelings and thoughts, and language uses – and construct them into a system of interpretations. This system includes as important concepts those mental states – perceptions, desires, beliefs, imaginings, dreams – that are referred to by specific names in conversation. Seeing, hearing, wanting, thinking, knowing, guessing, pretending, and dreaming are the stuff of everyday talk in which children participate. These words enter into their cognitions about social interactions and aid in establishing understanding of those interactions. However, except for those adults who specialize in psychology, philosophy, or related areas of scholarly activity, there is no evidence and no reason to believe that abstractions such as perception, belief, or intentionality, for which they do not have available language terms, enter into the everyday interpretations of adults, much less children.

Lessons from Autism

Autism is a rare disorder (affecting about 4 in 10,000 infants) characterized by atypical and delayed language and disturbance of interprersonal relations. Both the atypical language and disturbance of social relations have brought autism to the attention of those interested in theory of mind, and have suggested that the syndrome may reflect a specific ToM neurocognitive deficit; or, that the social and linguistic deficits in conjunction with ToM deficits may help to explain normal developments in understanding other minds.[10]

Autistic individuals typically have some degree of mental retardation, but some among them are of normal and even occasionally very high intelligence. The latter group are distinguished by distinctive disabilities, namely those associated with communication and intentionality.

Most children are not identified as autistic until well after infancy, usually in connection with delayed language. Although autistic children display some early signs such as lack of pretend play, their early development usually seems to be within the normal range. Autistic children may engage with objects and toys in somewhat repetitive, obsessive routines, such as arranging shapes in parallel lines. When the child reaches the age of $2\frac{1}{2}$, the incapacity to learn or use language, or indeed to use communicative signs for achieving ends, becomes evident, and a diagnosis of autism may be made.

Autistic individuals of 6 to 16 years show deficits on perspective-taking and false belief tasks compared with mentally retarded Down syndrome children and normal 4-year-olds. For example, Baron-Cohen, Leslie, and Frith (1985) used a series of pictures depicting an event and an outcome, showing a cause–effect sequence, a social sequence, or a sequence requiring a mental interpretation (e.g., a girl puts her toy down behind her and while her back is turned someone takes it–she turns around and registers surprise). The autistic children performed normally on the first two series, but showed poor understanding of the third series, and compared with Down syndrome children and with normal 4-year-olds they did significantly less well even though their average mental age levels were higher than either of the other groups. Studies using other tasks with these groups have reported similar findings.

A small proportion of autistic children develop some productive language; these children are higher functioning and generally more intelligent, as measured by IQ tests. Tager-Flusberg (1993) followed a group of six such children (all boys–four of five autistic children are male) between 3 and 6 years of age for a one- to two-year period, and compared their language development with that of a matched group of Down syndrome children. In many ways the language development of the two groups was similar, although the autistic children displayed some language peculiarities, such as pronoun reversals (using "I" for "you" and vice versa), and inappropriate question intonation. Both groups acquired words for emotions, perceptions, and desire, but the autistic children showed a marked lack of words for cognitive states in comparison with the Down syndrome children. Tager-Flusberg comes to an interesting conclusion with regard to autistic children's language and communication:

> From the onset of intentional communication through the acquisition of a formal linguistic system, autistic children demonstrate a fundamental impairment in their understanding that communica-

tion and language exist for the exchange of information or knowledge. Because understanding where information comes from is at the core of understanding belief, it is no wonder that autistic children show impairments in their acquisition of the theory of mind. (p. 153)

Tager-Flusberg's account is similar to Frith's (1989): It is not just that autistic children have problems with language; language problems emerge because they do not understand language as a communicative tool for conveying messages. According to Astington (1993), however, autistic "children do not discover the mind in the normal way and their social relations and communicative abilities are severely impaired, which supports the argument that children's discovery of the mind underlies their ability to communicate and interact with others" (p. 180). Yet precisely the opposite relation – that children's ability to communicate with others on these topics underlies their "discovery" of the mind – is implied by Tager-Flusberg's statement, and is also implicit in Astington's own emphasis on the importance, for normal children, of talking with others so as to share others' thoughts, wants, feelings, and perceptions.

In Hobson's (1993) view, the autistic child does not relate to caretakers in the normal way, a problem that develops with the failure to establish the I–thou relationship, and particularly with the lack of shared symbols, in play or in language. Hobson's account of normal early development is *"from* interpersonal relatedness (in terms of co-ordinated experiences as well as behaviour) *to* an increasing awareness of the distinctions among persons, *from* intersubjectivity *to* individual self-reflective awareness" [Hobson (1993), p. 188; italics in original]. The infant-person-environment relation established through joint attention and social referencing (see Chapter 4) is critical for the development of symbolization, and hence for the infant/child "to reflect on her own mind, and consciously to assign 'selfhood' (including a self's forms of mental state) to other people" (p. 189). According to Hobson, it is precisely this that is missing in autism: "The essence of autism is severe disturbance in intersubjective personal engagement with others. Autistic children are profoundly limited in their capacity for and experience of 'personal relatedness'" (p. 194).

Several points of interest to the present account may be found in Hobson's proposals. First, his theory recognizes that the self is established through the interpersonal differentiation that takes place in late infancy and toddlerhood, simultaneous with the critical developments in pretense and symbolic language. Intuitive knowledge of self, of self-perception, emotion, feeling, and psychological attitudes, emerges as the child becomes cognizant of differences between self and other. This awareness is a normal developmental achievement that takes place through human social and communicative interactions in all cultural environments. Its dependence on normal social life means that infants who are deprived of these experiences will not have the same understanding of other people in early childhood. Autistic children do not achieve this awareness because they are blocked from the interpersonal experience. They can no more achieve "selfhood" than they can attribute selfhood to others.

The achievement of this level of selfhood is critical to development of communicative language, Hobson claims, and it is through language that further understanding of others' perspectives and attitudes grows. In this sense knowledge of minds develops naturally and normally as interpersonal social exchanges, sharing knowledge of one's own and others' perspectives on the environment increases. Hobson's view of infant and toddler development provides a foundation for the evident direct intuition of the meaning of mental state terms, including emotion words and cognitive state words. These intuitions arise from experience with parents, siblings, and other close relations with whom the child shares psychological space, but whose attitudes are often divergent from her own. Long before the child reaches the advanced state of the 4-year-old's theory of mind, she will have conceptualized basic intentional concepts of perception, emotion, and cognition, as Dunn's (1988) observations firmly support. Harris's (1992) simulation theory, in which imagination does the work of interpreting others' perspectives, also fits well with Hobson's view of normal development.

For the 3-year-old, then, many psychological attitudes are directly intuited from behavior, facial expression, and so on, just as they are for the 1-year-old. But the 3-year-old has advanced much further. She communicates about the world of people and things using a shared symbolic language, in which her own behavior and feelings are frequently commented upon, and in which she is increasingly able to make her own feelings, wants, and thoughts explicit. This ability makes it possible for her to discover more about people's sources of knowledge, and to make predictions about their behavior by simulating what she would know if she were in their place. Beyond that, language makes it possible to represent in a conveniently manipulable way nonpresent realities and unreal and changeable states. Not only is language a medium through which the individual learns about others and about the cultural world, but it also becomes an invaluable representational medium for intrapersonal cognitive functioning, articulating, maintaining, and manipulating situational models. Five and 6-year-olds (and adults) may be able to construct representations from nonverbal presentations (although younger children – and apes – cannot), because they have had the requisite experiences with interpreting the relevant verbalizations of others in analogous situations and have thereby learned to think about the situations in these ways. The fact that symbolic representations may include information about the mental states and causal chains behind behavioral observations makes them uniquely suitable for interpretation of otherwise puzzling patterns of behavior.

It is plausible that metarepresentation, alleged by Perner (1991) and others to enable the child to solve false belief tasks, is dependent upon representation in language. Metarepresentation means not only representing to oneself a situation but also understanding that the representation is a stand-in for the situation, that is, understanding representing as representation (and not as reality). At the very least language greatly facilitates establishment of metarepresentation if it is not actually necessary to it. Language establishes a separate possible level of representation through the purely verbal, and thus establishes the possibility of using one level to articulate another. All these cognitive advances made possible by language as a representational system are closed to autistic children lacking a reasonable level of language competence. Thus their deficits in interpersonal understanding must be compounded by a severe conceptual deficiency.

Finally, it is worth considering still another specific biologically determined deficit possibly underlying autism, consistent with Donald's (1991) thesis, described in Chapter 3: a deficit in the mimetic capacity for representation. This speculation is consistent with the evidence that autistic children do not imitate [except for echoic language – see discussion by Meltzoff and Gopnik (1993)] and do not engage in social referencing, pointing, and other forms of joint attention, or in pretend play. Given the foundational significance attributed to mimesis by Donald, this deficit could explain their incapacity for acquiring language in a normal way. Their failure at theory of mind tasks is an indication that they are incapable of engaging in the normal human mimetic skills involved in sharing feelings and intentions of others. The more complex demands of the theory of mind tasks require, as argued here, not only knowledge of linguistic terms, but also a quite deep understanding of the mental and social schemes implied by those terms. Hobson's (1993) account of the autistic child's disconnection from the social world is consistent with these speculations.[11]

A Mediated Mind Account of the Developing Understanding of Self and Other

"Enculturation" as a theory of children's developing understanding of other people's perceptions and thoughts has been discounted by theory of mind researchers. Although cultures differ in the mental terms they employ, all cultures seem to view human minds in similar causal terms, and cross-cultural research (Avis & Harris, 1991) finds that theory of mind tasks tap children's developing understanding in both Western and non-Western societies. Nonetheless, as Astington (1993) notes, the Western folk theory of mind is at least in part a cultural invention; ideas of subjectivity and individual responsibility have their origins in Greek philosophy. "These ideas are captured in our folk psychology and are fundamental to our conception of ourselves and others. In this sense 'mind' is a cultural invention, and children discover the mind as they acquire the language and social practices of the culture" (p. 164). But, Astington also argues, "Although it may be true that 'mind' is a cultural invention, there is still a sense in which each child discovers the mind for herself" (p. 166). This does not imply that children do it all by themselves. Rather it is recognized that all children need exposure to the ideas of the culture expressed in its ways of speaking about the mind. The autistic research indicates that there is a critical human capacity for understanding other people's knowledge and intentions that is missing in autism. It does not tell us that that critical piece enables the normal child to construct a theory of mind by herself.

A social-cultural account of the development of understanding of the mental states of self and others must begin with self and social knowledge in infancy. As reviewed in Chapter 4, Meltzoff (1988) argues that the infant is equipped with the disposition to see that "Others are like me" and therefore is disposed to imitate their actions and to recognize their imitations of her actions. It is important that this is not an egocentric or solipsistic view; it is not that "Others are me" – rather, "They are other than me but like me." Harris's (1992) claim that the infant/child may build on this experience to simulate the perspective and experience of others requires that the infant go beyond the recognition that "Others are like me" to the insight that "Others are different from me."

If the beginning supposition is that others are like me, it may take considerable experience to come to the conclusion that others are different, and to distinguish how they are different and how alike and under what circumstances each is true. Early empathic responses may be simply extensions of the "like me" recognition. That is, infants and young children may respond to the distress (and delight) of others with similar responses of their own, without cognitive understanding of causes or effects. Language is used by parents, teachers, and peers to articulate differences between the child and the other in terms of likes, dislikes, wants, knowledge, memories, as well as possessions, both concrete and abstract. Shatz (1994) similarly emphasizes the achievement, through language experience in the years from 2 to 3, of recognizing that "there are both differences and commonalities between self and others and using the language of mental states to express those relations" (p. 327).

If we view the ToM problem as involving that of coming to understand when others are different, it is apparent that the various intentional states broadly considered in the theory of mind literature provide different interpretive clues. Feeling states are often projected through species-specific facial expressions and salient noises, linguistic and nonlinguistic ("oh no," "ow," "umm"). Perceptual perspective may be recognized as the infant/child moves about and experiences perceptual change. Wants/desires are frequently articulated in easily interpretable situations, or are readily inferable from another's actions (e.g., "Give me that," as one child grabs a toy from another). Primitive empathy, action, and perception can provide the young child with what Wellman (1990) refers to as a desire psychology, recognizing that others' desires may lead to actions to obtain a wanted object. They may also provide the child with the wherewithal to simulate the experience of another and thus to predict how that other will perform. Language used in these situations is relatively easily interpretable and is relatively frequent in the productions of children as young as 2 years, as Bartsch and Wellman (1995) have found.

The speculations of Donald (1991) on the prelinguistic mimetic capacity provide an alternative route for the child, as suggested earlier with regard to the deficits observed in autistic children. The nonlinguistic but socially symbolic mimetic capacity is revealed in imitative behaviors, games, rituals, and shared pretense. The symbolic forms – like language itself – are simultaneously "out there" in the social world, and "in there" in the representing mind. From this perspective, the disposition to engage in social games such as "peekaboo" and "pattycake" may be critical to the developing capacity for interpreting others' actions and intentions. The 3-year-old may build on such exchanges with parents and peers to construct a complex set of knowledge schemes about others' intentions, especially in familiar social situations. Engaging in pretense with objects is but an extension of such capacities and, as both Hobson (1993) and Leslie (1988) agree, is critically important.[12]

What is not readily apparent in action or nonlinguistic expression, and not readily simulatable on the basis of perceptual experience, are the belief states of other people – their thoughts, imaginings, and guesses. Language alone enables the child to gain insight into the knowledge/belief states of others. Therefore, representing others' beliefs as different from one's own requires some experience with the imparting of information from those others about their beliefs. We know what other people think, if it is different from what we think, only because they tell us about it. Even adults are frequently surprised – and even skeptical – that others believe something contrary to their own understandings. It is hardly surprising that young children have little experience with this kind of knowledge and little insight into differences of this kind. This is a kind of egocentrism: Assume others think the same way you do until you hear differently.[13] In the period between 3 and 4 years, children are just beginning to be able to use language as a narrative form that enables them to compare their own experience and understanding with that of others. And it is only in the reflection of their knowledge of others' thoughts that self-knowledge emerges. Such reflection depends to a large extent upon linguistic expression. Experience of self and other provides only a tacit understanding of difference; language makes the difference explicit.

Conclusion

A very complex developmental process drawing on direct experience, social interchanges, reorganization processes, linguistic forms, metarepresentations, and cultural knowledge structures is thus involved in social understanding. This developmental process is consistent with the developmental course – and the evolutionary analogue – already laid out in the preceding chapters. What emerges from this process during early childhood is the capacity to project knowledge of thoughts and feelings in understanding the actions of self and others. The evidence and arguments set forth here for the importance of language in developing social and self-knowledge provide firm support for the developmental progression envisioned. The variety of theories proposed as alternative explanations of these developments reflects the larger theoretical frame within which human development is viewed, and at the same time has implications for the interpretation of much other empirical work in cognitive development. The final chapter addresses these issues and implications.

IV. Conclusions

11. Collaborative Construction of the Mediated Mind

The previous chapters have traced cognitive, social, and linguistic developments between the years of 1 and 5 in human childhood with the aim of understanding how normally developing individuals make the transition from infancy to childhood. The basic underlying assumption of this effort is that to understand development, it is necessary to understand the developing system in all its complexity, including its organismic, experiential, social, and cultural history. This does not imply neglect of the separate parts of the developing system at particular phases of development. But as a theoretical enterprise it is important to see the pieces as parts of a whole that is an ongoing, historically constituted, forward-looking individual person within a social-cultural matrix. At this point, then, I return to the themes set out in the first section of the book.

Becoming an Encultured Individual

The destiny of human individuals (as stated in Chapter 1) is to enter into a cultural environment, complete with all the social institutions, symbolic forms, artifacts, activities, interpersonal scripts, rules, expectations, technologies, fashions, moral strictures, and so on. Not least of these are the languages of the groups within which participatory interactions take place. These languages – often two or more linguistic systems, always more than one social register (e.g., formal and informal, peer and adult) – become the vehicle of enculturation as well as the content and structure of internal representations and the tools of complex thinking. Thus to a large extent in the course of human childhood, between about 2 and 6 years of age, language and the surrounding culture take over the human mind. It is during these years that biology "hands over" development to the social world.

But not entirely. The developing individual has a history that predates the invasion of the linguistic world and extends beyond it. To a very significant extent the human mind – in terms of the basic neural structure in the brain–is tuned and shaped by experience in the world. Much of that tuning, of course, is general across individuals, in that the biological substrate expects certain environmental conditions, and develops in concert with them; but the particulars of these exchanges are unique to each individual. Thus with development each individual, beginning with common potentials and constraints of infancy, acquires a unique mentality that is carried into his or her interactions with the linguistic world. Each linguistic world is also unique, of course; thus the product of these interactions is always contingent and to some extent unpredictable.

The shaping of the prelinguistic mind of the infant takes place largely in terms of social experiences – through caretaking routines and play, as well as the simple sharing of social spaces with adults and other children. As Meltzoff (1990) stated, the infant appears to understand from the outset that "I am one of these, we are the same kind." The infant also comes to appreciate that one or some of these specific others are more important for love, sustenance, and security than are others. The specificity of the primary caretaker bond is an early key ingredient in the individuality of the infant's model of the world.[1]

The unstable balance between individuality and society is an inevitable product of the enculturation process. It is precisely because the human mind is so open to experience that it retains its individuality in the face of the overwhelming pressure to become a replica of society's mold. Each individual's experiential history dictates a different perspective on new encounters. But is individuality only an effect of history? Are human beings prisoners of their experience, as the radical behaviorists believed? The answer is no – this is the beauty of the human condition: Particularities from the beginning of life dictate that the same experience is incorporated in different ways by different individuals. And individuals maintain their own integrity even as they gain wisdom from the experience of others through their stories, instructions, explanations, and so on.

Infancy is the beginning of individuality, the tuning of the system to the particulars of the specific people and things of the individual's world. But, however impressive the analytic powers of the helpless infant have been shown to be, they are the foundation of experience, not the structure of thought or the "natural kind" of human cognition. On a different plane, the 3-year-old is an active, speaking, thinking creature; these thoughts and spoken words are based on a history as well as on present realities, and the constraints of that history determine to a large extent what the child understands in the present. The young child's brain implies the existence not only of a cognitive system, but also of a mind with expectations based on preconceived models of how the world is and should be, models that are as yet hardly modified by the ideas of others, simply because language is not developed sufficiently to enable the child to interpret others' ideas.

These considerations have important implications for theories of cognitive development, including in the first instance what these theories are about. For many researchers, theories address issues such as the development of language as a system, or the learning of arithmetic, or the acquisition of physical knowledge. In these cases theoretical models may be very formal, very abstract, and very static, confined to one domain of knowledge, elaborating how a final system of known (or hypothesized) constitution is constructed over time [see Valsiner (1987)]. The quirks of construction that depart from the ideal may tell us something about developing human minds that bears on other issues, but they do not provide an overarching developmental theory from this basis. Domain-specific theories and descriptions of this kind have proliferated in developmental psychology in recent years.

On the other hand, if theories of cognitive development are about the developmental process as it reveals itself in the complexities of human lives, as biologically constituted organisms growing in a socially constituted environment organized within a larger culture, and if the goal of such theories is to understand how cognition develops under these conditions, then the interplay of individual experience and the engulfing cultural communicative society must be the focus of analysis. Whereas this kind of theory draws on the wisdom afforded by behavioral developmental theories in general, it is necessarily specific to humanity because *Homo sapiens* is the only species that has constructed complex cultural environments, and thus the only species whose development is necessarily constituted within their constraints.

From this perspective the following section examines the ontogenetic course of development in terms of the phylogenetic model described in Chapter 2. Here the general, universal, and social are emphasized, but the individual and unique are always assumed to be the level wherein developments take place.

The Phylogenetic Model Revisited: Toward the Hybrid Mind

Donald's (1991) scheme envisioned four levels of representational potential, all of which are present in the modern adult human mind, and which evolved sequentially with different successive species of hominids after branching off from a general primate line. Early hominids were conceived to share the general event or episodic representation system of other primates. *Homo erectus* developed a nonlinguistic mimetic system of externalization of shared, motorically based representations, capable of internalization as a private as well as public symbolic system. Early *Homo sapiens* developed true language and used it prototypically as a narrative device, for sharing experience and constructing histories and mythologies. Modern minds developed written language systems useful for complex operations dependent upon externalization of representations, such as mathematics, logic, and scientific theories.

The attraction of such an evolutionary model as an analogue to the ontogenetic sequence is its clear connections to both the beginnings and the endings of the sequence, as well as its clear connections to social, cultural, and linguistic developments. It is now apparent that by late infancy children have good representations of repeated episodes – mental event representations (MERs) – and can formulate and hold in memory single episodes as well. Thus event representations appear to be the basic building blocks of cognitive development, as both Donald (1991) on the phyogenetic level and Nelson and Gruendel (1981; Nelson, 1986) on the ontogenetic level claim. Moreover, it is clear that complex theoretical thinking requires extensive practice with written forms, as the traditional claims (e.g., Piaget & Vygotsky) about formal thought emerging in adolescence imply.[2] Although for many, categorical thought might be placed in the role of "basic building block" rather than MERs, and some prefer to see theories in the minds of babes, the early event representation and late theoretical mind claims are not on the whole very controversial.

It is the intermediate stages that may give pause to some. The proposal of a mimetic mind as essential to the evolution of true human language is novel. In Chapters 3 and 4 the evidence for a developmental analogue was considered. First, it must be accepted that contemporary human infants are hardly equivalent to adult early hominids, and toddlers are not similar to adult *Homo erectus*. Modern human infants are more like other primate infants – in cognitive as well as motor development – than they are like adults of primate species (e.g., Diamond, 1991). But they are also different from other primate infants; not only do human infants live in a human world, but their brains are developing in human ways, including the capacity for processing speech sounds, a capacity that begins prenatally. They respond especially to the tonality of human speech as well as music. Thus they are never truly *prelinguistic*. They are surrounded by talk, even in groups in which the talk is not directed to the infant but to other adults. Unlike the infant *Homo erectus*, modern human infants are biologically and socially tuned to speech, and their social partners support their efforts to use speech as a communicative medium from infancy onward. For these reasons we can reject the idea that there is a "natural" course of development preceding the cultural (in the way that Vygotsky proposed).

Do we need a mimetic stage then? The answer rests on the true meaning of the mimetic stage in Donald's (1991) theory, which is twofold. First, it established a means of communicating intentions, plans, technical skills, and complex social rituals between members of a group. Without the mimetic capacity, the passing on of many complex cultural forms is not possible (Tomasello, Kruger, & Ratner, 1993). Second, because mimesis involves bodily movements and gestures, the external can be internalized and represented on a new level. Skills and routines can be practiced on the basis of internal models. The external social model then becomes the internal individual model. Likewise, the modern family group establishes for the human infant not only a communicative complex, but also a setting for practicing interpersonal routines, both caretaking (e.g., diapering, feeding, bathing) and playing (e.g., pattycake, roll the ball). Parents typically insert words into these routines, and use words to signal their onset or the partitioning of the event.

This is important: The language of the community becomes part of the two- or three-person games played in private. In contrast, Tomasello (1990) points out that in chimpanzee groups, mother and child may establish a gestural signal between themselves, but it is not communally shared, and is discarded and lost once its utility within a situation such as nursing is no longer needed. The situation with human parents and children is subtly different – however idiosyncratic the rituals they establish may be, they incorporate the language of the group, a language that has utility beyond the infant situation. Still, it is not the language that establishes the routines, but the coordinated actions within the activity. Both actions and objects take on symbolic social value in these exchanges. Most important, the establishment of mutual understanding within routines enables a level of intersubjectivity within which words can be used interchangeably by both infant and parent. The mimetic use of speech forms thus reinforces the sense that "We are the same."

In this way the basic capacity for representing events enables the practice of mimetic routines that incorporate symbolic objects and actions, as well as speech. When the infant begins to share mimetically the same speech forms in the routine, the path is paved for the onset of true language forms and structures. As many others[3] have argued, in the absence of the scaffolding that the mimetic routine provides, language forms rattle around inside human activities without becoming easily accessible to the young child. Other ways in are then needed. One sees these other ways in the practices of communities where language is not specifically included in caretaking and infant games (e.g., Heath, 1983; Ochs & Schieffelin, 1984), but where language is linked with other community practices and used in different kinds of routinized forms. However, in cases where children are unable to partake of such routinized games and activities – as with autistic children, who appear to lack some component that makes intersubjectivity possible – language remains inaccessible.[4]

The conclusion to the story is that in ontogenesis, as in phylogenesis, a prelinguistic establishment of shared symbolic activities is essential to the launching of language as a normal process. However, in human childhood such mimetic activities take place at the same time as language is being learned and established as an effective communicative medium, and they persist as the primary means by which activities are structured and carried out through the interim period from about 1 to 3 years of age. Thus, despite the onset and rapid development of language as a medium of propositional expression and pragmatic communication, language remains to be developed as a medium of narrative before it becomes an internal representational mode, that is, before the third representational stage analogous to Donald's mythic stage is reached.

The third stage is launched after basic language skills are sufficiently developed so that complex discourse may be held in memory and interpreted according to available mental models. Again, practice with the use of narrative to express one's own experience and to understand that of others is necessary, and again scaffolding by closely affiliated intimates is certainly helpful if not actually essential to the process. As Dorval (1990) has shown, sharing and sustaining a topic with a partner over extended discourse is not easily accomplished, and its development takes place over a long period of time, lasting into the adolescent years.

There are many observational data from parents and children demonstrating the process of establishing narratives of the past. But we don't know precisely how such practices affect the child's thinking. Indeed, much of the research with preschool children, including the recent research on children's theory of mind, takes these developments for granted. This research assumes that young children represent the world in the same ways that adults do and that they apply the same analyses to their knowledge, handicapped only by lesser knowledge than the adult possesses. In contrast, the implication of the present analysis is that the young child is working with representational systems that are still largely prelinguistic, and that linguistically formulated mental representations change the potential of the system dramatically, just as they change the structure of the models of the represented world (see Chapter 5).

In summary, Donald's phylogenetic model has provided many insights, particularly on the mimetic component and the primary contribution of language to cognition and culture. The years between 3 and 5 can now be seen as a significant period of transition in human development that replays, albeit in modern form, the move from mimetic to narrative representations, both social and mental. The problems faced and potentials opened in this transitional period, both psychological and theoretical, have been the main topics of the developments traced in this book.

Collaborative Construction of Language-Related Competence in Early Childhood

In this section, the findings from Chapters 6 through 10 are briefly reviewed to highlight the main themes and conclusions. As discussed in Chapter 6, memory in infancy displays many of the characteristics of what is generally referred to as implicit or involuntary memory, with deliberate recall evident in the latter part of the first year. Memory for objects and events – episodic and generic – is reliable as early as 1 year, but most episodic memories usually do not persist more than about 6 months during the early childhood years. A long-lasting narrative-based autobiographical memory system begins to emerge at about 4 years. Before 4 years there is evidence that children are easily confused as to the source of their knowledge, and may overwrite and thus effectively erase something experienced in a way that older children do not. This change in memory accounts is strongly influenced by the experience of exchanging memory with others, and is closely tied to the period when language becomes established as a complex mode of extended discourse.

Narrative competence is the most obvious of the language-dependent abilities. Narrative, which has its basis in the event representations of the infant and young child, can be realized through pictorial or dramatic means, but language is its primary medium; or, as Donald (1991) claims, narrative is the natural product of language. We have seen that children's abilities to engage in coherent narratives, and to extract a structured narrative from someone else's account, develops over the preschool years. It is not until the late preschool period that children engage in fluent personal episodic accounts, and not until the early school years that they generally are able to produce a short "made-up" story rather than a script. Much practice in listening to others' narratives, based on real-life experiences, as well as fictional stories in books, and contributing to these accounts from their own experience and knowledge, lies behind these developments. Emerging from them is a self-narrative or life history that begins as a social construction in collaboration with parents, teachers, and peers, and continues to develop thereafter at least in part in response to social sharing of viewpoints on experienced events. In consequence, the underlying cultural myths, themes, and values become part of the child's own ideology, embedded as they are in society's stories as told by adults.

Competence in constructing and using culturally defined categories of entities (objects, events, properties, etc.) has been shown to involve a number of different linguistic components, including superordinate labels and the vocabulary of inclusive hierarchies. These verbal components can account for aspects of conceptual development previously held to be perceptually based (e.g., grouping along lines of shape similarity), or logically based (e.g., set relations). The verbal contributions to the development of cultural categories are integrated with experientially derived categories, such as slot-fillers in scripts. The coordination and integration processes involved in the assembling of cultural taxonomies are evident in the residue of slot-filler categories found even in adult productions of familiar, everyday category members. These processes exemplify the more general problem encountered during the preschool years of reconfiguring individual experientially based representations established independently of linguistic input to accommodate knowledge systems displayed in language. This reconfiguration cannot be accomplished through individual constructive processes alone, but requires implicit and explicit collaboration with knowledge bearers, as was illustrated in Chapter 8.

Humans, like all organisms, have some inborn "clock" and "calendar" mechanisms that regulate their biological states with respect to temporal durations. Young children also regulate their actions in terms of sequences, with respect to both basic motoric actions and participation in socially established activities. They are sensitive to causal even more than temporally invariant relations, especially those causal relations involving the actions of agents. The language of time begins to enter the system at about 2 years. Children must eventually coordinate their earlier event-based temporal knowledge with the cultural knowledge system and its associated technologies. This coordination begins at about 4 years as children mark their event sequences with conventional terms for sequence and location ("before," "first," "yesterday," etc.). But this is only a beginning; acquiring the system in full requires years of explicit instruction involving artifacts for marking and measuring time. Unlike the hierarchies of object categories, or the linear plot structures of episodic narratives already described, temporal systems are organized in terms of recurrent cycles. It is not until the early school years that children begin to understand and participate in the several complex timekeeping and measuring systems that each culture establishes.

Research organized around the question of "theory of mind" implies that some new understanding of the intentional states of other people emerges at about 4 years. Prior to that age children engage in communicative interactions with closely related others and are able to predict the behavior of others in familiar situations, but they do not apply consistent rules to the predictions of others' actions on the basis of others' knowledge and belief states. Talking with others about their feelings and ideas, and learning the language of mental states and its implications, are critical to these developments. At the same time, the child's sense of self as different from others emerges and is nurtured by the reflection of self-knowledge in talk with others.

Consideration of these developments in relation to the developmental analogue of the phylogenetic scheme that Donald laid out (summarized in Table 3.4) in the end requires that the original projection be modified. The developments over the first 5 years of life are certainly dramatic in nature, but they now appear to be less stage-like, more complex, with representational processes more interwoven than sequential in nature. Event representations, mimetic representations, and language forms all begin to coexist in early forms toward the end of the first year of life, and become more elaborate and more firmly mastered over the next several years. They differ, however, in how easily the child can establish and use them in guiding action, coordinating action with others, and understanding the actions of others, in the beginning and over time. Event representations are basic and arise from the child's own organization of participation in routines. Mimetic representations depend upon the models provided by others, and an engagement with others in increasingly complex skills and games. Language, on the other hand, awaits the mastery of a complex system before it reveals its rich potentials.

Other Domains

Some domains that have been extensively studied by researchers in early cognitive development have not been examined in this volume. *Spatial* knowledge, such as orientation in a room or finding one's way in a maze, develops over the period in question (Acredolo, 1982; Liben, 1982). *Numerical* awareness, according to current research, begins in infancy, but is established gradually over the preschool period as the number names are learned and used to mark both order and cardinality (Gelman & Gallistel, 1978; Wynn, 1992b). Using *models* as representations of large spaces is a skill that shows a quite dramatic development between $2\frac{1}{2}$ and 3 years (DeLoache, 1990). Understanding the relation of *pictures* to things in the real world also undergoes development (Beilin & Pearlman, 1991; Robinson, Nye, & Thomas, 1994; Zaitchek, 1990), and drawing develops in predictable ways that may be related to cognitive change.[5] Each of these domains is certainly as important and as species-typical as those noted above and described in more detail in the previous chapters. These other domains may derive from specialized perceptuo-motoric-neural structures adapted to the functions of human cognition. They differ from those given separate consideration in this book in two ways: (1) They do not obviously derive from event knowledge; and (2) they are not obviously interconnected with language processes, although language may affect them in some way; in the case of number, for example, language labels appear critical to the establishment of the arithmetic system.[6] In the case of models and pictures, these may be precursor forms of later external symbol storage (ESS) system (Chapter 3) developments, including written language. But critical as language is to much of human cognition, concurrent development in these other domains indicates that it is not the entire story. Thus it is imperative to give closer attention to the ways in which language-specific processing is involved in cognition, particularly in cognitive representations, and ways in which it may not be.

The Importance of 4 Years

For each of the domains that have been given special consideration here, a level of functioning emerges or begins to emerge around the age of 4 years. A question of considerable interest is, "Why this particular age?" Campbell and Bickhard (1986) suggest that 4 years is the age at which a new level of knowing emerges. Karmiloff-Smith (1992) argues that different knowing levels emerge at different times in different domains or modules of functioning, although some may emerge in concert at 4 years. In their recent neo-Piagetian stages of cognitive development, both Fischer (Fischer & Rose, 1993) and Case (1992a) find a new level of functioning at 4 to 5 years, which accords as well with evidence from neurological studies of increased activity in integrative processes in the central nervous system at 4 to 5 years.

The general representational advance at around 4 years common to these theories is, I suggest, driven largely by the mastering of language for both communicative and cognitive purposes. Each domain of knowledge and skill undergoes development in response. In the process of representational change from a largely experientially based system to a potentially language-based system the child must coordinate and integrate her individually constructed knowledge with the culturally established knowledge systems that she meets through language. The claim here is that language is the key – that representation in language changes the cognitive system dramatically during this age period.

Limitations on Preschool Competence: Cultural Gaps

Impressive as the achievements of the preschool years are, there are strong limitations on the structure and function in each system, underscoring that much more is to be accomplished at the fourth level (analogous to Donald's theoretical stage); it is important to note what those limits are, lest we fall into the trap of thinking that once basic language skills are in place cognitive development is simply a matter of learning more.

- *Language.* There is much for children to learn about how to construct both oral and written discourse beyond the competence achieved at 4 years, in terms of vocabulary, pragmatics and even matters of grammar. As illustrated in Chapter 7, the ability to compose cohesive text, whether oral or written, continues to develop, and as Dorval (1990; Dorval &

Eckerman, 1984) has emphasized, conversational skills including topic-sharing require many years of practice beyond the early childhood period. Learning the written symbol system for interpretation of messages of course requires extensive periods of instruction and practice in both reading and writing. Automatic reading brings the cognitive potential to a new level of literate competence fundamental to much of advanced modern cognition.

- *Memory.* Research on memory in the school years indicates that metamemory skills generally come into play after the age of 6, and that the use of external notating devices, including the use of lists and other mnemonic practices, are learned then. Deliberate strategies of chunking and organizing are learned in the service of mastering material in specific cultural knowledge domains typically taught in school. As Donald (1991) suggested, schooling to a large degree is a matter of training to organize and use knowledge in internal and external memory.
- *Narrative.* Constructing narratives around one's own experience, taking others' points of view into account, making up stories, following an extended work such as a novel, all require vastly more experience with the narrative genre beyond that available to a 4-year-old. Alternative narrative genres, such as those of science and social science, and the expository forms that develop therefore, become part of the child's exposure to written forms.
- *Concepts and categories.* Elaboration of knowledge structures in terms of scientific and theoretical conceptual structures formulated as formal explanatory theories lies far beyond the abilities of the preschooler.
- *Time.* As indicated earlier, the preschooler has only the most tenuous understanding of the meaning of time in society, and the conventional temporal systems that measure and regulate time. Implicit knowledge established in the preschool years is transformed into explicit knowledge that extends far into the past and far into the future.
- *Social.* There is little need to document here the skills needed to anticipate the perspective of others, of self and other roles in different institutional situations, of obligation, reciprocity, friendship, moral and conventional behavioral rules, gender roles and relations, and so on.

A summary view of these limitations implicates the importance of the specific lack in the preschool years of external culturally designed symbolic systems, using artifacts such as clocks, written language, and graphic materials, which become mastered during the school years. More generally, the preschooler lacks access to the cultural knowledge systems contained in written works and archived in libraries, schools, and museums. During the preschool years the child begins to become a participant in larger cultural enterprises through such media as stories, television, and video. What the breakthrough into representational language at the age of 4 does is to establish the foundation for the entry into the more formal cultural knowledge systems through written and electronic media.

What Language Does for the Child

That language enters into and changes both cognition and communication between the years of 1 and 6 is the critical argument put forth here. As I have emphasized throughout this book, the roles of language change as language itself is mastered and organized and takes on functions in the child's life. At this point a summary of how language affects cognition during this transitional period that cross-cuts both functions and developmental levels brings out the critical importance of these roles to all aspects of the child's functioning.

Naming and Referring: Sharing Concepts

Referring is a function that can be achieved nonlinguistically through pointing and other gestures, for example, but it is a primary linguistic function. Referring points out what is to be attended to in the discourse. Naming is a natural corollary of referring, as shared naming practices make reference to things and events not present in the immediate context feasible. Much of the child's first language experience is spent in learning common names (see Chapter 5). One obvious function of establishing naming and referring is to build up a common vocabulary that serves as the base for simple communication between parents and children and for learning more words within familiar contexts. Another related function is to provide the base from which the child can interpret and produce word combinations and simple and complex sentences. Naming and referring are both fundamental to communicating with language.

A second important function of learning names for things – objects, actions, events, and other kinds – is to learn the categories of the social and cultural world. Prelinguistic infants recognize categorical similarity of objects and actions in experimental situations in which their attention to the dimensions of similarity is controlled. But children's use of words in early speech indicates that they are often indifferent to the categorical boundaries of these words, and cross ontological categories in using them. This is not surprising under the assumption that the child begins with event representations, in which objects are a part of the whole. Events are nonlinear and dynamic – action, actor, and object are only three aspects of the complex situation, in which many objects are visible at once, and many actions may take place at the same time. The practice of drawing attention to a specific object and naming it places it in a privileged class of named things that can be talked about in any situation. But the child often takes considerable time to learn this practice, and sometimes errs by using the name for objects and actions in the same situation but not in the same category. Also, often the child takes the name and applies it to other objects that bear little resemblance to the target object from the perspective of the adult.

Naming thus establishes categories, and shapes the child's initial categories to those of the shared culture. This practice and function is even more critical to the many terms the child learns on the basis of concrete everyday experience that do not refer to objects, but rather to actions, places, events, times, and so on. For these categories the child must learn the characteristic components and boundaries of the culture's definitions as displayed through the language terms used to refer to them in discourse contexts. It is not that the child cannot come to some preliminary understanding of these categories on her own, but that the categories are culturally defined; whatever understanding the child achieves independent of language does not guarantee that the categories are the same as those used by other cultural members. Of course this function of naming and referring does not end with the achievement of a first vocabulary, but extends throughout life as new vocabulary is learned for each new or expanding knowledge domain. From the beginning, however, it is dependent on a dialectic between individual conceptual representations and external linguistic representations. In this dialectic neither language nor cognition is primary; the two are interdependent and intertwined throughout the acquisition of language and the development of the conceptual knowledge base.

Linear Order: Slowing and Stabilizing

Experience is multidimensional, often with many different things displayed and many different actions taking place at the same time. Speech, on the other hand, is one-dimensional, linearly ordered through time. To express experience in language requires recomposing it into linear form, conforming to the syntax of one's own language. This means that there is no one-to-one mapping of experience on language; the adults' intuition that there is arises, no doubt, from their being fully inducted into the uses of language. Further, events that take place simultaneously or instantaneously take time to be expressed in full sentences. In other words, language slows down and stretches out thought into discrete parts in linear relations to each other.[7]

Can this slowing process be an advantage, or is it a drawback, a necessary outcome of the language process, albeit an unfortunate one? For the cognitive uses of language in thought the slowing down and stabilizing of experience in linguistic form is actually an enormous contribution to individual and group processing. Compared with nonlinguistic thought, language enables the establishment of explicit stable concepts, referring to parts of the world experience that can be contemplated, reflected upon, and put into articulated conjunction with other concepts. Ordering and reordering of categories becomes possible through manipulation of language and emerges from the nature of the language medium itself, which requires stable components and standard orders for expression.[8]

Many linguists and psychologists now recognize that thought might not be organized like language in terms of propositions and hierarchies but in more fluid forms (e.g., Lakoff, 1987). This realization appears to provide justification for the technologies (e.g., video techniques, hypertext) that break away from the logical linear forms traditionally imposed on written language. But the advantage that linear organization offers to thought – beginning with the sentence – should be recognized and preserved. It requires that one follow through with an ordered and completed argument or story rather than flying off in all directions at once. Sometimes, as in fantasy, dreams, or poetry it may be advantageous to follow one's wayward thoughts wherever they may go, but to think clearly about a problem or a plan, linear order helps to keep matters straight and provides the basis for more complex logical or theoretical thought.

Regulating Action: Planning

A primary function of private speech emphasized in Vygotsky's work and by his successors is the regulation of action, from the simple voluntary control of actions and reactions to elaborately planned activities. This function represents the "genetic law of cultural development" (Wertsch, Tulviste, & Hagstrom 1993, p. 338) in that action is first regulated by social others, before the child takes over the role of planning ahead and subsequently internalizing the function in inner speech. As postulated in Chapter 6, memory, especially generic or script memory, serves the basic function of prediction, thus supplying the internal support for action in the present and planning for the immediate future. But when a problem arises, when a script is not available or does not apply, problem-solving must be invoked and decisions made as to appropriate actions. When peers collaborate on a plan, beginning with simple nursery pretense play, they invoke scripts, and verbalize their intentions, calling on the partners to enter into a shared plan. Later elaborations of the planning function may become very complex and call on the ability to engage in extended discussion and to use external symbols.

Exchange of Expressions: Sharing Feelings and Beliefs

We do our best to make sense to each other by establishing shared contexts and making our utterances relevant (Sperber & Wilson, 1986). In the process, we tell each other what we think about things. When mother says, "that hurts" as the child is pinching her arm, the child learns something about her own actions, and about language that expresses pain. When mother says, "I think it's in the kitchen" the child learns something about the word "think." A difficulty is that mother is usually right. Thus "think" may appear to the child to be equivalent to "know." Talking about mental states, motives, pains, and other private experiences is part of everyday use of language, but it is often obscure to unpracticed language users such as young children (see Chapter 10).

Yet it is only through language that children can be sure that someone else's experience of a situation is different from their own. Much exchange of point of view must take place, using language terms that are only partially understood, before the child can build an appropriate model that enables her to project onto others (without their explicit expression) a view that is different from her own. As with the acquisition of categories and temporal expressions, the process is inevitably cyclical. Learning the vocabulary requires hearing the words used in relevant contexts in which their meaning can be interpreted, but interpreting the meanings of others' perspectives requires understanding the vocabulary. Because the words are used multifunctionally the learning cannot be straightforward. No doubt there comes a point where enough experience with such words in use has taken place that children can begin to accumulate models of social experience that enable them to project different experiences onto other actors based on what they know of the actor's access to information. Of course, this process continues throughout life.

Narrative World-making

Infants and young children from the beginning attempt to form cognitive models of aspects of the world they live in, models that are organized in terms of events that they are part of, or that they observe, including the people, objects, and actions that are components of these events. In infancy these models must be rather fragmented, consisting of pieces that are stable and reliable (e.g., mealtimes, bedtimes, bathtimes, outings) and others that appear and disappear or reappear in unpredictable manners. The child has good command of routines, but not of the overall structure of daily life, or of the meaning of novel settings and experiences or the behavior of strangers.

Narratives that tie experiences together come into play when language is used by adults to connect them into a whole. Parents use temporal and causal language to direct activities, and to lead from one activity to the next. As Emily's crib talk suggests (see Chapters 6 and 7), the fragmented models of scripted routines gradually become coherent narrative models of everyday experiences, incorporating the new and the old, the expected, and unexpected, the fantasied, and the lived. Evidence from other children indicates that narrative plays a crucial role in structuring experiences to make sense in the context of their own understanding, and enabling the retention of the experience in memory. Eventually, these experiences become woven together into a life story or set of stories that constitute a history as a background for a sense of continuing self. Further, stories of others – real life and fictional – provide the child with a rich background of alternative experiences with which to elaborate her world models. The narrative capacity made possible by language has been underestimated as a contribution to human cognition and knowledge, but has begun to be recognized as a force that is a source not only of pleasure but also of understanding, whether the object of understanding is the actions of other people, a self-concept, or more abstract constructions.

Reflective Articulation and Explanation

Piaget's later theory (Beilin, 1992) emphasized the importance of reflective abstraction for explicit understanding of relationships. Similarly, Karmiloff-Smith's (1992) theory posits a redescription process that brings representations to a new level, and she recognizes the critical role of language in this process. In this function language becomes a tool of thought, a means by which intuitive understanding can be articulated and new relationships can be established. Bringing implicit knowledge to consciousness and examining its implications is surely one of the most important intelligent activities, one that language is uniquely designed to perform. This move makes possible the generation of new relationships and thus the formation of new theoretical propositions.

In everyday life we say, "I have a theory" as easily as we say, "I have an idea" or "I have a dream." Yet what we mean by "theory" is usually no more than "I think the explanation for X is Y," that is, that there is a plausible cause for an observed effect. Young children of 3 and 4 years often state such explanations as well. Children in the late preschool years seem to be extraordinarily creative in finding and proposing what often appear to be very strange connections between experiences. As dialogue (6) in Chapter 8 suggests, their models of the world at times seem totally unconstrained by any physical laws.[9] The permeability of ontological boundaries seen in that example implies that proposals that the preschool child's mind contains coherent theoretical structures within a circumscribed domain are far off the mark. What emerges instead is a picture of a mind that engages in considerable constructive and imaginative activity, but that is incoherent in the sense that different conflicting parts can exist without disturbance, and that parts belonging to separate domains can merge without interference [see Harris (1994)]. Nonetheless, such thinking marks the beginning of using language as a reflective, articulating basis for explaining as well as representing.

The search for explanations is no doubt the beginning of the potential for forming valid theoretical structures that organize and explain within a domain of knowledge. But the latter require a level of articulation of elements and relations that is abstracted from the ongoing narrative construction of the world, which merges elements from many different domains. Donald (1991) claims that theories arise when written forms of language are available, making sustained reflection on an unchanging propositional structure feasible. The preschooler is far from this level of linguistic function. More important, as argued in Chapters 8 and 10, theories are based in cultural knowledge systems, which are formulated in language and conveyed therein.

Acquisition of Cultural Knowledge Systems

The most obvious cognitive use of language is for the acquisition of knowledge not attainable through direct experience. This case goes beyond the implicit functions involved in categorizing and interpreting experience to the explicit imparting of knowledge. This can begin very early as parents explain aspects of the world that are not within the child's experience. For example, parents look at pictures with children and explain the uses of kinds of machines, or the roles of firefighters and doctors. Before visiting the doctor, parents might explain what she will do and why. They talk about their workplaces, about airplanes, and other cities where relatives live. These mundane examples are meant to convey how much of what very young children come to know about the world (however inadequately they understand what is said) is conveyed to them explicitly through language.

As explicated in Chapters 6 through 10, much of the everyday cultural organization of knowledge ("folk theories") is displayed nonexplicitly in the language used by parents and others to direct activities and talk about experiences. Such talk embeds different kinds of systems of knowledge, from the familiar categories of food and clothes, to the complexities of temporal schemes, to the symbolism of religious institutions, to the rule systems of government. It conveys moral instructions as well as politeness formulas, systems of counting and measuring as well as judgments of character and aesthetics. All this is subtly displayed in ordinary talk to and around young children, and is imbibed by them as they begin to enter into the discussion themselves.

A point emphasized throughout this book, however, is that the child must reach a quite advanced state of language mastery before extensive explicit complex knowledge acquisition through language is feasible. Extended explanations, like extended stories, require on-line processing and representation of information presented, which are skilled linguistic activities. On the basis of studies of different knowledge domains it is apparent that this skill is not achieved usually until between the age of 3 and 5 years. It is a skill that must be attained if learning is to take place through verbal presentation in the classroom, and eventually through literate presentations.

Emergence of the Self in a Social World

All the cognitive functions of language just enumerated imply that the child's mind becomes mediated by cultural ways of thinking and speaking during the preschool years. At the heart of all these ways and effects is the emerging sense of self. The emerging self is glimpsed at many points along the way. It is especially in the set of concerns discussed in Chapter 10, in interpreting the actions of other people in terms of their thoughts and desires, that the child is seen most clearly as situated in a social world. Then the self must be differentiated from the activity if understanding of others is to be established. Taking a larger view, we can see that lurking behind all the developments discussed herein is an emerging self who learns to represent the categories of the culture, and not only those of her own egocentrically organized events. The same self learns to recognize that others have memories different from one's own, thus experiences that are not shared, and narratives to tell that one has not heard before and that speak of a world different from one's own experience. It is the self in a social world who tracks events through time, and learns that yesterday is no longer while tomorrow is yet to come. To understand the perspective of now one must have a sense of an enduring self existing through time (Nelson, 1989b, 1991b).

The social intelligence that enabled early humans to survive involved not only the individual's knowledge of and perspective on the social and cultural situation, but also the individual's knowledge and perspective on self and his or her own role in the specific situation. Self-knowledge and social knowledge proceed together, as Mead (1934) insisted: "The self, as that which can be an object to itself, is essentially a social structure, and it arises in social experience" (p. 140). In Mead's view also, language played the critical role in the construction of the self.

From one point of view, then, this book has been about the emerging self and its dependence on defining in social terms, terms conveyed and understood through communal language uses. As various authors have noted (see Chapter 4), self-awareness begins in earliest infancy, and by late in the second year the self is recognizable in mirrors and pictures. Hobson (1993) has provided a particularly persuasive account of the emerging sense of self in relation to the social other and joint interactions with objects, interactions that are key aspects of mimetic external representations. But until the various uses of language make it possible to imagine a past and future self, and to imagine that other people have different pasts and futures, as well as different presents, one cannot speak of a fully determined self distinct from ongoing experience. Event representations, like dreams, do not separate the self from the experience. Nor do mimetic activities like play, in which the self is still part of the experience, make this level of self-realization possible. Language uniquely enables contemplating a self that is different from present experience, and imagining a self that will grow older as well as a self that was once a little baby.

Domain Specificity, Children's Theories, and Conceptual Change

The chapters in this book have presented the developmental story in terms of processing (language, memory), organizing (narrative, category), and knowing (time, self, others) components of mind. These discussions might appear to be in tune with the now common partitioning of the child both vertically – in terms of domains and functions – and horizontally – in terms of focal ages. But at the same time, I have argued against attributing domain-specific theories to young children. Representing, processing, and organizing, I would argue, are applied to specific domains in ways that are both common and distinct, as the differences between the organization of temporal knowledge and knowledge of others' intentions illustrate. The outcome is distinctive and generally coherent systems within domains of knowledge, but this outcome is dependent as well on the collaborative construction of this knowledge, as explicated throughout this book.

Some domains such as space, number, and language appear to be specially designed by evolution to process information in distinct ways (see Chapter 2). Modularity of brain function is supported by evidence of specific aphasias and amnesias, as well as by specific deficits associated with brain damage at birth or later. However, evidence also supports the idea that the brain is extremely plastic in development and that modularity may be acquired rather than strictly preordained. Perceptual and motor skills, such as those involved in speech, are prime examples of modular functions, but so are culturally specific and late-acquired skills such as writing and reading. Similarities and differences among these and their relation to brain processing will become much clearer no doubt with new imaging technologies that can track ongoing processing, and enable the study of variation over different developmental periods.

Theories of domain specificity generalize from modularity to propose that ways of processing and organizing within specific knowledge domains[10] are properly thought of as theories. At present the ideas of innate modules, domain specificity, and theory structure of conceptual representation are interconnected within a common theoretical framework [see discussions in Hirschfeld & Gelman (1994a)]. The view presented here differs from those based on these constructs in important ways, as the following discussion attempts to clarify.

Domain specificity initially was studied in relation to areas of knowledge such as physics, biology, cosmology, economics, psychology, and so on, as a hypothesis from cognitive studies of expertise (Chi, 1978; Simon & Simon, 1978). This research indicated that experts and novices organize new learning within a domain in different ways, reflecting their different underlying structuring of the field. There is no implication that the way novices organize knowledge – in chess, for example – is somehow based on innate principles and that of experts is a cultural construction.

Knowledge domains of the kind to which expert systems and theories apply differ from cognitive processes such as memory or language processing, and from modes of organization such as narratives, categories, or theories. Narrative and category organization are ways of organizing memory and knowledge that are not specific to any particular knowledge domain. To the extent that they represent something universal and pervasive across domains, there is evidence for domain-general organization rather than domain-specific processing. As for the latter, at some very basic level general processing mechanisms must be at work, as in recently developed connectionist networks. The questions then turn on how such mechanisms are organized within domains to process information efficiently within those domains. But narrative and category organizations are higher-level organizing structures that apply to many different domains of knowledge. As we have seen, children's competence with the use of each develops in terms of complexity and abstraction over the preschool period and into the school years.

The domain of temporal knowledge was presented in this book as representative of some of the cultural knowledge systems that children must acquire. It was noted that some temporal sensitivity and understanding are innately available, as reflected in the parsing of events by infants and young children. But this knowledge is concretely tied to knowledge about human activities, involving people, actions, material objects, spaces, and so on. It is only after encountering the organization of temporal concepts in linguistic form that children begin to conceptualize time independently of the events to which it relates. As with the child's understanding of others' intentionality, their understanding of time is initially embedded in knowledge of activities and language. Abstraction of such knowledge into an organized system is a long-term process that begins only as the child gains control of the shared meanings of words – in the one case referring to hours, weeks, and years; in the other to thinking, saying, and knowing – and understands their reference to concepts as they are constructed in the adult world. This domain illustrates that the existence of some innate function relevant to domain knowledge cannot in itself constitute or grow into a theory within the cultural knowledge domain to which it is relevant. Rather, the cultural knowledge must be cognitively reconstructed to reorganize and regulate the basic processing function.

Equally important, the experientialist model set out here rests on the assumption that the formal structure of a domain may have little to do with how expertise within it is acquired. In a similar vein, Flanagan (1992) states:

> Much of what we are conscious of is culturally transmitted. The learning capacities that subserve the acquisition of knowledge are clearly adaptive. But the details of what we learn and how we use the information we acquire . . . may or may not be functional in the short or long run. . . . Many of our conscious capacities, for example, to do arithmetic or geometry, were probably not directly selected for. They are the fortuitous outgrowths of combining our linguistic capacities and our capacities for abstraction with our abilities to individuate objects, estimate quantities and display spatial savvy in manipulating objects and moving about in the world. (p. 139)

The extension of this idea to the acquisition of knowledge systems in early development is straightforward: The knowledge domains spontaneously acquired in childhood are the outgrowths of practical activities, not derivations from established principles. Children operate in a world that is subdivided not into knowledge domains but into activities, within which the knowledge is applicable. Knowledge specialists – for example, academicians and scientists – partition these domains and display them to students of all ages, beginning in the preschool years (e.g., dinosaur knowledge). But these domains are abstracted from the ongoing activities of everyday life, not abstractly constructed within it from innate principles, as much contemporary theory assumes.

Conceptual Change

Carey's (1985) idea of scientific theory change as a model of conceptual change in childhood requires the reorganization of knowledge within a theory domain, and consequent redefinition of concepts in terms of new relations within the domain. This theory change proposal is similar to the conceptual change problem discussed by Vygotsky (1986) in terms of spontaneous and scientific concepts, in that the existence of relevant concepts, using the same terms but different conceptual bases, is emphasized in both. However, Carey's model ignores the critical distinction that Vygotsky drew between spontaneous and scientific, and does not explicitly recognize the sociocultural/linguistic origin of either system.

Current views of conceptual change such as Carey's rest on the assumption that the individual encountering a new, more advanced, higher-order scientific body of knowledge has in place a prescientific conceptual system that applies to some of the same phenomena that the more advanced system does. But except for claims that children arrive in the world with naive theories, there has been little concern for the origin of those prescientific theoretical systems. Obviously if we wish to understand the problem of conceptual change it is necessary to understand both ends – the nature of spontaneous conceptual systems, as well as adult theoretical systems. Labeling all of the young child's knowledge as "theoretical" and then discussing any change as the move from one theory to another poses the danger of supposing that the autonomous mind creates theories from scratch and changes them at will.

As implied in the discussion in Chapter 8, two fundamental changes in conceptual systems may be found, the first a shift in the child's thought from the spontaneous presemantic, based in activities, to the conventional "folk" semantic, based in lexical meanings, which must precede a second shift from the "folk" system to a more formal or theoretical, directly conveyed through instruction. The first transition, outlined in Chapter 8 in terms of hierarchical categories, involves the child's achievement of a system that coordinates the event-based primitive system with the system revealed through adult language use. The second transition builds on the first folk cultural system and transforms it in terms of the established knowledge structures of the communities that define formal knowledge domains. Building on these observations, the proposal is that within all basic domains of knowledge (those open to encounter by the independent individual) two progressions are possible – from the individual to the folk/semantic, and from the semantic to the scientific.

The semantic level of knowledge organization is a product of the language-using community. It abstracts from activities to provide a generalized organization of related knowledge. The "folk taxonomies" observed across the world in different cultures (Berlin, 1978; Atran, 1990) are examples of this kind of knowledge structure, as are the general nonscientific practical taxonomies of the English language, such as those of food, clothes, furniture, and the natural kinds of animals and plants. These are systematically organized domains serving cultural purposes. An individual who has acquired knowledge at the level of the semantic organization of a domain has acquired the tools for viewing activities

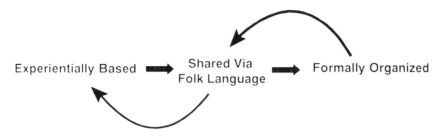

Figure 11.1. Changes in conceptual representation systems

within a larger context of relationships. Food is not only what one eats at lunch, but also anything edible by any organism. A day is not only a sequence of activities, but also a unit in an organized temporal system that can be counted, divided, multiplied, and located within an abstract temporal space.

Culturally organized knowledge of this kind tends to exist in an informal system that is conveyed to individuals partially through simple exposure to the concepts embedded in language use, and partially through informal instruction, in school, workplace, or other context. It may result, therefore, in partial conventional knowledge idiosyncratically organized, as the levels sketched in Figure 8.1 suggest. This figure indicates that a systematically organized body of knowledge exists in the community at large. Most adults possess part or all of it, and in discourse with children they convey, implicitly and explicitly, parts of the system. The child, operating with a differently organized body of experientially derived knowledge in the domain, attempts to align and reorganize her knowledge with that conveyed by the adult. The process results in partial and incompletely connected knowledge on the part of the child. As Valsiner (1993) has pointed out, this kind of indirect semiotic mediation may lead at first to confusion and increased complexity, rather than leading directly to clarification and reorganization.

In contrast, formally organized cultural knowledge systems as theoretical knowledge are not accessible informally to the individual through simple exposure to discourse in the domain, but must be mastered as an abstract system. There are, no doubt, distinctions to be made within this level of knowledge systems, and significant, often radical, conceptual change takes place as one formal system displaces another in the domain, as Carey (1991) and Chi (1992) have both discussed. These change levels both feed forward and then feed backward, as Figure 11.1 indicates.

In summary, making sense in the first instance involves practical knowledge derived from everyday activity. Eventually the child advances beyond simple observation and representation, with the substantial help of other people who provide explanations and systematic knowledge systems that the child can use to inform her own deeper understanding. All children acquire practical knowledge systems; not all children – or all adults – go on to acquire formal systematic theoretical knowledge systems in the most basic domains of experience. We should be wary of projecting our own academic images as scientists or epistemologists into the heads of universal children. Only by situating our inquiry within the child's frame of reference can we begin to make sense of how the child makes sense. How the child uses linguistic representations, as well as social guidance and feedback, as sources of knowledge is at this point poorly understood, and is a vital point toward which research should be directed.

Collaborative Construction of Mind, Self, and Knowledge

The ultimate challenge to cognitive development is to formulate a theory of both process and product that begins in infancy and extends into adulthood; that recognizes the unique social and cultural condition of humankind without losing sight of its biological-organismic individuality and evolutionary history. To do this is to trace how, at any point in development, the current state is an ongoing product of individual history and a specific complex of resulting competencies and potentials. Recognizing the continuity of the characteristics of human mentality does not mean attributing adult competence and knowledge organization to young children. Rather, recognition of growth and development of the biological in the context of specific social and cultural conditions of childhood necessitates a model that focuses on processes of change. The claim here is that language is the mediator, the medium, and the tool of change in the major cognitive transitions of early development.

The overarching thesis of this book is that the individual child constructs representations – of the real experienced world, of desired states, of pretend worlds, of others' worlds – and that these representations are from the beginning *constructed in collaboration* with social others, adults and peers. Thus the model outlined here is one of COLLABORATIVE CONSTRUCTION, emphasizing both individual construction (as in Piaget's model) and social construction (as in Vygotsky's model). Neither is adequate alone to account for human cognitive development. But both collaboration and construction change with development as the potential to engage in symbolic activities, including language, is realized.

In the beginning, the child's event representations are constructed from her experience in the world, experience that is dependent upon caretakers to assemble, arrange, and guide. Thus the infant is in a state of greatest dependency upon others, but at the same time she is in a cognitive state of greatest autonomy, being unable to call on others for help in constructing meanings of her experience.

As the infant becomes mature enough to engage in simple mimetic activities – routines, play – these serve as collaborative scaffolds for her individual reconstructions of experiences. During these early years the mimetic activities serve as a childhood adaptation to a symbolically organized world. Mnemonic representations of activities and routines provide the background for the implicit fallout of categories of material objects and social relations. Within these activities the roles of participants become understood (e.g., the hider and the peeker), but the internal perspectives of others remain hidden from view. Between 1 and 3 years speech mimesis and linguistic constructions become part of the mimetic activities. During this period children not only participate, but also transform in pretense; they engage in invention as well as imitation – both critical characteristics of emerging human minds.

Narrative begins to become a part of children's lives as parents and others collaborate with them in reconstructing past events, marking ongoing experiences with narrative structure, planning future happenings, and telling made-up stories or playing out dramas. These activities may begin as early as 2 years with children whose language is well advanced. Linguistic narratives can tie previously experienced activities (understood on a participant level) into stories that include motivations and goals. Through them, children's goals (previously private and egocentric) may begin to be coordinated with adults' goals, and a broader, more coherent understanding of the particulars of the experienced world may come into view. The language of narrative includes temporal, causal, intentional, and conditional forms that help to constitute the story, and in so doing make explicit relations that were previously obscure or only partially understood. These linguistic forms thereby also take on more of the meanings of the wider community and no longer are tied only to the child's understanding of events.

Three novel developments emerge thereafter: first, the possibility of incorporating other previously unknown worlds into one's representations. Not everything is assimilated to the child's own prior experientially based representations. Stories can be understood as *about* a different time and a different place, where the child herself has never been. Second, this level of linguistic achievement enables the use of language to turn back on experientially based representations and to reanalyze and re-represent them on another level, decontextualized from actual experience. Third, the collaborative constructions in narrative provide the basis for understanding perspectives, motivations, goals, and emotions of others in a way that is not possible on the mimetic level alone, when different roles in activities are understood, but not the internal states of the other actors.

Beyond this point, but to a very large extent dependent upon it, lies the use of all the material externalizations of symbolic forms, including but far from limited to written language, which makes the larger culture accessible to the mind of the individual. At this point the collaboration in constructing cognitive representations becomes culturewide. It comes into play especially in the school years, but has its beginning in the earlier period in the use of pictures, films, and models to represent things and states of the world both known and unknown.

As this final summary suggests, there is no discrete division of event, mimetic, narrative, and externalized symbolic stage, as originally hypothesized in Table 3.4. Rather, what we find is a seamless weaving together of individual experience-based constructions in collaboration with others, gradually incorporating the potential of social and cultural forms, including especially language in its first simple and later complex constructions. The shared meanings of the community thus gradually enter into the individual child's knowledge representations and to a large, but nonetheless limited, extent take over the child's mind. Thus individuality is balanced with sociality.

Notes

1. Language, Cognition, and Culture in Developmental Perspective

1. Note that the word "infant" derives from the Latin meaning "without language."
2. The child as an individual is referred to throughout this book as "she" and "her." This usage is in preference to the generic "he," "him" or the awkward "he/she," "him/her." I choose the individualizing "she" because among other reasons, it is appropriate to the many examples herein from the female child Emily.
3. Such as those documented by Brown (1991).
4. A similar reproach has been aimed at studies of child language – see Atkinson (1986) for the distinction between the Flats (formal language acquisition theorists) and the Sharps (those who study language as it is used by children). This distinction actually reflects a division between the fields of linguistics and psychology, and the study of language in use has yielded enormous quantities of theoretically important data from the perspective of understanding the psychology of language development.
5. In addition to Karmiloff-Smith's model, Bickhard (1987; Campbell & Bickhard, 1986) has developed a theory of "knowing levels" that is similar in many ways, and Perner (1991) has developed somewhat similar ideas within the theory of mind problem that is discussed in Chapter 10. Halford's (1993) theory of mental models also falls into this group, as does Mounoud's (1993) theory of shifts in knowledge modes from procedural to declarative.
6. The script terminology is unfortunate, suggesting as it does that there is a static, rigid formulation for how to play a role in a prespecified act. "Scenario" is much closer to the loose, flexible, but generally predictable skeletal outline of the event that is usually intended by the other term.
7. Activity theory was developed initially in the Soviet Union; now it is international, with a strong American representation [see Martin, Nelson, & Tobach (1995)].
8. See Lucy (1985, 1992) for informative discussion of this topic.

2. Emergence of Human Minds in Evolution and Development

1. Let me state at the outset, however, that my status is one of novice amateur. I have tried to present valid accounts of the issues and to check doubtful facts, but insiders can and no doubt will find fault, for which I apologize in advance.

2. There are many excellent discussions of the technical problems and interpretative pitfalls of these models; for recent developmental discussion see the exchange between Scarr (1992, 1993), Baumrind (1993), and Jackson (1993).
3. The notion of constraints on learning and development has taken on major significance in developmental theorizing in recent years, and is sometimes used inadvisedly in my opinion (Nelson, 1988). In the sense that we do not develop tails or wings, for example, there are obvious and clear constraints on biological development. On the other hand, it often seems more appropriate to talk about potentials rather than constraints, in the sense that we have the potential to acquire grammar (rather than being constrained to do so). Moreover, as suggested here, constraints on development emerge from the social and cultural world just as surely as they do from the biological, but so do potentials for further development. I use the term here advisedly because of its proliferation in the fields under discussion, without necessarily endorsing such widespread and undiscriminating uses.
4. Cognitive development in infancy is discussed in more detail in Chapter 4.
5. But see Antinucci (1990) for variations that reflect opportunities to handle and/or mouth objects.
6. This summary is based on current reviews in the literature, especially Bates et al. (1992), Dawson and Fischer (1994), and Turkewitz and Devenny (1993).
7. This view of restricted imitation by other primates is not universally accepted among comparativists (Gibson, King, & Parker, 1993), but it resonates with the position outlined by Donald (1991 – see chapter 3). Savage-Rumbaugh and colleagues (1993) present data from chimpanzee language learning that may call into question the conclusions Tomasello (1990) draws with respect to restrictions on chimpanzee learning capacities and strategies. However, the latter are based on observations in the wild and without human interventions, whereas the former are based on specific environmental interventions designed to elicit symbolic capacities.
8. This level was anticipated in Popper's (1972) "world 3," where "world 1" is the physical world and "world 2" is the world of conscious (individual) experience. It is noteworthy that Popper claims that *"full consciousness of self* depends upon . . . (world 3) theories, and that animals, although capable of feelings, sensations, memory, and thus of consciousness, do not possess the full consciousness of self which is one of the results of human language and the development of the specifically human world 3" (p. 74).
9. The following sketch is drawn from a variety of sources, primarily Durham (1991), Donald (1991), Gamble (1994), and Parker and Gibson (1990). Dates are approximate and subject to revision in line with further paleontological research.
10. These measurements are approximations subject to revision; some *Homo erectus* brain casts exceed the latter size. Neanderthal brains reached cranial capacities larger than those of *Homo sapiens*.
11. Parker and Gibson (1979) proposed that rather than stone tools used in hunting, early hominids first developed wooden tools for digging roots and bulbs and used naturally available containers (e.g., gourds) for carrying. They also emphasize the importance of food sharing among early hominids as social habits that pressed for development of tools. Like all stories presently available, this one is speculative, but no more so than the traditional hunting story as an explanation of the evolution of tools and human intelligence and language.

12. This results in some quite bizarre claims. For example, Barkow (1992) presents an analysis that the present-day American enjoyment of reading gossip about celebrities is based on adaptations in a social world where understanding the interactions of others (and, specifically, reflecting the significance of knowing who is having sex with whom) is important. But rather than reflecting functions relevant to the reproductive imperatives of hunting-gathering environments, it seems much more likely that gossip about movie stars is simply one of the many "spandrels" (see note 17) kicked up by our complex cognitive capacities. It is one way that present-day humans keep their brains busy when there are no more important tasks to be performed. It is also a use of language for storytelling, which, as the later discussion suggests, is basic to human cognitive activities.

13. It has come to my mind while reading similar claims that, given the assumption that reproductive success in these models is measured in terms of fecundity and survival, ancient adaptations must have prepared humankind extraordinarily well for modern conditions, based on the observation of exploding human populations over the past couple of centuries. Of course, this conclusion requires buying the premises. Otherwise one may indeed continue to question the degree to which the environments that we have (indubitably) constructed are *in the long run adaptive.*

14. The fact [Pinker & Bloom based on Falk (1983) and Tobias (1981)] that Broca's area is visible in cranial endocasts of 2-million-year-old fossils would speak only to the probability that there was some precursor of human language in the human line, but not language or speech as we know it.

15. According to Lieberman, these developments began with the emergence of upright posture, resulting in the lengthening of the larynx and the repositioning of the pharynx, but this conclusion is controversial. See Studdert-Kennedy (1991) for a discussion of the relation of these evolutionary developments to the ontogenetic course of speech development in normal human infants.

16. The rapidity of information presented in normal conversational speech can be intuitively understood when listening to native speakers conversing in a language that the listener has only partially learned. This experience may be useful as well in evaluating what young children may understand of speech they are casually exposed to.

17. Spandrels were introduced to evolutionary discussion by Gould and Lewontin (1979) in their discussion of inappropriate uses of the adaptationist arguments. The reference is to the spandrels of St. Marcos cathedral in Venice, triangular spaces formed by the intersection of arches supporting the dome. The spandrels are richly decorated in mosaics and have been widely admired and discussed by art historians. However, their existence is not a matter of design but a functional by-product of the architecture.

18. Pinker and Bloom also quote Konner (1982) to the effect that the !Kung (a contemporary hunter-gatherer culture) discuss "everything from the location of food sources to the behavior of predators to the movements of migratory game . . . knowledge critical to survival. A way of life that is difficult enough would, without such knowledge, become simply impossible" (p. 171). Does this claim (from Konner, endorsed by Pinker and Bloom) imply that hunter-gatherer groups could not have survived without language, and in particular without the complex language that enables them to "exchange great stores of knowledge" (Pinker & Bloom, 1992, p. 482)? If so, the usual

timetables ascribing the emergence of complex language to somewhere around 100,000 years B.P. and the $2\frac{1}{2}$ million years of hunter-gatherer culture alleged by Barkow, Cosmides, and Tooby to have determined human cognition are at odds. Pinker (1994) acknowledges this, opting for the emergence of language just after the splitting off of hominids from the primate line shared with chimpanzees 4 million years ago. There is no solid scientific basis for locating language at this point.

3. Evolution and Development of the Hybrid Mind

1. After this chapter was complete Raeithel's (1994) very similar conception came to my attention, with its explicit implications for development. I have not attempted to try to integrate it with Donald's work or to differentiate it therefrom. However, those who find the approach interesting should consult the source as well.

2. Although the earlier discussion of the probable common substrate of human and other primate cognition, and the evidence from Savage-Rumbaugh and colleagues' (1993) work that some chimpanzees can acquire receptive human language at a basic level, seems to argue against Donald's position on this, the matter is certainly not foreclosed.

3. See Mandler (1992) on the extraction of object knowledge from inspection by infants. See also discussion in Chapter 4.

4. This conception departs somewhat from my developmental model, and indeed I suggest that there is a contradiction lurking here. If apes remember specific episodes that are situation- and time-bound, specifying time and place, they are not bound to the present but live in the past as well, however much the past memory may be dependent for its recall on a specific present cue. It seems likely, however, that Donald's basic conception is right: Apes live in the present. This is understandable if they do not have specific episodic memory, but rather general event memory (Nelson, 1986, 1993a; Nelson & Gruendel, 1981). As argued in Chapter 6, general event memory is prior to both specific episodic memory and semantic memory in ontogeny, and no doubt it is in phylogeny as well. General event memory supports action in the present and planning for the future, which Savage-Rumbaugh and colleagues (1993) note is within the capacities of chimpanzees. What it fails to do is to differentiate past episodes one from another, and to abstract semantic categories from events.

5. This, however, seems not at all obvious. Rather, a mechanism must be capable of extracting the general from the specific; whether and where both are stored is a different question. These are quibbles about a formulation that is actually not central to Donald's basic concerns, however.

6. But see Tomasello's (1990) skeptical discussion on this point.

7. A similar position is taken by Noble and Davidson (1991), who note, "Part of the issue in theorizing about language origins involves considering how the discovery of the meaningfulness of meaningful signs could occur prehistorically" (p. 572). "Language is a form of behaviour in which meaningful signs are used symbolically, that is referentially, arbitrarily (yet conventionally), in the absence as well as the presence of what is referred to. . . . That meaningful signs can be used symbolically is a discovery young children . . . make in the course of the socialization as language-users. . . . It is not a discovery they could make unassisted by language-using older members" (p. 572). They go

on: "We have speculated . . . . that it arises as a perceptual consequence of a novel behaviour . . . involving visual representation of meaningful bodily signs . . . appropriate neural circuitry is required to enable a creature to witness the significance of its own forms of behaviour. But the capacity to provide an external representation of its actions seems to us a necessary precursor to its being aware of them" (p. 572).

8. See Olson (1994) for similar views along this line.

9. Of course, this is an oversimplification as theories in both literature and science contend; although the words and propositions may be maintained in the same form over the centuries, their interpretation is still subject to change over time as different cultures impose their different conceptual systems on similar forms.

10. We often complain of this explosion of potential information coming in the form of scholarly journals, computer networks, television, books, multimedia presentations, and whatever next year's technology promises. The human mind, it appears, is under considerable strain in attempting to adapt to all of the potential that ESS systems now present.

11. See Eisenstein (1993) for related discussion of the effect of printed text and graphics on theoretical achievements in the Renaissance. See also Olson (1994). See Freyd (1983) on the cognitive consequences of shareability.

12. For a related discussion of ontogenetic parallels with evolutionary sequence, see Studdert-Kennedy (1991).

13. The fact that reading becomes an automatic "modularized" skill among highly literate individuals suggests reorganization of the brain during the later school years, resulting in specialized brain organization for reading and writing that is evident in the deficits seen in some aphasias. To explore these possibilities it might be helpful to study brain activity in deaf children and illiterate children during the developmental years in question.

14. This stage sequence is different from the one that Van der Veer and Valsiner (1991) describe in terms of four stages of cultural use in the child, which was succeeded by the better-known natural (no use) to external use to internal use, applied to speech as well as to other mediational forms.

15. Because Bruner and his students did not continue to work out this theory and its implications, there remain a number of contradictions within it that need be of no concern here.

4. Early Cognition: Episodic to Mimetic Childhood in a Hybrid Culture

1. Research over the past 20 years has convincingly demonstrated that very young infants understand much more about the physics of objects, including causal mechanics, than Piaget or earlier psychologists imagined [see, e.g., Spelke (1991)]. The claim here is not that infants do not have such knowledge, but rather that what they learn about objects includes important understandings about the role of objects in human activities, and specifically in activities involving themselves, their desires and intentions.

2. Throughout this work (except when necessary in direct quotes from other authors) words will be enclosed in quotation marks, concepts will be italicized, and events as mentally represented will be in small capitals.

3. There is no implication here that such games are prerequisite to the establishment of speaker and listener roles. Rather, the dynamics of the system

suggest that such practices may provide the basis for the child to enter more easily into role exchanges on the linguistic level.

4. Susan Engel (personal communication, November 1994) and I hypothesize that the first symbolic play involving objects emerges in interactions with a social partner, who uses the object in a pretend action. This hypothesis has not been systematically investigated, however.

5. This discussion is not concerned with members of the species who are deprived of speech for some reason, for example, congenital deafness or birth into a family of deaf, nonspeaking parents. In the latter case infants are typically exposed to sign language and tend to engage in sign "babble" after an initial period of vocal production (Pettito & Marentette, 1991). Pettito has shown that children of deaf parents using sign language are equally sensitive to the patterns of sign, and babble in sign, beginning toward the end of the first year. Thus the sensitivity to language patterning does not appear to be specific to speech sounds, but may be specific to the communicative function and to the kinds of structural patterns (e.g., componential and clausal) that human languages employ. Goldin-Meadow and Mylander (1984) have provided evidence that children not exposed to either spoken or signed language will begin to develop their own structured gestural language, including the establishment of "rules" for making combinations of gestures, such as that the "topic" precedes its "comment." While this creativity is of considerable interest in emphasizing the disposition of human children to acquire a patterned communication system – and in the absence of a model, to invent one – nonetheless, it appears to be more similar to the kind of protolanguage that may have emerged in the prelinguistic mimetic period that Donald has described. These variations on the general scheme provide additional insight into its potentials and processes, but they are not considered further here.

6. Although experiments with other species have cast doubt on the claim that categorical perception of speech sounds is unique to the human species, it is extremely improbable that other species would discriminate the sound pattern of one human language from another at birth. That perception and production of speech is a biologically determined human characteristic, a product of evolution, is beyond question (Lieberman, 1984).

7. As Ochs and Schieffelin (1984) have emphasized, not all cultures indulge in this kind of response. The Kaluli of New Guinea, for example, do not interpret infant sounds as "talking" and do not respond to their infants in this way. It cannot be assumed that practices that are common in one culture are universal or necessary to the development of speech. The point is rather that adults in all cultures hold expectations that their children will grow up to join the speaking community. In some cultures, adults are eager to induct their children into that community from earliest infancy. Other communities, which provide ample opportunity for children to hear and observe the use of speech among community members, wait to encourage participation by children until the biologically driven process is farther along.

8. Fernald (1992) views these characteristics of infant-directed speech as themselves products of human evolution, providing parents with a specific register for vocal interactions with infants, but this view is somewhat controversial. Some characteristics of infant-directed speech, especially those that are seen during the period when the child is learning language, such as slow speed and loud tone, are found also in address to listeners with poor lan-

guage abilities, such as non–native language speakers or those with hearing impairments. Other characteristics, such as high pitch and exaggerated into-nation, are seen in use with pets. The latter might be considered extensions of the accommodations naturally made to infants, while the former might emerge for functional and pragmatic reasons.

9. These estimates also vary depending on the methodology used. Fenson and colleagues (1994) indicate that having parents recognize the words children know on checklists provides higher estimates of vocabulary at early ages.

10. Not all analysts agree with this conclusion, however; some would prefer a maturational explanation, such that the grammar "module" kicks in with abstract categories subsequent to the first two-word constructions, or that semantic categories are essential to the triggering of grammatical categories.

11. See Bloom (1993b); Bates Bretherton, & Snyder (1988); Gopnik and Choi (1990); Hampson (1989); Heath (1983); Lievien, Pine, and Dresner Barnes (1992); Nelson (1973b, 1981, 1991a); Ochs and Schieffelin (1984); Peters (1983) for relevant evidence and discussion.

12. See also Dromi (1987) for a similar account of early word use; see Nelson (1985) and Nelson and Lucariello (1985) for a general account of development proceeding from event representations to categorical uses.

13. I owe the cascading metaphor to an anonymous reviewer.

5. The Emergence of Mediating Language

1. That this is a likely response is indicated by findings such as the study of imitative responding by 2-year-olds, in which 15 to 28% of the requests, questions, and statements uttered by the adult in the course of joint play were simply ignored by children (Boskey-Olson, 1988).

2. The description here and throughout these chapters is based primarily on research with middle-class children in Western industrialized societies, most frequently monolingual English-speaking children. The cultural perspective taken here is an attempt to recognize simultaneously both the universals of human culture and their variations. It is clear that even within contemporary urban societies there is cultural variation in the conditions of social support for linguistic and cognitive development, and across cultures one finds even greater variation (Heath, 1983; Ochs & Schieffelin, 1984). The research thus far has focused primarily on conditions of language acquisition. What is less clear is the variation within and between cultures in representational func-tions of language. One of the aims of this book is to draw attention to the possible effects of such variations, but the description of development inevi-tably portrays the uniformities that are observed within the populations that have been most closely studied.

3. Mitchell (1991) reports on the remarkable capacity of preschoolers in solitary play to envoice a variety of different actors.

4. See *A Man without Words* (Schaller, 1991) for testimony to the differences between thinking without and with language. See also Donald's description of bouts of functioning without language as a result of epileptic seizure; Kertesz and Jansons in Weiskrantz (1988) for thinking with aphasia and dyslexia respectively. For bilingual thinking and "learning to think" in an-other language, see Hoffman (1989).

5. This terminology may seem awkward, and terms such as "concepts" and "utterances" might be preferred, as one reviewer has suggested. However,

the import of the representational levels is that there is no single level (such as the conceptual) at which mental representations can be located, but there may be multiple simultaneous levels of any information. Moreover, "utterance" suggests a single (although perhaps complex) proposition formulated in speech, whereas the LREP here may be an extended narrative, conversation, or theoretical text. In this sense this book is an LREP that the reader may be attempting to transform into an MREP, with what success I cannot guess.

6. This is termed "transformation" rather than "translation" because the latter term implies a one-to-one mapping between the MREP (conceptualized as the "language of thought") and the LREP in natural language.

7. Bloom (1991b; 1993b) has presented a related picture of the representation and expression of linguistic messages, focused on the early stages of the child's language development. She relies on Fauconnier's (1985) idea of "mental spaces" as the MREP that interprets and projects linguistic messages. This idea is formulated on a more microlevel but is readily adaptable to the model set forth here. Bloom is among the few who have considered the developmental problem of representing in language, and like the present account, she calls on Sperber and Wilson's (1986) relevance principle to explain interpretation of messages in the early phases of acquisition, as well as later.

8. Rice (1991) has studied this process of children's rapid acquisition of words in context in terms of "quick incidental learning" (QUIL).

9. The full quotation from Augustine suggests a much more complex process, as seen in the following:

> This I remember, and have since observed how I learned how to speak. It was not that my elders taught me words (as, soon after, other learning) in any set method; but I, *longing* by cries and broken accents and various motions of my limbs to *express my thought*, that so I might have my will, and yet unable to express all I willed, or to whom I willed, did myself, by the *understanding* which Thou, my God, gavest me, practise the sounds in my memory. When they named any thing, and as they spoke turned towards it, I *saw and remembered* that they called what they would point out, by the name they uttered. And that they meant this thing and no other, was plain from the motions of their body, the natural language, as it were of all nations, expressed by the *countenance, glances of the eye, gestures of the limbs, and tones of the voice,* indicating the affections of the mind as it pursues, possesses, rejects, or shuns. And thus by constantly hearing words, as they occurred in various sentences, I *collected gradually* for what they stood; and having broken in my mouth to these signs, I thereby gave utterance to my will. (Augustine, 1950/397, p. 9; emphases added)

Here it is clear that Augustine's child had a good deal more help in solving the problem than is currently assumed by constraints theorists, including support from adults and the use of words in discourse contexts that made their meaning clear.

10. See Bloom (1993b) for a similar interpretation.

11. The examples in this section are reprinted from Levy & Nelson (1994), and the text summarizes the analysis therein. Used with permission of the publisher, Cambridge University Press.

12. Parent and child conversations about the past and present are discussed in Chapter 6; narrative as a discourse genre is considered in Chapter 7.
13. See Fischer and Bidell (1991) for a good discussion of this point.

6. Memory in Early Childhood: The Emergence of the Historical Self

1. This chapter is based on previous publications concerned with the development of memory, especially of autobiographical memory. See Nelson, 1993a–d., in press. In some cases excerpts have been reproduced verbatim, but the material has been resynthesized for this chapter. Permission to use this material from Cambridge University Press (1993c), Lawrence Erlbaum Associates (1995a, b, and d) and University of Chicago Press (in press) is acknowledged.
2. This report casts an interesting light on the assumptions behind Donald's (1991) story of the importance of the written word for serving an ESS memory function. Rather, it appears that the ESS function of extending memory across time and space may have preceded the function of extending memory individually. For the individual, if Carruthers (1990) is correct, reliance on personal memory remained as important as it had been in antiquity. See Eisenstein (1993) for discussion of the impact of printed texts of graphic materials on Renaissance thinking.
3. One might even imagine that, as the neural connections at this point are still very labile, the connections first made for addressing the toy were themselves "overwritten" by other connections so that the memory of the toy literally no longer exists. This suggestion is highly speculative, of course, for lack of any neurological evidence to support it.
4. The number of infants who "fail" in the average experiment because of fussiness or crying is usually quite large, and is testimony to novelty and potential for affect arousal of such experiments.
5. Occasionally an individual reports an image from infancy, dated on the basis of being in a crib. There is no reliable experimental or documented case study for infant memory in adults, however.
6. Recently, Gopnik and Graf (1988) and Perner (1991) have suggested similar "overwrite" mechanisms.
7. Emily's memories were organized in this way from the age of about 23 months, earlier than any other child reported in the literature. Emily was a highly verbal child, skilled in language forms. In addition, the private speech monologues may have revealed more about her capability for formulating narrative than concurrent dialogic speech [see discussion in Nelson (1989c)]. It also seems likely that she received models of formulating narrative accounts, not only from parental talk about the past (infrequently observed in the data gathered, but presumably engaged in on other occasions) but also from stories, which she heard from an early age. Her capabilities as a memorist call out for further studies of this kind. Although Emily was a bright, charming, and verbal child, we have no reason to believe that she is unique.
8. Unstudied as yet is the effect of talk about future events on the child's memory for an experience. This is clearly an area that deserves close research.
9. Mullen also found that in children under the age of 4, there is a correlation between family moves and preschool attendance (earlier memories in each case). These factors are likely related to the ease with which adults can date their memories, as well as the organization of their life histories.

10. Mullen's studies support the hypothesized connection between social inter-action about memories, the emergence of autobiographical memory, and the establishment of a social self-concept and self-history (Nelson, 1993c). This position contrasts with that of Howe and Courage (1993), who propose the opposite temporal-causal relation, namely that self-concept is logically neces-sary and causal to the onset of autobiographical memory. Their proposal sets the requisite level of self-concept at 2 years, which does not match the age of offset of childhood amnesia, consistently found to average $3\frac{1}{2}$ years, and it does not allow for the achievement of language representation facility, as theorized here.

11. See Pillemer (1992) for a related functional analysis.

12. It is worth noting that most of the adult data on age of emergence are from educated middle-class adults, and most of the studies of early memory in children are based on middle-class children, often from highly educated families. It might well be that the considerable variability in establishing autobiographical memory already documented would be even greater if the populations studied were less homogeneous.

7. The Emergence of the Storied Mind

1. This claim is echoed in an interesting way in Feldman's (1989) location of logical problem solving in Emily's narratives, and it is also explicit in the claim of taxonomic categories emerging from event representations, detailed in Chapter 8.

2. "Mind-reading" is the term used by Whiten (1991) for "theory of mind," both concerned with how people, including children, understand other peo-ple's intentions. See Chapter 10.

3. Although this example is reported in present tense, frequently in our data it was only tense that differentiated between children's scripts and their memo-ries for the same event [see Hudson & Nelson (1986)]. What is clear is that this child's account, like many others, is temporally ordered but not tempo-rally located. In that sense it is timeless. The realization of temporal relations in scripts, memories, and stories is an important topic that will be considered more fully in Chapter 9.

4. See Chapters 1 and 4; also Schank & Abelson (1977); Bower, Black, & Turner (1979); Nelson & Gruendel (1981); and Nelson (1986).

5. Miller's research has been carried out mostly with working-class families in poor neighborhoods; we lack comparable data from middle-class families.

6. As noted in Chapter 6, Emily was a highly verbal, probably quite precocious child, and no claim is made that her monologic musings are typical or repre-sentative of children in general. However, they do suggest that even very young children may engage in reflection on, organization of, and interpreta-tion of the events of their lives as they try to make sense of their world.

7. There may be an interesting difference in the names of these practices. "Show and tell" suggests a focus on objects to be described and categorized, a paradigmatic function, while "sharing time" suggests the possibility of sharing personally significant happenings in narrative form.

8. In adult usage, cohesive pronouns are indexical in the sense that they point to something in the linguistic context. In spoken speech, cohesion is accom-plished by virtue of temporal contiguity with other linguistic elements. Cohe-sive pronouns are referential insofar as they pick out their referents by virtue

of semantic categories encoded in the forms. For example, *he* is encoded for the categories *singular, animate,* and *male.*

9. Perrier water.

10. One wonders what the equivalent figures for the reality of television characters might be.

11. See Kemper (1984) for a review and comparison of the structure of children's story productions from 2 to 10 years of age.

12. Some writers (e.g., Bettelheim, 1976) seem to assume that the eternal themes are available in unconscious knowledge as a kind of Jungian heritage. But the attribution of knowledge of adult-type experience of triumph and tragedy to the young unconscious mind has little backing. Rather, young children appear to be focused on the triumphs and tragedies of their own experiences and the fantasies that these may suggest, as Paley's (1990) reports indicate.

13. Of course, the anthropomorphizing of animals in children's stories may not provide a valid view of this domain and may mislead the child.

8. The Emergence of the Paradigmatic Mind

1. Class inclusion tasks have been very widely studied, and many hypotheses have been put forth and tested to explain the generally replicable results. Whether the results come from a logical "deficiency," a linguistic miscomprehension, or a perceptual centration (among the various possibilities) has not yet been decisively shown. This is one of those tasks that many adults consider "unfair" [see Donaldson (1978)], but overcoming the "conceptual delusion" that it presents is very difficult for the younger child. Indeed, Winer (1980) reported that a review of the literature indicated that it is not until the middle school years (8 to 10 years) that children could respond successfully to this task.

2. But children may form "child-basic" categories that differ from the adult's, as Mervis (1987) demonstrated.

3. The original form of this argument was based on Cassirer (1923). It has an obvious relation to the Quinean problem noted in Chapter 4 with regard to the indeterminacy of word meaning. Related problems of defining properties have been the basis for a number of contemporary arguments in philosophy as well as psychology (Schwartz, 1977).

4. Oddly, this whole history is being replayed in the controversy between those who hold that shape (and perceptual features in general) is the defining characteristic for young children's object words, and those who hold that "deeper" characteristics lie behind the child's reliance on shape as an index of category membership (Landau, Smith, & Jones, 1988; Soja, 1992; Gelman & Coley, 1991). Although the deeper knowledge in some of the research concerns theoretical domains such as the biological, in the word-learning literature the contrast to shape is usually assumed to be function.

5. Equivalent status of class members is assumed in the classical model of concepts in which all members have necessary and sufficient features as determinants of class membership. Category models like Rosch's, however, assume internal structure and therefore do not posit equivalent status but rather degrees of centrality of membership.

6. It is important to keep in mind, however, that extension alone does not define a superordinate. The child's "dog" extended to all four-footed animals

is not the equivalent of the adult's "animal," "mammal," or any other conventional linguistic inclusive term. Similarly, the child's "bug" is not the same as the category *insect,* which subsumes flies, mosquitoes, bees, and so forth, all of which are independently named and recognized at the basic level.

7. Saussure's structural analysis was very influential on subsequent structural theories in linguistics and the social sciences. Modern linguistics, following Chomsky (1965), abandoned this kind of structural analysis in favor of the generative transformational model of syntax, in which t._ generation of grammatical sentences from underlying rules is substituted for the static analysis implied in the Saussurian principles. A number of models of child grammar development, however, have been constructed along lines similar to the structuralists (e.g., Maratsos, 1982). In such models the child is viewed as attempting to construct grammatical principles from language in use, somewhat similar to the Saussurian, rather than the Chomskyan, goals.

8. The syntagmatic-paradigmatic shift is observed primarily for nouns. Verbs continue to elicit syntagmatic associates longer than do nouns, and for adults they remain the primary responses to adjectives. A number of factors besides age and form class, such as word frequency, affect the degree to which paradigmatic associates are dominant.

9. Although other part–whole structures such as scenes and collections may also be used as a basis for early categories (Mandler, 1979; Markman, 1981).

10. Greenfield and Scott (1986) found, in fact, that subjects of all ages made thematic choices in tasks using pictures.

11. Indeed, *food* is an ambiguous domain – it has biologically important properties, but it is also culturally defined and manufactured, and is consumed in settings that thoroughly embed the biological within cultural organizations.

9. The Emergence of the Temporal Mind

1. This chapter is based to a large extent on Nelson (1991c) and Levy and Nelson (1994). (Permission to use this material is granted by the publisher, Cambridge University Press.) Research from collaborations with Maureen Carbery, Lorraine Harner, Marta Korintos, Lea Kessler Shaw, and Roseanne Flores has been incorporated as well. The general characterizations of time through history and cultures is based primarily on Aveni (1989) and Fraser (1981, 1987); the history of clocks is covered in Boorstin (1983). The language of time is based on Lyons (1977) and Miller and Johnson-Laird (1976). Recent discussions of developmental time by Brockmeier (1991) and Valsiner (1993) provide historical and philosophical background important to the developmental story.

2. Why is time so neglected as a developmental topic when development itself is a temporally ordered concept? I believe the answer has two related parts: (a) Developmental psychologists have to a large extent neglected the study of developmental process; and (b) time concepts require linguistic and cultural mediation, which many psychologists have avoided in preference for the pursuit of universals of mind.

3. Some calendars, such as the Mayan, have been constructed in terms of planetary movement rather than the position of the sun, which is a more obvious time marker.

4. Color is a case in point: Bornstein (1975, 1985) showed that infants perceive

the color spectrum in divisible categories similar to those that are focal for adults, but it is several years before most children can reliably code these divisions in language. Yet color, unlike time, is visible and can be pointed to, named, and contrasted; indeed, adults frequently spend much time trying to teach color words (Rice, 1980). In contrast, time remains in the background until the child's verbalizations bring its incomplete understanding to the attention of adults.

5. Unfortunately, these cycles do not naturally mesh. The lunar month is approximately 29.5 days in length; the solar year is 365.24 + days. The division of the solar year by the lunar month yields 12.38 months per year, or 12 months plus 11 days. There are no neat solutions to this problem. The present Gregorian calendar dates from 1582 and has been adjusted several times since then by inserting or omitting the extra leap year day, so that at present the calendar is accurate to 1 day in 44,000 years.

6. Working with dual conceptions and representations of time is not unusual. For example, religious calendars, both Christian and Jewish, calculate annual observances according to schemes that differ from the secular calendar. To take a more extreme example, the Balinese observe celebrations dictated by 10 different "weeks" running simultaneously and ranging from 1 to 10 days, the whole forming a year of 210 days. At the same time they follow a Hindu calendar with a standard 12-month year similar to the Western calendar.

7. It is frequently noted by teachers of hearing-impaired children who have had little exposure to language, either sign or speech, that they have particular problems with concepts of time. They also have significant problems with hierarchical categories. See also Schaller (1991). Young children's fascination with dinosaurs cannot be interpreted as evidence for a sense of historical time. Recent reports of educational assessment suggest that even some young adults have a very vague conception of historical time.

8. Those that do not have tense as such have lexical forms for marking temporal perspective (Lyons, 1977). Even those languages without tense morphology (e.g., Chinese) have markers for indicating that something happened in the past as contrasted with the present. Lyons (1977) argues that English (and Indo-European languages in general) makes a fundamental distinction only between past/not-past. This appears to be a basic contrast in all human languages. The past/not-past contrast is apparently more universal than past/present or present/future. In English, for example, future constructions incorporate modal meanings such as intentionality, rather than simple futurity. An even more basic contrast is the now/not-now which distinguishes between the ongoing event of the present and events that have taken place or might take place at some other time. Some evidence from Emily's very early narratives suggests that this contrast was in place before the past/not-past contrast was established (Nelson, 1989b).

9. "Tomorrow" is a very elusive term, as was illustrated vividly by a colleague's 3-year-old daughter who asked repeatedly every morning for a month "Is this tomorrow?" only to be told "No, now it's today" (Carbery, personal communication). Anecdotal evidence from other parents suggests that children as old as 3 years may have a poor understanding of *morning* and *night.*

10. It is not feasible to review here the extensive literature on the complexities of the acquisitional course of the comprehension of the terms "before" and "after" and their use to express relations between events. [See Clark (1983); French & Nelson (1985).]

11. Or, from another perspective, to set up foreground and background relations in the narrative [see Hopper (1979)].
12. These implications are currently being examined by Flores and Nelson.
13. After all, it was Newton in the sixteenth century, not Aristotle in the fourth century B.C. (a clockless society), who formulated the relation.
14. The claim here can be seen to accord to no small degree with Whorfian ideas [see Whorf (1956); Lakoff (1987); Lucy (1985); Silverstein (1985); see also Bowerman (1985) and Slobin (1987) for related ideas]. This relation is complex, however, as indicated later in this chapter.
15. See Bowerman (1982, 1989) for related research and discussion.
16. Malotki (1983) reanalyzed the data on which Whorf based his claims and argued that the Navaho language does not represent time in a way different from the English language. This argument may be correct, but it does not imply uniformity of cultural systems of time.

10. The Emergence of the Projective Mind

1. Humans not infrequently generalize their social intelligence inappropriately to situations in which the phenomena are not responsive, to nature in particular. A highly intelligent, educated person might make a statement such as, "It's raining because I did not bring my umbrella." It is understood that he does not really believe that weather is pernicious in this way, yet there is a lingering doubt that somewhere there is a control system that can read his mind and trip him up. Certainly the widespread human propitiation of the gods, belief in magic and the power of the stars to control human events, is evident proof of the basic human assumption that systems are reactive, an assumption that is based on the realities of the social world.
2. This language is meant to distinguish the folk theory from scientific theories, but note that "theory theorists" attribute the characteristics of scientific theorizing to child theorists, as discussed later in this chapter.
3. For an excellent, clear, and balanced introduction to the research and the basic and applied theoretical issues surrounding it, Astington's (1993) book is the best choice. For further reading, Astington, Harris, and Olson (1988) is the first in a series of edited works, followed by Frye and Moore (1991), Whiten (1991), and Butterworth and colleagues (1991). Wellman (1990) and Perner (1991) have published their research in book form as well. Lewis and Mitchell (1994) have edited a volume that attempts to go beyond the basic findings to trace origins and development. Much work is ongoing in this area, and no review can stay up-to-date. This chapter was completed in 1994 and represents findings and ideas up to that point. It should be noted that Astington chaired a symposium at the 1995 meetings of the Society for Research in Child Development on the topic of language and theory of mind; and Harris has written a paper (in press) on the contributions of conversation to understanding other minds. This evidence suggests that the arguments in this chapter may soon find additional support, both theoretical and empirical.
4. In some ways this is a quite sophisticated notion (Chandler & Hala, 1994). Take, for example, the characterization of Piaget's stage of Concrete Operations (Piaget, 1970). Here it is claimed the child can operate logically on objects in the world, but not on propositions. Piaget's own conception of this stage did not account for the fact that children were operating on representa-

tions of objects, and that these representations might differ in ways that would affect their operations. Piaget did of course entertain the alternative possibility – that constraints of operational thought might affect the child's representations (see Piaget & Inhelder, 1973). It has been only in recent work that contextual, cultural, and developmental factors have been seen as relevant to the representation of logical problems and thus to their solution. On these grounds, among others, I am somewhat skeptical of the claims that the common folk theory – including the young child's theory – is based on a conception of mental representations of the kind that psychologists and philosophers entertain.

5. It is interesting that such a theory has been applied to the problem of autism, which seems well described in just such terms – the problem of the autistic child often seems to be that the child is in a state of being a mechanistic, autonomous unit unconnected to the social world through normal human relations. See discussion in the section "Lessons from Autism."

6. This is not an incontrovertible fact. Other investigators have found that children have more difficulty reporting others' false beliefs than their own (e.g., Mitchell & Lacohee, 1991; Plesa, Goldman & Edmondson, 1995).

7. The arguments here apply specifically to preschool children and in particular to the problem of other minds. A related controversy can be found in differing views of children's concepts and reasoning about the physical world during the school years. Arguments pro and con on that question may differ from the present ones because of the difference in age, knowledge states, and cultural inputs.

8. Russell says "human cultural system," but clearly more than one system exists.

9. However, the data presented in their tables (3.10 and 4.10 of Bartsch & Wellman, 1995) are not so conclusive; 9 of 10 of the children studied produced utterances referring to their own desires prior to or during the same month as those of others, and 5 of 7 children also referred to their own beliefs before or during the same month as others.

10. Leslie (Leslie & Roth, 1993) believes that autistic individuals lack the ToMM that he has defined. Uta Frith (1989) views the deficit in terms of a lack of interest in or capacity to search for coherence or meaning; thus the autistic child lives in a world of surface significance, where things – including people – are what they are in themselves but do not stand for anything; they have no symbolic significance.

11. Oliver Sacks (1995) appears to subscribe to this theory to some extent. He also speculates that autistic individuals may develop neurocognitive systems in which modules that are normally coordinated in an overall cognitive organization are disconnected and develop independent of other systems. Thus from his perspective, the specific domain development theories so popular in current research are applicable to abnormal but not normal development, explaining the spectacular feats of drawing or numerical calculation displayed by some otherwise retarded or autistic individuals.

12. See Harris and Kavanaugh (1993) for evidence of 3-year-olds' capacities to engage in imaginary action sequences. Under the event representation thesis, such capacities require that the child invoke a script in accordance with the verbal cue from the experimenter, and then carry out the expected or violated sequence as called for. This is all expected in terms of Donald's (1991) mimetic symbolism. It may be noted that Leslie's (1988) frequent

reference to the situation in which a mother holds a banana to her ear in pretense that it is a telephone (which the 18-month-old allegedly interprets, providing evidence of metarepresentation) supposes that the infant represents the telephone as a *telephone,* that is, as an object with some meaning beyond that of the infant's experience. However, for the infant the real telephone arguably has no more meaning (and perhaps less) than the banana. Thus one object is used in action analogously to another. The real pretend challenge in this situation may be not that the banana is simultaneously represented as both telephone and banana, but that the banana as an edible object is being used in an anomalous way.

13. The child is not (necessarily) ego-centered. Rather, simulation is engaged in in order to understand the actions of others, and to become a more accomplished player in the social world oneself.

11. Collaborative Construction of the Mediated Mind

1. It is probably no coincidence that as Western society has grown more complex, and as individual styles of caretaking no longer replicate in exactitude the patterns found in a small well-knit society, that individuality of the self has emerged as an important distinction, whereas in more traditionally oriented groups the self is merged more completely into the purposes of the group (Markus & Kitayama, 1991).

2. Cairns (1983) reminds us that Rousseau also saw "reason" arriving at puberty, as did both Hall (1904) and Baldwin (1895).

3. For example, Bruner (1983), Trevarthen (1980), and Lock (1991).

4. Recall that it was hypothesized in Chapter 10 that such children might lack the "mimetic module" on which symbolic forms are based. In contrast to autistic children, deaf children do make use of mimetic forms in communication (Goldin-Meadow & Mylander, 1984). On the other hand, Hobson (1995) claims that children blind from birth suffer problems similar to the autistic, presumably because they find it difficult to imitate movements they cannot see.

5. On the other hand, the domain of elementary physical knowledge, shown to be present in infancy by researchers such as Spelke and colleagues (1992) and Baillargeon (1993) and reflected at 7 to 10 years in the conservations of mass, weight, and volume, does not, according to present understanding, undergo significant development during the early childhood years.

6. Although simple arithmetic calculations can be carried out even in the absence of numeral knowledge (Khan, 1994).

7. Related but in contrast to this observation is a passage in Piaget's *Play, Dreams, and Imitation in Childhood* (1962), in which he claims that with development the child's thought is speeded up. It begins, he says, as discrete pictures, and becomes a moving picture as the sensorimotor infant grows into the representational child. This seems exactly backward. The infant must experience the world in all its dynamic qualities, whereas mastery of language enables the child to grab hold of stable parts and manipulate them in slow time.

8. Infants and young children are capable of mapping serial order in events through time, although they appear to have difficulty ordering objects in space. It may be that order in time is a specific capacity that underlies the human capacity for language.

9. See also Chukofsky (1968) for many examples from natural speech.
10. Chomsky (e.g., 1988) (and many others who follow his practice) refers to language as a "knowledge system"; by this he means the system that linguistics defines in terms of phonology, semantics and syntax. This is the basic language competence that is required to use language for communicative and cognitive purposes. In this sense, language is a system of symbols that may be used to represent knowledge. The symbols themselves have no semantic content until they are interpreted, given meaning within a language community. Such meaning rests on shared knowledge systems, but these are not part of language per se. For these reasons talk of language as a knowledge domain seems appropriate only for linguists, for whom the system is the object of study – not for those who use language but do not have particular knowledge of it. (Of course, linguists maintain that all adults have implicit knowledge equivalent to the linguists explicit knowledge, but this is not proved.) The confusion of these levels of knowing leads to such unfounded claims as: The knowledge underlying spiders' web-spinning is equivalent to that underlying preschoolers' counting or color-naming.

References

Abelson, R. P. (1981). Psychological status of the script concept. *American Psychologist, 36,* 715–729.

Acredolo, L. P. (1982). The familiarity factor in spatial research. In R. Cohen (Ed.), *New directions for child development: Children's conceptions of spatial relationships* (pp. 19–31). San Francisco: Jossey-Bass.

Adams, A. K., & Bullock, D. (1986). Apprenticeship in word use: Social convergence processes in learning categorically related nouns. In S. A. Kuczaj II & M. D. Barrett (Eds.), *The Development of word meaning* (pp. 155–197). New York: Springer-Verlag.

Ainsworth, M. D. S. (1973). The development of infant-mother attachment. In B. M. Caldwell & H. N. Ricciuti (Eds.), *Review of child development research* (vol. 3). Chicago: University of Chicago Press.

Ames, L. B. (1946). The development of the sense of time in the young child. *Journal of Genetic Psychology, 68,* 97–125.

Andersen, E. S. (1975). Cups and glasses: Learning that boundaries are vague. *Journal of child language, 2,* 79–104.

Anderson, R. C., & Nagy, W. E. (1989). *Word meanings,* Technical Report No. 485. Urbana-Champaign: Center for the Study of Reading, University of Illinois.

Anglin, J. (1977). *Word, object and conceptual development.* New York: Norton.

Antinucci, F. (Ed.). (1989). *Cognitive structure and development in nonhuman primates.* Hillsdale, NJ: Erlbaum.

Antinucci, F. (1990). The comparative study of cognitive ontogeny in four primate species. In S. Parker & K. R. Gibson (Eds.), *"Language" and intelligence in monkeys and apes: Comparative developmental perspectives* (pp. 157–171). New York: Cambridge University Press.

Antinucci, F., & Miller, R. (1976). How children talk about what happened. *Journal of Child Language, 3,* 169–189.

Applebee, A. N. (1978). *The Child's Concept of Story.* Chicago: University of Chicago Press.

Arlin, M. (1990). What happens to time when you sleep? Children's development of objective time and its relation to time perception. *Cognitive Development, 5,* 71–88.

Astington, J. W. (1993). *The child's discovery of the mind.* Cambridge, MA: Harvard University Press.

Astington, J. W., Harris, P. L., & Olson, D. (Eds.). (1988). *Developing theories of mind.* Cambridge: Cambridge University Press.

Atkinson, M. (1986). Learnability. In P. G. Fletcher M. (Ed.), *Language acquisition, 2d ed.* (pp. 90–108). Cambridge, Cambridge University Press.

Atran, S. (1990). *Cognitive foundations of natural history: Towards an anthropology of science.* Cambridge: Cambridge University Press.

Augustine, S. (1950/397). *The confessions of St. Augustine.* Translated by E. B. Pusey. New York: Dutton.

Aveni, A. F. (1989). *Empires of time: Calendars, clocks, and cultures.* New York: Basic Books.

Avis, J., & Harris, P. L. (1991). Belief-desire reasoning among Baka children. *Child Development, 62,* 460–467.

Bahrick, L. E., & Pickens, J. N. (1988). Classification of bimodal English and Spanish language passages by infants. *Infant Behavior and Development, 11,* 277–296.

Baillargeon, R. (1993). The object concept revisited: New directions in the investigation of infants' physical knowledge. In C. E. Granrud (Ed.), *Visual perception and cognition in infancy.* Hillsdale, NJ: Erlbaum.

Baillargeon, R., Spelke, E. S., & Wasserman, S. (1985). Object permanence in five-month-old infants, *Cognition, 20,* 191–208.

Bakhtin, M. M. (1981). *The dialogic imagination: Four essays by M. M. Bakhtin.* Translated by C. Emerson & M. Hoquist. Austin: University of Texas Press.

Bakhtin, M. M. (1986). *Speech genres and other late essays.* Austin: University of Texas Press.

Baldwin, J. M. (1895). *Mental development in the child and the race: Methods and processes.* New York: Macmillan.

Barkow, J. H. (1992). Beneath new culture is old psychology: Gossip and social stratification. In J. H. Barkow, L. Cosmides, & J. Tooby (Eds.), *The adapted mind: Evolutionary psychology and the generation of culture* (pp. 627–637). New York: Oxford University Press.

Barkow, J. H., Cosmides, L., & Tooby, J. (1992). *The adapted mind: Evolutionary psychology and the generation of culture.* New York: Oxford University Press.

Baron-Cohen, S., Leslie, A. M., & Frith, U. (1985). Does the autistic child have a "theory of mind?" *Cognition, 21,* 37–46.

Barrett, M. D. (1986). Early semantic representations and early word-usage. In S. A. Kuczaj II & M. D. Barrett (Eds.), *The development of word meaning: Progress in cognitive development research* (pp. 39–68). New York: Springer-Verlag.

Barsalou, L. W. (1991). Deriving categories to achieve goals. In G. H. Bower (Ed.), *The psychology of learning and motivation: Advances in research and theory* (vol. 27, pp. 1–64). New York: Academic.

Bartlett, F. C. (1932). *Remembering: A study in experimental and social psychology.* Cambridge: Cambridge University Press.

Bartsch, K., & Wellman, H. M. (1995). *Children talk about the mind.* New York: Oxford University Press.

Bates, E. (1979). *The Emergence of Symbols.* New York: Academic Press.

Bates, E. Bretherton, I., & Snyder, L. (1988). *From first words to grammar: Individual differences and dissociable mechanisms.* New York: Cambridge University Press.

Bates, E., & Carnevale, G. F. (1993). New directions in research on language development. *Developmental Review, 13,* 436–470.

Bates, E., Thal, D., & Janowsky, J. S. (1992). Early language development and its neural correlates. In I. Rapin & S. Segalowitz (Eds.), *Handbook of neuropsychology* (vol. 7: *Child Neuropsychology,* pp. 69–110). Amsterdam: Elsevier.

Bates, E., Thal, D., & Marchman, V. (1991). Symbols and syntax: A Darwinian approach to language development. In N. A. Krasnegor, D. M. Rumbaugh, R. L. Schiefelbusch, & M. Studdert-Kennedy (Eds.), *Biological and behavioral determinants of language development* (pp. 29–66). Hillsdale, NJ: Erlbaum.

Bauer, P. J. (1993). Memory for gender-consistent and gender-inconsistent event sequences by twenty-five-month-old children. *Child Development, 64,* 285–297.

Bauer, P. J., Dow, G. A., & Hertsgaard, L. A. (1995). Effects of prototypicality on categorization in 1- to 2-year-olds: Getting down to basics. *Cognitive Development, 10,* 43–68.

Bauer, P. J., Hertsgaard, L. A., & Dow, G. A. (1994). After 8 months have passed: Long-term recall of events by 1- to 2-year-old children. *Memory, 2,* 353–382.

Bauer, P. J., & Mandler, J. M. (1989a). One thing follows another: Effects of temporal structure on one- to two-year-olds' recall of events. *Developmental Psychology, 25,* 197–206.

Bauer, P. J., & Mandler, J. M. (1989b). Taxonomies and triads: Conceptual organization in one- to two-year-olds. *Cognitive Psychology, 21,* 156–184.

Bauer, P. J., & Mandler, J. M. (1992). Putting the horse before the cart: The use of temporal order in recall of events by one-year-old children. *Developmental Psychology, 28,* 441–452.

Bauer, P. J., & Shore, C. M. (1987). Making a memorable event: Effects of familiarity and organization on young children's recall of action sequences. *Cognitive Development, 2,* 327–339.

Bauer, P. J., & Thal, D. J. (1990). Scripts or scraps: Reconsidering the development of sequential understanding. *Journal of Experimental Child Psychology, 50,* 287–304.

Baumrind, D. (1993). The average expectable environment is not good enough: A response to Scarr. *Child Development, 64,* 1299–1317.

Behrend, D. A. (1994). Review of Tomasello, M.: First verbs: A case study of early grammatical development. *Journal of Child Language, 21,* 748–752.

Beilin, H. (1992). Piaget's new theory In H. Beilin and P. B. Pufall (Eds.), *Piaget's theory: Prospects and possibilities* (pp. 1–17). Hillsdale, NJ: Erlbaum.

Beilin, H., & Pearlman, E. G. (1991). Children's iconic realism: Object vs. property realism. In. H. W. Reese (Ed.), *Advances in child development and behavior* (vol. 23). New York: Academic.

Benelli, B. (1988). On the linguistic origin of superordinate categorization. *Human Development, 31,* 20–27.

Benson, J. B. (1994). The origins of future-orientation in the everyday lives of 9- to 36-mo-old infants. In M. M. Haith, J. B. Benson, R. J. Roberts, & B. Pennington (Eds.), *The development of future-oriented processes* (pp. 375–409). Chicago: University of Chicago Press.

Berlin, G. (1978). Ethnobiological classification. In E. Rosch & B. B. Lloyd (Eds.), *Cognition and categorization* (pp. 9–26). Hillsdale, NJ: Erlbaum.

Berman, R. A., & Slobin, D. I. (1994). *Relating events in narrative: A cross-linguistic developmental study.* Hillsdale, NJ: Erlbaum.

Bettelheim, B. (1976). *The uses of enchantment: The meaning and importance of fairy tales.* New York: Knopf.

Bickerton, D. (1984). The language bioprogram hypothesis. *Behavioral and Brain Sciences, 7,* 173–188.

Bickerton, D. (1990). *Language and species.* Chicago: University of Chicago Press.

Bickhard, M. H. (1987). The social nature of the functional nature of language. In M. Hickmann (Ed.), *Social and functional approaches to language and thought.* New York: Academic.

Bijou, S. W., & Baer, D. M. (1965). *Child development. Volume II: Universal stage of infancy.* New York: Appleton-Century-Crofts.

Bjorklund, D. F. (1985). The role of conceptual knowledge in the development of organization in children's memory. In C. J. Brainerd & M. Pressley (Eds.), *Basic processes in memory development: Progress in cognitive development research.* New York: Springer-Verlag.

Blewitt, P., & Toppino, T. (1991). The development of taxonomic structure in lexical memory. *Journal of Experimental Child Psychology, 51,* 296–319.

Bloom, L. (1973). *One word at a time.* The Hague: Mouton.

Bloom, L. (1991a). *Language development from two to three.* New York: Cambridge University Press.

Bloom, L. (1991b). Representation and expression. In N. A. Krasnegor, D. M. Rumbaugh, R. L. Schiefelbusch, & M. Studdert-Kennedy (Eds.), *Biological and behavioral determinants of language development* (pp. 117–140). Hillsdale, NJ: Erlbaum.

Bloom, L. (1993). *The transition from infancy to language: Acquiring the power of expression.* New York: Cambridge University Press.

Bloom, L., & Capatides, J. B. (1987). Expression of affect and the emergence of language. *Child Development, 58,* 1513–1521.

Bloom, L., & Harner, L. (1989). On the developmental contour of child language: A reply to Smith and Weist. *Journal of Child Language, 16,* 207–216.

Bloom, L., Lahey, M., Hood, L., Lifter, K., & Fiess, K. (1980). Complex sentences: Acquisition of syntactic connectives and the semantic relations they encode. *Journal of Child Language, 7,* 235–261.

Blum-Kulka, S., & Snow, C. (1992). Developing autonomy for tellers, tales, and telling in family narrative events. *Journal of Narrative and Life History, 2,* 187–218.

Boorstin, D. J. (1983). *The discoverers: A history of man's search to know his world and himself.* New York: Vintage Books.

Booth, J. R., & Hall, W. S. (1995). Development of the understanding of the polysemous meanings of the mental state verb *know. Cognitive Development, 10,* 529–549.

Bornstein, M. H. (1975). Qualities of color vision in infancy. *Journal of Experimental Child Psychology, 19,* 401–419.

Bornstein, M. H. (1985). Colour-name versus shape-name learning in young children. *Journal of Child Language, 12,* 387–393.

Boskey-Olson, M. L. (1988). *Young children's response to novel words in a play setting.* Ph.D. Dissertation, City University of New York.

Bower, G. H., Black, J. B., & Turner, T. (1979). Scripts in memory for text. *Cognitive Psychology, 11,* 177–220.

Bower, T. G. R. (1989). *The rational infant: Learning in infancy.* San Francisco: Freeman.

Bowerman, M. (1976). Semantic factors in the acquisition of rules for word use and sentence construction. In D. M. Moorehead & A. E. Moorehead (Eds.), *Normal and deficient child language.* Baltimore: University Park Press.

Bowerman, M. (1982). Reorganization processes in lexical and syntactic development. In E. Wanner & L. Gleitman (Eds.), *Language acquisition: The state of the art.* New York: Cambridge University Press.

Bowerman, M. (1985). What shapes children's grammars? In D. I. Slobin (Ed.), *The cross-linguistic study of language acquisition* (vol. 2: *Theoretical Issues*, pp. 1257–1319). Hillsdale, NJ: Erlbaum.

Bowerman, M. (1989). Learning a semantic system: What role do cognitive predispositions play? In M. L. Rice & R. L. Schiefelbusch (Eds.), *The teachability of language* (pp. 133–170). Baltimore: Paul H. Brookes Publishing Co.

Boyer, M. E., & Rollins, H. A., Jr. (1991). *Examining the role of taxonomic, event-based and ad hoc categories on young children's memory.* Poster presented at the biennial meeting of the Society for Research in Child Development. Seattle, WA.

Braine, M. D. S. (1976). Children's first word combinations. *Monographs of the Society for Research in Child Development, 41*, (1).

Brainerd, C. J. (1978). The stage question in cognitive developmental theory, with commentary. *Behavioral and Brain Sciences, 1*, 178–214.

Brainerd, C. J., & Reyna, V. F. (1990). Gist is the grist: Fuzzy-trace theory and the new intuitionism. *Developmental Review, 10*, 3–47.

Bretherton, I. (1987). New perspectives on attachment relations: Security, communication, and internal working models. In J. Osofsky (Ed.), *Handbook of infant development* (pp. 1061–1100). New York: Wiley.

Bretherton, I., & Beeghly, M. (1982). Talking about internal states: The acquisition of an explicit theory of mind. *Developmental Psychology, 18*, 906–921.

Brewer, W. F. (1986). What is autobiographical memory? In D. C. Rubin (Ed.), *Autobiographical memory* (pp. 25–49). Cambridge: Cambridge University Press.

Brockmeier, J. (1991). The construction of time, language, and self. *The Quarterly Newsletter of the Laboratory of Comparative Human Cognition, 13*, 42–52.

Brown, D. E. (1991). *Human universals.* New York: McGraw-Hill.

Brown, R. (1958a). How shall a thing be called? *Psychological Review, 65*, 14–21.

Brown, R. (1958b). *Words and things.* New York: Free Press.

Brown, R. (1973). *A first language: The early stages.* Cambridge, MA: Harvard University Press.

Bruner, J. S. (1975). From communication to language: A psychological perspective. *Cognition, 3*, 255–287.

Bruner, J. S. (1983). *Child's talk: Learning to use language.* New York: Norton.

Bruner, J. S. (1986). *Actual minds, possible worlds.* Cambridge, MA: Harvard University Press.

Bruner, J. S. (1990). *Acts of meaning.* Cambridge, MA: Harvard University Press.

Bruner, J. S., & Lucariello, J. (1989). Monologue as a narrative recreation of the world. In K. Nelson (Ed.), *Narratives from the crib.* Cambridge, MA: Harvard University Press.

Bruner, J. S., Olver, R. R., & Greenfield, P. M. (1966). *Studies in cognitive growth.* New York: Wiley.

Burke, K. (1945). *Grammar of motives.* New York: Prentice-Hall.

Butterworth, G. (1990). Self-perception in infancy. In D. Cicchetti & M. Beeghly (Eds.), *The self in transition* (pp. 99–119). Chicago: University of Chicago Press.

Butterworth, G. E., Harris, P. L., Leslie, A. M., & Wellman, H. M. (Eds.). (1991). *Perspectives on the child's theory of mind.* Oxford: Oxford University Press.

Byrne, R., & Whiten, A. (Eds.). (1988). *Machiavellian Intelligence.* Oxford: Oxford University Press.

Byrnes, J. P. (1991). Acquisition and development of if and because: Conceptual and linguistic aspects. In S. A. Gelman & J. P. Byrnes (Eds.), *Perspectives on language and cognition: Interrelations in development* (pp. 354–393). New York: Cambridge University Press.

Cairns, R. B. (1983). The emergence of developmental psychology. In W. Kessen (Ed.), *History, theory and methods* vol. I, of P. H. Mussen (Ed.), *Handbook of Child Psychology,* 4th ed. (pp. 41–102). New York: Wiley.

Cairns, R. B. (1990). Developmental epistemology and self-knowledge: Towards a reinterpretation of self-esteem. In G. Greenberg & E. Tobach (Eds.), *Theories of the evolution of knowing* (pp. 69–86). Hillsdale, NJ: Erlbaum.

Cairns, R. B. (1993). Belated but bedazzling: Timing and genetic influence in social development. In G. Turkewitz & D. A. Devenny (Eds.), *Developmental time and timing* (pp. 61–84). Hillsdale, NJ: Erlbaum.

Callanan, M. A. (1985). How parents label objects for young children: The role of input in the acquisition of category hierarchies. *Child Development, 56,* 508–523.

Callanan, M. A., & Oakes, L. M. (1992). Preschoolers' questions and parents' explanations: Causal thinking in everyday activity. *Cognitive Development, 7,* 213–233.

Campbell, D. T. (1982/1974). Evolutionary epistemology. In H. C. Plotkin (Ed.), *Learning, development and culture* (pp. 73–107). New York: Wiley.

Campbell, D. T. (1990). Levels of organization, downward causation, and the selection-theory approach to evolutionary epistemology. In G. Greenberg & E. Tobach (Eds.), *Theories of the evolution of knowing* (pp. 1–18). Hillsdale, NJ: Erlbaum.

Campbell, J. H. (1985). An organizational interpretation of evolution. In D. J. Depew & B. H. Weber (Eds.), *Evolution at a crossroads* (pp. 133–168). Cambridge, MA: MIT Press.

Campbell, R. L., & Bickhard, M. H. (1986). *Knowing levels and developmental stages.* Basel: Karger.

Campos, J. J., & Stenberg, C. R. (1981). Perception, appraisal and emotion: The onset of social referencing. In M. E. Lamb & L. R. Sherrod (Eds.), *Infant social cognition* (pp. 273–314). Hillsdale, NJ: Erlbaum.

Carbery, M. (1989). *Children's representation of a day's events.* Unpublished research report, City University of New York Graduate Center.

Carbery, M. (1992). *The development of objective time: The integration of logical and cultural conceptual systems.* Unpublished Ph.D. Dissertation, City University of New York Graduate Center.

Carey, S. (1985). *Conceptual change in childhood.* Cambridge, MA: MIT Press.

Carey, S. (1991). Knowledge acquisition: Enrichment or conceptual change? In Carey, S., & Gelman, R. (Eds.), *The epigenesis of mind: Essays on biology and cognition* (pp. 257–292). Hillsdale, NJ: Erlbaum.

Carey, S., & Gelman, R. (1991). *The Epigenesis of mind: Essays on biology and cognition.* Hillsdale, NJ: Erlbaum.

Carni, E., & French, L. A. (1984). The acquisition of before and after reconsidered: What develops? *Journal of Experimental Child Psychology, 37,* 394–403.

Carrithers, M. (1991). Narrativity: Mindreading and making societies. In A. Whiten (Ed.), *Natural theories of mind: Evolution, development and simulation of everyday mindreading* (pp. 305–318). Oxford: Basil Blackwell.

Carruthers, M. J. (1990). *The book of memory: A study of memory in medieval culture.* Cambridge: Cambridge University Press.

Case, R. (1992a). *The mind's staircase: Exploring the conceptual underpinnings of children's thought and knowledge.* Hillsdale, NJ: Erlbaum.

Case, R. (1992b). The role of the frontal lobes in the regulation of cognitive development. *Brain and Cognition, 20,* 51–73.

Caselli, M. C., Bates, E., Casadio, P., Fenson, J., Fenson, L., Sanderl, L., & Weir, J. (1995) A cross-linguistic study of early lexical development. *Cognitive Development, 10,* 159–200.

Cassirer, E. (1923/1953). *Structure and function and Einstein's theory of relativity.* (Trans. W. C. Swaby & M. C. Swaby). New York: Dover.

Ceci, S. J., & Bruck, M. (1993). Suggestibility of the child witness: A historical review and synthesis. *Psychological Bulletin, 113,* 403–439.

Chafe, W. L. (1986). Cognitive constraints on information flow. In R. Tomlin (Ed.), *Coherence and grounding in discourse.* Amsterdam: John Benjamin.

Chandler, M. (1988). Doubt and developing theories of mind. In J. W. Astington, P. L. Harris, & D. R. Olson (Eds.), *Developing theories of mind* (pp. 387–413). New York: Cambridge University Press.

Chandler, M., & Hala, S. (1994). The role of personal involvement in the assessment of early false belief skills. In C. Lewis & P. Mitchell (Eds.), *Children's early understanding of mind: Origins and development* (pp. 403–425). Hillsdale, NJ: Erlbaum.

Chase, W. G., & Ericsson, K. A. (1982). Skill and working memory. In G. H. Bower (Ed.), *The psychology of learning and motivation* (vol. 16, pp. 1–58). San Diego, CA: Academic.

Chi, M. T. H. (1978). Knowledge structures and memory development. In R. S. Siegler (Ed.), *Children's thinking: What develops?* Hillsdale, NJ: Erlbaum.

Chi, M. T. H. (1992). Conceptual change within and across ontological categories: Examples from learning and discovery in science. In R. Giere (Ed.), *Cognitive models of science: Minnesota studies in the philosophy of science* (pp. 133–189). Minneapolis: University of Minnesota Press.

Chi, M. T. H., & Koeske, R. D. (1983). Network representation of a child's dinosaur knowledge. *Developmental Psychology, 19,* 29–39.

Chomsky, N. (1965). *Aspects of a theory of syntax.* Cambridge, MA: MIT Press.

Chomsky, N. (1988). *Language and problems of knowledge: The Managua lectures.* Cambridge, MA: MIT Press.

Chomsky, N. (1991). Linguistics and cognitive science: Problems and mysteries. In A. Kasher (Ed.), *The Chomskyan turn* (pp. 26–53). Cambridge, MA: Basil Blackwell.

Chukovsky, K. (1968). *Reflections on language.* Glasgow, Scotland: Fontana.

Clark, E. V. (1971). On the acquisition of the meaning of before and after. *Journal of Verbal Learning and Verbal Behavior, 10,* 266–275.

Clark, E. V. (1973). What's in a word? On the child's acquisition of semantics in his first language. In T. E. Moore (Ed.), *Cognitive development and the acquisition of language.* New York: Academic.

Clark, E. V. (1983). Meanings and concepts. In J. Flavell & E. Markman (Eds.), *Cognitive development* vol. 3 of P. H. Mussen (Ed.) *Handbook of Child Psychology,* 4th ed. New York: Wiley.

Clark, H. (1973). Space, time, semantics and the child. In T. E. Moore (Ed.), *Cognitive development and the acquisition of language* (pp. 27–63). New York: Academic.

Clements, W., & Perner, J. (1994). Implicit understanding of belief. *Cognitive Development, 9,* 377–396.

Cohen, L. B., & Younger, B. A. (1983). Perceptual categorization in the infant. In E. Scholnick (Ed.), *New trends in conceptual representation: Challenges to Piaget's theory?* (pp. 197–220). Hillsdale, NJ: Erlbaum.

Cole, M. (1991). Conclusion. In L. B. Resnick, J. M. Levine, & S. D. Teasley (Eds.), *Perspectives on socially shared cognition* (pp. 398–417). Washington, DC: American Psychological Association.

Cole, M., John-Steiner, V., Scribner, S., & Souberman, E. (Eds.). (1978). *Mind in society: The development of higher psychological processes.* Cambridge, MA: Harvard University Press.

Comrie, B. (1985). *Tense.* Cambridge: Cambridge University Press.

Cosmides, L., & Tooby, J. (1994). Origins of domain specificity: The evolution of functional organization. In L. A. Hirschfeld & L. A. Gelman (Eds.), *Mapping the mind* (pp. 85–116). New York: Cambridge University Press.

Cosmides, L., Tooby, J., & Barkow, J. H. (1992). Introduction: Evolutionary psychology and conceptual integration. In J. H. Barkow, L. Cosmides, & J. Tooby (Eds.), *The adapted mind: Evolutionary psychology and the generation of culture.* New York: Oxford University Press.

Cromer, R. F. (1968). *The development of temporal reference during the acquisition of language.* Ph.D. Dissertation, Harvard University.

Cromer, R. F. (1989). The cognition hypothesis revisited. In F. S. Kessel (Ed.), *The development of language and language researchers: Essays in honor of Roger Brown* (pp. 223–248). Hillsdale, NJ: Erlbaum.

Dawkins, R. (1976). *The selfish gene.* NY: Oxford University Press.

Dawson, G., & Fischer, K. W. (Eds.). (1994). *Human Behavior and the developing brain.* New York: Guilford Press.

DeCasper, A. J., & Fifer, W. P. (1980). Of human bonding: Newborns prefer their mothers' voices. *Science, 208,* 1174–1176.

DeLoache, J. S. (1990). Young children's understanding of models. In R. F. & J. Hudson (Eds.), *Knowing and remembering in young children.* New York: Cambridge University Press.

Dennett, D. (1978). Beliefs about beliefs. *Behavioral and Brain Sciences, 1,* 568–570.

Depew, D. J., & Weber, B. H. (1985). Innovation and tradition in evolutionary theory: An interpretive afterword. In D. J. Depew & B. H. Weber (Eds.), *Evolution at a crossroads: The new biology and the new philosophy of science* Cambridge, MA: MIT Press, 227–260.

Diamond, A. (1991). Neuropsychological insights into the meaning of object concept development. In S. Carey & R. Gelman (Eds.), *The epigenesis of mind: Essays on biology and cognition* (pp. 67–110). Hillsdale, NJ: Erlbaum.

Diamond, A. (1993). Neuropsychological insights into the meaning of object concept development. In M. H. Johnson (Ed.), *Brain development and cognition: A reader* (pp. 208–247). Oxford: Blackwell.

Diaz, R. M., & Berk, L. E. (Eds.). (1992). *Private speech: From social interaction to self-regulation.* Hillsdale, NJ: Erlbaum.

Donald, M. (1991). *Origins of the modern mind: Three stages in the evolution of culture and cognition.* Cambridge, MA: Harvard University Press.

Donald, M. (1993b). Precis of origins of the modern mind: Three stages in the evolution of culture and cognition. *Behavioral and Brain Sciences, 16,* 737–791.

Donald, M. (1995). Hominid enculturation and cognitive evolution. *Archaeological Review from Cambridge* (Special volume: "Hierarchy of being human").

Donaldson, M. (1978). *Children's minds.* Glasgow, Scotland: William Collins & Sons, Inc.

Dore, J. (1989). Monologue as reenvoicement of dialogue. In K. Nelson (Ed.),

Narratives from the crib (pp. 231–262). Cambridge, MA: Harvard University Press.

Doris, J. (1991). *The suggestibility of children's recollections.* Washington, DC: American Psychological Association.

Dorval, B. (1990). A dialogized version of Piaget's theory of egocentric speech. In B. Dorval (Ed.), *Conversational organization and its development* (pp. 131–164). Norwood, NJ: Ablex.

Dorval, B., & Eckerman, C. O. (1984). Development trends in the quality of conversation achieved by small groups of acquainted peers. *Monographs of the Society for Research in Child Development, 49* (2, Serial No. 206).

Dromi, E. (1987). *Early lexical development.* Cambridge: Cambridge University Press.

Dudycha, G. J., & Dudycha, M. M. (1941). Childhood memories: A review of the literature. *Psychological Bulletin, 38,* 668–682.

Dunn, J. (1988). *The beginnings of social understanding.* Cambridge, MA: Harvard University Press.

Dunn, J. (1991). Young children's understanding of other people: Evidence from observations within the family. In D. Frye & C. Moore (Eds.), *Children's theories of mind: Mental states and social understanding.* Hillsdale, NJ: Erlbaum.

Dunn, J. (1994). Changing minds and changing relationships. In C. Lewis & P. Mitchell (Eds.), *Children's early understanding of mind: Origins and development* (pp. 297–310). Hillsdale, NJ: Erlbaum.

Dunn, J., Brown, J., Slomkowski, C., Tesla, C., & Youngblade, L. (1991). Young children's understanding of other people's feelings and beliefs: Individual differences and their antecedents. *Child Development, 62,* 1352–1366.

Durham, W. H. (1991). *Coevolution: Genes, culture, and human diversity.* Stanford, CA: Stanford University Press.

Eco, U., Santambrogio, M., & Violi, P. (Eds.). (1988). *Meaning and mental representations.* Bloomington: Indiana University Press.

Eisenstein, E. (1993). *The printing revolution in early modern Europe,* canto ed. New York: Cambridge University Press.

Engel, S. (1986). *Learning to reminisce: A developmental study of how young children talk about the past.* Unpublished Ph.D. Dissertation, City University of New York Graduate Center.

Ericsson, K. A., & Chase, W. G. (1982). Exceptional memory. *American Scientist, 70,* 607–619.

Evans, M. A., & Schmidt, F. (1991). Repeated maternal book reading with two children: Language-normal and language-impaired. *First Language, 11,* 269–287.

Fagan, J. F. I. (1984). Infant memory: History, current trends, relations to cognitive psychology. In M. Moscovitch (Ed.), *Infant memory: Its relation to normal and pathological memory in humans and other animals* (pp. 1–28). New York: Plenum.

Falk, D. (1983). Cerebral cortices of East African early hominids. *Science, 221,* 1072–1074.

Fauconnier, G. (1985). *Mental spaces: Aspects of meaning construction in natural language.* Cambridge, MA: MIT Press.

Feldman, C. F. (1989). Monologue as problem-solving narrative. In K. Nelson (Ed.), *Narratives from the crib* (pp. 98–122). Cambridge, MA: Harvard University Press.

Fenson, L., Dale, P. S., Reznick, J. S., Bates, E., Thal, D. J., & Pethick, S. J.

(1994). Variability in early communicative development. *Monographs of the Society for Research in Child Development, 59* (5).

Fernald, A. (1992). Human maternal vocalizations to infants as biologically relevant signals: An evolutionary perspective. In J. H. C. Barkow, L. Cosmides, & J. Tooby. (Eds.), *The adapted mind: Evolutionary psychology and the generation of culture* (pp. 391–428). New York: Oxford University Press.

Fischer, K. W. (1980). A theory of cognitive development: The control and construction of hierarchies of skills. *Psychological Review, 87,* 477–531.

Fischer, K. W., & Bidell, T. (1991). Constraining nativist inferences about cognitive capacities. In S. Carey & R. Gelman (Eds.), *The epigenesis of mind: Essays on biology and cognition* (pp. 199–236). Hillsdale, NJ: Erlbaum.

Fischer, K. W., & Farrar, M. J. (1988). Generalizations about generalization: How a theory of skill development explains both generality and specificity. In A. Demetriou (Ed.), *The neo-Piagetian theories of cognitive development: Toward an integration* (pp. 103–137). Amsterdam: North Holland.

Fischer, K. W., & Rose, S. P. (1993). Development of coordination of components in brain and behavior: A framework for theory and research. In G. Dawson & K. W. Fischer (Eds.), *Human behavior and the developing brain,* New York: Guilford Press.

Fivush, R. (1984). Learning about school: The development of kindergarteners' school scripts. *Child Development, 55,* 1697–1709.

Fivush, R. (1988). The functions of event memory: Some comments on Nelson and Barsalou. In U. Neisser & E. Winograd (Eds.), *Remembering reconsidered: Ecological and traditional approaches to the study of memory* (pp. 277–282). New York: Cambridge University Press.

Fivush, R. (1993). Emotional content of parent-child conversations about the past. In C. A. Nelson (Ed.), *Memory and affect in development* (vol. 26, pp. 39–77). Hillsdale, NJ: Erlbaum.

Fivush, R. (1994). Constructing narrative, emotion, and self in parent-child conversations about the past. In U. Neisser & R. Fivush (Eds.), *The remembering self: Construction and accuracy in the self-narrative* (pp. 136–157). New York: Cambridge University Press.

Fivush, R., & Fromhoff, F. A. (1988). Style and structure in mother-child conversations about the past. *Discourse Processes, 11,* 337–355.

Fivush, R., & Hamond, N. R. (1989). Time and again: Effects of repetition and retention interval on two year olds' event recall. *Journal of Experimental Child Psychology, 47,* 259–273.

Fivush, R., & Hamond, N. R. (1990). Autobiographical memory across the preschool years: Toward reconceptualizing childhood amnesia. In R. Fivush & J. A. Hudson (Eds.), *Knowing and remembering in young children* (pp. 223–248). New York: Cambridge University Press.

Fivush, R., & Hudson, J. A. (1990). *Knowing and remembering in young children.* New York: Cambridge University Press.

Fivush, R., & Slackman, E. (1986). The acquisition and development of scripts. In K. Nelson (Ed.), *Event knowledge: Structure and function in development* (pp. 71–96). Hillsdale, NJ: Erlbaum.

Flanagan, O. (1992). *Consciousness reconsidered.* Cambridge, MA: MIT Press.

Flavell, J. H. (1971). First discussant's comments: What is memory development the development of? *Human Development, 14,* 272–278.

Flavell, J. H. (1988). The development of children's knowledge about the mind: From cognitive connections to mental representations. In J. Astington, P.

Harris, & D. Olson (Eds.), *Developing theories of mind*. New York: Cambridge University Press.

Flavell, J. H., Beach, D. H., & Chinsky, J. M. (1966). Spontaneous verbal rehearsal in memory tasks as a function of age. *Child Development, 37*, 283–299.

Flavell, J. H. Friedrichs, A. G., & Hoyt, J. D. (1970). Developmental changes in memorization processes. *Cognitive Psychology, 1*, 324–340.

Flavell, J. H., Green, F. L., & Flavell, E. R. (1986). Development of knowledge about the appearance-reality distinction. *Monographs of the Society for Research in Child Development, 51* (1), Serial No. 212.

Flores, R. L. (1993). *Urban preschool children's understanding of temporal and causal relations*. Unpublished Ph.D. Dissertation, City University of New York.

Fodor, J. A. (1975). *The language of thought*. New York: Crowell.

Fodor, J. A. (1981). *Representations*. Cambridge, MA: MIT Press.

Fodor, J. A. (1983). *Modularity of mind*. Cambridge, MA: MIT Press.

Fraisse, P. (1963). *The psychology of time*. New York: Harper & Row.

Fraser, J. T. (Ed.). (1981). *The voices of time*, 2d ed. Amherst: University of Massachusetts Press.

Fraser, J. T. (1987). *Time the familiar stranger*. Amherst: University of Massachusetts Press.

French, L. A. (1988). The development of children's understanding of "because" and "so." *Journal of Experimental Child Psychology, 45*, 262–279.

French, L. A., Boynton, M., & Hodges, R. (1991). Beginning to talk with peers: The roles of setting and knowledge. In S. A. Gelman & J. P. Byrnes (Eds.), *Perspectives on language and thought: Interrelations in development* (pp. 485–510). New York: Cambridge University Press.

French, L. A., & Nelson, K. (1985). *Young children's understanding of relational terms: Some ifs, ors and buts*. New York: Springer-Verlag.

Freud, S. (1963). Three essays on the theory of sexuality. In J. Strachey (Ed.), *The standard edition of the complete works of Freud* (vol. 7). London: Hogarth Press.

Freyd, J. J. (1983). Shareability: The social psychology of epistemology. *Cognitive Science, 7*, 191–210.

Friedman, W. J. (Ed.). (1982). *The developmental psychology of time*. New York: Academic.

Friedman, W. J. (1990a). *About time: Inventing the fourth dimension*. Cambridge, MA: MIT Press.

Friedman, W. J. (1990b). Children's representations of the pattern of daily activities. *Child Development, 61*, 1399–1412.

Frith, U. (1989). *Autism: Explaining the enigma*. Oxford: Basil Blackwell.

Frye, D., & Moore, C. (Eds.), (1991). *Children's theories of mind*. Hillsdale, NJ: Erlbaum.

Furrow, D., Moore, C., Davidge, J., & Chiasson, L. (1992). Mental terms in mothers' and children's speech: Similarities and relationships. *Journal of Child Language, 19*, 617–632.

Gallistel, C. R. (1989). Animal cognition: The representation of space, time and number. In M. R. Rosenzwig & L. W. Porter (Eds.), *Annual Review of Psychology* (vol. 40, pp. 155–189). Palo Alto, CA: Annual Reviews Inc.

Gallistel, C. R., Brown, A. L., Carey, S., Gelman, R., & Keil, F. C. (1991). Lessons from animal learning for the study of cognitive development. In S. Carey & R. Gelman (Eds.), *Epigenesis of mind* (pp. 3–36). Hillsdale, NJ: Erlbaum.

Gallup, G. G., Jr. (1970). Chimpanzees: Self-recognition. *Science, 167*, 86–87.

Gamble, C. (1994). *Timewalkers: The prehistory of global colonization*. Cambridge, MA: Harvard University Press.

Garvey, C. (1990). *Play*. Cambridge, MA: Harvard University Press.

Garvey, C., & Hogan, R. (1973). Social speech and social interaction: Egocentrism revisited. *Child Development, 44*, 562–568.

Gee, J. P. (1991). Memory and myth: A perspective on narrative. In A. McCabe & C. Peterson (Eds.), *Developing narrative structure* (pp. 1–25). Hillsdale, NJ: Erlbaum.

Gelman, R., & Baillargeon, R. (1983). A review of some Piagetian concepts. In J. Flavell & E. Markman (Eds.), *Cognitive Development*, vol. 3 of P. H. Mussen (Ed.) *Handbook of Child Psychology* 4th ed. New York: Wiley.

Gelman, R., & Gallistel, R. (1978). *The young child's understanding of number*. Cambridge, MA: Harvard University Press.

Gelman, S. A., & Coley, J. D. (1991). Language and categorization: The acquisition of natural kind terms. In S. A. Gelman & J. P. Byrnes (Eds.), *Perspectives on language and thought: Interrelations in development* (pp. 146–196). Cambridge: Cambridge University Press.

Gelman, S. A., & Markman, E. M. (1986). Categories and induction in young children. *Cognition, 23*, 183–209.

Gerhardt, J. (1989). Monologue as a speech genre. In K. Nelson (Ed.), *Narratives from the crib* (pp. 171–230). Cambridge, MA: Harvard University Press.

Gesell, A. L. (1940). *The first five years of life*. New York: Harper.

Gibson, E. J., & Spelke, E. S. (1983). The development of perception. In J. Flavell, E. M. Markman, (Eds.), *Cognitive development* P. Mussen (Ed.) *Handbook of Child psychology*, 4th ed. (vol. 3, pp. 1–76). New York: Wiley.

Gibson, J. J. (1979). *The ecological approach to visual perception*. Boston: Houghton Mifflin.

Gibson, J. J. (1982). The concept of stimulus in psychology. In E. Reed & R. Jones (Eds.), *Reasons for realism: The selected essays of James J. Gibson*. Hillsdale, NJ: Erlbaum.

Gibson, K. R., & Ingold, T. (Eds.) (1993). *Tools, language and cognition in human evolution*. Cambridge: Cambridge University Press.

Gibson, K. R., King, B., & Parker, S. T. (1993). *Symposium on primate and human cognition: Continuities and discontinuities, Part I*. Washington DC, 92nd Annual Meeting of the American Anthropological Association.

Gleitman, L. (1990). The structural sources of verb meanings. *Language Acquisition, 1*, 3–56.

Goldin-Meadow, S., & Mylander, C. (1984). Gestural communication in deaf children: The effects and noneffects of parental input on early language development. *Monographs of the Society for Research in Child Development, 49*, 3–4.

Goldman-Rakic, P. Isseroff, A., Schwartz, M. L., & Bugbee, N. M. (1983). The neurobiology of cognitive development. In M. M. Haith & J. J. Campos (Eds.), *Infancy and developmental psychobiology* vol. 2 of P. H. Mussen (Ed.) *Handbook of Child Psychology* 4th ed. (pp. 281–344). New York: Wiley.

Golinkoff, R., Mervis, C. B., & Hirsh-Pasek, K. (1994). Early object labels: The case for a developmental lexical principles framework. *Journal of Child Language, 21*, 125–156.

Gomez, J. C. (1990). The emergence of intentional communication as a problem-solving strategy in the gorilla. In S. T. Parker & K. R. Gibson (Eds.), *"Language" and intelligence in monkeys and apes: Comparative devel-*

opmental perspectives (pp. 333–355). Cambridge: Cambridge University Press.

Gopnik, A. (1993a). How we know our minds: The illusion of first-person knowledge of intentionality. *Behavorial and brain sciences, 16,* 1–14.

Gopnik, A. (1993b). Theories and illusions. *Behavioral and Brain Sciences, 16,* 90–100.

Gopnik, A., & Choi, S. (1990). Language and cognition. *First Language, 10,* 199–216.

Gopnik, A., & Choi, S. (in press, 1996). Cross-linguistic differences in early semantic and cognitive development. *Cognitive Development.*

Gopnik, A., & Graf, P. (1988). Knowing how you know: Young children's ability to identify and remember the sources of their beliefs. *Child Development, 59,* 1366–1371.

Gopnik, A., & Meltzoff, A. (1986). Words, plans, and things: Interactions between semantic and cognitive development in the one-word stage. In S. Kuczaj & M. Barrett (Eds.), *The development of word meaning* (pp. 199–223). New York: Springer-Verlag.

Gopnik, A., & Wellman, H. (1994). The theory theory. In L. A. Hirschfeld & S. A. Gelman (Eds.), *Mapping the mind* (pp. 257–293). New York: Cambridge University Press.

Gottlieb, G. (1992). *Individual development and evolution: The genesis of novel behavior.* New York: Oxford University Press.

Gould, S. J. (1977). *Ontogeny and phylogeny.* Cambridge, MA: Harvard University Press.

Gould, S. J. (1987). *Time's arrow, time's cycle: Myth and metaphor in the discovery of geological time.* Cambridge, MA: Harvard University Press.

Gould, S. J., & Lewontin, R. C. (1979). The spandrels of San Marco and the Panglossian program: A critique of the adaptationist programme. *Proceedings of the Royal Society of London, 250,* 281–288.

Gould, S. J., & Vrba, E. S. (1982). Exaptation – a missing term in the science of form. *Paleobiology, 8,* 4–15.

Graesser, A. C., Woll, S. B., Kowalski, D. J., & Smith, D. A. (1979). Memory for typical and atypical actions in scripted activities. *Journal of Experimental Psychology: Human Learning and Memory, 6,* 503–515.

Greene, T. R. (1994). What kindergartners know about class inclusion hierarchies. *Journal of Experimental Child Psychology, 57,* 72–88.

Greenfield, D. B., & Scott, M. S. (1986). Young children's preference for complementary pairs: Evidence against a shift to a taxonomic preference. *Developmental Psychology, 22,* 19–21.

Greenfield, P. M. (1991). Language, tools and brain: The ontogeny and phylogeny of hierarchically organized sequential behavior. *Behavioral and Brain Sciences, 14,* 531–551.

Grieve, R., & Hughes, M. (Eds.). (1990). *Understanding children.* Oxford: Blackwell.

Gruendel, J. M. (1980). *Scripts and stories: A study of children's event narratives.* Unpublished Doctoral Dissertation, Yale University.

Guralnik, D. B. (Eds.). (1974). *Webster's new world dictionary of the American language,* 2d ed. New York: William Collins & World Publishing Co. Inc.

Haeckel, E. (1905). *The evolution of man.* Translated by J. McCabe. London: Watts & Co.

Haith, M. M. (1992). Future-oriented processes in infancy: The case of visual expectation. In C. E. Granud (Ed.), *Visual perception and cognition in infancy* (pp. 235–264). Hillsdale, NJ: Erlbaum.

Halford, G. S. (1993). *Children's understanding: The development of mental models.* Hillsdale, NJ: Erlbaum.

Hall, E. T. (1983). *The dance of life: The other dimension of time.* Garden City, NY: Doubleday.

Hall, G. S. (1904). *Adolescence: Its psychology and its relation to physiology, anthropology, sociology, sex, crime, religion, and education.* New York: Appleton.

Halliday, M. A. K. (1975). *Learning how to mean.* London: Edwin Arnold.

Hampson, J. (1989). *Elements of style: Maternal and child contributions to the expressive and referential styles of language acquisition.* Unpublished doctoral dissertion. City University of New York Graduate Center.

Hampson, J., & Nelson, K. (1993). The relation of maternal language to variation in rate and style of language acquisition. *Journal of Child Language, 20,* 313–342.

Harkness, S. (1990). A cultural model for the acquisition of language: Implications for the innateness debate. *Developmental Psychobiology, 23,* 727–740.

Harnad, S. (Eds.). (1987). *Categorical perception: The groundwork of cognition.* New York: Cambridge University Press.

Harner, L. (1975). Yesterday and tomorrow: Development of early understanding of the terms. *Developmental Psychology, 11,* 864–865.

Harner, L. (1982). Talking about the past and future. In W. J. Friedman (Ed.), *The developmental psychology of time.* New York: Academic.

Harner, L., Nelson, K., Korintus, M., & Kessler Shaw, L. (1992). *From bedtime to Eastern Standard Time.* Unpublished manuscript. City University of New York.

Harris, P. L. (1992). From simulation to folk psychology: The case for development. *Mind and Language, 7,* 120–144.

Harris, P. L. (1994). Thinking by children and scientists: False analogies and neglected similarities. In L. A. Hirschfeld & S. A. Gelman (Eds.), *Mapping the mind* (pp. 294–315). New York: Cambridge University Press.

Harris, P. L. (in press). Desires, beliefs, and language. In P. Carruthers and P. K. Smith (Eds.), *Theories of theories of mind.* Cambridge: Cambridge University Press.

Harris, P. L., & Kavanaugh, R. D. (1993). Young children's understanding of pretense. *Monographs of the Society for Research in Child Development, 58*(1), Serial No. 231.

Hasher, L., & Zacks, R. T. (1979). Automatic and effortful processes in memory. *Journal of Experimental Psychology: General, 108,* 356–388.

Heath, S. B. (1982). What no bedtime story means: Narrative skills at home and school. *Language in Society, 11,* 49–76.

Heath, S. B. (1983). *Ways with words.* Cambridge: Cambridge University Press.

Hirschfeld, L. A. & Gelman, S. A. (Eds.). (1994a). *Mapping the mind: Domain specificity in cognition and culture.* New York: Cambridge University Press.

Hirschfeld, L. A., & Gelman, S. A. (1994b). Toward a topography of mind: An introduction to domain specificity. In L. A. Hirschfeld & S. A. Gelman (Eds.), *Mapping the mind: Domain specificity in cognition and culture.* New York: Cambridge University Press.

Hirsh-Pasek, K., Kemler Nelson, D. G., Jusczyk, P. W., Cassidy, K. W., Druss, B., & Kennedy, L. (1987). Clauses are perceptual units for young infants. *Cognition, 26,* 269–286.

Hobson, R. P. (1993). *Autism and the development of mind.* Hillsdale, NJ: Erlbaum.
Hobson, R. P. (1995). Through feeling and sight to self and symbol. In U. Neisser (Ed.), *The perceived self* (pp. 254–279). New York: Cambridge University Press.
Hodge, R., & Kress, G. (1988). *Social semiotics.* Ithaca, NY: Cornell University Press.
Hoffman, E. (1989). *Lost in translation: A life in a new language.* New York: Dutton.
Hood, L., & Bloom, L. (1979). What, when, and how about why: A longitudinal study of expressions of causality in the language of two-year-old children. Chicago: *Society for Research in Child Development Monographs 44* (6, Serial No. 181).
Hopper, P. (1979). Aspect and foregrounding in discourse. In T. Givon (Ed.), *Discourse and syntax* (vol. 12: *Syntax and semantics,* pp. 213–241). New York: Academic.
Horton, M. S., & Markman, E. M. (1980). Developmental differences in the acquisition of basic and superordinate categories. *Child Development, 31,* 708–719.
Howe, M. L., & Courage, M. L. (1993). On resolving the enigma of infantile amnesia. *Psychological Bulletin, 113,* 305–326.
Howe, M. L., Courage, M. L., & Bryant-Brown, L. (1993). Reinstating preschoolers' memories. *Developmental Psychology, 29,* 854–869.
Hudson, J. A. (1986). Memories are made of this: General event knowledge and the development of autobiographic memory. In K. Nelson (Ed.), *Event knowledge: Structure and function in development* (pp. 97–118). Hillsdale, NJ: Erlbaum.
Hudson, J. A. (1990). The emergence of autobiographic memory in mother-child conversation. In R. Fivush & J. A. Hudson (Eds.), *Knowing and remembering in young children* (pp. 166–196). New York: Cambridge University Press.
Hudson, J. A. (1993). Reminiscing with mothers and others: Autobiographical memory in young two-year-olds. *Journal of Narrative and Life History, 3,* 1–32.
Hudson, J. A., Gebelt, J., Haviland, J., & Bentivegna, C. (1992). Emotion and narrative structure in young children's personal accounts. *Journal of Narrative and Life History, 2,* 129–150.
Hudson, J. A., & Nelson, K. (1986). Repeated encounters of a similiar kind: Effects of familiarity on children's autobiographical memory. *Cognitive Development, 1,* 253–271.
Hudson, J. A., & Shapiro, L. R. (1991). From knowing to telling: The development of children's scripts, stories, and personal narratives. In A. McCabe & C. Peterson (Eds.), *Developing Narrative Structure* (pp. 89–136). Hillsdale, NJ: Erlbaum.
Hudson, J. A., & Sheffield, E. (1993). *Effects of re-enactment on toddlers' memory after 2, 8, and 12 months.* Paper presented at Society for Research in Child Development Conference New Orleans, LA.
Humphrey, N. K. (1976). The social function of intellect. In P. P. G. Bateson & R. A. Hinde (Eds.), *Growing points in ethology.* Cambridge: Cambridge University Press.
Hunt, E., & Love, T. (1972). How good can memory be? In A. W. Melton & E. Martin (Eds.), *Coding processes in human memory* (pp. 237–260). Washington, DC: Winston & Sons.
Huttenlocher, J., & Higgins, E. T. (1978). Issues in the study of symbolic development. In W. A. Collins (Ed.), *Minnesota symposium on child psychology* (vol. 11, pp. 98–140). Hillsdale, NJ: Erlbaum.

Hymes, D. (1974). *Foundations in sociolinguistics: An enthographic approach.* Philadelphia: University of Pennsylvania Press.

Inhelder, B., & Piaget, J. (1958). *The growth of logical thinking from childhood to adolescence.* New York: Basic Books.

Istomina, A. M. (1975). The development of voluntary memory in preschool age children. *Soviet Psychology, 13,* 5–64.

Iverson, J. M., Capirci, O., & Caselli, M. C. (1994). From communication to language in two modalities. *Cognitive Development, 9,* 23–44.

Jackendoff, R. S. (1983). *Semantics and cognition.* Cambridge, MA: MIT Press.

Jackendoff, R. S. (1988). Conceptual semantics. In U. Eco, M. Santambrogio, & P. Violi (Eds.), *Meaning and mental representations* (pp. 81–98). Bloomington: Indiana University Press.

Jackson, J. F. (1993). Human behavioral genetics, Scarr's theory, and her views on interventions: A critical review and commentary on their implications for African American children. *Child Development, 64,* 1318–1332.

Jakobson, R. (1960). Linguistics and poetics. In T. A. Sebeok (Ed.), *Style in language* (pp. 350–357). Cambridge, MA: MIT Press.

James, W. (1950/1890). *The principles of psychology.* New York: Dover Publications.

Jansons, K. M. (1988). A personal view of dyslexia and of thought without language. In L. Weiskrantz (Ed.), *Thought without language* (pp. 498–503). Oxford: Clarendon Press.

Jenkins, J. M., & Astington, J. W. (In press). Cognitive factors and family structure associated with theory of mind development in young children. *Developmental Psychology.*

Johnson, C. N., & Maratsos, M. P. (1977). Early comprehension of mental verbs: Think and know. *Child Development, 48,* 1743–1747.

Johnson, M. (1987). *The body in the mind.* Chicago: Chicago University Press.

Johnson, M. H. (Ed.). (1993). *Brain development and cognition.* Oxford: Blackwell.

Johnson, M. H., & Morton, J. (1991). *Biology and cognitive development: The case of face recognition.* Oxford: Blackwell.

Johnson-Laird, P. N. (1987). The mental representation of the meaning of words. *Cognition, 23,* 189–211.

John-Steiner, V., & Panofsky, C. (1992). Narrative competence: Cross-cultural comparisons. *Journal of Narrative and Life History, 2,* 219–233.

Karmiloff-Smith, A. (1979). *A functional approach to child language: A study of determiners and reference.* Cambridge: Cambridge University Press.

Karmiloff-Smith. A. (1986a). From meta-processes to conscious access: Evidence from children's metalinguistic and repair data. *Cognition, 23,* 95–147.

Karmiloff-Smith, A. (1986b). Language development beyond age five. In P. Fletcher & M. Garman (Eds.), *Language acquisition.* Cambridge: Cambridge University Press.

Karmiloff-Smith. A. (1992). *Beyond modularity.* Cambridge, MA: MIT Press.

Keil, F. C. (1987). Conceptual development and category structure. In U. Neisser (Ed.), *Concepts and conceptual development: Ecological and intellectual factors in categorization* (pp. 175–200). New York: Cambridge University Press.

Keil, F. C. (1989). *Concepts, kinds, and cognitive development.* Cambridge, MA: MIT Press.

Keil, R. C. (1991). The emergence of theoretical beliefs as constraints on concepts. In S. Carey & R. Gelman (Eds.), *The epigenesis of mind: Essays on biology and cognition* (pp. 237–256). Hillsdale, NJ: Erlbaum.

Kemler Nelson, D. G. (1995). Principle-based inferences in young children's categorizations: Revisiting the impact of function on the naming of artifacts. *Cognitive Development, 10,* 347–380.

Kemper, S. (1984). The development of narrative skills: Explanations and entertainments. In S. A. Kuczaj II (Ed.), *Discourse development: Progress in cognitive development research* (pp. 99–124). New York: Springer-Verlag.

Kertesz, A. (1988). Cognitive function in severe aphasia. In L. Weiskrantz (Ed.), *Thought without language* (pp. 451–463). Oxford: Clarendon Press.

Kessen, W., & Kuhlman, C. (Eds.). (1962). Thought in the young child, *Monographs of the Society for Research in Child Development, 27* (2). Chicago: University of Chicago Press.

Khan, F. (1994). *Cultural contexts and mathematical practices: A study of New Delhi school children, newspaper vendors and cigarette sellers.* Ph.D. Dissertation, City University of New York Graduate Center.

Kinsbourne, M., & Hiscock, M. (1983). The normal and deviant development of functional lateralization of the brain. In M. M. Haith & J. J. Campos (Eds.), *Infancy and developmental psychobiology* vol. II of P. H. Mussen (Ed.) *Handbook of Child Psychology,* 4th ed. (pp. 157–280). New York: Wiley.

Kohlberg, L., Yaeger, J., & Hjertholm, E. (1968). Private speech: Four studies and a review of theories. *Child Development, 39,* 691–736.

Konner, M. (1982). *The tangled wind: Biological constraints on the human spirit.* New York: Harper.

Korintus, M. (1992). *Studies of young children's time knowledge.* Seville, Spain, Vth European Conference on Developmental Psychology.

Kozulin, A. (1986). Vygotsky in context, In A. Kozulin (Ed.), *Thought and language* (pp. xi–lvi). Cambridge, MA: MIT Press.

Krackow, E., & Blewitt, P. (1989, March). *What determines order of acquisition of taxonomic relationships?* Paper presented at the annual meeting of the Southeastern Psychological Association, Washington, DC.

Krackow, E., & Gordon, P. (1992). *What contributes to the superior recall of event-based categorical relationships?* Paper presented at Conference on Human Development, Atlanta, GA.

Kuczaj, S. A., II, & Barrett, M. D. (Eds.). (1986). *The development of word meaning: Progress in cognitive developmental research.* New York: Springer-Verlag.

Kuhn, T. S. (1970). *The structure of scientific revolutions,* 2d ed. Chicago: Chicago University Press.

Kyratzis, A. (1989). *The role of language in superordinate category formation.* Unpublished Ph.D. Dissertation, City University of New York Graduate Center.

Laboratory of Comparative Human Cognition (1983). Culture and cognitive development. In W. Kessen (Ed.), *History, Theory and Methods.* P. H. Mussen (Ed.), *Handbook of child psychology,* 4th ed. (vol. 1, pp. 295–356). New York: Wiley.

Labov, W., & Waletzky, J. (1967). Narrative analysis. In J. Helm (Ed.), *Essays on the verbal and visual arts* (pp. 12–44). Seattle: University of Washington Press.

Lakoff, G. (1987). *Women, fire and dangerous things.* Chicago: University of Chicago Press.

Lakoff, G., & Johnson, M. (1980). *Metaphors we live by.* Chicago: Chicago University Press.

Landau, B., Smith, L. B., & Jones, S. S. (1988). The importance of shape in early lexical learning. *Cognitive Development, 3,* 299–331.

Leontiev, A. N. (1978). *Activity, consciousness, personality.* Englewood Cliffs, NJ: Prentice-Hall.

Leslie, A. M. (1987). Pretense and representation: The origins of "theory of mind." *Psychological Review, 94*, 412–426.

Leslie, A. M. (1988). Some implications of pretence for mechanisms underlying the child's theory of mind. In J. W. Astington, P. L. Harris, & D. R. Olson (Eds.), *Developing theories of mind* (pp. 19–46). Cambridge: Cambridge University Press.

Leslie, A. M., German, T. P., & Happe, F. G. (1993). Even a theory-theory needs information processing: ToMM, an alternative theory-theory of the child's theory of mind. *Behavioral and Brain Sciences, 16*, 56–57.

Leslie, A. M., & Roth, D. (1993). What autism teaches us about metarepresentation. In S. Baron-Cohen, H. Tager-Flusber, & D. Cohen (Eds.), *Understanding other minds: Perspectives from autism* (pp. 83–111). New York: Oxford University Press.

Levy, E. (1989). Monologue as development of the text-forming function of language. In K. Nelson (Ed.), *Narratives from the crib* (pp. 123–170). Cambridge, MA: Harvard University Press.

Levy, E., & Nelson, K. (1994). Words in discourse: A dialectical approach to the acquisition of meaning and use. *Journal of Child Language, 21*, 367–389.

Levy, Y., Schlesinger, I. M., & Braine, M. D. S. (Eds.). (1988). *Categories and processes in language acquisition.* Hillsdale, NJ: Erlbaum.

Lewis, C. (1994). Episodes, events, and narratives in the child's understanding of mind. In C. Lewis & P. Mitchell (Eds.), *Children's early understanding of mind: Origins and development* (pp. 457–480). Hillsdale, NJ: Erlbaum.

Lewis, C., Freeman, N. H., Hagestadt, C., & Douglas, H. (1994). Narrative access and production in preschoolers' false belief reasoning. *Cognitive Development, 9*, 397–424.

Lewis, C., & Mitchell, P. (Eds.). (1994). *Children's early understanding of mind: Origins and development.* Hillsdale, NJ: Erlbaum.

Lewis, C., & Osborne, A. (1991). Three-year-old's problem with false-belief: Conceptual deficit or linguistic artifact? *Child Development, 61*, 1514–1519.

Liben, L. S. (1982). Children's large-scale spatial cognition: Is the measure the message? In R. Cohen (Ed.), *New directions for child development: Children's conceptions of spatial relationships* (pp. 51–64). San Francisco: Jossey-Bass.

Lieberman, P. (1984). *The biology and evolution of language.* Cambridge, MA: Harvard University Press.

Lieven, E. V. M., Pine, J. M., & Dresner Barnes, H. (1992). Individual differences in early vocabulary development: Redefining the referential-expressive distinction. *Journal of Child Language, 19*, 287–310.

Lillard, A. S. (1993). Pretend play skills and the child's theory of mind. *Child Development, 64*, 348–371.

Linton, M. (1982). Transformations of memory in everyday life. In. U. Neisser (Ed.), *Memory observed: Remembering in natural contexts.* San Francisco: Freeman.

Lock, A. (1991). The role of social interaction in early language. In N. A. Krasnegor, D. M. Rumbaugh, R. L. Schiefelbusch, & M. Studdert-Kennedy (Eds.), *Biological and behavioral determinants of language development* (pp. 287–300), Hillsdale, NJ: Erlbaum.

Lorenz, K. (1966). *On aggression.* London: Methuen.

Lucariello, J. (1987). Concept formation and its relation to word learning and use in the second year. *Journal of Child Language, 14*, 309–332.

Lucariello, J. (1990). Canonicality and consciousness in child narrative. In B. K. Britton, & A. D. Pelligrini (Eds.), *Narrative thought and narrative language* (pp. 131–150). Hillsdale, NJ: Erlbaum.

Lucariello, J., Kyratzis, A., & Nelson, K. (1992). Taxonomic knowledge: What kind and when. *Child Development, 63*, 978–998.

Lucariello, J., & Nelson, K. (1985). Slot-filler categories as memory organizers for young children. *Developmental Psychology, 21*, 272–282.

Lucariello, J., & Nelson, K. (1986). Context effects on lexical specificity in maternal and child discourse. *Journal of Child Langauge, 13*, 507–522.

Lucariello, J., & Nelson, K. (1987). Remembering and planning talk between mothers and children. *Discourse Processes, 10*, 219–235.

Lucariello, J., & Rifkin, A. (1986). Event representations as the basis for categorical knowledge. In K. Nelson (Ed.), *Event knowledge: Structure and function in development* (pp. 189–204). Hillsdale, NJ: Erlbaum.

Lucy, J. A. (1985). Whorf's view of the linguistic mediation of thought. In E. Meertz & R. Parmentier (Eds.), *Semiotic mediation: Sociocultural and psychological perspectives* (pp. 73–97). Orlando, FL: Academic.

Lucy, J. A. (1992). *Language diversity and thought: A reformulation of the linguistic relativity hypothesis.* New York: Cambridge University Press.

Luria, A. R. (1961). *The role of speech in the regulation of normal and abnormal behavior.* Oxford: Pergamon Press.

Luria, A. R. (1968). *The mind of a mnemonist.* New York: Avon.

Luria, A. R. (1976). *Cognitive development: Its cultural and social foundations.* Cambridge, MA: Harvard University Press.

Lyons, J. (1977). *Semantics.* Cambridge: Cambridge University Press.

MacNamara, J. (1982). *Names for things.* Cambridge, MA: MIT Press.

Malotki, E. (1983). *Hopi time: A linguistic analysis of the temporal categories of the Hopi language.* Berlin: Mouton.

Mandler, J. M. (1979). Categorical and schematic organization in memory. In C. R. Puff (Ed.), *Memory organization and structure* (pp. 259–302). New York: Academic.

Mandler, J. M. (1983). Representation. In J. H. Flavell & E. M. Markman (Eds.), *Cognitive development* P. H. Mussen (Ed.) *Handbook of Child Psychology*, 4th ed. (vol. III, pp. 420–494). New York: Wiley.

Mandler, J. M. (1984a). Representation and recall in infancy. In M. Moscovitch (Ed.), *Infant memory: Its relation to normal and pathological memory in humans and other animals* (pp. 75–101). New York: Plenum.

Mandler, J. M. (1984b). *Stories, scripts, and scenes: Aspects of schema theory.* Hillsdale, NJ: Erlbaum.

Mandler, J. M. (1988). How to build a baby: On the development of an accessible representational system. *Cognitive Development, 3*, 113–136.

Mandler, J. M. (1992). How to build a baby II: Conceptual primitives. *Psychological Review, 99*, 587–604.

Mandler, J. M., & Johnson, N. S. (1977). Remembrance of things parsed: Story structure and recall. *Cognitive Psychology, 9*, 111–151.

Mandler, J. M., & McDonough, L. (1993). Concept formation in infancy. *Cognitive Development, 8*, 291–319.

Maratsos, M. (1982). The child's construction of grammatical categories. In E. Wanner & L. Gleitman (Ed.), *Language acquisition: The state of the art.* New York: Cambridge University Press.

Maratsos, M. P. (1990). Innateness and plasticity in language acquisition. In M.

Rice & R. Schiefelbusch (Eds.), *The teachability of language* (pp. 105–125). Baltimore: Paul H. Brookes.

Markman, E. M. (1981). Two different principles of conceptual organization. In M. Lamb & A. Brown (Eds.), *Advances in developmental psychology* (vol. I). Hillsdale, NJ: Erlbaum.

Markman, E. M. (1987). How children constrain the possible meanings of words. In U. Neisser (Ed.), *Concepts and conceptual development: Ecological and intellectual factors in categorization* (pp. 255–287). New York: Cambridge University Press.

Markman, E. M. (1991). The whole-object, taxonomic, and mutual exclusivity assumptions as initial constraints on word meanings. In S. A. Gelman & J. P. Byrnes (Eds.), *Perspectives on language and thought: Interrelations in development*. New York: Cambridge University Press.

Markman, E. M., & Hutchinson, J. E. (1984). Children's sensitivity to constraints on word meaning: Taxonomic vs. thematic relations. *Cognitive Psychology, 16* (1–27).

Markus, H., & Kitayama, S. (1991). Culture and the self: Implications for cognition, emotion, and motivation. *Psychological Review, 98,* 224–253.

Marler, P. (1991). The instinct to Learn. In S. Carey & R. Gelman (Eds.), *The epigenesis of mind: Essays in biology and knowledge* (pp. 37–66). Hillsdale, NJ: Erlbaum.

Martin, L., Nelson, K., & Tobach, E. (Eds.), (1995). *Sociocultural psychology: Theory and practice of doing and knowing.* New York: Cambridge University Press.

Mayr, E. (1982). *The growth of biological thought: Diversity, evolution, and inheritance.* Cambridge, MA: Harvard University Press.

McCabe, A., & Peterson, C. (1991). *Developing narrative structure.* Hillsdale, NJ: Erlbaum.

McCune, L., DiPane, D., Fireoved, R., & Fleck, M. (1994). Play: A context for mutual regulation within mother-child interaction. In A. Slade & D. P. Wolf (Eds.), *Children at play: Clinical and developmental approaches to meaning and representation* (pp. 148–166). New York: Oxford University Press.

McCune-Nicolich, L. (1981). Toward symbolic functioning: Structure of early pretend games and potential parallels with language. *Child Development, 52,* 785–797.

McDonough, L., & Mandler, J. M. (1994). Very long-term recall in infants: Infantile amnesia reconsidered. *Memory, 2,* 339–352.

McGrath, J. E., & Kelly, J. R. (1986). *Time and human interaction: Toward a social psychology of time.* New York: Guilford Press.

McNamara, T. P., & Miller, D. L. (1989). Attributes of theories of meaning. *Psychological Bulletin, 106,* 355–376.

Mead, G. H. (1934). *Mind, self, and society.* Chicago: Chicago University Press.

Medin, D. L. (1989). Concepts and conceptual structure. *American Psychologist, 44,* 1469–1481.

Mehler, J., & Dupoux, E. (1994). *What infants know.* Cambridge, MA: Blackwell.

Meltzoff, A. N. (1988). Infant imitation and memory: Nine-month-olds in immediate and deferred tests. *Child Development, 59,* 217–225.

Meltzoff, A. N. (1990). Foundations for developing a concept of self. In D. Cicchetti & M. Beeghly (Eds.), *The self in transition* (pp. 139–164). Chicago: University of Chicago Press.

Meltzoff, A. N., & Gopnik, A. (1993). The role of imitation in understanding persons and developing theories of mind. In S. Baron-Cohen, H. Tager-Flusberg, & D. Cohen (Eds.), *Understanding other minds: Perspectives from autism* (pp. 335–366). New York: Oxford University Press.

Mervis, C. B. (1987). Child-basic object categories and early lexical development. In U. Neisser (Ed.), *Concepts and conceptual development: Ecological and intellectual factors in categorization* (pp. 201–233). New York: Cambridge University Press.

Mervis, C. B., & Crisafi, M. (1982). Order of acquisition of subordinate-, basic-, and superordinate-level categories. *Child Development, 53,* 258–266.

Miller, G. A. (1956). The magical number seven, plus or minus two: Some limits on our capacity for processing information. *Psychological Review, 63,* 81–97.

Miller, G. A. (1978). Pastness. In G. A. Miller & E. Lenneberg (Eds.), *Psychology and biology of language and thought: Essays in honor of Eric Lenneberg* (pp. 167–186). New York: Academic.

Miller, G. A. (1990). The place of language in a scientific psychology. *Psychological Science, 1,* 7–14.

Miller, G. A., & Johnson-Laird, P. N. (1976). *Language and perception.* Cambridge, MA: Harvard University Press.

Miller, J. L., & Eimas, P. D. (1983). Studies on the categorization of speech by infants. *Cognition, 13,* 135–165.

Miller, P. J. (1994). Narrative practices: Their role in socialization and self construction. In U. Neisser & R. Fivush (Eds.), *The remembered self: Construction and accuracy in the self-narrative.* New York: Cambridge University Press.

Miller, P. J., & Hoogstra, L., Mintz, J., Fung, H., & Williams, K. (1993). Troubles in the garden and how they get resolved: A young child's transformation of his favorite story. In C. A. Nelson (Ed.), *Memory and affect in development: Minnesota symposium on child psychology* (vol. 26, pp. 87–114). Hillsdale, NJ: Erlbaum.

Miller, P. J., & Moore, B. B. (1989). Narrative conjunctions of caregiver and child: A comparative perspective on socialization through stories. *Thos, 17,* 428–449.

Miller, P. J., Potts, R., Fung, H., Hoogstra, L., & Mintz, J. (1990). Narrative practices and the social construction of self in childhood. *American Ethnologist, 17,* 292–311.

Mitchell, G. (1991). *Private voices, other rooms.* Unpublished paper, City University of New York Graduate Center.

Mitchell, P., & Lacohee, H. (1991). Children's early understanding of false belief. *Cognition, 39,* 107–127.

Moore, C., Bryant, D., & Furrow, D. (1989). Mental terms and the development of certainty. *Child Development, 60,* 167–171.

Moore, C., Pure, K., & Furrow, D. (1990). Children's understanding of the modal expression of speaker certainty and uncertainty and its relation to the development of a representational theory of mind. *Child Development, 61,* 722–730.

Morgan, J. L. (1986). *From simple input to complex grammar.* Cambridge, MA: MIT Press.

Mounoud, P. (1993). The emergence of new skills: Dialectic relations between knowledge systems. In G. J. P. Savelsbergh (Ed.), *The development of coordination in infancy* (pp. 13–46). Amsterdam: North Holland.

Mullen, M. K. (1994). Earliest recollections of childhood: A demographic analysis. *Cognition, 52,* 55–79.

Mullen, M. K., & Yi, S. (1995). The cultural context of talk about the past: Implications for the development of autobiographical memory. *Cognitive Development, 10,* 407–419.

Murphy, G. L., & Medin, D. L. (1985). The role of theories in conceptual coherence. *Psychological Review, 92,* 289–316.

Myers, N. A., Clifton, R. K., & Clarkson, M. G. (1987). When they were very young: Almost-threes remember two years ago. *Infant Behavior and Development, 10,* 123–132.

Myers, N. A., Perris, E. E., & Speaker, C. J. (1994). Fifty months of memory: A longitudinal study in early childhood. *Memory, 2,* 383–416.

Neisser, U. (1962). Cultural and cognitive discontinuity. In T. E. Gladwin & W. Sturtevant (Eds.), *Anthropology and human behavior* (pp. 54–71). Washington DC: Anthropological Society of Washington.

Neisser, U. (Ed.). (1987). *Concepts and conceptual development: Ecological and intellectual factors in categorization.* New York: Cambridge University Press.

Nelson, K. (1973a). Some evidence for the cognitive primacy of categorization and its functional basis. *Merrill-Palmer Quarterly, 19,* 21–39.

Nelson, K. (1973b). Structure and strategy in learning to talk. *Monographs of the Society for Research in Child Development, 38* (1–2, Serial No. 149).

Nelson, K. (1974). Concept, word, and sentence: Interrelations in acquisition and development. *Psychological Review, 81,* 267–285.

Nelson, K. (1977a). Cognitive development and the acquisition of concepts. In R. C. Anderson, R. J. Spiro, & W. E. Montague (Eds.), *Schooling and the acquisition of knowledge* (pp. 215–253). Hillsdale, NJ: Erlbaum.

Nelson, K. (1977b). The syntagmatic-paradigmatic shift revisited: A review of research and theory. *Psychological Bulletin, 84,* 93–116.

Nelson, K. (1978a). How young children represent knowledge of their world in and out of language. In R. S. Siegler (Ed.), *Children's thinking: What develops?* (pp. 225–273). Hillsdale, NJ: Erlbaum.

Nelson, K. (1978b). Semantic development and the development of semantic memory. In K. E. Nelson (Ed.), *Children's language* (vol. I). New York: Gardner.

Nelson, K. (1979). Explorations in the development of a functional semantic system. In W. Collins (Ed.), *Children's language and communication: Minnesota symposium on child psychology* (vol. 12). Hillsdale, NJ: Erlbaum.

Nelson, K. (1981). Individual differences in language development: Implications for development and language. *Developmental Psychology, 17,* 170–187.

Nelson, K. (1982). The syntagmatics and paradigmatics of conceptual development. In S. Kuczaj (Ed.), *Language development (Vol. 2): Language, thought, and culture* (pp. 335–364). Hillsdale, NJ: Erlbaum.

Nelson, K. (1983). The derivation of concepts and categories from event representations. In E. Scholnick (Ed.), *New trends in conceptual representation: Challenges to Piaget's theory?* (pp. 129–149). Hillsdale, NJ: Erlbaum.

Nelson, K. (1985). *Making sense: The acquisition of shared meaning.* New York: Academic.

Nelson, K. (1986). *Event knowledge: Structure and function in development.* Hillsdale, NJ: Erlbaum.

Nelson, K. (1988). Where do taxonomic categories come from? *Human Development, 31,* 3–10.

Nelson, K. (1989a). Monologue as representation of real-life experience. In K. Nelson (Ed.), *Narratives from the crib* (pp. 27–72). Cambridge, MA: Harvard University Press.

Nelson, K. (1989b). Monologue as the linguistic construction of self in time. In K. Nelson (Ed.), *Narratives from the crib* (pp. 284–308). Cambridge, MA: Harvard University Press.

Nelson, K. (Ed.). (1989c). *Narratives from the crib.* Cambridge, MA: Harvard University Press.

Nelson, K. (1990). Event knowledge and the development of language functions. In J. Miller (Ed.), *Research on child language disorders.* New York: Little, Brown.

Nelson, K. (1991a). Concepts and meaning in language development. In N. A. Krasnegor, D. M. Rumbaugh, R. L. Schiefelbusch, & M. Studdert-Kennedy (Eds.), *Biological and behavioral determinants of language development* (pp. 89–116). Hillsdale, NJ: Erlbaum.

Nelson, K. (1991b). The matter of time: Interdependencies between language and thought in development. In S. A. Gelman & J. P. Byrnes (Eds.), *Perspectives on language and cognition: Interrelations in development.* New York: Cambridge University Press.

Nelson, K. (1991c). Remembering and telling: A Developmental story. *Journal of Narrative and Life History, 1*, 109–127.

Nelson, K. (1992). *Contexted relevance and the acquisition of shared meaning.* Invited Presentation to the British Child Language Seminar, Glasgow, Scotland.

Nelson, K. (1993a). Developing self-knowledge from autobiographical memory. In T. K. Srull & R. Wyer (Eds.), *The mental representation of trait and autobiographical knowledge about the self* (vol. 5, pp. 111–120). Hillsdale, NJ: Erlbaum.

Nelson, K. (1993b). Events, narratives, memories: What develops? In C. Nelson (Ed.), *Memory and affect in development: Minnesota symposium on child psychology* (vol. 26, pp. 1–24). Hillsdale, NJ: Erlbaum.

Nelson, K. (1993c). The psychological and social origins of autobiographical memory. *Psychological Science, 4*, 1–8.

Nelson, K. (1993d). Towards a theory of the development of autobiographical memory. In A. Collins, M. Conway, S. Gathercole, & P. Morris (Eds.), *Theories of memory.* Hillsdale, NJ: Erlbaum.

Nelson, K. (1994). Long-term retention of memory for preverbal experience: Evidence and implications. *Memory, 2*, 467–475.

Nelson, K. (1995). The dual category problem in lexical acquisition. In W. Merriman & M. Tomasello (Eds.), *Beyond names for things* (pp. 223–250). Hillsdale, NJ: Erlbaum.

Nelson, K. (In press). Memory development from 4 to 7 years. In A. Sameroff & M. Haith (Eds.), *Reason and responsibility: The passage through childhood.* Chicago: University of Chicago Press.

Nelson, K., & Gruendel, J. (1979). At morning it's lunchtime: A scriptal view of children's dialogue. *Discourse Processes, 2*, 73–94.

Nelson, K., & Gruendel, J. (1981). Generalized event representations: Basic building blocks of cognitive development. In M. Lamb & A. Brown (Eds.), *Advances in developmental psychology* (vol. 1). Hillsdale, NJ: Erlbaum.

Nelson, K., Hampson, J., & Kessler Shaw, L. (1993). Nouns in early lexicons: Evidence, explanations, and implications. *Journal of Child Language, 20*, 61–84.

Nelson, K., & Levy, E. (1987). Development of referential cohesion in a child's monologues. In R. Steele & T. Threadgold (Eds.), *Language topics: Essays in honour of Michael Halliday* (vol. I, pp. 119–136). Amsterdam: John Benjamins Publ. Co.

Nelson, K., & Lucariello, J. (1985). The development of meaning in first words.

In M. D. Barrett (Ed.), *Children's single word speech*. Chichester, England: Wiley.

Nelson, K., & Nelson, A. J. (1990). Category production in response to script and category cues by kindergarten and second grade children. *Journal of Applied Developmental Psychology, 11,* 431–446.

Nelson, K., & Ross, G. (1980). The generalities and specifics of long term memory in infants and young children. In M. Perlmutter (Ed.), *Children's memory: New directions for child development* (vol. 10, pp. 87–101). San Francisco: Jossey-Bass.

Nelson, K. J. (1969). The organization of free recall by young children. *Journal of Experimental Child Psychology, 8,* 284–295.

Newell, A. (1980). Physical symbol systems. *Cognitive Science, 4,* 135–183.

Noble, W., & Davidson, I. (1991). Evolving remembrance of times past and future. *Behavioral and Brain Sciences, 14,* 572.

Norton, D. G. (1990). Understanding the early experience of black children in high risk environments. *Zero to Three,* 1–7.

Oakley, D. A. (1983). The varieties of memory: A phylogenetic approach. In A. Mayes (Ed.), *Memory in animals and humans*. Workingham, England: Van Nostrand Reinhold.

Ochs, E., & Schieffelin, B. (1984). Language acquisition and socialization: Three developmental stories. In R. Schweder & R. LeVine (Eds.), *Culture theory: Essays on mind, self and emotion* (pp. 276–320). Cambridge: Cambridge University Press.

O'Connell, B., & Gerard, A. (1985). Scripts and scraps: The development of sequential understanding. *Child Development, 56,* 671–681.

Ogura, T. (1991). A longitudinal study of the relationship between early language development and play development. *Journal of Child Language, 18,* 273–294.

Olquin, R., & Tomasello, M. (1993). Twenty-five month old children do not have a grammatical category of verb. *Cognitive Development, 8,* 245–272.

Olson, D. R. (1988). On the origins of beliefs and other intentional states in children. In J. W. Astington, P. L. Harris, & D. R. Olson (Eds.), *Developing theories of mind*. Cambridge: Cambridge University Press.

Olson, D. R. (1994). *The world on paper.* New York: Cambridge University Press.

Olson, G. M., & Strauss, M. S. (1984). The development of infant memory. In M. Moscovitch (Ed.), *Infant memory: Its relation to normal and pathological memory in humans and other animals* (pp. 29–48). New York: Plenum.

Ong, W. J. (1982). *Orality and literacy: The technologizing of the word.* London: Routledge.

Paley, V. G. (1990). *The boy who would be a helicopter.* Cambridge, MA: Harvard University Press.

Parker, S. T., & Gibson, K. R. (1979). A developmental model for the evolution of language and intelligence. *Behavioral and Brain Sciences, 2,* 367–408.

Parker, S. T., & Gibson, K. R. (Eds.). (1990). *"Language" and intelligence in monkeys and apes: Comparative developmental perspectives.* New York: Cambridge University Press.

Parker, S. T., Mitchell, R. W., & Boccia, M. I. (Eds.). (1994). *Self-awareness in animals and humans: Developmental perspectives.* New York: Cambridge University Press.

Passingham, R. E. (1982). *The human primate.* New York: Freeman.

Perner, J. (1991). *Understanding the representational mind.* Cambridge, MA: MIT Press.

Perner, J., Ruffman, T., & Leekam, S. R. (1994). Theory of mind is contagious: You catch it from your sibs. *Child Development, 65,* 1228–1238.

Perris, E. E., Myers, N. A., & Clifton, R. K. (1990). Long-term memory for a single infancy experience. *Child Development, 61,* 1796–1807.

Peters, A. (1983). *The units of language acquisition.* Cambridge: Cambridge University Press.

Peterson, C., & McCabe, A. (1983). *Developmental psycholinguistics: Three ways of looking at a child's narrative.* New York: Plenum.

Peterson, C., & McCabe, A. (1991). Linking children's connective use and narrative macrostructure. In A. McCabe & C. Peterson (Eds.), *Developing narrative structure* (pp. 29–54). Hillsdale, NJ: Erlbaum.

Pettito, L. A., & Marentette, P. F. (1991). Babbling in the manual mode: Evidence for the ontogeny of language. *Science, 251,* 1397–1536.

Piaget, J. (1926). *The language and thought of the child.* New York: Harcourt, Brace.

Piaget, J. (1952). *The origins of intelligence in children.* New York: Norton Library.

Piaget, J. (1962). *Play, dreams, and imitation in childhood.* New York: Norton.

Piaget, J. (1969). *The child's conception of time.* London: Routledge & Kegan Paul.

Piaget, J. (1970). Piaget's theory. In P. H. Mussen (Ed.), *Carmichaels' handbook of child development* (vol. I, pp. 703–732). New York: Wiley.

Piaget, J., & Inheldu, B. (1973). *Memory and Intelligence.* New York: Basic Books.

Piattelli-Palmarini, M. (Eds.). (1980). *Language and learning: The debate between Jean Piaget and Noam Chomsky.* Cambridge, MA: Harvard University Press.

Piattelli-Palmarini, M. (1989). Evolution, selection, and cognition: From "learning" to parameter setting in biology and the study of language. *Cognition, 31,* 1–44.

Pillemer, D. B. (1992). Preschool children's memories of personal circumstances: The fire alarm study. In E. Winograd & U. Neisser (Eds.), *Affect and accuracy in recall: The problem of "flashbulb" memories.* New York: Cambridge University Press.

Pillemer, D. B., & White, S. H. (1989). Childhood events recalled by children and adults. In H. W. Reese (Ed.), *Advances in child development and behavior* (vol. 21, pp. 297–340). New York: Academic.

Pine, J. M., & Lieven, E. V. M. (1990). Referential style at thirteen months: Why age-defined cross-sectional measures are inappropriate for the study of strategy differences in early language development. *Journal of Child Language, 17,* 625–632.

Pinker, S. (1994). *The language instinct: How the mind creates language.* New York: William Morrow.

Pinker, S., & Bloom, P. (1990). Natural language and natural selection. *Behavorial and Brain Sciences, 13,* 707–784.

Pinker, S., & Bloom, P. (1992). Natural language and natural selection. In J. H. Barkow, L. Cosmides, & J. Tooby (Eds.), *The adapted mind: Evolutionary psychology and the generation of culture* (pp. 451–494). New York: Oxford University Press.

Pitcher, E. G., & Prelinger, E. (1963). *Children tell stories: An analysis of fantasy.* New York: International Universities Press.

Plaut, D. C., & Karmiloff-Smith, A. (1993). Representational development and theory-of-mind computations. *Behavioral and Brain Sciences, 16,* 70–71.

Plesa, D. N., Goldman, S., & Edmondson, D. (1995, April). *Negotiation of meaning in a false belief task.* Poster Presentation, Society for Research in Child Development Biennial Meeting, Indianapolis, IN.

Plotkin, H. C. (Ed.). (1982). *Learning, development, and culture: Essays in evolutionary epistemology.* Chichester, NY: Wiley.

Plotkin, H. C. (1988). An evolutionary epistemological approach to the evolution of intelligence. In H. J. Jerison & I. Jerison (Eds.), *Intelligence and evolutionary biology* (pp. 73–91). New York: Springer-Verlag.

Plotkin, H. C. (1993). *Darwin machines and the nature of knowledge.* Cambridge, MA: Harvard University Press.

Polkinghorne, D. E. (1988). *Narrative knowing and the human sciences.* Albany: State University of New York Press.

Popper, K. R. (1972). *Objective knowledge: An evolutionary approach.* London: Oxford University Press.

Pouthas, V. (1985). Timing behavior in young children: A developmental approach to conditioned spaced responding. In J. A. Michon & J. L. Jackson (Eds.), *Time, mind and behavior* (pp. 100–109). New York: Springer-Verlag.

Premack, D., & Dasser, V. (1991). Perceptual origins and conceptual evidence for theory of mind in apes and children. In A. Whiten (Ed.), *Natural theories of mind: Evolution, development and simulation of everyday mindreading* (pp. 253–266). Oxford: Blackwell.

Premack, D., & Woodruff, G. (1978). Does the chimpanzee have a theory of mind? *Behavioral and Brain Sciences, 1,* 515–526.

Propp, V. (1968). *The morphology of the folk tale.* Austin: University of Texas Press.

Quine, W. V. O. (1960). *Word and object.* Cambridge, MA: MIT Press.

Raeithel, A. (1994). Symbolic production of social coherence. *Mind, Culture and Activity, 1,* 69–88.

Ratner, H. H. (1980). The role of social context in memory development. In M. Perlmutter (Ed.), *Children's memory: New directions for child development* (vol. 10, pp. 49–68). San Francisco: Jossey-Bass.

Ratner, H. H. (1984). Memory demands and the development of young children's memory. *Child Development, 55,* 2173–2191.

Reed, E., & Jones, R. (Eds.). (1982). *Reasons for realism: The selected essays of James J. Gibson.* Hillsdale, NJ: Erlbaum.

Reed, E. E. (1995). The ecological approach to language development: A radical solution to Chomsky's and Quine's problems. *Language and Communication, 15,* 1–29.

Reese, E., & Fivush, R. (1993). Parental styles of talking about the past. *Developmental Psychology, 29,* 596–606.

Reese, E., Haden, C. A., & Fivush, R. (1993). Mother-child conversations about the past: Relationships of style and memory over time. *Cognitive Development, 8,* 403–430.

Reichenbach, H. (1947). *Elements of symbolic logic.* New York: Free Press.

Rescorla, L. A. (1976). *Concept formation in word learning.* Unpublished Ph.D. Dissertation, Yale University.

Rescorla, L. A. (1980). Overextension in early language development. *Journal of Child Language, 7,* 321–335.

Resnick, L. B., Levine, J. M., & Teasley, S. D. (Eds.). (1991). *Perspectives on socially shared cognition.* Washington, DC: American Psychological Association.

Reznick, J. S., & Kagan, J. (1983). Category detection in infancy. In L. P. Lipsitt & C. K. Rovee-Collier (Eds.), *Advances in infancy research* (vol. 2). Norwood, NJ: Ablex.

Rice, M. (1980). *Cognition to language: Categories, word meanings and training.* Baltimore: University Park Press.

Rice, M. L. (1991). Children with specific language impairment: Toward a model of teachability. In N. A. Krasnegor, D. M. Rumbaugh, R. L. Schiefelbush, & M. Studdert-Kennedy (Eds.), *Biological and behavioral determinants of language development* (pp. 447–480). Hillsdale, NJ: Erlbaum.

Richie, D. M., & Bickhard, M. H. (1988). The ability to perceive duration: Its relation to the development of the logical concept of time. *Developmental Psychology, 24*, 318–323.

Robinson, E. J. (1994). What people say, what they think, and what is really the case: Children's understanding of utterances as sources of knowledge. In C. Lewis & P. Mitchell (Eds.), *Children's early understanding of mind: Origins and development* (pp. 355–384). Hillsdale, NJ: Erlbaum.

Robinson, E. J., & Nye, R., & Thomas, G. V. (1994). Children's conceptions of the relationship between pictures and their referents. *Cognitive Development, 9*, 165–191.

Rogoff, B. (1990). *Apprenticeship in thinking: Cognitive development in social context.* New York: Oxford University Press.

Rosch, E. (1973). On the internal structure of perceptual and semantic categories. In T. E. Moore (Ed.), *Cognitive development and the acquisition of language.* New York: Academic.

Rosch, E. (1975). Cognitive representation of semantic categories. *Journal of Experimental Psychology: General, 104*, 192–233.

Rosch, E. (1978). Principles of categorization. In E. Rosch & B. Lloyd (Eds.), *Cognition and categorization.* Hillsdale, NJ: Erlbaum.

Rosch, E., Mervis, C., Gray, W., Johnson, D., & Boyes-Braem, P. (1976). Basic objects in natural categories. *Cognitive Psychology, 8*, 382–439.

Rosner, S. R., & Smick, C. (1989). *Cueing maintenance of slot-filler and taxonomic categories.* Poster presented at meetings of Society for Research in Child Development, Kansas City, MO.

Ross, G. (1980). Concept categorization in 1 to 2 year olds. *Developmental Psychology, 16*, 391–396.

Rothstein, L. (1991). *Three-year-olds' symbolic representation of familiar events: Factors of decontextualization, discrepant action and order.* Unpublished Ph.D. Dissertation, Cornell University.

Rovee-Collier, C. (1995). Time windows in cognitive development. *Developmental Psychology, 31*, 147–169.

Rovee-Collier, C., & Hayne, H. (1987). Reactivation of infant memory: Implications for cognitive development. In H. W. Reese (Ed.), *Advances in child development and behavior* (vol. 20, pp. 185–283). New York: Academic.

Rozin, P. (1976). The evolution of intelligence and access to the cognitive unconscious. In J. M. Sprague & A. N. Epstein (Eds.), *Progress in psychobiology and physiological psychology.* New York: Academic.

Russell, J. (1992). The theory theory: So good they named it twice? *Cognitive Development, 7*, 485–519.

Sachs, J., Goldman, J., & Chaille, C. (1984). Planning in pretend play: Using language to coordinate narrative development. In A. D. Pellegrini & T. D. Yawkey (Eds.), *The development of oral and written language in social contexts* (pp. 110–128). Norwood, NJ: Ablex.

Sacks, O. (1995). A neurologist's notebook: Prodigies. *The New Yorker,* January 9, 1995, 44–51.

Salthe, S. N. (1993). *Development and evolution: Complexity and change in biology.* Cambridge, MA: MIT Press.

Saussure, F. D. (1959/1915). *Course in general linguistics*. New York: The Philosophical Library, Inc.

Savage-Rumbaugh, E. S., Murphy, J., Sevcik, R. A., Brakke, K. E., Williams, S. L., & Rumbaugh, D. M. (1993). Language comprehension in ape and child. *Monographs of the Society for Research in Child Development, 58*, 3–4.

Scarr, S. (1992). Developmental theories for the 1990s: Development and individual differences. *Child Development, 63*, 1–19.

Scarr, S. (1993). Biological and cultural diversity: The legacy of Darwin for development. *Child Development, 64*, 1333–1353.

Schachtel, E. (1947). On memory and childhood amnesia. *Psychiatry, 10*, 1–26.

Schacter, D. L. (1992). Understanding implicit memory. *American Psychologist, 47*, 559–569.

Schacter, D. L., & Moscovitch, M. (1984). Infants, amnesics, and dissociable memory systems. In M. Moscovitch (Ed.), *Infant memory: Its relation to normal and pathological memory in humans and other animals* (pp. 173–216). New York: Plenum.

Schaller, S. (1991). *A man without words*. New York: Summit Books.

Schank, R. C. & Abelson, R. P. (1977). *Scripts, plans, goals, and understanding*. Hillsdale, NJ: Erlbaum.

Schank, R. C., & Abelson, R. P. (1995). Knowledge and memory: The real story. In R. S. Wyer Jr. & T. Srull (Eds.), *Advances in social cognition* (vol. 8, p. 1–88). Hillsdale, NJ: Erlbaum.

Schwartz, S. P. (Ed.). (1977). *Naming, necessity, and natural kinds*. Ithaca, NY: Cornell University Press.

Scribner, S. (1974). Developmental aspects of categorized recall in a West African society. *Cognitive Psychology, 6*, 475–494.

Searle, J. R. (1983). *Intentionality*. Cambridge: Cambridge University Press.

Sebris, S. B. (1992). *Autobiographical childhood narratives: Processes of remembering and reconstructing*. Unpublished Ph.D. Dissertation, City University of New York.

Seidman, S., Nelson, K., & Gruendel, J. (1986). Make believe scripts: The transformation of ERs in fantasy. In K. Nelson (Ed.), *Event knowledge: Structure and function in development* (pp. 161–187). Hillsdale, NJ: Erlbaum.

Sell, M. A. (1992). The development of children's knowledge structures: Events, slots, and taxonomies. *Journal of Child Language, 19*, 659–676.

Shatz, M. (1994). Theory of mind and the development of social-linguistic intelligence in early childhood. In C. Lewis & P. Mitchell (Eds.), *Children's early understanding of mind: Origins and development* (pp. 311–331). Hillsdale: NJ: Erlbaum.

Shatz, M, Wellman, H. M., & Silber, S. (1983). The acquisition of mental verbs: A systematic investigation of first references to mental state. *Cognition, 14*, 301–321.

Shaw, R. E., & Hazelett, W. M. (1986). Schemas in cognition. In V. McCabe & G. J. Balzano (Eds.), *Event cognition: An ecological perspective* (pp. 45–58). Hillsdale, NJ: Erlbaum.

Sheffield, G., Sosa, B. B., & Hudson, J. A. (1993). *Narrative complexity and 2- and 3-year-olds' comprehension of false belief*. Poster presented at the biennial meeting of the Society for Research in Child Development, New Orleans, LA.

Sherry, D. F., & Schacter, D. L. (1987). The evolution of multiple memory systems. *Psychological Review, 94*, 439–454.

Shore, C., O'Connell, B., & Bates, E. (1984). First sentences in language and symbolic play. *Developmental Psychology, 20*, 872–880.

Shweder, R. A., & LeVine, R. A. (Eds.). (1984). *Culture theory: Essays on mind, self and emotion.* New York: Cambridge University Press.

Siegal, M., & Peterson, C. C. (1994). Children's theory of mind and the conversational territory of cognitive development. In C. Lewis & P. Mitchell (Eds.), *Children's early understanding of mind: Origins and development* (pp. 427–456). Hillsdale, NJ: Erlbaum.

Silverstein, M. (1985). The functional stratification of language and ontogenesis. In J. V. Wertsch (Ed.), *Culture, communication, and cognition: Vygotskian perspectives* (pp. 205–235). Cambridge: Cambridge University Press.

Simon, D. P., & Simon, H. A. (1978). Individual differences in solving physics problems. In R. S. Siegler (Ed.), *Children's thinking: What develops?* (pp. 325–348). Hillsdale, NJ: Erlbaum.

Simon, H. A. (1972). On the development of the processor. In S. Farnham-Diggory (Ed.), *Information processing in children.* New York: Academic.

Slackman, E. (1985). *The effect of event structure on children's ability to learn an unfamiliar event.* Ph.D. Dissertation, City University of New York.

Slobin, D. I. (1982). Universal and particular in the acquisition of language. In E. Wanner & L. R. Gleitman (Eds.), *Language acquisition: The state of the art* (pp. 128–170). Cambridge: Cambridge University Press.

Slobin, D. I. (1987). Thinking for speaking. In J. Askew, N. Berry, L. Michaelis, & H. Filip (Eds.), *Proceedings of the Thirteenth Annual Meeting of the Berkeley Linguistics Society* (pp. 435–445). Berkeley: University of California.

Smith, C. (1980). The acquisition of time talk: Relations between child and adult grammars. *Journal of Child Language, 7,* 263–278.

Smith, E. E., & Medin, D. L. (1981). *Categories and concepts.* Cambridge, MA: Harvard University Press.

Smith, L. B., & Thelen, E. (Eds.). (1993). *A dynamic systems approach to development: Applications.* Cambridge, MA: MIT Press.

Smith, M. D., & Locke, J. J. (1988). *The emergent lexicon: The child's development of a linguistic vocabulary.* New York: Academic.

Snow, C. (1986). The social basis of language development. In P. Fletcher & M. Garman (Eds.), *Language acquisition.* Cambridge: Cambridge University Press.

Snow, C., & Ferguson, C. A. (Eds.). (1977). *Talking to children: Language input and acquisition.* Cambridge: Cambridge University Press.

Snow, C., & Goldfield, B. (1983). Turn the page please: Situation-specific language acquisition. *Journal of Child Language, 10,* 551–571.

Soja, N. N. (1992). Inferences about the meanings of nouns: The relationship between perception and syntax. *Cognitive Development, 7,* 29–46.

Spelke, E. (1988). The origins of physical knowledge. In L. Weiskrantz (Ed.), *Thought without language.* New York: Oxford University Press.

Spelke, E. S. (1991). Physical knowledge in infancy: Reflections on Piaget's theory. In S. Carey & R. Gelman (Eds.), *The epigenesis of mind: Essays on biology and cognition* (pp. 133–170). Hillsdale, NJ: Erlbaum.

Spelke, E. S., Breinlinger, K., Macomber, J., & Jacobson, K. (1992). Origins of knowledge. *Psychological Review, 99,* 605–632.

Spence, M. J., & DeCasper, A. J. (1987). Prenatal experience with low-frequency maternal-voice sounds influences neonatal perception of maternal voice samples. *Infant Behavior and Development, 10,* 133–142.

Sperber, D., & Wilson, D. (1986). *Relevance: Communication and cognition.* Cambridge, MA: Harvard University Press.

Squire, L. R. (1992). Memory and the Hippocampus: A synthesis from findings with rats, monkeys, and humans. *Psychological Review, 99,* 195–231.

Starkey, P., & Cooper, R. G. (1980). Perception of number by human infants. *Science, 200,* 1033–1035.

Starkey, P., Spelke, E. S., & Gelman, R. (1990). Numerical abstraction by human infants. *Cognition, 36,* 97–127.

Stein, N., & Glenn, C. (1979). An analysis of story comprehension in elementary school children. In R. Freedle (Ed.), *New directions in discourse processing* (pp. 53–120). Norwood, NJ: Ablex.

Stein, N. L. (1988). The development of children's storytelling skill. In M. B. Franklin & S. S. Barton (Eds.), *Child language: A reader* (pp. 282–297). NY: Oxford University Press.

Stein, N. L., & Trabasso, T. (1981). What's in a story: Critical issues in story comprehension. In R. Glaser (Ed.), *Advances in the psychology of instruction.* Hillsdale, NJ: Erlbaum.

Stein, N., Trabasso, T., & Liwag, M. (1993). The representation and organization of emotional experience. Unfolding the emotion episode. In M. Lewis & J. Haviland (Eds.), *Handbook of emotion* (pp. 279–300). New York: Guilford.

Stern. D. N. (1985). *The interpersonal world of the infant: A view from psychoanalysis and developmental psychology.* New York: Basic Books.

Sternberg, R. J., & Powell, J. S. (1983). Comprehending verbal comprehension. *American Psychologist, 39,* 878–891.

Sternberg, R. J., & Wagner, R. K. (Eds.). (1994). *Mind in context.* New York: Cambridge University Press.

Stigler, J. W., Shweder, R. A., & Herdt, G. (Eds.). (1990). *Cultural psychology: Essays on comparative human development.* New York: Cambridge University Press.

Studdert-Kennedy, M. (1991). Language development from an evolutionary perspective. In N. A. Krasnegor, D. M. Rumbaugh, R. L. Schiefelbusch, & M. Studdert-Kennedy (Eds.), *Biological and behaviorial determinants of language development* (pp. 5–28). Hillsdale, NJ: Erlbaum.

Sugarman, S. (1983). *Children's early thought.* New York: Cambridge University Press.

Tager-Flusberg, H. (1993). What language reveals about the understanding of minds in children with autism. In S. Baron-Cohen, H. Tager-Flusberg, & D. Cohen (Eds.), *Understanding other minds: Perspectives from autism* (pp. 138–157). New York: Oxford University Press.

Taylor, C. (1985). *Philosophy and the human sciences: Philosophical papers.* Cambridge: Cambridge University Press.

Taylor, M., & Gelman, S. A. (1988). Adjectives and nouns: Children's strategies for learning new words. *Child Development, 59,* 411–419.

Tessler, M. (1986). *Mother-child talk in a museum: The socialization of a memory.* Unpublished manuscript. City University of New York Graduate Center.

Tessler, M. (1991). *Making memories together: The influence of mother-child joint encoding on the development of autobiographical memory style.* Unpublished Ph.D. Dissertation, City University of New York Graduate Center.

Tessler, M., & Nelson, K. (1994). Making memories: The influence of joint encoding on later recall. *Consciousness and Cognition, 3,* 307–326.

Thelen, E. (1989). Self-organization in developmental processes: Can systems approaches work? In M. R. Gunnar & E. Thelen (Eds.), *Systems and development* (vol. 22, pp. 77–117). Hillsdale, NJ: Erlbaum.

Thelen, E. (1993). Timing and developmental dynamics in the acquisition of early motor skills. In G. Turkewitz & D. A. Devenny (Eds.), *Developmental time and timing* (pp. 85–104). Hillsdale, NJ: Erlbaum.

Thelen, E., & Smith, L. (1994). *A dynamic systems approach to the development of cognition and action.* Cambridge, MA: MIT Press.

Tobias, P. V. (1981). The emergence of man in Africa and beyond. *Philosophical Transactions of the Royal Society of London B, 292,* 43–56.

Tomasello, M. (1990). Cultural transmission in the tool use and communicatory signaling of chimpanzees? In S. T. Parker & K. R. Gibson (Eds.), *"Language" and intelligence in monkeys and apes* (pp. 274–311). New York: Cambridge University Press.

Tomasello, M. (1992). *First verbs: A case study of early grammatical development.* New York: Cambridge University Press.

Tomasello, M. (In press). Joint attention as social cognition. In C. D. Moore P. (Ed.), *Joint attention: Its origins and role in development.* Hillsdale, NJ: Erlbaum.

Tomasello, M., & Farrar, M. J. (1986). Joint attention and early language. *Child Development, 57,* 1454–1463.

Tomasello, M., & Kruger, A. C. (1992). Joint attention on actions: Acquiring words in ostensive and non-ostensive contexts. *Journal of Child Language, 19,* 313–333.

Tomasello, M., Kruger, A. C., & Ratner, H. H. (1993). Cultural learning. *Behavioral and Brain Sciences, 16,* 495–552.

Tomasello, M., & Olquin, R. (1993). Twenty-three-month-old children have a grammatical category of noun. *Cognitive Development, 8,* 465–494.

Tooby, J., & Cosmides, L. (1992). The psychological foundations of culture. In J. H. Barkow, L. Cosmides, & J. Tooby (Eds.), *The adapted mind: Evolutionary psychology and the generation of culture.* New York: Oxford University Press.

Trabasso, T., & Stein, N. L. (In press). Narrating, representing, and remembering event sequences. In P. van den Broek, P. Bauer, & T. Bourg (Eds.), *Developmental spans in event comprehension and representation: Bridging fictional and actual events.* Hillsdale, NJ: Erlbaum.

Trabasso, T., Stein, N. L., Rodkin, P. C., Munger, M. P., & Baughn, C. R. (1992). Knowledge of goals and plans in the on-line narration of events. *Cognitive Development, 7,* 133–170.

Trabasso, T., & van den Broek, P. (1985). Causal thinking and the representation of story events. *Journal of Memory and Language, 24,* 612–630.

Traugott, E. C. (1978). On the expression of spatio-temporal relations in language. In J. H. Greenberg (Ed.), *Universals of human language* (vol. 3: *Word Structure,* pp. 369–400). Stanford, CA: Stanford University Press.

Trevarthen, C. (1980). The foundations of intersubjectivity: Development of interpersonal and cooperative understanding in infants. In D. R. Olson (Ed.), *The social foundations of language and thought* (pp. 316–342). New York: Norton.

Tulving, E. (1972). Episodic and semantic memory. In E. Tulving & W. Donaldson (Eds.), *Organization of memory* (pp. 382–403). New York: Academic.

Tulving, E. (1983). *Elements of episodic memory.* New York: Oxford University Press.

Tulving, E. (1993). What is episodic memory? *Current Directions in Psychological Science, 2,* (3), 67–70.

Tulviste, P. (1991). *The cultural-historical development of verbal thinking.* Translated by M. Jaroszewska Hall. Commack, NY: Nova Science Publishers, Inc.

Turkewitz, G. (1993). The influence of timing on the nature of cognition. In G.

Turkewitz & D. A. Devenny (Eds.), *Developmental time and timing* (pp. 125–142). Hillsdale, NJ: Erlbaum.

Turkewitz, G., & Devenny, D. A. (Eds.). (1993). *Developmental time and timing.* Hillsdale, NJ: Erlbaum.

Valsiner, J. (1987). *Culture and the development of children's action.* New York: Wiley.

Valsiner, J. (1993). Making of the future: Temporality and the constructive nature of human development. In G. Turkewitz & D. A. Devenny (Eds.), *Developmental time and timing* (pp. 13–40). Hillsdale, NJ: Erlbaum.

Van der Veer, R., & Valsiner, J. (1991). *Understanding Vygotsky: A quest for synthesis.* Cambridge, MA: Blackwell.

Van Geert, P. (1991). A dynamic systems model of cognitive and language growth. *Psychological Review, 98,* 3–53.

Van Geert, P. (1993). A dynamic systems model of cognitive growth: Competition and support under limited resource conditions. In L. B. Smith & E. Thelen (Eds.), *A dynamic systems approach to development: Applications* (pp. 265–332). Cambridge, MA: MIT Press.

Varela, F. J., Thompson, E., & Rosch, E. (1991). *The embodied mind.* Cambridge, MA: MIT Press.

Vygotsky, L. S. (1978). *Mind in society: The development of higher psychological processes.* Cambridge, MA: Harvard University Press.

Vygotsky, L. S. (1986). *Thought and language.* Cambridge, MA: MIT Press.

Waddington, C. H. (1957). *The strategy of the genes.* New York: Macmillan.

Walkenfeld, F. F., & Nelson, K. (1995). *Reinstatement effects on preschoolers' event recall.* Poster presented at Biennial Meeting of the Society for Research in Child Development, March 1995, Indianapolis, IN.

Watson, R. (1985). Towards a theory of definition. *Journal of Child Language, 12,* 181–197.

Waxman, S., & Gelman, R. (1986). Preschoolers' use of superordinate relations in classification and language. *Cognitive Development, 1,* 139–156.

Weinert, F. (1991). *Stability in change of memory functions in childhood.* Paper presented at the International Conference on Memory, Lancaster University, Lancaster, England.

Weiskrantz, L. (Ed.). (1988). *Thought without language.* Oxford: Oxford University Press.

Weist, R. M. (1986). Tense and aspect: Temporal systems in child language. In P. Fletcher & M. Garman (Eds.), *Language acquisition.* Cambridge: Cambridge University Press.

Weist, R. M., Wysocka, H., Witkowska-Stadmik, K., Buczowska, E., & Konieczna, E. (1984). The defective tense hypothesis: On the emergence of tense and aspect in child Polish. *Journal of Child Language, 11,* 347–374.

Wellman, H. M., & Bartsh, K. (1994). Before belief: Children's early psychological theory. In C. Lewis & P. Mitchell (Eds.), *Children's early understanding of mind: Origins and development* (pp. 331–354). Hillsdale, NJ: Erlbaum.

Wellman, H. M. (1988). First steps in the child's theorizing about the mind. In J. W. Astington, P. Harris, & D. Olson (Eds.), *Developing theories of mind.* New York: Cambridge University Press.

Wellman, H. M. (1990). *The child's theory of mind.* Cambridge, MA: MIT Press.

Wellman, H. M., & Gelman, S. A. (1992). Cognitive development: Foundational theories of core domains. *Annual Review of Psychology, 43,* 337–375.

Wertsch, J. V. (Eds.), (1985a). *Culture, communication and cognition: Vygotskian perspectives.* New York: Cambridge University Press.

Wertsch, J. V. (1985b). *Vygotsky and the social formation of mind.* Cambridge, MA: Harvard University Press.

Wertsch, J. V. (1990). Dialogue and dialogism in a socio-cultural approach to mind. In I. Markova & K. Foppa (Eds.), *The dynamics of dialogue* (pp. 62–82). London: Harvester/Wheatsheaf.

Wertsch, J. V., Tulviste, P., & Hagstrom, F. (1993). A sociocultural approach to agency. In E. A. Forman, N. Minick, & C. A. Stone (Eds.), *Contexts for learning: Sociodynamics in children's development* (pp.336–356). New York: Oxford University Press.

Wertsch, J. V. (1991). *Voices in the mind.* Cambridge, MA: Harvard University Press.

Whiten, A. (Ed). (1991). *Natural theories of mind: Evolution, development and simulation of everyday mindreading.* London: Basil Blackwood.

Whorf, B. L. (1956). *Language, thought and reality: Selected writings of Benjamin Lee Whorf.* Cambridge, MA: MIT Press.

Wierzbicka, A. (1994). Cognitive domains and the structure of the lexicon: The case of the emotions. In L. A. Hirschfeld & S. A. Gelman (Eds.), *Mapping the mind* (pp. 431–452). New York: Cambridge University Press.

Wilson, E. O. (1975). *Sociobiology: The new synthesis.* Cambridge, MA: Harvard University Press.

Wilson, P. J. (1980). *Man the promising primate: The conditions of human evolution.* New Haven: Yale University Press.

Wimmer, H., & Perner, J. (1983). Beliefs about beliefs: Representation and constraining function of wrong beliefs in young children's understanding of deception. *Cognition, 13,* 103–128.

Winer, G. (1980). Class inclusion reasoning in children: A review of the empirical literature. *Child Development, 51,* 309–328.

Wittgenstein, L. (1953). *Philosophical investigations.* New York: Macmillan.

Wolf, D., & Gardner, H. (1979). Style and sequence in symbolic play. In M. Franklin & N. Smith (Eds.), *Early symbolization.* Hillsdale, NJ: Erlbaum.

Wolf, S. A., & Heath, S. B. (1992). *The braid of literature: Children's worlds of reading,* Cambridge, MA: Harvard University Press.

Wozniak, R. H., & Fischer, K. W. (Eds.). (1993). *Development in context: Acting and thinking in specific environments.* Hillsdale, NJ: Erlbaum.

Wynn, K. (1992a). Addition and subtraction by human infants. *Nature, 358,* 749.

Wynn, K. (1992b). Children's acquisition of the number words and the counting system. *Cognitive Psychology, 24,* 220–251.

Yu, Y. (1993). *Effects of category knowledge, strategies, and social interaction on children's memory performance.* Unpublished Ph.D. Dissertation, City University of New York.

Yu, Y., & Nelson, K. (1993). Slot-filler and conventional category organisation in young Korean children. *International Journal of Behavioral Development, 16,* 1–14.

Zaitchek, D. (1990). When representations conflict with reality: The preschooler's problem with false beliefs and "false" photographs. *Cognition, 35,* 41–68.

Zazanis, E. (1991). *Remembering a story with and without pictures by young children.* Unpublished paper, City University of New York Graduate Center.

Zukow, P. G. (1986). The relationship between interaction with the caregiver and the emergence of play activities during the one-word period. *British Journal of Developmental Psychology, 4,* 223–234.

Name Index

Subject Index

413